BUFFALO BILL CODY, A MAN OF THE WEST

BUFFALO BILL CODY, A MAN OF THE WEST

PRENTISS INGRAHAM

EDITED WITH AN INTRODUCTION BY
SANDRA K. SAGALA

UNIVERSITY PRESS OF KANSAS

© 2019 by the University Press of Kansas
All rights reserved

Published by the University Press of Kansas (Lawrence, Kansas 66045), which was organized by the Kansas Board of Regents and is operated and funded by Emporia State University, Fort Hays State University, Kansas State University, Pittsburg State University, the University of Kansas, and Wichita State University.

Library of Congress Cataloging-in-Publication Data

Names: Ingraham, Prentiss, 1843–1904, author. | Sagala, Sandra K., editor.
Title: Buffalo Bill Cody, a man of the west / Prentiss Ingraham, edited with an introduction by Sandra K. Sagala.
Description: Lawrence, Kansas : University Press of Kansas, 2019. | Includes bibliographical references and index.
Identifiers: LCCN 2018051540
ISBN 9780700627615 (cloth : alk. paper)
ISBN 9780700627622 (pbk. : alk. paper)
ISBN 9780700627639 (ebook)
Subjects: LCSH: Buffalo Bill, 1846–1917. | Pioneers—West (U.S.)—Biography. | Scouts (Reconnaissance)—West (U.S.)—Biography. | Frontier and pioneer life—West (U.S.)
Classification: LCC F594 .I54 2019 | DDC 978/.02092 [B]—dc23
LC record available at https://lccn.loc.gov/2018051540.

British Library Cataloguing-in-Publication Data is available.

Printed in the United States of America

10 9 8 7 6 5 4 3 2 1

The paper used in this publication is recycled and contains 30 percent postconsumer waste. It is acid free and meets the minimum requirements of the American National Standard for Permanence of Paper for Printed Library Materials Z39.48-1992.

To Jen, Jeremy, and Bill once again

CONTENTS

Acknowledgments *ix*
Introduction *1*
Part 1. "A Man of the West" *13*
Part 2. "Led by Destiny" *139*
Part 3. "Honors Easy" *275*
Appendix: Prentiss Ingraham's Buffalo Bill Novels *311*
Notes *323*
Bibliography *337*
Index *343*

ACKNOWLEDGMENTS

It is not merely for this book that I appreciate these specific individuals, but for all the encouragement and support my family, friends, librarians, and archivists have given me over the years.

Many thanks to Mary Robinson, Karling Abernathy, Charlotte Gdula, Samantha Harper, Jeremy Johnston, and Linda Clark at the Buffalo Bill Center of the West; to Jen Moriarty, Doreen Chaky, and JoAnne Bagwell, my first readers. Thanks to Steve Friesen for the insightful chats at WWA; another thumbs up to the Interlibrary Loan Department at the Erie County Library, especially Janet Wolf. Always, gratitude goes to the late Joseph Rosa whose wise observations I miss. I'm also grateful to Kim Hogeland of the University Press of Kansas for seeing value in this manuscript and to Larisa Martin for her careful guidance to publication.

INTRODUCTION

In the preface to his book *American Spirit: Who We Are and What We Stand For*, David McCullough writes that "history . . . is about people, and they speak to us across the years. Our history, our American story, is our definition as a people and a nation."[1] One version of America's story is handed down through the eyes of William F. "Buffalo Bill" Cody, a resourceful and ambitious man who came to regard himself not only as an entertainer but, arguably, as a historian.

He first brought the story to the American public through his colossal Wild West show comprising horsemanship and sharpshooting displays. Fit into a narrative structure, the show illustrated events from America's western frontier, a time and place he knew well. Born in 1846, he spent his childhood and young adult years on the midwest prairies and began working at age eleven to support his mother and sisters after his father died. He served in the Union Army and as a civilian scout in the Indian wars. After marriage and brief career as a landlord, he reenacted frontier adventures for fourteen years in melodramas onstage. Beginning in 1883, Cody's Wild West outdoor arena program showcased for Americans, and eventually for Europeans, the life of frontier settlers. He devoted over thirty years to his show and toured throughout the United States and Europe, exhibiting his cowboys and Indians in small towns for one-night stands and in metropolises for weeks at a time. He performed for Queen Victoria at Windsor, met Pope Leo XIII, and transported European royalty around the show's arena in his Deadwood stagecoach. His name was synonymous with showman; he was beloved by family, friends, employees, and strangers young and old.

Prentiss Ingraham's biography of Cody reveals the man who, unlike thousands of plainsmen with similar prospects for fame, capitalized on his role in America's story in an extraordinary fashion. The biography, serialized in the *Duluth Press* from July 13, 1895, through May 16, 1896, and transcribed here, was an attempt to popularize Cody's story. Actuality juxtaposed with fiction filled the gap between Cody's candid autobiography and the swashbuckling derring-do of dime novels. Scholar and editor Charles Rankin has observed that if the public knows a little bit about a subject, they're going to want to know more.[2] Despite the miles of newsprint and thousands of book pages devoted to Cody's adventures, historic and modern audiences have always looked for more. Ingraham's *Duluth Press* pieces are presented here together in book form for the first time; readers will appreciate how Ingraham's positioning of Cody's celebrity and historical impact provides insight into the development of the American story.

Because Cody had been a part of significant events—such as the Kansas border wars fought over the issue of permitting slavery in new states, the Civil War, and Indian wars waged over possession of land—and because he was personally acquainted with military commanders like George Armstrong Custer, Philip Sheridan, and Nelson Miles, and American Indian chiefs, like Rain-in-the-Face, Yellow Hair, and Sitting Bull, he had indisputably participated in shaping history. Taking as his basis Cody's retelling of his contribution to those events in his 1879 autobiography, *The Life of Hon. William F. Cody, Known as Buffalo Bill*, Ingraham embellished the stories, embroidering details gleaned from his association with the plainsman as publicist and dramatist. Ingraham confesses that, at times, he dwelt on minor incidents in Cody's life until they took on a larger-than-life quality not incompatible with Cody's significance in Western lore.[3]

Prentiss Ingraham's own life story was as action-packed as any fiction. No academic biography of him has been published, but details of his life are revealed in contemporary newspapers and his obituaries. He was born near Natchez, Mississippi, in December 1843, son of clergyman Joseph Holt Ingraham, and attended Maryland's St. Timothy's Military Academy, Mississippi's Jefferson College, and the Mobile Medical College in Alabama. When the Civil War began, he enlisted in the Confederate Army in the 1st Mississippi Light Artillery then in the Texas Cavalry as commander of scouts, during which time he received a foot wound that afflicted him the rest of his life.[4] Following capture during the siege at Port Hudson, Louisiana, Ingraham escaped and was wounded a second time at the Battle of Franklin, Tennessee, in November 1864.

His firsthand account of an early experience as a soldier illustrates his flair for sensationalism. He found himself in

> hand to hand, or rather musket to sabre [combat] with a Yankee on a horse that looked to me as big as a haystack. He came at me cutting and slashing to kill and murder . . . and the best I could do was to punch viciously at him with my bayonet. . . . He struck the hammer of my musket with his sword blade, and the gun went off with an explosion that threw it out of my hands and sent the entire charge square into the cavalryman's face. We went down together, both covered with blood—his blood. But only one of us got up again.[5]

Despite his being a staunch Confederate, his contemporaries noted Ingraham's broadmindedness toward Unionists.[6] In Saratoga Springs, New York, Ingraham's home for six years, a city father remarked that Ingraham "spoke of the many brave men, both north and south, who were engaged in that terrible conflict . . . but all are now united and we are all Americans under the glorious star[s] and stripes."[7]

After the Civil War Ingraham traveled abroad, from Mexico and Austria to Crete and Egypt, to satisfy his appetite for adventure so, it was said, he "knows Cairo like he knows Manhattan and the Riviera as the Rialto."[8] By 1869, his travels brought him to London where he wrote satirical sketches about the English as seen through an American's eyes.[9] He found writing lucrative, but the call of the military remained strong, so he set off again to join Cuba's fight for independence from Spain.[10] All his travel and exotic military experiences provided background material for scores of dime novels.

The small (4 by 6 inches in size, approximately three hundred pages) paperbacks, published by two New York firms—Beadle and Adams, as well as Street & Smith—were introduced as cheap and portable reading for Civil War soldiers. They capitalized on readers' voracious appetite for sensational stories of seagoing or frontier adventurers, an appetite Ingraham believed would never die.[11] In addition to the adrenaline-raising tales, dime novels introduced readers to real-life frontier characters like Jesse James or Texas Jack. Though ostensibly incorporating biographical information, the exciting and entertaining stories helped create their legends with little regard for fact.

Ingraham's novels featuring the adventures of Buffalo Bill proved the author's savvy in combining real adventures with fiction to produce a saleable commodity but, most notably, they contributed to Cody's elevation to mythic hero. Another dime novelist, Ned Buntline, first catapulted Cody to the nation's attention when his story "Buffalo Bill, King of the Border Men" was serialized in the *New York Weekly* in 1869. Though Buntline wrote only four Buffalo Bill books, audiences hankered for more, and other writers soon took up the standard. To the question of whether Buntline had "invented" Buffalo Bill, Ingraham argued that "heroes are born, not made, and circumstances bring them out of obscurity."[12] Before he was discovered by Buntline, his "pluck" was already legendary. Although Cody's adventurous life and interactions with other western characters—from fellow plainsmen and army commanders to hostile Indians and black soldiers—lent themselves to sensationalism, authors often used literary license to make his exploits even larger than life.

At first reluctant, Cody ultimately accepted his celebrity and acknowledged his role in America's frontier myth defined by Richard Slotkin as "a wide-open land of unlimited opportunity for the strong, ambitious, self-reliant individual to thrust his way to the top." Cody even alluded to himself as the "link between savagery and civilization."[13] In his Wild West show, he capitalized on his amalgam of legendary and authentic heroism by encapsulating the frontier as a reality in which he had participated, a time and place dangerous yet theatrical.

Throughout his lifetime, Ingraham wrote six hundred novels—over a third of which include the Buffalo Bill character—and nearly that many novelettes, poems, magazine articles, and plays, often based on his experiences and occasionally under aliases, such as Maj. Dangerfield Burr, Dr. Noel Dunbar, T. W. King, or Alfred B. Taylor.[14] The speed at which he wrote—churning out seventy thousand words in longhand per month—prompted one columnist to observe, "If speed of composition did not allow for niceties of plot, neither did it permit subtlety of character. Indians are invariably treacherous, foreigners foolish, beautiful young women good."[15] Seemingly, Ingraham was more interested in money, productivity, or volume than in creating nuanced characters, except for, perhaps, his leading man Buffalo Bill. Because of his prolific literary output, which netted him $5,000–$7,000 annually (about $140,000 today), another newsman fantasized that Ingraham "writes a novel before breakfast. Another between orange and coffee. Stops in a hotel on his walk downtown and dashes off forty or fifty thousand words in the reading room."[16]

His fiction was occasionally panned as cheap and flamboyant, appealing to the uneducated. "Blood and thunder, impossible situations and impossible heroes. . . . That he was so liberally rewarded for his industry is a severe commentary on American literary taste," denounced one newsman.[17] Rebuffing criticism that his was worthless literature demoralizing the nation's youth, Ingraham argued how newspapers daily published accounts of crime with the potential to inspire similar activity in their readers. Instead, he believed that his own stories "were clear cut in the lesson taught and never made crime attractive, or wickedness or blasphemy other than detestable." He modeled his heroes after men he knew and then allowed imagination to take over.[18] "It's what the people want," he said when interviewed for New York's *Morning Telegraph*. "He ought to know," concluded the reporter. "He's written an average of a novel a day for a good many years. And he has 'local color' down fine. . . . I asked him the other day how he came to write adventure tales, his father having been a famous preacher. 'Somebody had to uphold the reputation of the family,' he replied."[19] To his credit, a perusal of Ingraham's dime novels—some synopses and examples of which are included in this volume's appendix—proves he is a more gifted writer than this biography might lead one to believe.

How or when Ingraham first met Cody is uncertain, but Ingraham claims he accompanied the Fifth Cavalry's expedition to the West as Cody's guest in 1876.[20] Although they had served on opposite sides of the Mason-Dixon line, no animosity seems to have existed between them over past allegiances, and soon Ingraham was working for Cody. The press described Ingraham as one who "looks like the popular idea of a Kentucky colonel. . . . Manners so polished you can see your reflection in them. A way with him that makes men want to shake hands with him, and women ask him to call again."[21] Besides his charisma, Ingraham's literary talents impressed Cody, particularly when he found himself in print in *New York Weekly* as the hero of Ingraham's novel *The Crimson Trail; or, On Custer's Last Warpath* (1876). Consequently, he commissioned Ingraham to write dramas for his theatrical company (*Red Right Hand*, 1876; *Knight of the Plains*, 1879; and *Buffalo Bill at Bay*, 1880).[22]

However, sources hint that the association may have teetered between tolerance and aversion. In letters to a friend, Cody intimated that he never entirely trusted Ingraham, characterizing him as a "bad egg, or that he is a forked tongue [sic]." However, enough confidence must have existed that Ingraham acted for Cody's interest in court in 1884 when disputes arose between Cody and a former partner over ownership of the name of the Wild West show.[23] Ingraham's expertise as publicist also proved advantageous when Cody was touting his Wild West at Chicago's 1893 World's Fair. Although Cody's troupe performed outside the official fairgrounds, Ingraham's publicity helped to bring in over four million people to his show, and Cody walked away a rich man.

However, after the Wild West performed exclusively in Brooklyn's Ambrose Park the next summer, finances were in the red. Cody's partner Nate Salsbury recommended that the show return to its original itinerant arrangement, daily exhibiting in a different city with an untapped audience but, because the park was an excellent showground, it was unreasonable for it to remain idle. Therefore, when Cody toured with the Wild West, Salsbury introduced another program to utilize the park, titled *Black America*, in which over five hundred black performers sang and danced to antebellum melodies.[24] The press numbered it among the century's successes, but Cody later claimed *Black America* lost $78,000. Sanctioning Ingraham's biography provided an opportunity to sell it at Wild West concessions to recoup the losses. Indeed, shortly after the first installments appeared, Cody wished he had fifty thousand more copies of the newspaper to sell, proving that his instincts were correct.[25]

Despite constantly worrying about money to keep the Wild West going and his myriad investments profitable, Cody continued to be financially generous to his family. When his widowed sister Helen married Hugh Wetmore in 1893, Cody bankrolled a $30,000 (over $700,000 today) publishing plant in Duluth, Minnesota, for them, adding his name to the roster of financial investors in the city. The next year, Cody Street was added to the city's map.[26] In return, Wetmore advertised his brother-in-law's business ventures as well as printing a long-running biographical story titled "The Silver Star."[27] Such serialization of fiction was popularized in Britain when the industrial revolution introduced new printing technology and literacy increased. Following the trend, American newspapers printed stories in installments, increasing circulation for the press as well as providing sustaining income for writers who excelled at creating cliffhangers to keep interest high.

When Wetmore serialized Ingraham's Cody biography in the *Duluth Press* in 1895–1896, Helen supplemented the profile with an article titled "Life in Our Childhood Home." The Cody name was prominent in Duluth—his namesakes also included the Cody Sanatorium, one of Helen's pet businesses—but perhaps not everyone knew of his boyhood despite his show business years being well documented. By 1895, Buffalo Bill was, if not the richest, by all accounts the most publicized figure of the West and perhaps the most famous American alive.[28] Besides his Wild West show, he held investments in a tungsten mine in Oracle, Arizona; Panmalt Coffee; the Shoshone Land and Irrigation Company; and the Big Horn Basin & National Park Transportation Company. The new biography, it was hoped, would increase readership as well as interest in Cody's businesses. It worked. By the last installment, an editorial claimed that the newspaper now reached 200,000 readers worldwide.[29]

However, since the point was to make money, Cody became exasperated at Helen's claims on his familial generosity after her various business schemes failed. He paid for her barely two-year-old Cody Sanatorium to be converted into a summer hotel. Five months later, when it burned to the ground, Helen "witness[ed] thousands of my brother's hard earned money go up in smoke." The next year on the same site, Cody built a home for her that she called Cody View, then he ended up paying property liens for the contractors' labor and materials. Finally, he wrote to his older sister begging her to urge Helen to leave him alone. "When she gets financially embarraced [*sic*] which happens often, I raise the money in some way to help her out. . . . My brain is nearly gone thinking how I can tide over my financial trouble."[30]

Thus, for two reasons, Cody anticipated that Ingraham's biography could be sold at the Wild West show as an additional source of income. But, since Cody was familiar with Ingraham's inclination to sensationalism, before Ingraham began, he supposedly reminded him to write only the truth and not to "depict me with an ax in one hand and a warclub in the other, knocking out the brains of all the people I meet."[31] In reality, however, Cody cared not for absolute accuracy but engaged in what historian James Cook called "artful deception . . . a mix of authentic and sham, a momentary suspension of disbelief."[32] In other words, he might not be deliberately untruthful, but neither was he particular about strict adherence to history.

That Cody should issue such instruction is ironic since his autobiography, from which Ingraham drew inspiration, was itself full of confused chronology, misspelled names, and others' adventures misremembered as his own. Nevertheless, knowing that was exactly what his readers expected, Ingraham circumvented the directive by enhancing facts with hyperbole. In his *Adventures of Buffalo Bill: From Boyhood to Manhood* published in *Beadle's Boy's Library* in December 1881, Ingraham had also recklessly borrowed from Cody's autobiography, including stories of his first love, his trapping calamity and broken leg, and his duel with Cheyenne chief Yellow Hair. In some instances in the Duluth biography, Ingraham quotes Cody nearly word for word, including one in which he neglects to substitute the third-person pronoun "he" for Cody's "I."[33] Beyond Cody's own tendency to confuse and exaggerate, Ingraham added an extra layer of fiction, expanding stories Cody told, adding dialogue, and making Cody more intrepid than Cody himself did.

That Ingraham idolized his subject, at least in print, appears obvious from recurring references to "my hero," encouraging readers to regard Cody likewise. In *Adventures of Buffalo Bill*, Ingraham introduced his subject: "Knowing the man well, having seen him amid the greatest dangers, shared with him his blanket and campfire's warmth, I feel entitled to write of him as a hero of heroes," but whether the adulation was, in fact, Ingraham's unbridled sentiment or if, like Buntline, he capitalized on Cody's fame for his own profit may never be known. His myriad novels featuring a Cody character suggests the latter.[34]

Despite their somewhat strained relationship, Ingraham presented Cody in print as a model subject. Cody could do nothing wrong or embarrassing and was never anything but cooperative, kind, and thoughtful of others. His family and military comrades constantly praised him; his frontier wit made him a universal favorite. When Cody confessed to some questionable actions in his autobiography, Ingraham either excluded these in his retelling or amended them to negate any suggestion of imperfection. For example, when General Whistler asked him to carry dispatches to General Sheridan, Cody admitted he objected. According to Ingraham's version, however, Cody promptly consented.[35] When Cody and Wild Bill Hickok brought a wagon of beer into camp for General Carr's troops, "the result was one of the biggest beer jollifications I ever had the misfortune to attend," wrote Cody.[36] Ingraham neglects to report the good time. When Cody, as a nervous justice of the peace, was to perform a wedding ceremony, he admitted he "'braced up' for the occasion by imbibing rather freely of stimulants."[37] Ingraham details the event but overlooks Cody's preparations. He also ignores Cody's admission that, in his jayhawking days of clashing with pro-slavery groups, he had "entered upon a dissolute and reckless life—to my shame be it said—and associated with gamblers, drunkards, and bad characters generally."[38]

On the other hand, if Cody reported that he was part of a group lauded for an impressive Indian fight, Ingraham took it one step further, informing the others, "You were fortunate to have Cody along."[39] Whenever Cody credits a guide or soldier for an auspicious tactic, Ingraham makes the success Cody's own. After one treacherous rescue, Ingraham has a wagon master proclaim, "'You wouldn't have found us alive, boys, if it hadn't been for Billy's dream.' . . . Three extra cheers were given for Will."[40]

Those Duluth readers of the biography unfamiliar with dime novels may have wondered if Ingraham's grammar and punctuation were representative of the genre. He consistently uses passive voice and reverse sentence construction, as in: "The creek where the herder's camp was he well knew." Occasionally, Ingraham breaks the fourth wall and injects his own commentary on a scene, as when he writes, "It may be of interest to the reader just here to know that. . . ." As Orson Welles once said, "There's no biography so interesting as the one in which the biographer is present."[41] Given that criterion, Ingraham's biography is quite remarkable.

Inconsistent capitalization and misuse of commas may be blamed on the typesetter running with free rein or maybe he was simply unable to decipher Ingraham's handwriting. However, readers are likely to be confused by some of his syntax, such as this line: "Recognizing him as a man who had once been in his father's employ and always been friendly with him, he did not doubt what he had told him," leaving it unclear to whom "he" and "him" refers.

Despite the convolutions, that Ingraham grew up as a preacher's son and read widely is apparent from his many biblical and literary refer-

Introduction : 9

ences. He divided the biography into three parts: "A Man of the West" (Cody's childhood years); "Led by Destiny" (his army career); and "Honors Easy" (Cody's theatrical career and intermittent scouting for the army), similar to his father's three volumes of biblical tales: "Prince of the House of David," "The Pillar of Fire," and "The Throne of David." Ingraham alludes to Lot's wife, Balaam's ass, Gabriel's horn, and Nimrod, Noah's great grandson. He indicates that Cody "search[ed] the scriptures."[42] References from secular literature, such as Shakespeare and Thoreau, also proliferate.

Following his father's example, Will Cody was very much an abolitionist, and indications point to his respect for African Americans. Several black cowboys became famous in his Wild West show. Nevertheless, in his autobiography he mimicked contemporary authors, like Mark Twain and Joel Chandler Harris, by ascribing to African Americans a black dialect. Ingraham did not deviate from that tradition. Even though nearly 200,000 African Americans served honorably in the Civil War, Ingraham, possibly with a deep-seated Confederate prejudice, wrote of them as less-than-skilled or -courageous soldiers.

Parts of the biography feature Cody's many perilous encounters with American Indians in his role as army scout. Whether the stories are factual, apocryphal, or hyperbolic, Ingraham seems to have anticipated criticism, particularly of the army's treatment of Indians (the latest massacre—Wounded Knee—occurred only four years prior to the biography's publication), from "those who, in their ignorance of facts and mistaken judgment, carp at the army and such men as Buffalo Bill." Ingraham insists that "the savage nation [is] doomed to fall before the one of civilization."[43] Consequently, modern readers must remember that the account is a product of its time and cultural context, and some language may be offensive.

Ingraham's biography was not the final word on the plainsman-turned-showman. Four years later, Helen Wetmore also wrote a biography of her brother, which included many details she had shared with Ingraham. Peddling her book at the Wild West show, she earned $80,000 in one season.[44] One critique calls her *Last of the Great Scouts* "a vapid book . . . cluttered with sentimentality, accounts of Cody's tenderheartedness, stories of devotion to his mother, and a sterling pedigree for the family." Buffalo Bill, who had not publicly commended Ingraham's work, nevertheless in a brotherly show of affection, applauded Helen's tome as the "only one true book about me . . . all the rest is fiction."[45]

After Ingraham's death in 1904, his wife, the former Rosa Langley, told a reporter, "My husband often wished to confine his literary work to that for which he was best fitted," presumably referring to his plays or poems. "But," she continued, "the other kind was the more lucrative."[46] Regardless of how he exaggerated, or even invented, facts about Buffalo Bill Cody, Ingraham presented Cody's perspective on American history, carefully curated for reading audiences.

The text of Ingraham's biography has been transcribed from the original and includes accompanying illustrations by Alice M. Cooke. While care has been taken to ensure the integrity of the original, many typographical errors have been corrected, such as *trouble* for *trouple* and *won't* for *wont*. Ingraham's footnotes, designated with asterisks, are left intact, as are stray punctuation marks, particularly commas and quotation marks, except those noted for clarity. The notes provide background information on Ingraham's references as well as on historical events and characters mentioned; the bibliography lists works consulted in preparing the notes and suggests further reading on Buffalo Bill Cody and Prentiss Ingraham. Digitized versions of several of Ingraham's Buffalo Bill novels can be found at https://swco-ir.tdl.org/swco-ir/handle/10605/395 and https://dimenovels.org/Series/162/Full Text.

Prentiss Ingraham, Buffalo Bill Center of the West, Cody, Wyoming, USA; P.69.0143

"A MAN OF THE WEST"

An Authentic History of the Remarkable and Romantic Career of
Col. W. F. Cody—"Buffalo Bill"
—From—
Boyhood to Manhood.
by Col. Prentiss Ingraham.
Author of "Montezuma," "The Mutineer," "A Knight of the Plains,"
"Florette," "Love and Duty," "A Child of the Street," Etc., Etc.

There is no more unique character and picturesque personage in American history today, than is Col. W. F. Cody—Buffalo Bill, the hero of this true story of the romantic realities of a most phenomenal career.

Of the earlier boyhood of William F. Cody, of home life and influences, the brave father, the noble mother and the loving sisters, true daughters of the west, that aided so well to shape the destiny of the son and brother, this beau ideal of the "Land of the Setting Sun," comparatively little is known to the world, and hence this story has been written to place before the public the scenes, incidents, aspirations, and deeds that led the boy step by step up the arduous path of fame, fortune, and honor.

William F. Cody stands today as the last typical Knight of the Plains, a man whose deeds will send his name down through ages indelibly stamped upon the pages of American history, as a Pilot of the Border, one who was a Pioneer into the wilderness, standing as a barrier be-

A Man of the West

tween the savage and the emigrant, who daringly followed the "Star of Empire" on its way into western wonderland, and winning for himself laurels that will never fade.

The Author.[1]

CHAPTER I.
A HERO IN EMBRYO.

Standing upon the banks of the Mississippi river, where its waters wash the shores of Scott county, Iowa, was a boy of ten, gazing with face all aglow from the tints of the setting sun, as well as lighted up with thoughts that were then crowding upon him.[2]

At his side stood a dog patiently awaiting the will of his young master, while a pony was cropping at the bunches of juicy grass near by, yet now and then casting longing glances toward the barn of a pleasant farm house standing back from the river.

The boy's attitude was one of perfect repose, as he was leaning upon his little rifle, and lost in deepest reveries, for he was just then a dreamer, as in his heart that day aspirations had been awakened for a brighter life than that led in the farm house where his boyhood life had been spent.

Who can tell the thoughts then busy in the brain of the Boy Dreamer?

Today, in manhood's prime, having passed through scenes of death and danger, of hardships untold, sorrows that left their impress upon his life and drunk from the cup of joy and fame as well, having won a name among men, the man recalls vividly that day forty years ago, when he stood gazing at the swiftly plowing Mississippi as it glided at his feet, and felt the first glow of kindling ambition to some time become more than a mere country lad.

In our childhood it is that we dream our dreams of ambition, alas! so many of them to have but a sad awakening as we find our hopes are blasted and we are fitted only for the common routine of life.

But Will Cody, the boy, builded greater than he knew, and his after years more than fulfilled the ambitions of his early youth.

And the reason of his ambitious dream? The night before his father, a well-to-do farmer and honored citizen,[3] thinking to better his fortunes, and thus more liberally provide for his large family, had made known

A Hero in Embryo

his intentions to his wife and children to give up his home in Iowa, and penetrate further to the westward.

This expressed determination of Isaac Cody, to leave a pleasant home, where he was popular with the people and held several positions of trust and honor, and seek a new home and new associations in the then Territory of Kansas, gave joy to the heart of his little son, who saw in it the consummation of his hopes to penetrate western wilds, the home of the Indian, and behold frontier life as it really was, as he had heard stories told of it, and had listened by the hour to tales read to him of the brave deeds of the Pioneers.

Now had come to him the opportunity to live amid the scenes and people of the far frontier, and all that day as he had ridden along through forest and valley in search of birds and squirrels to bring down with his rifle, for once the game was unnoticed, and he returned homeward in the gathering gloom without the string it was his usual good fortune to supply the larder with.

"And we are going to Kansas," were the words repeated over and over by the boy, who could he have known what sorrow and suffering was to come to those he loved by "going west," would have gladly then and there awakened from his dreaming and been content to remain upon the old farm in Iowa.

And could Isaac Cody only have had a premonition of the fate that was to be his in the then wild land of Kansas, he too would have lingered there on the Mississippi near the graves of his dead loved ones, content to remain in the sunshine of a humble, yet happy life, rather than venture into the untried and unknown.

But Isaac Cody was no ordinary man, he possessed pluck and determination, he had decided to take the step, be it for better or worse, and thus was Will Cody's dream of "Westward ho" realized, the die was cast for good or evil, and there was no back-down in the blood of the Codys.

CHAPTER II.
WESTWARD HO!

A pleasant abiding place was the farm of Isaac Cody, near the little village of LeClaire, Iowa,[4] and where in the little burying ground, sleep the loved ones Death called away from the family circle before their removal to Kansas.

One incident in the life of Will Cody that left a deep impress upon him young as he was, I may mention here.

It was the death of his elder brother, Sam, a handsome, daring youth full of adventure and pluck, whom Will looked up to as his guide and good comrade.[5]

As Sam was killed by being thrown from his horse while riding with Will, the blow made a deeper impression than it otherwise would have done upon his younger brother, who was thus left upon his own resources for outdoor sports and comradeship.

But this was the means of making Will Cody more self-reliant and manly, and with his brother dead he naturally looked upon himself as the one his mother and sisters should call upon in the absence of his father from home, or his being wrapped up in the cares and duties that were his.

The home of Mr. Isaac Cody in Iowa was a fine old farmhouse. Surrounded by many comforts, and yet with the western fever upon him he gave up all to penetrate into what was at that time almost a terra incognita.

Having a brother[6] living in Missouri, near the Kansas border line Mr. Cody determined to first visit him and make that his starting point to go forth in search of a home.

"A Man of the West" : 17

A man of fine physique, determined pluck, energy and endowed with brain to think and act, he believed that he could grow up, as it were, with a new country and make his influence felt.

So the venture was made, and one bright morning with Mrs. Cody and the girls packed away in the old family carriage, drawn by two stout horses, three wagons, known as "prairie schooners," drawn by mules, and riding in the lead, with Will mounted on his pony, at whose heels trotted Turk, a magnificent dog and faithful pard[7] of the boy, the start on the long trail was begun.*

To say that the "young hopeful" of the Cody family was happy at the prospect of a long and dangerous journey into the wilds of the far west, would be to express his feelings most mildly.

He was simply in ecstasies, in his self-contained way, a virtue I may here say has ever clung to him, for, learning in boyhood to command himself he has thus been an able commander of others.

With his pony, and his other boon companion, Turk, the dog, his rifle and puffed up with the importance of being a youthful Pioneer, his cup of bliss was full to overflowing.

In those days, away back in the fifties, overland travel over bad roads, and through sparsely settled country was very different from what it is now.

But Mr. Cody knew all that was before him, and his good wife realizing it also, put her shoulder to the wheel with all the pluck and energy of the noble wife and mother that she was.

They both knew that at first their way would be along roads where at night they could find shelter in farm houses, accommodations which young William, and several of his more adventurous sisters did not care for, as their hearts were set upon "camping out."

"It won't be any fun until we can camp out at night," sagely remarked my hero, to his sister Helen, who promptly agreed with him.

The line of march continued slowly but surely along the roads point-

---

*The family at that time were Isaac Cody, his wife, five daughters and Will.

Martha, the oldest girl, was then eighteen and died several years after in Kansas. Julia, a girl of thirteen, is now Mrs. J. A. Goodman and lives with her husband on a ranch near North Platte, Neb. Will Cody came next in age, then Helen, now Mrs. Wetmore the partner with her brother of the Duluth Press, and the youngest was May, now Mrs. E. C. Bradford, of Denver, Col. —The Author.

ing to the southwest, Mr. Cody's intention being to cross into Missouri at a point near the Kansas line, his brother Elijah Cody living in Platte County, Missouri.

It was with much interest that the father watched his young son, and saw how eager he was to make himself useful and do a man's share in the care of the wagon train.

The elder boy, Sam, had been taken from them, as has been told, and Will had become their idol, and was a young hero in the eyes of his sister, Martha, the eldest, being completely wrapped up in him.

With feelings of misgiving, therefore, remembering Sam's sad end, the parents and sisters were wont to see the boy ride away each day from the trail of travel to secure game for them, and seldom returned empty handed.

At length as they journeyed on the farmhouses grew like Angel's visits, few and far between, and the face of the boy brightened as he whispered to his sisters: "I heard father tell mother that he expected we would have to camp tomorrow night, and won't I be glad."

And so the anticipation was fulfilled, for they came to a stream where there was a lone ferryman and his boat, in the midst of a dense wilderness, and night was coming on.

The nearest habitation across the river was a dozen miles away, and the ferryman said he could not more than get the wagons across by dark.

The carriage went first, and Will was deputized by his father to select a good camping ground across the river, and he was eminently successful, for it has been said by Army officers whom he has since guided on many a long trail, that it is a talent with him to pick his way through an unknown country and select good campgrounds, and certainly there is an art in it.

The camp was pitched on the river bank, in a sheltered wood, with plenty of grass at hand for the horses, wood nearby for the camp fires, and altogether it made a most comfortable and picturesque recess.

His first task well done the boy shouldered his rifle, whistled to Turk, and set out on foot to find some game to make the camp scene more complete.

A quail or two, rabbit and a squirrel would have satisfied him, for thus far his ambition scarce dared soar to larger game, so he was fairly started when Turk gave a warning note, and there, not a hundred feet away came bounding along a graceful deer.

So dazed was the boy at sight of his first deer, that he was seized at once with what hunters call the "buck fever," and stood rifle in hand gazing at the beautiful creature until it disappeared from sight with Turk in full cry after him.

But Turk was running a losing race, and realizing the fact he quickly returned, disgusted with his young master and himself.

Seeing the dog's reproachful look, Will's face flushed with shame, and he muttered in apologetic tone:

"I know, Turk—it's too bad I couldn't shoot him and you couldn't catch him, but next time—"

Another warning yelp from the dog, a crashing of bushes near at hand, and there bounded into view a fine stag.

Stopping a moment to gaze at the young hunter in a surprised way, his curiosity was fatal to him, for the boy's rifle went up to his shoulder, there was an instant of suspense, then a sharp report and bounding into the air the stag fell dead.

The boy had redeemed himself in his own and in Turk's eyes.

Will Cody had killed his first deer, brought to earth his first big game.

CHAPTER III.
A BRAVE RESCUE.

William Cody has said that he does not remember when he first learned to swim, or that he learned at all, for it came as natural to him as it does to an Indian.

That he could swim and well before the time he is presented to my readers, is proven by the fact that he once saved a schoolmate several years his senior, from drowning when they were attending the country school on the Mississippi.

A cry for help from the boy who had ventured beyond his strength, and it was "little Will Cody" that went to his aid and assisted to the shore, thus placing to his credit the saving of a human life.

Cultivating the art of swimming, he had often gone in a skiff in the

Mississippi, and leaping overboard made his way to a landing far below, a comrade paddling after him.

I have thus spoken of him as a youthful swimmer to show that he had confidence in himself young as he was, and it will not be surprising to know that he risked his life for a dumb brute as he had for a comrade.

It was several days after the first night's camp on the trail to Kansas, then at the lonely ferry, and when "camping out" still held its dreams for him, growing instead of lessening in interest with each occurrence.

His first camp, and his first deer, coming at one time as it were, had filled his heart with joy, and he had long remained awake, wrapped in his blanket, gazing at the twinkling stars, listening to the rippling of the water, and building castles high in the air of what he would make of the future.

Continuing on the next day the boy felt himself more of a man than he had ever dreamed of becoming for years, and he saw though he did not seem to do so, that his parents and sisters regarded him with more pride than ever before, even the men who drove the wagons seeming to feel his added importance.

But what has this to do with swimming some may ask. Simply that I dwell upon the incidents of minor importance, though many occur that went to shape the life of the man whose name today is known the world over.

"There is a divinity that shapes our ends,
Rough hew them how we will,"[8]

expresses a great deal, and it was the minor happenings in Will Cody, the boy's life, that made him famous as a man.

It was the third day after the first camp out, and the little party had camped over Sunday on the banks of a stream that was swift and deep.

Turk, anxious to distinguish himself had crossed with the ferryman and gone in chase of a rabbit.

It was a long, hard chase, and though the Sabbath Day Turk had run down his game, and with it in his mouth, as proof of his success, returned to the river to find the boat had returned to the shore.

He had slipped away, and feeling guilty, at the same time being very warm, he had plunged in to swim across.

But a cry from one of the girls told Will that his dog pard was in distress, and running to the river he saw him there, struggling violently, but still clinging to the rabbit.

Unheeding the warning cry of the Ferryman, the boy sprang into the river, and with a few bold strokes reached the drowning dog, for Turk was game, and though chilled by the cold water would not release his hold upon the rabbit, and was nearly gone when he felt the grasp of his young master upon him.

"Come, help me with the boat! The rapids are just below and he'll be drowned," shouted the Ferryman, and a rush was made for the boat.

Will Cody heard the warning cry, gave a quick glance toward the rapids, and with his left arm supporting Turk struck out for the further shore, to which he was nearest.

Just as he staggered out of the water the boat touched the shore, and the Ferryman called out with angry energy:

"You was a fool, boy, to do that, for this haint no river to swim in."

"I wouldn't let my dog die," was the modest reply, and it appeased the anger of the Ferryman who responded:

"Well, you has got grit, to risk your life for a dog, and some day you'll be heerd from.[']"

And Will Cody never forgot the prophecy, and it gladdened his heart to hear his father reply:

"It was a risk, Ferryman, but the boy was right, for he loves that dog as though he were a human being."

Taken to camp Turk was kindly cared for and soon came around all right, though he fought shy of the water after that for awhile, and sat in the very middle of the boat crossing the stream the next day.

CHAPTER IV.
A SABLE APPARITION.

The overland journey daily increased interest for the young emigrants, whatever Mr. Cody and his wife might think of it for theirs was the responsibility, the vigil, the care of their loved ones and dread of what the future might bring forth.

The loss of a horse now and then, the breaking down of a wagon, a delay by storms and swollen streams all went to make up events that

A Sable Apparition

were, to the young adventurer of the outfit, of greatest interest and importance.

Daily he became more hardened in muscle, more thoughtful of all duties devolving upon him; he rode his pony with a firmer seat, and the way he handled a rifle, young as he was, made him an expert in its use, and fitted him to face many a deadly danger in after years, when his life, and the lives of others depended upon his deadly aim and iron nerve.

The journey was a revelation to the boy, a schooling he never forgot, and which formed the foundation of his after life.

From the scattering settlements found along the trail, Mr. Cody learned that he must be on his guard against rough characters that infested the road, for several times of late emigrants had been attacked and robbed, in some cases killed.

Will Cody heard his father tell the wagon drivers to be on the guard, and though he was not taken into their confidence, he was told to keep closer to the wagons on the march.

The boy kept his own council [sic], but from that moment was as watchful on the way and in the camp, as was his father, and Turk shared in this watchfulness with him.

It was true that they did meet a band or two of rough men, but were not molested, for there was something about Mr. Cody that showed he would stand no nonsense.

Refusing to allow several suspicious characters to share their camp one night, Mr. Cody felt sure that they meant later to come and attack them, and all were put on their guard.

Will Cody and Turk constituted themselves special guardians, and all through the night the dog would growl, bristle up and bark, and if an attack was intended at first, the men thought better of it.

"You and Turk saved us last night, Will," said Mr. Cody the next morning, and both boy and dog showed their appreciation of the praise bestowed upon them; but after their night's vigil Will was half asleep as he rode along, swerving at times to a dangerous angle in his saddle, while Turk allowed rabbits and squirrels to go unnoticed, and even a deer darted by without a shot.

At last they drew near the end of their long trail, and night found them on the Missouri line, near a comfortable farm house where dwelt a widow.

To their surprise they were refused shelter, until Mr. Cody told that he was on his way to his brother's home, and was glad that the end of their journey was near at hand.

The name of Elijah Cody proved an "open sesame" to the widow's hospitality, as she knew him well, and the travelers were at once invited to make themselves at home.

When Mr. Cody returned to his halted train he saw that something was wrong, and he hastened to discover the cause of the excitement and seeming fear of his children, for even Will had a half-awed expression upon his face, and Turk was all bristled up, and his tail, usually carried high in air had a decided droop that betokened fear.

Mrs. Cody was there, and about her clung the girls, while my hero and his dog stood slightly apart gazing at the object of their dread.

At first Mr. Cody was alarmed, but the face of his wife reassured him, for it was an amused expression.

And no wonder, for it was the Cody children's first sight of a negro.

There before them amazed at the reception he had met, stood a negro in whose veins no drop of blood other than African flowed.

Black! Ebony would appear a dull slate color by comparison.

Large-featured, shining white teeth revealed in a broad grin, eyes that looked like black balls floating in miniature cups of milk, jetty wool that clung close to his scalp, a hickory shirt open to the waist, knee pants held up by one suspender, a ragged straw hat twisted nervously in his black hands, and feet of enormous size and the big toes boring holes into the ground, as though to hide, made up the picture of the first negro Will Cody and his sisters had ever seen.

An Indian in full war paint would not have startled them more, and Mr. Cody enjoyed the picture.

The man was a slave, belonging to the widow whose home was near, and he had come suddenly out of the bushes on the roadside, appearing like a black apparition before the startled young emigrants, taking all aback, even to Turk.

Mr. Cody spoke pleasantly to the negro, who answered respectfully, and was most willing to help in making the strangers feel at home, though he kept an anxious look upon Turk the while.

Somewhat reassured by his father's action, Will went up the negro and offered his hand very much as he would have done to a performing bear at a show, and said boldly:

"I think I shall like you."

"Yes Massa, all childers likes Nigger Jim."

"Is your name Jim?"

"Yes Massa, Nigger Jim."

"Is a nigger a negro?"

"No Massa, only a nigger."

Will seemed proud of being called "Massa," and would have continued the conversation ad infinitum, had he not been called to supper in the widow's hospitable home, where the table fairly groaned with edibles he had never seen before, for nearly all states, peopled by different nationalities, have their distinct dishes as well as customs.

That night Will tossed uneasily in a feather bed, for he preferred camp life and blankets to the comforts of a farmhouse, and Turk did not enjoy sweet repose either, as three separate times "Nigger Jim" had to beat the farm dogs off of him, for they had not been influenced by their mistress to extend the same hospitality to the strange canine which she had to her most welcome guests.

The next day the trail was renewed and pushing along at a good pace they reached the comfortable and hospitable home of Elijah Cody in Platte County, Missouri, where the welcome that awaited them more than made up for the hardships of the long journey.

CHAPTER V.
WILL CODY'S FIRST MEETING WITH "POOR LO."[9]

It took several days to rest up after the long trip to Missouri, but Mr. Cody was anxious to get to work as soon as possible, and, advised by his brother, he decided to cross the river upon a prospecting tour.

Will and Turk were most anxious to go along, but a compromise was reached which resulted in the boy accompanying his father, while the dog remained behind.

Will was more reconciled to this arrangement by his uncle telling him that Turk would have whole tribes of Indian curs on the warpath after him, to which the ill treatment of the widow's dogs would be a picnic.

Mounted upon good horses the father and boy set forth upon the prospecting tour, crossing the Missouri River and striking up the Kickapoo Indian Agency in what is now Leavenworth County, Kansas.[10]

At that time there were a number of Indian Reservations in Kansas, through which ran the great Overland Trail to Salt Lake City and California.

Thousands of "gold seekers," on their way to find fortunes, also passed through the territory via Fort Leavenworth, then a most important Military Post, as in fact it really is today, though not from the same causes.[11]

Mormons also on their hegira[12] from Illinois, made use of this trail, so that constantly there was a stream of humanity flowing westward and eastward.

Mr. Cody was wise enough to see that this constant ebb and flow of people made their line of march the very spot for a Trading Post, and after a few days of search he found a place to his liking four miles from the Kickapoo Agency and in the beautiful Salt Creek Valley.

It was here that Will Cody made the acquaintance of his first Indian, and the introduction was more startling than his meeting with "Nigger Jim."

Worn out with hard riding his father had left him asleep in a noon day halting place, while he and the guide rode away to find just the place for the proposed post.

How long the boy slept he did not know, but he awoke with what to him was a nightmare.

Could he believe his eyes, when they opened upon the fact that an Indian was about to mount his pony and ride away, leaving in his stead a most wretched specimen of the genus horse.

But it was no dream, no nightmare conjured up by a very generous lunch, but a stern reality.

The boy gave a shout and sprang to his feet, his rifle in hand.

"That's my horse," he shouted, though he made no attempt to use his rifle.

The Indian stood looking at him and said:

"Me swap pony with pale face boy."

Will Cody had heard his father tell a story once of an Indian and a white man going hunting together, when the former killed a fine turkey, the latter a turkey buzzard.

With the usual method of the pale face treating the redskin, the white man proposed a division of the game as follows:

"You take buzzard and give me turkey, or I take turkey and give you the buzzard."

But "Poor Lo" saw through the generous proposition of the white man, and replied:

"Pale face no say turkey to me once."

So it seemed now to Will Cody, that in the "swap" proposed he was in the position the Indian referred to, for the redskin before him was going to take the "turkey," his good horse, and leave him the animal that would soon be food for buzzards.

Must he submit to the bargain that was all one-sided?

There he was, face to face with one of the race of whom he had heard stories read and tales told. He had longed for that meeting with a real American citizen.

His ambition had been to gaze into the cunning eyes of the fierce and untamed "child of forest and plains," and the moment had come.

What should he do; what could he do?

The Indian was armed, he saw that; but must he allow him to walk off with his Uncle Elijah's fine horse and leave instead "a bag of bones"?

What would his uncle think, and what would his father say?

What opinion would his sisters have of him?

Oh! that Turk were only there to help him out!

And how far away were his father and the guide?

But Turk was across the Missouri River, doubtless sampling Missouri rabbits, and Mr. Cody and the guide were not within sight, perhaps not within hearing.

And so Will Cody felt that the ordeal had been thrust upon him, that he must work out his own salvation.

CHAPTER VI.
PROSPECTING IN KANSAS.

I left my young hero in a predicament by no means an enviable one, for he stood face to face with a redskin who was making a forced trade of horses with him, the bargain being all on his side.

But Will Cody was not one to be robbed even by an Indian, and so he said boldly:

"No, I won't swap."

"Pale face boy fool."

Just then Will did not care to argue that matter, especially as he thought the Indian might be right, as he had been foolish in preferring a nap to going with his father.

But the horse question he would argue, and so replied:

"Don't you take my horse."

"Pale face horse no good."

This was a slander upon a most excellent animal, and it lowered the redskin in the boy's estimation, for he had had an impression that what an Indian did not know about the qualities of a horse was really not worth knowing.

"He's good enough for me," was the cautious reply, and he boldly added:

"You take your old crow roost and go."

The Indian quickly let go of the rein he held, turned to his pony and mounting rode away in silence, but with a weather eye cast backward as though to watch any hostile movement of the boy's gun.

"Why I scared him!

"What an Indian," muttered Will in mingled triumph and contempt.

But hardly had he uttered the words when he caught sight of the guide returning for him, and muttered:

"I guess HE scared him."

And Will was about right in his guess.

The guide had returned to tell him that his father had found a place to pitch his tent and was there awaiting him, and gave a blow to Will's pride by adding:

"That redskin jist see me a comin' and lit out.

"If I hadn't come as I did, he'd hev tuck yer critter."

"I'm glad you came," muttered Will, and the Indian was replaced upon the pinnacle he had formerly occupied in his estimation, and from which he had momentarily been dethroned.

When he reached the spot where the guide had left his father, they found him standing as though spell bound, gazing at the scene of beauty spread out before him, for he was looking upon Salt Creek Valley, a vale of beauty that has few rivals in the scenery of our land.

Standing upon the brow of what today is known as Government Hill, the view of Salt Creek Valley opened before the vision of Isaac Cody in all its grand and picturesque beauty.[13]

There he remained in silent admiration at the sight, so lost in fact that he failed to notice the return of his guide with Will, and unheeding the former's words:

"Yer've got the right spot ter see it all, and yer can't beat it, Pard, go whar yer will."

Will Cody gave one look over the scene and uttered an exclamation of pleasure, for he has ever been a devoted lover of Nature.

So there he also stood and gazed up on the scene, then grand in its loneliness and unbroken natural beauty, so different today where it is broken by the artificial work of puny man.

But it is of what it was then that I would speak, for with the advantages of civilization the world can gaze on it as it is today.

Stretching away for miles the western boundary line of the valley the hill that today bears his name—Cody Hill—met the vision of the man who then little dreamed what changes time would make there, that it would be the theatre of such busy action as followed close upon the establishment of his home in a spot so peaceful and inviting to the travel-worn Pioneer, still following the Star of Empire[14] as untiringly as did the Three Wise Men follow the Star of Bethlehem in the Land of the Rising Sun.

Adown [sic] the centre of the valley wound Salt Creek, like a silver belt as the stream glided over the pebbly bottom to mingle with the murky waters of the Missouri River, rushing onward toward the Gulf.

Afar off the little hamlet of the Kickapoo Agency nestled close to the Missouri, the smoke from the fires curling upward to mingle with the blue haze above.

Still further off Fort Leavenworth, then a frontier fort in every particular, frowned down up on the scene, with the Stars and Stripes floating over it, the only bit of bright coloring in the scene.

Such was the landscape upon which Isaac Cody gazed, and it was no wonder that his little son stood also looking with awe-struck eyes upon the scene.

They were at last in Kansas—there was to be their future home. In that scene of beauty the man was to toil hard for his family, the boy to lay the foundation for his future years.

What thoughts, dreads, hopes, longings crowded upon the man as he stood there, what ambitions upon the boy?

Who can tell?

They had come out of the Land of the Rising Sun—they had ventured into the Land of the Setting Sun.

The eyes of the man as he stood there were resting upon the spot that was to be his grave.

To him it was to be the Valley of Shadows.

CHAPTER VII.
WILL'S INTRODUCTION TO A WILD WESTERNER.

Settling his family temporarily upon a farm in Missouri, Mr. Cody moved into Kansas to establish himself upon the spot selected in Salt Creek Valley.

Of course Will accompanied him, for the boy would not have it otherwise, and he had seen just enough of the busy life along the border to make an existence on a farm decidedly tame to him.

He was playfully called his father's shadow, and was proud of the title, while Mr. Cody found him most useful to have with him.

"The boy has a level head, and if not studying his books just now, as he will have to do when we get settled, he is learning much by rough experience and it will do him good.

"Let him go along with me."

Thus said the father, and with such a backing Will Cody was again to cross the river into Kansas, but not without a series of admonitions, entreaties and commands from his mother and sisters to keep out of the way of Indians and wild westerners.

Now this was good advice only it was the wrong country in which the boy could follow it, for it was the land of wild westerners and redskins, of big game and lawlessness, hardships and dangers.

The cabins were built there in the beautiful valley, the stores sent for, and the Trading Post established, with every prospect that it would be a most successful undertaking.

Roughing it had been the order of the day, but this Will liked, and it was while the post was being established that he came in contact with the typical westerner.

His first acquaintance with an out and out man of the Plains, who might be anything fancy pictured him, from his general make up, was not reassuring.

The boy was seated on the side of the trail, in the little camp, when with a wild war-whoop up dashed a horseman in all the picturesque wildness of the Plains.

His horse came bounding along, the man yelling at each bound, while he slung his lariat around and around his head.

Will was delighted at the sight, for he beheld a man with large sombrero, buckskin leggings and top boots, the heels armed with massive spurs, a woolen shirt, belt of arms about his waist and the general make-up of a "terror."

He seemed too large for his little horse, which the saddle nearly covered, and Will felt that barring this fact he gazed up on a real "Hero of the Plains."

As he sat there in open-mouthed wonder and admiration the Westerner suddenly spied him, gave a wild whoop, and swerving from his direct way launched his lariat with the cry:

"Hoop la! I've roped you young'un."

And he had, for the noose settled down over Will's head and shoulders, the horse was brought to a sudden halt and the lariat drawn suddenly taut the boy was pulled from the log forward upon his face.

"Halt thar! Git down off that critter an' ax thet boy's pardon and set him loose, or I'll put a bullet inter yer coward heart."

Will heard the words and wondered who it was that had dared speak to the great sombrero hero.

He struggled to his feet, half stunned by the fall, and what he saw amazed him, for his champion was a mere nobody, a young man with red hair, freckled face and with nothing of the hero about him, while he was engaged by his father for the humble work of cutting brush from about the cabin.

And yet he it was who had dared face the bold horseman, the picturesque desperado.

But Will saw that the young gentleman who answered simply to the name of "Red-Head," had a revolver covering the mighty man who had so skillfully attached him to the end of his lariat, and what happened surprised him the more.

"I were playin' with the kid," sheepishly said the horseman.

"Waal I haint playin' with you—quick! or I'll pull the trigger."

"Ef I has hurt him I is sorry, for I is tender hearted."

"That don't go!"

"You is coward hearted, and you asks his pardon or yer hands in your chips right here.

"Now do it."

There was that about Red Head, simple and humble as he looked that showed he meant what he said, and the bully dismounted and approached the boy, excusing his doing so by saying:

"I wouldn't harm yer fer nothin', kid, and asks yer pardon—come, shake hands."

"No, I won't, for you are a coward to bully a boy and back down from a man," was the bold reply, and it brought a yell of delight from Red Head who called out:

"Now git, or my gun goes off!"

The man muttered a threat, threw himself into his saddle and was off like a shot, while Will walked up to his defender and warmly thanked him for what he had done.

Will's Introduction to a Wild Western Terror

"I knowed he were nobody when he came whoopin' up here, hopin' ter scare some folks, and when I see him yank you off thet log, I concluded it would be a fight or a footrace."

Will disliked to be under obligations, and tried to even matters by saying he hoped some day he could do something for his defender, and years later, to his great delight, he was able to repay the debt of gratitude two fold.

CHAPTER VIII.
EARLY DAYS IN KANSAS.

After his introduction to the typical "wild westerner," Will Cody was not so impressed with the rude and fractious elements of adventurers pioneering the west, and which attached themselves to the forts, settlements and wagon trains of the Overland.[15]

His father explained to him that this ruffian element was apparently a necessary adjunct to the caravans westward bound and the border settlements, where were also many honest and noble hearted men.

Tares[16] would grow among the wheat he told the boy, and no man must be judged by his garb, but by his actions, for the roughest appearing men might possess the noblest of natures, and his defender, Red Head, for if he had another name he did not claim it, had shown that his heart was in the right place.

Anticipating that what was known as the "Enabling Act of Kansas,"[17] which would permit settlers to enter the Territory, would soon be passed by Congress, Mr. Cody, prospering at his Trading Post, took his family from the farm in Missouri and established them with him, at once commencing to build a suitable home for them.

It was a cabin home, built of stout logs, with the necessary out buildings, garden plot and farm lands; but it was a home, however humble and primitive, and each member of the family set to work to make it all that circumstances would permit.

The Post had become a general rendezvous for all traders, emigrants and Indians as well, and witnessing daily feats of daring horsemanship that filled him with admiration, beholding men make the most marvelous shots with rifle and revolver, throw a lasso unerringly, and listening to thrilling deeds done by the true men of the border, the boy longed to emulate them and become also a true Hero of the Plains.

Few as his years were, he had learned a lesson in reading character, begun to understand human nature, and was able to sift the chaff from the wheat, to know bluster from modest courage, to pick out the man who would talk from the one who would act, and each day the schooling he was under, rough though it might be, was the foundation of his character for future years.

Among Mr. Cody's good patrons were the Kickapoo Indians from the Agency, and they all seemed to take a fancy to the boy, youths of his age teaching him how to follow a trail, shoot with a bow and arrow, snare birds and other game, all of which he became most expert in, and enjoyed to such an extent that his mother and sisters found it a hard task to "round him up" for household duties.

But the boy never forgot the days when he had to go on rides to the fort, Indian Agency, and take messages to other points for his father, whom he always was proud to serve and often was trusted with missions of a most important nature.

Though in a wilderness as it were, Mrs. Cody never forgot her duty to her children and her household, but did all in her power to instruct each one in all they owed to their parents and themselves, and to make an ideal and happy home, crude though it necessarily was.

In this praiseworthy effort, busy as he was by day and night, Mr. Cody gave a willing helping hand, and the "Cody family" became respected by the roughest element that ever found a hospitable reception under their roof, while "Cody's boy," as Will was called, became a favorite with all who met him, and his pluck was the talk of bearded men, as often there occurred little things to call it forth.

"The boy don't know what fear is," was a common expression among the men who frequented the Trading Post, and overhearing the remark at times, from men he respected, it made him anxious to bear the same record through life.

Those who know William F. Cody today, and remember something of his career, know well that his nerve has never failed him, no matter what the trying ordeal through which he has had to pass.

When the "Enabling Act" was passed by Congress then the rush into Kansas begun.[18]

Anticipating what would be done thousands of settlers gathered upon the Missouri border, awaiting the tocsin[19] to sound that bade them "go."

At night the campfires could be seen along the Missouri for miles, and those in the territory already, the officers at Fort Leavenworth, the traders and others knew well that when the day of coming should come there would be turned loose upon Kansas a horde that would be hard indeed to manage.

Mr. Cody made all arrangements for pre-empting his claim the moment the Act should become a law.

At last came the news, the claim was pre-empted, and Isaac Cody became a citizen of the territory of Kansas, and could not but watch with deepest interest the rush of the human tide across the border for homes.

Honest men most of them were, with their families, some worldly goods, household furniture, cattle and all that went to make up a home.

A few were well-to-do, others poor, and a number were adventurers, outcasts from other homes and associations, who avoided work as they would a pestilence, living by their wits or a game of bluff, believing that the world owed them a living and determined to have it at no matter what cost to others.

Both Mr. and Mrs. Cody found the realization far worse than the anticipation, and felt a foreboding of what the future might be for their children; but the die had been cast and they were there to stay, so like the brave man and woman they were they faced the alternative fearlessly.

When the first mad rush was over, the fierce struggle for claims, a better feeling followed and the element of law-abiders were anxious to rule.

But alas! there were two parties of the very people who were law-lovers, and the seeds of discord were at once planted to bring forth a harvest of bitter fruit.

The gulf that divided them was "slavery," and the question was not laid to rest until the soil of Kansas was reddened with the blood of hundreds of brave men, and a stain was put upon the land which tears of regret can never blot out.

CHAPTER IX.
FACING THE ORDEAL.

In the early settlement of Kansas nearly all who crossed the river from Missouri, or came from other states of the Southwest, were in favor of slavery, while the settlers from Indiana, Illinois and the northern states were against having a slave state.

It was this very question which caused the "Kansas war,"[20] in my humble opinion, the direct cause of the civil struggle that followed years after.

With bitterness thus engendered between the two elements, it increased day by day, the shadows deepened over the fair land, and thinking men fully understood that a single imprudent act would precipitate a war to the knife, and knife to the hilt.

Having firmly established himself in Kansas, made its interests his interests, Mr. Cody went on in the even tenor of his way hoping against hope that all would yet be well.

But the storm was gathering, though slowly, and though Mr. Cody hoped it would never break upon their beautiful valley, by a strange coincidence he was the innocent cause of the first blow being struck, the first victim of the war of vengeance, for such it was.

Near the Salt Creek Trading Post there had been a store established and kept by a man by the name of Rively,[21] and around it a number of settlers had made their home.

Rively was a pro-slavery man, and his near neighbors were also of his way of thinking, and at his store one day a large crowd had gathered.[22]

Mr. Cody had gone there, accompanied by Will, and as the crowd soon worked themselves up into a fervor, it was decided to hold a meeting and have speakers.

Mr. Cody would have departed, not caring to express his views, but it had leaked out that he had been known as an excellent speaker in Iowa, he was supposed to hold views similar to those about him, and he was actually forced to address the crowd.

The "platform" was a large drygoods box, and mounting it, he gazed over the sea of faces about him.

He knew that his words would not please, that he was against bringing slavery into Kansas, but he was no coward, he had the courage of his convictions, and he would not flinch from the ordeal forced upon him.

He would firmly and plainly, wishing to offend no man, express his views.

His brother Elijah, a Missourian, holding slaves, it was supposed that Isaac Cody held his view.

But not so, and how great the amazement and anger of those who listened to his utterances.

He saw the sensation his words were creating, knew that he was taking his life in his own hands to utter the sentiments he did; but he was man enough not to fly false colors, and ably went on to denounce slavery as a curse to the land, and begged that it be forced to remain in the states where the laws of the land made it a legal institution and not to force it upon the states yet to be brought into the union.

But he could not go on, for a great roar of voices went up against him, and suddenly a bearded ruffian[23] leaped to his side upon the box, his bowie knife in his hand, and drove it, before anyone realized his intention, once twice into the body of the brave but unfortunate speaker.

With a groan he staggered backward and fell off the box into the arms of several men who, though differing from him, but seeing that he yet lived, were determined to protect him from the fury of the now maddened mob.

Thus had Isaac Cody been made the first victim, shed the first blood in the long and cruel war that deluged Kansas with blood, held no pity, brought anguish to every home while the besom[24] of death and destruction clouded the land.

And in this sad school of man's inhumanity to man the boy Will Cody learned the stern lessons of life.

CHAPTER X.
FOR A FATHER'S LIFE.

Mr. Cody was not killed by the two severe wounds, inflicted by the knife of the cowardly assassin, who thus made his debut into the field of desperadoism.

Though protected from instant death by Rively and others he was left to the care of his son, and wounded seriously though he was, for eventually it caused his death, he crawled away through the long grass to his own home, guided by the devoted boy who was thus learning such cruel and bitter lessons of life.

The next day the pathway of the wounded man was seen, the red stains of ebbing life being visible, and "Cody's Crimson Trail" was long remembered by the dwellers in Salt Creek Valley, destined to have the fair face of nature blotted by deeds such as savages might be guilty of, yet hardly men who claimed the enlightenment of a boasted civilization, which then existed only in name.

And thus the border war was inaugurated, and the demon of destruction was abroad in the land.

Men were shot down while tilling their fields, again a shot would pierce the heart of a father while seated at his own fireside, industries were palsied, the torch of the incendiary lit up happy homes, laying them in ashes, women were left husbandless, orphans multiplied, and anguish and despair hovered over every household.[25]

The Cody family for awhile were left alone, while its head lay upon a bed of suffering, slowly recovering from his wounds.

The universal popularity of Isaac Cody, his many deeds of kindness, all that he had done for the settlement, his calm dignity and noble nature, had made it hard for many to continue the fight against him which the desperado had begun.

But when he was again able to attend to business his foes begun to persecute him and his family, and all knew that at any moment he might be attacked, for threats were constantly made against his life.

One night Will came running into the house and told his father that a large number of horsemen were coming.

Defense, with his wife and daughters about him would have been madness, and his brave wife at once put her bonnet and shawl upon him, a wrap served as a skirt, and with a bucket in his hand he coolly walked out before the eyes of the coming horsemen, who took him for a woman.

He wended his way toward the outhouses, thus escaping to a large cornfield, while his enemies, told by Mrs. Cody that he was away from home, frankly confessed that they had come to hang him.

As proof that they meant what they threatened, they robbed the house of all that was valuable, and going to the pasture drove off the horses, among them Prince, Will's pony whom he loved as fondly as he did Turk.

It was no use for the boy to beg for his pony, for they laughed at him and threatened as he was a "chip of [sic] the old block" he might suffer too.

Finding that they intended to keep a watch, expecting her husband's return, Mrs. Cody got a couple of blankets and some provisions, and watching his chance Will stepped out with them, called Turk, and passing along the cornfield the dog picked up the trail of Mr. Cody and soon after the brave boy was with his father.

"I will be comfortable with what you have brought me, Willie, and you are a brave boy.

"Soon I hope these clouds will pass away and we will all have a happy home once more," said the unhappy man sadly.

The boy could not speak, for his heart was full, and he returned to the house as he did not wish his absence to be noted.

The next morning, to the delight of Will, his pony Prince came flying home at full speed, having escaped from his captors.

"Now I can save Father, for he must not come home," said the boy.

Mounted upon Prince he boldly rode to Rively's store for provisions, for Isaac Cody's Trading Post had been robbed of all in it, and thus gathered what news he could pick up.

There were provisions hidden away in the Cody home, but the devoted wife wished to know just what was going on, and so Will was sent on his errand.

When he returned he told his mother that his father must remain in hiding, that he must not come home, as men were on the watch for him.

So three long days and nights of suspense passed. Mr. Cody remaining hidden in the cornfield and the brave boy, acting a man's part, carrying him food by night.

Realizing that he must not return home, and wishing to relieve his family of the strain of suspense upon them, Mr. Cody said:

"Will, I shall go to Fort Leavenworth tonight."

"I'll get Prince."

"No, I would be taken if I went mounted, and you need Prince at home.

"I'll go on foot, and there I will be safe and can plan for the future.

"You will be the man of the house now, and I know you will do all you can for your good mother and sisters, and boy though you are you have a wise head on your young shoulders."

So Isaac Cody started off in the darkness for Fort Leavenworth while Will returned home and reported what his father had done, to the great relief of the anxious wife and daughters.

He reached the fort in safety, and soon after, finding that he dare not return home, and that Kansas had now entered upon a bitter fight, he took passage on a boat going up the river, landing at Doniphan, where he had heard that Colonel Jim Lane, with several hundred Free State men, were coming from Indiana.[26]

Mr. Cody was cordially welcomed by the leaders of the Free State Party, and joining them was in the battle of Hickory Point, where the pro-slavery men were defeated.[27]

Sometime after, suffering from the wounds he had received, and anxious to be as near his family as possible, he left Colonel Lane and went to Grasshopper Falls, west of Leavenworth thirty-five miles.[28]

There he began the erection of a sawmill, hoping that he would be unmolested.

But vain the hope, for it came to Mrs. Cody's ears that another plot had been hatched to kill him, that a party were going to ride over to Grasshopper Falls and capture him.

Will was in bed with a high fever, and aching in every joint.

To Save a Father's Life

But he overheard all that was said by his mother and sisters in the adjoining room, and rising quietly dressed himself, appearing before them all with fever-flushed face, and a handkerchief, which he held forth and said: "Tie it tight around my head, mother, or it will burst, it aches so."

"Why Willie, where are you going?" all cried as they saw that he had his hat in his hand also.

"I am going to ride Prince to Grasshopper Falls and save my father," was the determined reply of the young hero.

CHAPTER XI.
A MIDNIGHT RIDE.

It was a dark night and a storm was threatening.

The wind swept fiercely about the house, and flashes of lightning now and then lit up the gloom.

But illness, a long ride of thirty-five miles alone, the darkness or the threatened storm held no terrors for the young hero.

He was determined to go, and the entreaties of mother and sisters were of no avail, go he would for a father's sake.

As he could scarcely stand from weakness, two of his sisters went out and bridled and saddled Prince, leading him to the door.

"Don't mind me, Mother, I'm all right and Prince is as fresh as a prairie flower—goodbye," and with a wave of the hand in farewell the young horseman was off, followed by the fervent prayers of the devoted mother and her brave daughters, who knew but too well that, ill as he was, caught in a storm, and even worse, liable to be halted by evil men, the chances were against the boy as well as his father.

But the violent exercise of a rapid run, with the cool night air fanning his fevered face, made Will feel better, and the excitement kept him up.

"I'll do it! I'll do it! Come Prince we must do it," he said through his shut teeth and seeming to realize that as much depended upon him as upon his rider, Prince bounded on with no sign of fatigue.

Seven miles from home Stranger's Creek was reached, and right at the crossing there was a small camp, half a dozen men being gathered about a fire cooking supper.

The splash of the pony in the water caused them to spring away from the firelight, not knowing who, or what to expect, and as the boy rode within a few paces of one of them there came a vivid and prolonged flash of lightning.

Instantly a voice called out:

"Halt, or I will kill you, Boy!"

But Will did not halt and a man shouted:

"Pards, it's Cody's boy!

"Kill him, or we will never get his father!"

There were flashes here and there, as shots rang out, and Will Cody heard for the first time in his life the angry whiz of a bullet fired to kill.

But Prince was going at lightning speed, the boy lay low upon his neck, and of the dozen shots fired not a bullet hit him, though several came uncomfortably near.

Once beyond range and unhurt there arose in the heart of the young rescuer of a father from death, a flush of pride at having been fired upon, that he had passed through an ordeal a man would shrink from.

But he soon realized that his enemies, whose words had told him were going after his father, were pursuing him with all the haste that they could mount their horses and do so.

He at once saw the importance then of escaping them to warn his father of their coming.

All depended upon his pony Prince.

But Prince was as fleet as a deer and had the powers of endurance of a hound, and it would take a very fast horse to overtake him the boy knew.

Thus the midnight ride, the flight of the young rescuer, the pursuit of the armed foes of his father, was kept up mile after mile, and Prince showed no sign of flagging.

Halting a moment to give his pony a breathing spell, and to listen how near the hoofs of the pressing horses sounded, to his joy he found he could not hear them.

Then came the dread that they might have cut across by a trail unknown to him, but after darting along a couple of miles further, he felt that the men had at least given up the chase as far as he was concerned, and Prince was allowed to go at a more leisurely pace, for just then the threatening storm burst in all its fury.

The wind howled along, almost lifting him from his saddle, and causing Prince to stagger under its force.

The lightning was blinding in its vividness, and peals of thunder that were appalling fairly shook the earth.

But the boy still held on his way, though his pace now was a slow walk, and he had to leave to Prince the duty of keeping the trail, for the blaze of lightning one moment, and inky darkness the next rendered his sight unavailing.

Next came the rain, and how it rained, coming down in torrents and drenching him to the skin in an instant.

Still he did not hesitate, did not try to seek shelter in the timber he now and then passed, but held on unswervingly to his purpose—to save his father.

At last he was cheered by a light ahead, and soon after reached Grasshopper Falls, where his father was aroused from bed and told of his danger.

A silent grasp of the hand, a resting of the arm upon the boy's shoulder showed how deeply the father felt what his little son had risked for him, for he dared not trust himself to speak.

And out into the darkness and storm went the hunted man and his noble boy, riding on to Lawrence that same night for there were the quarters of the Free State men.

That night ride was a terrible strain upon the boy, sick as he was, and for days he suffered from the effects of it, but was most tenderly nursed by his father.

At Lawrence was Jim Lane, beside other leading men of Kansas who were organizing what was known as the "Lecompton Legislature."

Isaac Cody was at once elected a member of that body, and took an active part in organizing the First Legislature of Kansas under Governor Reeder.[29]

As agents were being sent East to induce emigrants to come to Kansas, Mr. Cody was selected to go to Ohio, and having fully recovered from his illness, Will Cody started upon his return home by Fort Leavenworth, accompanied by two men who were going that far on his way.

CHAPTER XII.
A FIRE FROM AMBUSH.

It was with a glad heart that Will Cody started upon his return home, to tell the glad news of his father's escape to Lawrence, his having been made a member of the First Kansas Legislature and been sent East as a special agent.

He was sorry to have had to remain so long away from his mother and sisters, but his illness had prevented his returning sooner, and his father was glad to be able to send back by him news that would relieve his family of all suspense just then about himself.

So Will started back with the two men going to Fort Leavenworth.

As they rode into the stream known as "Little Stranger," and their horses were quietly drinking, suddenly out of some bushes on the bank came several shots, and the man nearest to Will Cody dropped dead from his horse.

"He is dead!"

"Ride for your life, Boy!" shouted the other man and away went the horses of the man and boy, plunging through the water, and with the animal of the dead man following.

Several other shots were fired, but missed their aim, and Will and his companion sped on like the wind.

"I wonder what they had against us," said the man as they drew rein

44 : *Part One*

to breathe their horses, and he caught the animal a short while before ridden by his comrade in full health and strength.

Will made no reply, but was busy thinking, for he felt sure that those shots had been fired at him, doubtless by some of the men he had foiled in their attempt to capture and kill his father.

"Poor fellow, his life ended mighty sudden, and I don't know who he is, for we were only traveling pards like you and me.

"But somebody will mourn for him and wait in vain for his coming back.

"This is a hard country, my boy, very hard."

"Yes sir," and though he said no more Will was still busy thinking.

"You are a cool one under fire, for you didn't scare a little bit," continued the man.

Then said Will with the air of a veteran:

"It was not the first time I've been under fire, sir."

"Ah indeed? You are a young one to be going about where men are at war with each other.

"Take my advice and stay at home."

"I went to Lawrence on important business and am returning home now, sir."

"Well, I only hope you'll get there," was the rather ominous reply, and as the man took a close survey of the boy and his pony, he added:

"And I guess you will."

Arriving at Fort Leavenworth Will left his companion to report the fatal ambush to the commanding officer, and rode on his way alone, reaching his home after nightfall without further adventure.

He was greeted with a glad and loving welcome, for not having heard of him, or his father since the night of his departure, their suspense had been terrible, as they did not know whether they were dead or alive.

Not knowing who to trust, Mr. Cody had not been able to send any word home, so was compelled to await the return of Will to carry back the news of his safety.

When Mrs. Cody had read aloud the long letter Will had brought her, and had partaken of a hearty supper, mother and sisters gathered around the young hero and until long after midnight listened to all he had to tell, while, with a modesty that has clung to him through life, when speaking of his own deeds, he dwelt but lightly upon his part in the rescue to his father, and the dangers he had faced.

But the mother and sisters who knew his nature so well, were fully aware that the dangers had been greater than he cared to tell.

The weeks and months then dragged along, the Cody home being often visited by lawless men, who made no secret of their intention to kill Mr. Cody if he returned to Kansas.

Time and again these unwelcome visitors would demand food, which Mrs. Cody and her daughters prepared for them, and when they could rob the house of anything they did so.

Elijah Cody, and other friends across the border came and urged Mrs. Cody to move to Missouri, saying that the lives of her family were in danger if she remained there, but she refused to leave, stating that their foes had robbed her of all but her home, and there she should remain, and not be driven from it.

Mr. Cody had done no wrong, he had established a home there, had only expressed his honest convictions and thus had become the victim of the fate of those who feared his influence.

It was her home and there she would remain.

And there she did remain through all.

There were two families in the Salt Creek Valley who were friendly to the Codys, the Lawrences and the Hathaways, while the Indians whom Isaac Cody had always befriended, visited them at times.

Mr. Elijah Cody could only befriend them by his sympathy and sending provisions, and so it can be readily seen that the lot of Mrs. Cody and her children, with the husband and father absent from home, and their lives in danger, dwelling in the midst of foes, was anything but a happy one.

Was it a wonder that living around such scenes the boy Will Cody was learning lessons that would make or mar his future life?

Returning from his mission to Ohio, Mr. Cody again went to work upon his saw mill at Grasshopper Falls, and Will started on a visit to his father, arriving there in safety.

Determined to return with the boy to visit his family, though he well knew that he was taking his life in his hands, the two started secretly by night, avoided the trails and before daylight reached the home.

His horse was securely hidden by Will, that his presence might not be suspected, and thus passed several days with those he loved and from whom a cruel destiny separated him.

One day while he was there a party of horsemen, fully armed, rode up to the house, and all believed that they knew of his presence there.

Mr. Cody and Will made ready for a bold resistance, but the first words of the leader of the party showed his ignorance of the real facts, for he remarked to Mrs. Cody:

"I hear your husband is again at Lawrence, so we may get him yet.

"But we want dinner."

So dinner was prepared for them, and after eating it they took their departure to the great relief of all.

Unwilling to risk placing his family in a scene of carnage should his presence be known, Mr. Cody started that night upon his return, his faithful son again accompanying him in his long and dangerous night ride.

Will returned in safety, and soon after a party of marauders visited his home, one of whom, against all entreaties, took his pony Prince.

The man who stole Prince Will Cody took a mental photograph of and never forgot and in speaking of it in later years to the writer, said:

"He afterwards branched out from the low level of a horse thief, into the dignity of a Justice of the Peace, to dispense the laws which he had broken in every instance when opportunity offered."

CHAPTER XIII.
THE YOUNG HERDER.

With his pony gone Will Cody felt that he was bankrupt in business.

He had Turk, it is true, but Turk was not a pony, and the boy only wished he had a magic wand to transform him into one.

Horses there were none, for the marauders had taken them all, and Will Cody began to have the same opinion of himself that he had heard was peculiar to the Comanche Indians—that is, dismounted, he was of no earthly use.[30]

Walking to Fort Leavenworth to mail a letter to his father telling him of his dire misfortune, Will met a gentleman whom he knew was most friendly to his family.

"A Man of the West" : 47

It was Mr. Waddell, of the great Overland Freighting Company of Waddell & Majors* and into his ears the boy told the whole story of his parents' misfortunes.[31]

Mr. Waddell listened with deepest interest and then said:

"Well, Will, I cannot see that you can be of any particular use at home just now, you cannot keep a horse, and the bitterness against your father may be visited upon you, young as you are, so tell your mother to let you come to me and I will send you off as a herder of cattle, paying you twenty-five dollars a month and giving you a camp outfit."[32]

Will could hardly believe his ears, and eagerly accepting the offer hurried home with the good news.

But his mother would not hear of his going notwithstanding his wages would be a great help to her.

Will felt as though he had been enveloped in a wet blanket, for his aspirations to help his mother were crushed.

But he called into council two of his sisters, urged [sic, argued?] that he had accepted Mr. Burrell's [sic] offer, that he was doubtless lying awake at night awaiting his coming, that twenty-five dollars a month was a fortune, and he must go.

So he quietly slipped away in the night, walked to Leavenworth, and reporting for duty, was sent out to herd cattle, mounted on a little gray mule, armed, and with a full camping outfit.

When he was gone his mother, knowing that his knowledge of the world and experience were far in advance of his years, and feeling that he would at least be away from the danger of having visited upon him the hatred of his father's foes, accepted with resignation the situation, and awaited in fond anticipation for his return home.

When, after two months the herd came in from the plains, Will Cody reported to Mr. Waddell, the wages due him, fifty dollars, were paid to him all in half dollar pieces.

With the silver tied in a sack and fastened to his saddle, the happy

---

*Alexander Majors, now a well preserved man of 86, and a prominent citizen of Denver, Col.

In a book entitled "Seventy Years upon the Frontier," and issued lately by Rand & McNally of Chicago, Mr. Majors pays a high tribute to Colonel Cody, whom he has known from boyhood and today holds in the highest esteem, affectionately speaking of him as "My boy Billy." —The Author.

boy started for home by night, mounted upon his little gray mule, and accompanied by a fellow herder who had taken a great fancy to the boy, and been invited to go home with him.

Never did any act of his life give William Cody more real joy than when he poured into his mother's lap the fifty dollars in silver which he had earned.

But in the midst of the joy over his return, and the warm welcome extended to his friend the herder, the tramping of hoofs was heard without and a loud voice commanded:

"Open this door; for we know that you have returned home, Isaac Cody, and your minutes are numbered."

CHAPTER XIV.
A WOMAN'S NERVE.

Mob rule had by no means subsided in Kansas, during the time that Will Cody was away from home, engaged in the laudable enterprise of earning money for the help of his mother and sisters.

Persecutions of various kinds still continued, and the Cody family had their share of night alarms and sufferings.

With Mr. Cody away from home, and his brave boy also absent, even their worse foes could not regard the noble mother and daughters, still clinging to their abiding place, as being very dangerous to Kansas, and hence they had not been molested to any very great extent since Will's departure.

But the night of the return, accompanied by the man who had been his warm friend while herding cattle the past two months, the tramp of the marauder was heard without and then came the stern demand for the door to be opened.

Will and the herder were for firing upon the mob, but Mrs. Cody's cool judgment prevailed, she saw beyond the present, she wished no more bloodshed, desired no more cruel persecution than they had already suffered, and she answered the demand.

Will's dog Turk had first given an alarm and then coming to a rear door had whined appealingly to be let in.

His being there proved that no foe was near enough to enter, so the door was opened and Turk bounded in, his joy being shown by his actions.

Opening a window Mrs. Cody called out, in a voice that held no tremor of fear, whatever she might feel:

"Who are you, and what do you wish here?"

"We want your husband," came the reply in a threatening tone.

"He is not in the house, and has not been home for a long time."

"We know better.

"He is at home and we are going to take him."

"I have told you the truth, my husband is not here; but I warn you now that this persecution of women and children has got to come to an end, for though Isaac Cody is a hunted man and dare not come home to protect us, there are those here who will.

"Come, heed my warning and be off, or the result be upon your own heads."

This determined stand, the brave words of the fearless woman brought to bay to protect her own, had its effect, and the circle about the house at once enlarged, as the men sought a safer distance.

It was afterward learned that Will Cody and the herder had been seen going there, and in the night they were supposed to be Isaac Cody and some friend.

Mrs. Cody, after saying what she had turned to the herder and said:

"They are in doubt, and I know their leader.

"He is an errant coward, as his action tonight reveals, so do you come to the window and warn them off for it will have a good effect.

"As well as I can see there are more than a dozen of them, and their leader is John Green."

As the Herder was about to obey her, she checked him for a moment and called out:

"Once more I warn you John Green that if our neighbors dare not protect us, men from Leavenworth will.

"Will you go?"

A voice was heard outside:

"She knows you, John."

It was evident that John Green did not relish being known, and equally as clear that the marauders had been nonplussed by the nerve of a woman.

At this moment the Herder, Luke Field, spoke.

He had taken his cue from what Mrs. Cody had said about men from Leavenworth protecting them, and decided to carry out the intimation that they were from the fort.

Luke Field had once been a soldier, holding the rank of Sergeant, and he had the sharp ring of an officer to his voice, as he commanded:

"Come, men, get away from here or take the consequences, and quick too!"

Mrs. Cody, Will and his sisters were in hopes that the ruse would be successful; but they were not prepared for such prompt obedience on the part of the marauders, for the way in which John Green et al got away from the Cody home set them all to laughing in spite of the seriousness of the situation, and Will said:

"Come, Turk, we'll go out and see which one wins the race."

"You'll do nothing of the kind," cried his sister Martha dragging him back from the door, though Turk managed to skip out and ran baying deeply after the skedaddlers.

"You have saved us, sir," said Mrs. Cody in her modest way grasping the Herder's hand.

"No indeed, a man's voice only helped, but it was your splendid nerve that balked [sic] them down," replied Luke Field, and all slept that night without dread of being again disturbed.

CHAPTER XV.
WILL STANDS GUARD.

The morning after the visit of the marauders, Will, who was up bright and early, made a very important discovery.

He found in the yard, left by the ruffians in their rapid flight, a keg of powder with a fuse attached, which they had intended to put in the cellar beyond all doubt and blow up the house.

"We are in the powder," muttered Will, trying to gain some comfort out of their visit.

After a couple of days spent at home, Will returned to Leavenworth with Luke Field, to go out with another herd of cattle, his mother feeling convinced that it was best to have him away from home, though she did not so express herself to him.

When he again returned home on a visit, once more bringing every dollar of his wages to his mother, he saw that something was wrong.

But his sister Nellie[33] quickly told him that their father was there, and lying very ill, suffering from the effects of his wounds, and which had brought on a high fever.

To his delight Will found that his father was improving, under the rest and kind nursing at home, and he said:

"I will soon be able to return, my son, but I feared the worst when I came home, for one of the wounds I received, gives me much trouble.

"I am glad to hear that you are doing so well.

"You are a noble hearted, brave boy, and will one day make a name for yourself."

This praise from his father filled Will Cody's heart with pride and he began to think deeply.

"Mother and Martha tell me that unless I study hard I will never make a man of any account, and they gave me my books to take herding with me so I could study.

"Well, I try to, but just when I go to study geography some old steer stampedes, and I've got to take a day to round him up.

"If I take up my history, I'm called off by the Boss Herder to look up stray cattle, and when I get down to verbs and nouns, adjectives and participles the whole herd seems to feel sorry for me, so their tails go up, their heads go down, and away they go on a general stampede.

"So it goes, and I wonder if I ever will climb the ladder of fame which Martha says, as the only son and brother I should climb.

"Maybe no, and maybe so."

Thus it was that my young hero soliloquized, and I may add that no matter what the set backs, like every boy who felt that it rested within himself to make a name, he still kept his eye on the future.

As long as his father lay ill in the house Will would not return to herding, and one day he saw riding alone up to the house his old enemy who had stolen his pony Prince.

"I'll be near if you want me, Martha," he said to his eldest sister, and a moment after he was on guard at the top of the stairs, leading to the

"He Shall Not Go Up These Stairs"

room where his father was confined to his bed, and he was resolved to kill the man if he attempted to ascend those stairs.

Mrs. Cody, with Turk by her side, met the man at the door and asked his business.

"I'm come after your husband," was the bold reply.

"I'm going to search the house, and it's war if I find him; but I'm as hungry as a wolf, so you girls get me some dinner."

"Certainly, you shall have something to eat, sit down," said Mrs. Cody, and Will who heard the words from where he sat on guard thought if he only had the getting of that meal the man would quickly hurry away to find a Doctor.

The man was evidently under the influence of some intoxicating Kansas beverage, which he had taken to stimulate himself with in the duty he had set out to perform.

Being "tired" he accepted the invitation to sit down, and to appear like a very bad man—for he beyond all doubt would not have come there alone if he had supposed Isaac Cody was really at home—he began to sharpen his bowie knife on the sole of his shoe.

The effort was too much for him and he fell off the chair in a heap upon the floor, while Turk, not knowing, or in that instance at least if knowing, not recognizing the unwritten code "never to strike a man when down," made a bound for him as though he considered him his game.

But a stern call from Mrs. Cody, and a chorus of terrified cries from the girls, caused Turk to realize that he had been mistaken in his intentions, and he skulked away with a look of utter dejection.

But the man had received a fright that nearly sobered him, and he arose, picked up his knife, and in silence ate his dinner, after which he mounted his horse and rode away.

"It was a big bluff to get fed," said Will, as he left his post of duty; but had the man attempted to search the house as he had threatened, he would have found a barrier in the way more dangerous than Turk.

As soon as Mr. Cody was able to travel, Will went with him back to Grasshopper Falls, for the boy seemed to consider himself the self-constituted protector of his father, as well as of his mother and sisters.

From Grasshopper Falls my hero returned again to his herding, but upon his next visit home found himself "rounded up," to use a term of cattle men, and was forced to go to school.

CHAPTER XVI.
SCHOOL DAYS.

In the early settlement of Kansas, and when lawless deeds, such as I have described, ran riot through the border land, common school advantages were not to be had.

But the settlers in Salt Creek Valley had numerous children growing up, and fully realizing that they should have the advantages of an education, be it ever so crude, a subscription school[34] was started, and though under a ban, as it were, Mrs. Cody gladly subscribed for the sake of her children.

A school house was built on the banks of a creek near the Cody home, a teacher was employed and the session opened with a fair number of scholars.

There it was that Will, upon his return from herding found himself, as he expressed it, "rounded up and corralled."

His suggestion to the effect that Messrs. Waddell & Majors might not be able to replace him, as well as the remark that he could not earn twenty-five dollars a month at school, unless he turned teacher, went for naught, as his mother felt sure that a man could be found to take the place of a boy, as a herder, and she felt assured that he would not be called upon to teach the school, so the twenty-five dollars monthly must be dispensed with.

"If it was to teach riding, rifle and pistol shooting and throwing a lasso, I have no doubt, my son, but that you could do it, but as for school teaching I am sure you are not fitted for it, as you are backward in your books, though the fault is not your own."

So Will laid his weapons, his lariat and wild life of a herder aside, and the following Monday started out bright and early with his younger sisters, to attend the school picturesquely situated upon the little stream.

Turk considered that he should go also, and though driven back by Will, as he might be needed at home, was curious to see his young master cross the threshold of learning and skulked along after him, keeping just out of sight.

Perhaps Turk understood enough of the situation, who knows, to wish to know how it was the "young idea was taught to shoot,"[35] conflicting the teacher's birch rod with a gun.

At any rate he went along and when he saw the Cody children enter the school house he made a run for it and camped underneath.

It is supposed that Turk heard the teacher, an out and out "Down-Easter" with the face of a hawk, and the reach of a lariat, finding out what his young master knew, or to be more correct, what he did not know, for Will found himself cornered, when Geography, History, Spelling and Arithmetic were thrown at him like an Orderly Sergeant calling a Company's Roll, and like the Pinafore twins, he got "all mixed up."[36]

But Turk came to the rescue nobly just then.

Another dog had followed children to school, and he was a large animal, a cross between meanness and general ugliness.

Furthermore, he belonged to a family unfriendly to the Codys, and when he came under the school-house, with a grin on his face as though he enjoyed my young hero's being in a pillory of despair, it was more than Turk could, or at least would, stand, and he fired himself at the sneering canine in a way that startled the children just over the scene of the fracas.

Up through the cracks between the planks came clouds of dust, while heavy blows, as the dogs' heads struck the flooring, wild ki yi's, fierce growls, savage yelps and the snapping of teeth, all together made up a pandemonium that was simply beyond the power of young human nature to stand without joining in.

"It is Turk!" shrieked the Cody girls.

"And our dog Nigger!" yelled the contingent who recognized their dog's growls and howls.

Just where he was in geography, whether Columbus had yet discovered the new world in History, or what were vulgar fractions, Will Cody never recalled, for he darted out of the school-house with a whoop-em-up cry learned in herding cattle, and shouted to his dog:

"Eat him up, Turk!"

Whether Turk wanted his young master to see fair play, or not there suddenly came rolling from under the school house a cloud of dust and twisting, snapping, snarling quantity of dog that was a sight to behold.

The owners of the other dog were now on the spot too, and each combatant had his champions, while the rest of the school children sang out in chorus a constant:

"Sic 'em! Sic 'em!"

Finding entreaties to Turk were unheeded the Cody girls began to cry, the teacher, black in the face with rage, for he could see nothing in a dog fight, danced about like a wild Indian, waving his birch stick like a war club, and bringing it down upon an innocent boy whenever he got within reach of his arm, and to add to the scene cries from the young sports of:

"Go for him, Turk!"

"Tear him, Nigger!"

"Bully for Turk!"

"Nigger's licked!"

This last assertion no one disputed, for a bundle of black hair suddenly shot away from the arena, tail drooping, and with a dismal howl went flying across the little foot bridge spanning the creek, missed his footing and falling into the water, was followed by Turk in his flight, plunge and race until they disappeared from sight.

But Steve Gobel, the owner of Nigger, a large boy and a bully, at once sought to resent his dog's defeat upon Will Cody, when the teacher joined in and whipped both boys for bringing their dogs to school with them, and this ended the fight, though it caused a feeling of enmity between Steve Gobel and my hero that at a later day culminated in serious trouble.

Thus Will Cody's school days began under a cloud.

CHAPTER XVII.
BOY RIVALS.

When the children returned home that evening from school, Turk was found with a mingled look of shame at his disobedience and triumph over his victory struggling for mastery in his much disfigured face.

Martha had bound up one of his front paws, and dressed a bite or two in his side and neck, at the same time looking after his somewhat disfigured countenance and ears.

But when he saw Will's reproachful look at his injuries, as plainly as a dog could express himself without words, he said:

"You just ought to see Nigger—he's a total wreck.

"Get sent over on some excuse and take me along just to have a look at him—it's worth it."

However Will read the expression he did not go, but turned to explain to his mother how it all happened, Nellie helping it out with:

"It was all that Steve Gobel's fault, mother, for he has told me time and again Nigger could whip Turk, and I'd see sometime."

"Well you saw today, and it was just the dandiest fight I—"

Will paused, for he caught his mother's reproachful eyes upon him and continued:

"Turk shant [sic] go to school again, Mother, I promise you, for Teacher says he'll lick me if he does," and he whispered to his sister:

"But did you see Nigger run, and when he fell off the bridge Turk went right in after him."

As the days passed at school Will buckled down to hard work.

He had had just what little teaching that his mother and eldest sister could give, and realized that he must study hard, for he did not wish to appear more backward than boys of his age.

But the teacher had never forgiven him for the dog fight, and was more severe toward Will who would not seek to curry favor with him, feeling that he did not treat him with justice.

But he studied hard so as not to give him any cause for complaint, and was making good progress in his studies, to the great joy of his mother, when suddenly he had his first attack of juvenile heart disease, in other words he fell in love.

The object of his adoration was a young girl by the name of Jessie Kane,[37] and of course his senior by a couple of years, as all boys fall in love the first time with girls older than they are.

Jessie Kane was a very pretty girl, and had a number of lovers, among them Steve Gobel, the owner of the fleet-footed "Nigger," and who was three years older than Will, and a large boy for his age.

But Jessie Kane was a "hero worshipper," and she had heard much of Will Cody, and her eyes told her that he was fair to look upon, being a handsome, dark-haired boy with large black eyes full of expression, and so her heart was touched, and unmindful of the dog fight rivalry existing between the boys she yearned for my hero as her beau cavalier.

This preference upon her part Steve Gobel was no more pleased with than he had been with the scrimmage of Turk vs Nigger, and when it was hinted to him in no gentle manner by a girl whom he had once loved, but deserted for Jessie Kane, that:

"Will Cody has cut you out," he waxed wroth and decided to straightway go upon the warpath for the said successful rival.

Now, in lieu of flowers, cakes and candies for sweethearts in these days, as now, it was the fashion at the school house on the little stream, for the boys to build arbors for their fair lady loves, and anxious to be up-to-date in the fashion Will Cody had erected a bower of boughs, leaves and wild flowers, as he only knew how to build one, for the fair Jessie.

Then, with a gallantry that has never deserted him, he led the fair Jessie to the bower to find, alas! that it was in ruins.

And there stood Steve Gobel with a smile of defiance upon his face.

Then followed a short but pithy dialogue.

"Steve Gobel, did you pull that arbor down?"

"Suppose I did?"

"Did you do it?"

"What if I did?"

"Then you did a mean thing, Steve Gobel, and are too great a coward to admit it," chimed in Jessie Kane indignantly.

Thus nettled by the word coward from the lips of the girl he loved, Steve Gobel said:

"Yes, I did it, Will Cody, and what are you going to do about it?"

Actions speak louder than words, and so it was in this instance, for, without measuring the years and strength against him, Will Cody threw himself then and there upon his sneering rival, to fight it out before the eyes of their sweetheart, and other children hastening to the scene.

CHAPTER XVIII.
THE YOUNG FUGITIVE.

What William Cody the boy was, and William Cody the man is [is] a contrast that is more striking than that usually presented by mankind.

What an American youth can aspire to is presented to great advantage in the anomalous character of the man of whom I write, the very embodiment of diversity, and a representative type of the antipodal phases of society, for upon the frontier his deeds won him to become the hero of song and story, and though reared amid surroundings that tried men's souls to the utmost tension, when brought into the salons of the aristocrat they found him versed in all the subtleties of polished etiquette, courteous to all, full of a natural effervescence of spirit most refreshing, witty, a good raconteur and as modest withal as became one upon whose brow justly rested the laurel wreath of the hero.

The varying shades and traits of his character will be evidenced by the eventual incidents of his life, the scenes he was called upon to face with undaunted front.

The quarrel forced upon him in the scene at the little school house on the creek, was not of his seeking, but of another's, his disappointed rival's, Steve Gobel's act.

There was suddenly thrust upon him a chance to maintain his rights, or back down before the eyes of his sweetheart, simply because he dared not meet one who was in every way his superior physically.

So he determined to then and there make the fight of his life, and with a bound he confronted the large boy, who thrust his hand into his pocket, as though to frighten him off from an attack.

If so intended it had the contrary effect, for with a leap Will Cody was upon him, his grasp upon his throat, and, hampered as he was with his hand in his pocket, and driven backward by the weight of his young adversary, Steve Gobel went down backward.

Just how it happened even Jessie Kane did not know, or whether Steve Gobel drew the knife to use upon his small adversary; but certain it was that Will Cody got hold of it, and as they struggled on the ground the sharp blade was driven into the thigh of his rival, who instantly cried out:

"Oh! Oh! you have killed me!"

Perhaps if the blade had entered his body it might have proven fatal, but as it was serious only to the youthful lookers-on, and it put an end very quickly to the trouble between Jessie Kane's rivals, for loud rang the cries:

"Will Cody has killed Steve Gobel!"

The alarm reached the ears of the teacher, and Will Cody who was now on his feet saw him coming with vengeance in his eye and a stick in his hand, and having no desire to be interviewed just then he turned suddenly and bounded away like a deer.

Just where he intended going he did not know; but the fear that he had really killed Steve Gobel sent him flying along to escape he knew not what, to go he cared not whither.

The teacher started in pursuit but was quickly distanced, long-legged though he was, and the boy disappeared in the distance.

Suddenly he halted, for just over a rise he saw a wagon train winding along, and the "Boss" was riding not far away, and he recognized him as John Willis,[38] a wagon master of Russell, Majors & Waddell's overland freight train, and whom he had several times met while herding cattle.

Calling out to the wagon master, who quickly rode up to him, he told his story, and found a most sympathetic friend in John Willis, who said:

"That's all right, Billy, we'll go over and lick the teacher and stampede the larnin' outfit."

"Oh no, it was my fault, Mr. Willis, for I was to blame; but I thought he intended to kill me, and I only wanted to scare him, and not to kill him; but what shall I do, for it will break my poor mother's heart, and do you think they'll hang me, for you know they don't like my father around here?"

"I'll tell you what to do, Billy, just get in that head wagon and come along with me."

"But I must risk it and go home to tell mother."

"No you don't, though I can't believe the boy is much hurt, for bad boys is hard to kill as cats; but when we camp for the night, I'll go back with you and tell your mother I'll take care of you."

With this promise Will Cody got into a wagon and the train moved on.

A couple of hours later the boy who kept an eye back on the trail saw some horsemen coming and called out:

"It's Mr. Gobel and some men and they are after me."

"Bein' after you and gettin' you is two different things, Billy, for I've got a say in this matter.

"You jist lay low in that wagon and leave it to me."

Soon after the party rode up and Mr. Gobel demanded the boy to arrest him.

"Well you can't get him and that goes," was the answer.

Finding that John Willis meant what he said, and that his men were as determined as he was to protect the boy, the party rode away and the train soon after went into camp.

Mounting Will upon a mule, as soon as it was dark, John Willis rode back with him to his home, and he was welcomed with joy, for his sisters having returned from school and told what had happened his mother was fearful that he had fallen into the hands of the Gobels.

As it was not known how badly Steve Gobel had been hurt, and John Willis promised to take Will with him to Fort Kearney [sic][39] and bring him safely back within two months, Mrs. Cody yielded a reluctant consent to this going, and then quickly set to work fitting him out for the long and perilous journey.

Then farewells were said, the grieving mother keeping up a bold front however, though she saw her only son going away from her as a fugitive, while his father even then dared not venture under his own roof, so bitter was the hatred of the pro-slavery men for the bold stand he had taken against them.

And so the boy turned his back upon his home and those he loved, to go forth in the world, young as he was as a fugitive.

"A Man of the West" : 61

CHAPTER XIX.
"BUFFALO BILLY."

Anxious to protect his young protege, should Steve Gobel really be seriously, or fatally injured, John Willis upon returning to camp at once gave orders to pull out on the march.

He wished to get as far away from the vicinity of Will's home as quickly as possible.

Knowing that the boy had had experience in herding cattle, that he was a fine rider, and could be of a great deal of assistance to him, he at once put him on the rolls as one of his hands, a kindness my hero fully appreciated.

Proud of the position he held Will Cody was anxious to do all in his power for his kind benefactor, and was soon most popular with all of the men in the train.

He liked the life he led, the moving by day and camping by night, while there was a spice in the thought that they were passing through a dangerous country and had to stand guard at night.

But this duty John Willis would not allow him to do, saying that he was too young and needed all the sleep he could get.

Will however was allowed to perform one duty that he was much pleased with, and that was to get what game he could while on the march.

There was one kind of game he had stood something in awe of, and never had tried over hard to get a shot at, and that was buffalo.

But he soon made up his mind that he must kill a buffalo, and one day started out with this intention, though he was discreet enough to keep the secret to himself, in case he failed to bring down one of these mighty rovers of the prairies.

The train was in the midst of a buffalo country, and had gone into camp at noon, when just over a rise Will Cody came upon a large herd of buffalo.

It was a startling sight at first, enough to awe any one, but the boy had been told by John Willis that the horse he rode was a good buffalo hunter, and he was anxious to find out just what that meant in a horse.

He had a double-barrel gun, one barrel rifled, the other loaded with slugs, for in those days repeaters were not known, and revolvers even had been but a few years in use.

In his holster he carried a large single-barrel pistol, and thus armed he rode for the herd.

He had not gotten fairly into the trouble before he regretted that he rode a well-trained buffalo horse, for the animal quickly carried him into the midst of the herd, which started across the prairie directly toward the wagon-camp.

This fact at least was encouraging to the boy, and as the herd of a thousand buffalo, swept over the rise at a full run, there in their midst was seen Will Cody, and his gun and pistol were heard cracking away.

Swerving from their headlong rush, at sight of the camp, the boy dropped back and the men beheld him halt as a wounded buffalo stood at bay.

They beheld him re-load his gun, then change his mind, apparently, for John Willis called out.

"He's going to lasso him!"

The lasso was thrown, caught on the horns of the huge beast, which, with a bound was away, and dragging side-ways upon the horse pulled him off his feet.

Down went horse and boy and gun, but Will Cody nimbly sprung to his feet, picked up his gun and fired both shots into the wounded and maddened brute, dropping him dead in his tracks just as John Willis and a dozen of the train men dashed up.[40]

"Hurrah, boy, you've got your buffalo!" shouted the wagon master in delight, and though brim full of delight he replied modestly:

"There are two more of them over the rise, sir, but I hope the horse is not hurt."

"It was you I was troubled about, Buffalo Billy, not the horse, for he's all right, only scared and shaken up.

"Come boys. Three cheers for our Boy Buffalo Hunter," cried John Willis, and they were given with a will, the boy flushing with pride at the honor done him, and that night in camp greatly enjoying the fruits of his prowess in the shape of a fine buffalo steak.

In good time Fort Kearney was reached, and there a halt was made before the return trip was begun, the delay giving Will a good insight into life at a frontier fort, and he was charmed with the music of the band, the cavalry drills and the parades, while he became a decided favorite with the soldiers.

The time being up John Willis started his train on the back trail, and though Indians gave them several alarms at night, they met with no adventure to speak of, greatly to the young buffalo hunter's regret.

True to his promise to Mrs. Cody the wagon master returned her son in safety to his home, where he was delighted to find the wounding of Steve Gobel had been but a slight affair, and the family were again upon friendly terms, and so ever remained, and thus ended the first love affair of my hero.

CHAPTER XX.
THE DEATH OF ISAAC CODY.

Finding that he could not live at home, without being in constant danger of his life and causing his family no end of trouble and anxiety, Mr. Cody went to Ohio and organized a company of some sixty families, returning with them to Kansas and locating them in the vicinity of Grasshopper Falls.

In the meantime all had been progressing fairly well at his home, his children were going to school and Will, in spite of his having shown his ability to earn money, (as he had been well paid for his overland trip with John Willis), was devoting himself assiduously to his studies, and had mastered, as he believed then, a great deal of knowledge.

Just as the skies seemed brightening for Isaac Cody, and his devoted wife began to hope that the clouds of civic strife in Kansas would soon roll by, another shadow fell upon them.

Mr. Cody, whose wound in the lung had never ceased to trouble him, caught a severe cold, and he seemed to feel that it would be a fatal illness, and faced the danger of going home to be once again with those he loved and from whom a merciless destiny had kept him apart.

When he reached home he was suffering greatly, but tender hands were there to nurse him and loving hearts to care for him.

In all haste Will rode for the nearest physician, and all that his skill, and the care of those about him could do was done for the sufferer, and at one time all hoped that the cup held to their lips, that they might drink still deeper of the dregs of bitterness and sorrow, might pass away.

But vain the hope, for the knife wound in the lung, though late, had done its work, and unable to rally the bold Pioneer of Kansas lay in his bed, looking out over the beautiful valley where he had stood with raptured gaze upon the scene where he was to make his home, the scene where his life was to end.

As slowly as the sun sunk beyond the hills, the life of Isaac Cody ebbed away, and what remained bore upon it the sacred seal of Death, where the hatred and malice of man dare not intrude.

Over on Pilot Knob, where his eyes had rested that day at sunset, when he first came into the Valley, the mortal remains of the fearless Pioneer, the first martyr to the cause of making Kansas a Free State, the victim of man's inhumanity to man, were laid to rest, his burial being attended by many from far and wide, for when the blow had fallen and he had been taken from their midst, those who had wronged him were quick to realize that they had made a sad mistake, at least those did who had not become hardened in their deeds of inhumanity and lawlessness.

Ill herself at the time of Mr. Cody's death, and with his affairs all in a chaotic state, the widow rallied from the shock and the terrible pressure upon her, and vowed that she would live for her children, that she should not leave them homeless and impoverished.

Brave as she had ever shown herself, her determined courage and undaunted energy shone forth now with greater power and her untiring devotion to her duty, her home and her children was the one aim of her life.

And true children she had, who appreciated her struggles, and were anxious to lend their aid in doing all they could to relieve her of every care they could take upon themselves.

Then it was that Will Cody showed the material of which he was made, that he felt that the responsibility rested upon him, and so it was he rode away one morning, rifle in hand, as though bound upon a hunt for game.

But the game he sought was of a different kind from that he had formerly hunted, for now he was looking for work.

Straight to the Headquarter camp of Russell, Majors & Waddell, the Overland Freighters, he rode, and boldly dismounted before the tent of Alexander Majors,[41] then in charge of the trains.

Alexander Majors was a splendid type of manhood, large-framed, an athlete and one who had been reared on the plains, yet had never in

Will Cody Applies for Work

the slightest degree become contaminated by the rough life he had been forced to live.* A man who never uttered an oath, and of temperate habits he commanded the full respect of his men, for he was an able leader, kind, generous to a fault but firm as iron.

"Well, my lad, what can I do for you," Alexander Majors asked in his kindly way, as Will Cody stood before him, his rifle in one hand, his bridle rein in the other.

"I am Isaac Cody's son, sir, and my father is dead. I have the care of my mother and sisters, so please sir, give me work to do," was the manly response.

"Well said, my lad, to wish to aid your mother and sisters.

"I knew your father and he was a fine man and his death is a great loss to Kansas in these stirring times; but you are very young to go out into the world."

"I am in my twelfth year, sir," said Will proudly thinking to impress Col. Majors with his great age.

The Colonel smiled and said:

"What can you do?"

---

*Today Col. Alexander Majors lives in Denver, Col., and though over four score years is a hale, hearty man in the full enjoyment of life, one of the last of the men of the Plains. Col. Majors' recent book, "Seventy Years on the Frontier," is a history of the stirring life of those days. —The Author.

Guiding a Wagon Train

"I can ride, sir, and shoot game, can herd cattle, but would like to be Train Messenger."

"All are duties for men to perform, and on the trail are attended with much danger; but I wish to keep you, so if you will bring me a letter from your mother giving her permission for you to go, I will make you a Messenger, and if you do a man's work you shall have a man's pay."*

Doffing his slouch hat to Colonel Majors, for he was too full for utterance, Will Cody sprang into the saddle and was off like the wind for home to tell the good news to his mother, that he was to ride Messenger on the Overland trail, between wagon trains, stretched out on the long line of march into Utah to General Albert Sidney Johnston's Army then preparing to fight the Mormons.[42]

CHAPTER XXI.
A YOUTHFUL PLAINSMAN.

There is no doubt but that Mrs. Cody fully realized that she was giving up much to allow her brave boy Will to assume the duties of man's estate, and go forth as a "bread winner" for his mother and sisters as he had determined to do, and yet she felt that the force of circumstances must cause her to yield, that she must give him up to a cruel Fate as it were.

In the midst of her suspense, her heartaches and sufferings in her new home, the devoted woman had become again a mother, a second

---

*Colonel Majors himself told me this story of William Cody's applying to him for work, and said that the boy's face was a study as he stood in doubt as to what his answer would be. From that day the two have been devoted friends. —The Author.

"A Man of the West" : 67

son[43] having been born to her, and as an argument in favor of his going on "extra" with the wagon train, Will said:

"But mother, you have Charlie, if anything should happen to me."

"Ah! my dear boy, I had your noble father but a short while ago, but he is gone, and soon we are to lose your sister Martha, for she will leave us as soon as she is married, and now you wish to go out from our midst into the dangers and temptations of a wild life."

"Don't fear for me, mother, for I'll take care of myself, see if I don't, and just think what a big sum of money I'll bring you when I come back, so you can pay the claim they have brought against the home since father died, to try and rob you."[44]

"Yes, and I fear we may lose all, my son, all, and be left without home or friends."

"Don't talk that way mother, for you must fight them, yes fight them hard, for Mr. Douglass* says you can win, and the money I earn will help you oh! so much.

"Yes, mother, don't give up after being brave so long, and let me go and earn a man's wages, for only think Colonel Majors says I shall have full pay—why it makes me feel big to think of it—say I can go, mother, for sister Martha thinks it is best, and Julia and Nellie, and the other girls say they ar'n't afraid to trust me, only Liza and May say they wish I could take Turk along as a pard, but he'll stay here to protect you."

Thus appealed to, and with the majority against her, Mrs. Cody was too good an American not to yield, and so gave her consent, and the letter was written to Colonel Majors, containing the maternal sanction for Will's debut in life in the capacity of a real "bread winner" for those he loved, and to play the part of a man in the long and dangerous trip across the Plains.

When all fitted out for his long journey, Will went home to say goodbye, and the proud consciousness that he was doing his duty, that he was to play a manly part, alone prevented him showing how bitter the parting was from those he loved.

When he was looked upon as the one who might be taken off, he lit-

---

*Hon. John C. Douglass now a prominent lawyer of Leavenworth, then a struggling young lawyer, whom I may here notice did fight the battle of Mrs. Cody and won, mentioning in his speech in Court the part Will Cody had played in aiding his mother in her hard struggle. —The Author.

tle dreamed that there was a loved form that would be missing from the family circle upon his return, a fair face that had ever beamed upon him in all his boyish sorrows to soothe away real and imaginary troubles from his young life.

But farewells were said, and when Will had again and again urged his mother to "fight the claim," he rode away from the little home, his own heart full, yet how much deeper and more poignant the sorrow of the mother and sisters whom he was leaving behind to miss him at morn, noon and night, and long and pray for his return.

Riding slowly along the road, Will turned from time to time to wave a farewell to those still watching him, and his face was set and stern as he tried not to yield to the natural weakness that throbbed up from his heart.

At last, as a turn in the highway would shut him out from home and loved ones, he turned his horse, waved his hat cheerily, and then disappearing quickly from view—broke down.

With the loving eyes no longer upon him, the heart overflowed, the tears welled up into the eyes, and the brave boy yielded to a flood of tears, tears which he would not have had his mother and sisters see for a fortune.

Shortly after when he rode up to Headquarters and reported to Colonel Majors as ready for duty, his face showed no sign of the emotion he had yielded to, when the hill shut the last sight of home and dear ones from his vision.

"Well, my boy, I am glad to see you, and I have no doubt, though very young indeed, for such work, that you will do your duty well.

"You are to go along with the wagon train, and ride courier when needed from train to train; and there will also be a large herd of cattle along, so you will be kept busy.

"Remember, you are going to aid in the support of your mother and sisters, and your love for them must keep you from going wrong; be not tempted by wicked men, utter no oath, be ever ready to obey those in authority over you, and one of these days I predict that you will rise to fortune and to fame.

"Upon your return be sure and report to me—goodbye, and success to you," and Colonel Majors shook hands warmly with the "Boy Plainsman" to whom he had given such good advice, and uttered a prophecy that has been fulfilled.

That night Will Cody slept on his blanket under a wagon, and at dawn the train pulled out on its long trail into the Land of the Sunset.

CHAPTER XXII.
ON THE TRAIL.

In his former short trips from home Will Cody had felt that the work was temporary, that he had not launched out upon his career for life, that he was nothing more than a mere boy parted for the time being from his home and youthful associations.

But now the situation was changed, all seemed wholly different to him.

He felt that he had embarked for life to build up his fortune, to make or mar his future.

His father was dead, his mother, with a large family had thrust upon her the worry and care of its support, she had a claim to fight, or be robbed of that which was her own, and upon him, he believed, fell the responsibility in a great degree for the future happiness of those he was glad to think depended in a great measure upon his efforts.

In spite of his years the boy felt that he was crossing the threshold of a new life, thrust upon him by circumstances beyond his control far too young.

But he did not shrink from the task, and then would rise constantly before him the cheerful sense of doing his duty, that he was making money, that his name was upon the pay-roll as an "extra," yet with a man's pay set against it.

As the train pulled slowly along he was anxious to be making better time, but he soon began to understand that man's and beast's powers of endurance had their limit, that, with the long trail before them the cattle could do no more, that with care, watchfulness and duty the men had all they could do.

"Go to the rear train and then to the herd, and tell them that I have decided to make four miles further today, to a better camp than the one where I had intended to halt, and to push on more rapidly to make it before dark."

Such was Will's first order to ride courier back over the trail, and he was off in a swooping gallop.

A few miles back he came upon the Boss of the rear train, and delivering his message pushed on once more to carry the orders given him to Frank McCarthy the chief of the cattle outfit.

Rapidly he rode the few miles, and telling Frank McCarthy the change of program, he wheeled his horse and went swiftly along to catch up with the advance.

Some of the men gave the "Boy Extra" a cheer as he passed the wagon train, and it made his heart thrill with pride.

Dashing up to Bill McCarthy, the Boss who had given him his instructions, he said simply:

"I told them, sir, and they said all right."

"You made a good ride of it, my boy.

"Now ride here at the head of the outfit while I go on in advance to select a camp."

And as Bill McCarthy rode on Will Cody riding at the head of the train, began to picture to himself the day when he should rise to the position of one upon whom such a responsibility could be placed as "Wagon Boss," for the Head Wagon Master, in the boy's opinion was a most exalted trust to hold.

The camping place was reached before sunset by the leading train, and soon after by the others of the outfit, and having staked his horse out and cared well for him, Will stood watching with greatest interest the going into camp, building of fires, looking after horses and cattle, his whole being wrapped up in the thrilling and picturesque scene, a scene he has never tired of to this day.

When supper time came he was promptly on hand with tin cup and tin plate, knife and fork, and having already won favor in the eyes of the mess cook he was helped most bountifully, for as he had been put on the roll in the full pay column, he wanted "full rations" as well, and not only got them but disposed of them.

Then followed the tones of a violin in one camp, a flute in another, the soft notes of a guitar, and here and there a solo in a manly voice, singing some ballad of home that touched not only the boy's heart, but the hearts of those made of sterner stuff.

Wrapped in his blanket, his saddle bags for a pillow, his couch the ground, his roof a wagon body, the boy sunk to sleep lulled by music in camp that to him was most beautiful.

CHAPTER XXIII.
INDIANS ON THE WAR-PATH.

Day after day the wagon train toiled on its westward way, and night after night camps were made where the best grass and water could be found.

There were days of sunshine and of storm, there were nights when the winds swept through the camps most dismally, when the rains descended and made all wet and uncomfortable, and the Boy Plainsman began to see life on the trail as it really was stripped of all the glamour of sentiment and romance.

There were swollen streams to cross, stampeded cattle to round up, night watches to keep, to guard against a surprise from Indians, and an alert lookout kept by day from dread of running into an ambush.

With eyes and ears open my young hero was drinking in sustenance for future years, building on experience a foundation that would withstand rude shocks that must be met in days to come.

He made his rides when ordered be the weather what it might, scorned to show fatigue, slept in rain drenched clothing, ate his meals when he could get them, made no complaint when he could not, and each day became more and more infatuated with the free life he was leading.

Thus far there had been no alarms from Indians, but each night's camp was bringing them nearer and nearer to the country through which they might have to fight their way.

Without giving expression to such thoughts, Will Cody was longing to discover just what an Indian fight was like.

He has since said that he was as glad, when the first fight with Indians came, as he was sorry soon after that a redskin had ever been created.

It was the boyhood romance in him that longed to see Mister Lo in all the glory of warpaint, feathers and blood-curdling yells.

Then it was the anticipation tinged with some of adventure; later it was with realization imbued with sorrow, suffering and death.

It was on Plum Creek on the South Platte River, some two score miles to the westward of old Fort Kearney, that Will Cody had his first experience with the noble red man on the hunt for pale face scalps.

The train had gone into camp for the noon meal, the horses and mules were staked out, the cattle were scattered over the grasslands feeding, the tired trainmen, many of them had gone to sleep under the wagons and only a few guards were on the alert around the camp, while the cooks were preparing dinner.

No Indians had been seen and no one was dreaming of any being near.

Will was watching the cook of his mess preparing dinner, educating himself for "future reference," when he would have to do his own cooking or go hungry and redskins were just then wholly effaced from his mind.

It is the unexpected that happens and so he found it, for without any warning a number of shots suddenly rang out from a distant thicket, followed by a chorus of wild yells that made Will shiver and lose his appetite with surprising quickness.

The Indians, with all the watchfulness of the train men, had caught them napping, and visited upon them a most unwelcome surprise.

The sleepers awoke quickly, the idlers were on their feet in an instant, and the men seized their arms to resist the attack.

One glance was sufficient to show all how completely had the Indians surprised them for the cattle had been stampeded, having crept upon and killed the three men on duty, and while a number of braves were driving off the herds, the greater number were charging down upon the camps with wild whoops and shots to try and frighten the pale faces into full flight.

There stood Will Cody at the fire, but with no thought then of the cook or the edibles.

He was gazing like one transfixed upon the magnificent yet terrible sight of the charging redskins.

It may be that he had the "Indian ague" as he had been stricken with the "buck-ague" at first sight of a deer, for now he stood with no thought of his rifle, riveted to the spot.

Before him swept the fears of his mother that he might be killed or captured by Indians, the warnings of his sisters to "run if he saw a redskin" flashed before him.

That last advice he felt somewhat inclined to follow, only he did not just know where to run.

But glancing about to see what the men were doing, he was instantly reassured, for no one seemed to be alarmingly excited, and though rallying quickly the men seemed very cool and determined.

Both Bill and Frank McCarthy were cool as icicles, and gave their orders to their men with no show of dread as to the result.

Seeing this, and realizing that safety lay in discipline, obedience to orders and calm courage, Will Cody ran for his rifle and took his stand by the side of Bill McCarthy, the men having formed a line for defense with the wagons as a shelter.

All were well armed, the men mostly carrying besides their Colt's revolvers, a Mississippi yager[45] which was loaded with buck shot as well as a bullet and were deadly weapons.

At the proper moment Bill McCarthy gave the order to fire, and the well aimed yagers checked the advance of the Indians, who, however, returned the shots, wounding several of the men slightly.

When the Indians halted the McCarthy brothers held a consultation as to what was best to be done, for it could now be seen that the train men were outnumbered ten to one and more warriors were coming into view each moment.

The spot held by the train was no place for a fight, and though they deeply regretted the necessity, the leaders decided that there was but one thing to be done, as their mules and cattle had been stampeded and there was even then a possibility that they could not retreat in safety.

"Boys, we must run for the creek bank yonder, and take it for a breast work[46]—if they drive us from there we must try and follow the stream back to Fort Kearney."

Every man saw that this was all that could be done, and at the word from Bill McCarthy they started in a run for the creek, Will Cody keeping well up with the leaders in the race for life, for the Indians seeing their intention again charged them with wild yells and shots.

CHAPTER XXIV.
A RETREAT UNDER DIFFICULTIES.

The run of Bill McCarthy and his band of trainmen for the creek bank, was made in safety and then and there Will Cody congratulated himself that he had always been fleet of foot, in fact he ran so rapidly that he felt sure of reaching the goal and turned and aided one of the wounded men in his flight, who however was already being assisted by a comrade.

The creek bank was reached without a mishap, the wounded being safely gotten there also, and then came the order:

"Shelter yourselves, men, and turn and give them another taste of your yagers!"

Will Cody found shelter, but not being armed with a yager, he did not fire.

His not doing so however was not noted, but as the Indians were again checked, and with considerable lost, he could not and did not claim the credit of having aided in the good work.

As the Indians were steadily showing an increase of numbers, the cattle had been stampeded beyond recall, and there was nothing else to be done, the McCarthy Brothers decided to retreat under the shelter afforded by the creek bank, which was about the height of a man's head.

Taking to the stream, which was shallow, but giving the redskins reason to believe that they intended to hold their position, the men began slowly to wade down the creek.

Every man was eagerly watched by the boy of the band, for he wished to see just what would be done in circumstances when the danger threatened was of a desperate nature.

"Well, Billy, you don't scare much," said Frank McCarthy and Will was proud of the praise thus bestowed upon him, and he was determined to keep cool though he could not but understand that every man felt that the chances of escape were against them.

They had not long left their position before the Indians discovered their going and at once made another charge.

But again the Mississippi yagers drove them back.

Thus they pushed on, keeping in the water, the bank making a most effective breastwork and their weapons holding their red foes at a safe distance.

After several miles the creek emptied into the Platte River, but the bank still afforded shelter though at times the water was quite deep for wading.

Another trouble that confronted them was carrying the wounded men, but this was gotten over by gathering driftwood, constructing a raft and placing them upon it, then pushing it along with them.

Bill McCarthy urged Will to also get upon the raft, but he said he was not wounded, and if the water got too deep for him he could swim, and he even insisted upon sticking to his rifle, instead of allowing one the of [*sic*] wounded men to carry it.

Later on Will was only too glad that he had stuck to his resolve about the rifle.

As they proceeded on their way they found places where the water was too deep to wade, to ascend to the bank would be certain death, and so, after firing a few shots at the Indians, they were compelled to put their weapons and ammunition upon the raft and swim over such places.

Several of the men could not swim, and as the raft was already loaded deep those who could had to carry them over the deep places in the river.

Thus the hours passed away, and mile after mile had been left behind, but fatiguing danger-haunted miles they were.

"How goes it, Boy Pard?" was the question frequently asked the young hero as no word of complaint came from his lips, and he struggled on with a pluck and energy that won the admiration of the men who know from experience how hard was the trail they were traveling.

"I'm all right," was the unfailing reply, and on he trudged through the water, swimming when it was too deep for him to wade.

Night fell at last to find the band still on their way in the bed of the river, one of the number constantly ascending to the bank to see just where the Indians were, who doggedly hovered after them, just out of range of the rifles.

But Will, though a hardy boy, had not a man's endurance, and without apparently observing that he did so, he began to lag behind the others.

The moon had come up so its light aided them on their way, as well as enabled them to see the Indians when they approached nearer, which at times they did.

It was while lagging behind the others, very tired, but determined not to give up, for awhile at least, that Will Cody caught sight of a head peering over the bank a few paces down the stream from where he was, the face being turned toward the men who had passed on.

CHAPTER XXV.
WILL CODY'S DEADLY AIM.

To this day William Cody says he can feel the shock the sight of that Indian's head peering over the bank gave him.

There was the war bonnet, the head, the shoulders, and the Indian, who had daringly slipped in close to the bank and was following the men wading in the stream, he was bringing his rifle up for a shot.

But unlike Lot's wife[47] he had not looked behind him, and therein was his mistake.

He had looked over the bank between the men and the tired boy.

Quick to think, and equally ready to act Will Cody took in the situation and mastered it.

He knew if he did not fire quickly the Indian would kill one of his comrades.

He also knew that if he did not fire with deadly aim the consequences would doubtless be that the Indian would fire and at him.

To call out to his companions he might have done, and the thought flashed through his mind, to be at once dismissed as cowardly.

No, he had been brought face to face with a deadly danger, he had full knowledge that it would be the life of a comrade, the Indian's life or his own.

Having to meet the situation, though it was to take a human life, to make a grave in the world, he did not flinch from the alternative, but met it bravely.

Standing knee deep in the water, with the Indian within twenty feet of his rifle muzzle, the moonlight shining fully upon him, he moved to get a better aim, and the splash he made betrayed him.

There was a quick turn of the bonneted head, a reversing of the rifle, a yell, and before the Indian could take aim the boy's finger touched the trigger.

The report rang out sharp, yells answered it back from the river, while with a wild clutching at the air the Indian came tumbling over the bank, his heavy fall in the water splashing Will all over.

"Who fired that shot?" came in the voice of Bill McCarthy from a few hundred feet ahead.

Then Will Cody missed the chance of his life to emulate the illustrious Father of his Country and reply:

"A Man of the West" : 77

Will Kills His First Indian

"I cannot tell a lie—I did it with my little rifle."

But he was not in an emulating humor just then, as the Indian was writhing in the water, and as the boy said afterwards, he "was afraid he would drown," and so was trying to pull him ashore.

Getting no answer to his question and missing his young pard, Bill McCarthy called to some of the men to take position on the bank to fire upon the Indians, while he ran back up stream to find that Will had gotten his redskin out on dry land, only to find that his struggles had ceased, that he had left the warpath on earth to travel the trails of the Happy Hunting grounds.

"Well done, Boy Pard, you've killed your first Injun, and done it like a man," and Bill McCarthy grasped the boy's hand, and then called out:

"Pards, Little Billy has killed a red."

A cheer greeted the words, but it seemed to jar on the ears of the boy, to rejoice over the death even of an Indian, and he said by way of excuse:

"I was behind, and saw him look over the bank to fire at the men ahead, so I shot him."

"Good for you, lad, and you are mighty cool about it too."

"Come, we must be getting on."

"Won't you bury him, sir?"

"Bury him?

"No indeed, his companions will do that, for they'll soon find him, when we push on; but the thought shows your heart is all right, Billy. Now come with me."

Will obeyed in silence, glancing back at the dead Indian as he lay in the moonlight, while strange thoughts crowded upon his mind at having for the first time raised his hand against a human life.

That the other Indians understood that the single shot had laid their daring scout low was shown by another charge, which however was checked as before by the hot fire of the yagers.

Pushing on then more rapidly, Bill McCarthy leading, and his brother bringing up the rear to see that there was no more lagging behind, the trainmen kept more steadily on their way, making a halt only when it was absolutely necessary to rest.

And all through that night Will Cody struggled on with the others, more determined than before, after what had occurred, not to yield to the fatigue he could not but feel more than those of matured years.

At last the Indians gave up their pursuit, knowing that they were getting in a dangerous locality; but Bill McCarthy would not halt and keeping on reached Fort Kearney just at sunrise, a worn-out, haggard-faced band, full of joy however at their escape, and each one of the men loud in his praise of the young hero who had faced every hardship and danger without a word, and so ably done his part in killing an Indian, thus saving the life beyond doubt of one of his companions, and giving the redskins to understand that they must not be pressed too hard.

CHAPTER XXVI.
A SECOND VENTURE.

The trainmen received a warm welcome at Fort Kearney, the wounded men at once cared for by the surgeon and Will found himself a hero in the eyes of both officers and soldiers.

Hearing the story Bill McCarthy had to tell, the commanding officer at once dispatched a force of cavalry and infantry, with a couple of howitzers, by a forced march to Plum Creek, hoping to recapture the cattle from the Indians, and tired though they were, some of the party of trainmen, at the request of the agent Russell, Majors & Waddell had at Fort Kearney, started back with the troops, all being well mounted.

Determined not to desert his comrades, Will Cody also went along, though urged to remain and seek much needed rest.

Arriving at the scene of the stampede the wagons were found half burned, the bodies of the three herders were lying where they had fallen, but scalped and otherwise mutilated.

The bodies of the unfortunate men were buried, and while the troops pressed on after the Indians the trainmen began a search for cattle.

Some were found, but many that the Indians had not driven off had gone with the numerous herds of buffalo that were everywhere found on the plains at that time.

The Indian trail led south toward the Republican River,[48] but so quickly had they made themselves scarce, anticipating the coming of the soldiers, that though the commanding officer pressed on to the head of Plum Creek, there was not a redskin overtaken and the men returned to Fort Kearney without seeing one.

As there was no further use for McCarthy's men, the company's agent sent them back to Leavenworth, the loss of the cattle and wagons being assumed by the government as it made itself responsible for losses through the acts of the Indians.

Will returned with the men, and an enterprising newspaper man at Leavenworth at once interviewed him upon his exploit and wrote him up as the "Boy Indian Slayer."*

Reading the account in print Will felt considerably set up, though he hardly recognized himself from what the reporter said of him, and it is my personal opinion confidentially expressed to the public, that it left an impression upon Will Cody the boy regarding the capabilities of newspaper men which has never been obliterated.

He over and over again reminded the author of this biography that he must remember to write only the truth and that he was not writing a romance, even if founded on fact.

Still for all the report being exaggerated, Will Cody read it over and

---

*The reporter who first brought Col. Cody before the public by Printer's Ink, is Mr. John Hutchinson, a well known resident of Wichita, Kansas. —The Author.

over again, and felt how proud his mother and sisters would be to see that when the time came he had done his duty well.

With only a flying visit home Will returned again to duty, for the Overland Freighter had entered into a contract with the government to transport stores and beef cattle across the plains to General Albert Sidney Johnston's army, then massing against the Mormons.

Determined to send a large enough force to prevent a disastrous result, such as had happened to the McCarthy Brothers, a large number of teamsters were required, with other needs in a large wagon train.

The trail was known to be one full of danger, especially since the affair on Plum Creek, and men were offered forty dollars a month in gold.[49]

Will's heart beat high with the hope of gaining such a large sum for his services, and he could scarcely believe what he heard when told that he had been put down as an "extra" to go with an old wagon master by the name of Lew Simpson, one of the best men that ever commanded a train.

The train was to start at once, Salt Lake being its destination, and Lew Simpson told Will that his duties would be very light, simply to aid him, unless he had to take the place of some driver who might be ill, wounded or killed.

There was no flinching from the responsibility, and Will knew that all of the men were aware of his exploit on the last expedition, they had read that report of his heroism and he was only afraid he would fall short of expectations.

He was furnished with a good mule, a complete outfit and was to be subject only to the orders of Simpson himself.

Of course there were at once objections raised at home to his going, he was told to remember his last painful experience, reminded how bitter the Mormons would be toward those taking supplies to General Johnston's army, that Indians would beset the way, and his mother urged that he accept his escape before as a warning not to tempt Providence too far.

But Will reminded his mother that money was sorely needed by her, that he could not back down at the first danger, that he was determined to become a plainsman, and though he would do almost anything to obey he felt that in this case he was doing only what was right in going against her commands.

At last a reluctant consent was given, upon condition that Mrs. Cody should see Lew Simpson and ask him to look after her boy, in case they should have to winter in the mountains.

To her dismay Mrs. Cody learned that Simpson had killed a number of men, and appealing to Colonel Majors,[50] he told her that the man had only acted in self-defense and the discharge of duty, that no better wagon master could be found, and Will would be well taken care of.

After a talk with Lew Simpson Mrs. Cody felt reassured, and bidding her daring young son goodbye she returned home wondering if she would ever see him again.

"All ready, boy?" called out Lew Simpson soon after, and Will replied:

"I only wish to see Colonel Majors, sir."

Away he dashed on his mule to Headquarters, and dismounting said:

"I may be gone a long time, sir, perhaps a year, so if I do not come back I want to ask you to pay all my wages to my mother."

Colonel Majors held out his hand and answered:

"I will, my lad, and let me tell you now that the boy who is true as you are to your mother can never go far wrong.

"You have put your name down upon the company's roll, but I wish you to sign this also,"[51] and Colonel Majors handed a printed slip of paper to the boy, who signed it modestly remarking that he could not use a pen as he could a rifle.*

With a farewell grasp of the hand to Colonel Majors Will Cody mounted his mule and rode to the head of the train to join Lew Simpson who had already started upon his long and perilous trail.

As the boy moved further and further away, he glanced backward again and again to look at the distant hill that was near his home and

---

*"I, William F. Cody, do hereby solemnly swear, before the Great and Living God, that during my engagement, and while I am in the employ of Russell, Majors & Waddell, that I will under no circumstances use profane language; that I will drink no intoxicating liquors of any kind; that I will not quarrel or fight with any other employee of the firm and that in every respect I will conduct myself honestly, be faithful to my duties, and so direct all my acts as will win the confidence and esteem of my employers, so help me God."

In spite of the many wild and reckless spirits he had under his command, Col. Majors caused all to sign this oath, and to their credit be it said many of them kept it as far as it was in their power to do so, and yet drive bull teams and mules. The oath at least shows Col. Major's nature and good intentions. —The Author.

his thoughts were busy, for before him came the sweet face of his loving mother, the anxious look his sisters wore at his going, and the admiration of him in the countenance of his little brother Charlie, because he could do what was impossible to him.

Even Turk was not forgotten, and only the presence of Lew Simpson kept my hero from giving away to his feelings in a burst of tears and revealing that he was still only a boy.

CHAPTER XXVII.
A WAGON TRAIN ON THE OVERLAND TRAIL.

The more he saw of the free, wild life of the plains, the more Will Cody liked it.

There was something to him almost fascinating in the nightly camps, the watching for danger, the care of the cattle and in being among the rough but noble spirits that made up the train people.

He reveled in the broad expanse of scenery, the immense herds of buffalo, the fleet-footed antelope and the fact that the train was pushing further and further into what was almost a terra incognito, save near the overland trails.

It may be of interest just here to make my readers acquainted with just what a "freight train" was.

The wagons in use were made especially for the plains, were large, strongly built and could carry seven thousand pounds of freight in the large wagon boxes, which were covered by two hoods of heavy canvas to protect the goods from the weather.

Each wagon was drawn by several yokes of oxen, under one driver, and a full train consisted of twenty-five wagons, all under a chief who was known as the wagon-master.

Then there was an assistant wagon-master, next the extra hands, the night herders, and the cavallard drivers* in the order named.

The men were divided into messes and did their own cooking, getting wood and water, washing up the tins, and one standing guard from each mess.

---

*It was the duty of the cavallard drivers to drive the loose cattle. —The Author.

All were heavily armed, and were ready to fight when called upon.

The "outfit" was known as a bull-train, the drivers being called bull-whackers, the whip they carried bearing the same name, and its crack was as loud as the report of a musket.

There must be something in the air, surrounding, life or associations to sharpen a man's wit, for nearly all plainsmen have a dry humor about them that is irresistible, a drawling a la Mark Twain way of talking that is irresistibly funny.

Those of the "bull outfit" that Will Cody formed the smallest part of were no exception, and he enjoyed listening at night around the campfire to their droll anecdotes, stories of remarkable escapes, and he has an irresistible way of relating today the tales he heard in boyhood, seldom even telling of any scene, adventure or hair-breadth escape in his own life, unless it is something against himself.

The trail to Salt Lake led through Kansas in a northwest direction, crossing the Big Blue, the Big Sandy and Little Sandy Rivers, and entering Nebraska near the Big Sandy.

Then the Little Blue River was crossed and the trail ran along its banks for sixty miles to old Fort Kearney.

From there the trail led along the South Platte River to Ash Hollow Crossing, thence to North Platte River, striking it in the neighborhoods of the scene of General Harney's big battle with the Cheyenne and Sioux Indians in 1855, near the mouth of the Blue Water.[52]

Still following the North Platte the trail led to Fort Laramie or the river of the same name.

The North Platte was crossed later, then the Red Buttes, Willow Creek, the Sweet Water, Independence Rock, Devil's Gate and the Cold Springs where ice can be found three feet underground the warmest of summer days.

Next the trail wound by the Hot Springs, Rocky Ridge, through the Rocky Mountains, and Echo Canyon on to Salt Creek Valley.

As a further item of interest to the reader, after following the long wagon trail, I may mention that Russell, Majors & Waddell, used some seven thousand wagons, seventy-five thousand oxen, a great number of mules and horses and employed eight thousand men in their gigantic overland freighting business.

Following the train which my hero accompanied, nothing of importance occurred until they reached the fateful camp where the McCarthy Brothers' outfit had been surprised, and where as a sad reminder was the grave in which the three slain herders had been buried.

Camping here a day for a grand buffalo hunt, the party captured a dozen or more of the cattle that had been stampeded by the Indians, while they also killed plenty of the big game which now stamps William Cody with the name known the world over—"Buffalo Bill."

Pulling out of camp the next morning, the last wagon had not yet started when a party of horsemen were seen in the distance, charging down upon an enormous herd of buffalo between them and the train.

The herd of giant game stampeded at once and hundreds of them dashed like a black avalanche down upon the train, the oxen in their fright trying to run off with the wagons, while wagon-tongues were broken and no end of damage was done.

For awhile it looked as though the whole train was wrecked, for the oxen were wild, yokes were broken and one old buffalo got entangled in the chains and went off toward the hills with the debris hanging to his horns.

Of course the train had to return to camp to repair damages, the horsemen who had caused the stampede camping with the outfit, they proving to be a party of returning Californians.

CHAPTER XXVIII.
LOST.

From the camp which had a second time proven an unfortunate one, the train pulled out as soon as repairs were all made, and days passed away without any happening of moment.

As he had much spare time on his hands Will was wont to go off the trail to hunt, and he was generally successful in bringing home game of some kind, which he always shared with the other messes.

On one of these hunts he got excited over a deer chase, and went miles further than he had intended.

But he got his stag, whose grand antlers were what had lured him into an act of imprudence.

He had already learned fairly well how to "butcher" his meat, and

Seemingly without warning there came a peal of thunder not only startling him greatly but causing his mule to dash away in fright

having cut the choicest bits and severed the heads with its fine horns, fastening all to his saddle, he was about to mount his mule when seemingly without any warning, there came a terrible peal of thunder, not only startling him greatly, but causing his mule to dash away in fright.

Whether the swaying antlers striking the mule caused him to run the faster, or he was still frightened at the thunder, Will could not tell, but he saw the animal dash away through the timber like mad, and at a speed which caused the boy to mutter:

"It would take a bird to catch that mule."

Had he been a man, and not a subscriber to Col. Majors' "oath" he might then and there have expressed himself with more vehemence at the mule's desertion of him.

Watching the swiftly running animal until he disappeared from view, Will then decided to make the best of his unfortunate situation.

But other peals of thunder were following the first one, the lightning incessantly flashed and over the mountain range there rolled a mass of inky storm-clouds that had a very destructive look.

The boy took in the situation, saw that there was a shelter near him in the shape of a large boulder, and if he left it he might be killed by falling timber, and he wisely determined to remain where he was, for the trees on the range were swaying wildly before a wind that was howling savagely.

The clouds shutting out the sun made the day almost as dark as night, and as Will shrank close in among the rocks for shelter the roar of the wind, crashing of the thunder and blazing of the lightning were appalling.

Down the mountain swept the storm, snapping off large trees like pipe stems, hurling rocks from their resting places to descend in mighty bounds down the range, and filling the air with sticks, leaves and dust.

Appalled, the boy stood gazing upon the scene, with awe not unmixed with some admiration at its grandeur, and in spite of all he saw a humorous side when he thought of his runaway mule, and wondered how fast he was going.

Following the first onslaught of the storm came the rain, and Will decided that never in his life before had he known what rain was, for the first downpour drenched him to the skin, and he discovered that the boulder afforded no shelter whatever.

For more than an hour the rain came down in the same unbroken sheet, and then the clouds swept away and a gleam of sunlight came.

But it was a last expiring ray, for the sun was on the horizon and with a sinking heart Will knew that darkness would soon be upon him.

Miles from the trail, not knowing in just which direction the train was in camp, for he was sure the storm had forced them to encamp, wet, on foot with night coming on, his condition was most deplorable.

At first he determined to follow on after the mule, but he gave this up, feeling confident that nothing short of a sudden shock of heart disease, or the falling of a tree upon him had stopped that animal.

Then he decided to remain where he was and make the best of it.

Fortunately his box of matches was safe and dry, and a search about among the rocks unearthed a few leaves and sticks from crevices that he knew would burn.

Wood was collected and brought up to the boulder, some brush cut with his knife to make a shelter and then he lighted the fire.

Then he cut off a steak from the deer, and just as darkness settled down he began to cook his supper, such as it was.

"If mother and the girls could only see me now," kept coming into his thoughts, for he could imagine the effect upon them.

"Well, this is dark," he muttered, as, after eating his venison steak he stepped away from his brush shelter and looked about him.

Returning to the fire he stood close to it to dry his clothes, until at last the heat made him very sleepy and he sat down with his back to the boulder, his rifle across his lap and dropped off to sleep.

CHAPTER XXIX.
CAPTURED BY DANITES.

It was a long, terrible night to the lost boy, for, after his first nap he got but little sleep.

In spite of the fire he was chilly, his clothes being still wet, and then too the noises he heard were not reassuring.

Wolves howled dismally up the mountains, then something passed near with heavy tread that at first he thought was his mule returned in a repentant mood, but as he stepped out to see he beheld a huge black object he was sure was a bear until it bounded away with a startled snort and he knew it was a stray buffalo or elk.

Several times he had to scare the wolves away from the body of the slain deer, and at last fearing he would have no breakfast he cut off another steak and then decided to cook it just to pass away time.

Broiling it on the coals he ate heartily, and was glad to see that the firelight was growing dim under the approach of dawn.

At last he shouldered his rifle and started to "find himself" as he expressed it.

The rain had washed away all trail left by the mule, yet after a walk of several miles he came directly upon the animal.

But the sight was a shock to him, for there lay the mule dead, while a huge bear was devouring him.

If Will was startled the bear was more so, for at sight of a human being he went scampering away at a speed the boy did not think Bruin was capable of.

The mule had been dead for some time, and had evidently fallen prey to the bear as one of his forelegs was broken.

The antlers had been torn from the saddle, but Will thought no more of them, for he was anxious to get away.

"If I can only get my saddle and skip before that bear comes back to see what scared him, it is all I want," he muttered, and throwing the saddle and bridle across his shoulders he quickly left the spot.

It was just noon when tired out he came upon the trail, and discovered that the wagon train had gone by.

Turning back along the trail a walk of a mile brought him in sight of the camp, just as Lew Simpson and half a dozen others were riding out to search for him, having already been looking for him all the morning.

He was greeted with a wild cheer by the men, and his story soon told, Lew Simpson remarking:

"I tell you, boy, if harm had come to you I'd never been the man to go back and face your mother; but don't mind the mule, for he ran off from you, and you can ride another, so get your dinner and we'll push along on the trail, for here's where we halted when the storm caught us, and I guess you know how bad that was."

Will guessed so too, and getting something to eat was soon once more mounted and riding along with Lew Simpson who had him tell his story of the night all over again.

Day after day the march continued, until a halt was made at noon some miles from Green River in the Rocky Mountains, where the magnificent scenery impressed Will greatly.

It was a "dry camp," for the cattle had to be driven about a mile to water, Simpson, George Woods, his assistant wagon-master and Will driving them.

When on the way back with the cattle they suddenly saw a number of horsemen who came unexpectedly upon them and at a point where the camp could not be seen.

Suspecting no danger Lew Simpson and the others halted as the horsemen rode up to them; one who was their leader calling out:

"How are you, Lew Simpson?"

"You've got the advantage of me, Pard," said Simpson, failing to recall where he had ever seen the man before.

"Yes, and I intend to keep it," was the reply of the man, with a malignant look coming over his face.

"What do you mean?" asked Lew Simpson, angrily, dropping his hand on his revolver, his example being followed by Will and George Woods.

"Hands off your guns, all of you, for we've got you covered!" sternly

Captured by Danites

ordered the leader, and half a dozen guns were aimed at them. Lew Simpson saw that he was taken wholly at a disadvantage, and his party were greatly outnumbered.

To resist would be to bring an instant fire upon all of them, and he said in his quiet way: "I rather guess you have got the advantage of us."

"Yes, and as I said, I shall keep the advantage."

"Say, who are you anyway?" and Simpson seemed to at last recall that he had met the leader of the party before.

"I am Joseph Smith,"[53] was the calm response.

"What! Joe Smith the leader of the Mormon Danites?" and in spite of his nerve Lew Simpson turned pale as the answer came:

"Yes, Joe Smith, the Danite."

CHAPTER XXX.
THE MORMONS.

Lew Simpson's face was a study as he realized that he was fairly caught, Will Cody, who had regarded the wagon-master as one capable of meeting any emergency felt pity for him, knowing how deep must be his chagrin and sorrow.

They were fairly caught, there was no denying that, and the trainmen were not within sight to see their predicament and come to their relief.

What the result would be could only be conjectured, but Will, ever hopeful, confidently looked for Simpson to find some way out of the difficulty.

Lew Simpson was a man of resources, he always had been able to take care of himself in any danger, but just how he was to do so now, Will could not discover, and he awaited developments with anxiety, though abiding faith for his leader was uppermost in his mind.

"So you are Joe Smith, the Danite?

"Yes, I know you now as a spy and all else that is mean," said Lew Simpson, nettled at his capture.

"You came to my train in distress and I cared for you, fed you and gave you a mule to ride on your way, and now you come back with a clean shaven face and a gang of Danites at your back.

"Oh yes, I know you Joe Smith, and if you don't kill me now, you have the chance, someday you will know me, too," and the wagon master was becoming excited, now that he knew just who the man was he had befriended.

Joe Smith only laughed, and ordered his men to disarm the prisoners, remarking:

"What did you bring that boy out in this wild country for?"

"Never mind the boy for he's all right," Simpson replied.

When the Danites had taken the arms of the three prisoners, Simpson asked:

"What are you going to do with us?"

"I'll soon show you. Bring them along, men."

To the surprise of the three trainmen Joe Smith rode straight out toward the wagon camp and their hearts beat with hope that the men there would rescue them.

But vain the hope, for as they went over the ridge and came in full view of the camp, their hearts sank within them at beholding it in the possession of a large band of Danites, all the men being prisoners.

It was a painful surprise and Joe Smith said:

"You see, I captured your camp, and without a shot.

"Your men were all asleep, and woke up to find that we had them covered, so they wisely surrendered."

"And what is your purpose now you've got us, Joe Smith?"

"You are carrying supplies to General Johnston, who is fighting our people, so, as we cannot take your train with us, we shall burn it and run off your cattle and horses."

"And will turn us adrift here without horses, arms or food?"

"No, I'll give you provisions to last you to Fort Bridger, and you can start as soon as you have them."

"You will give us horses?"

"No sir, you go on foot."

"And allow us our weapons?"

"No sir."

"See here, Joe Smith, if you treat us like that you are worse than the brute men say you are.

"You have captured our train, and you must give us a wagon to carry our provisions, six yoke of oxen and our weapons.

"Don't prove yourself a coward by treating men at your mercy as you threaten."

"See here, Lew Simpson, I know you as a brave man, and I will not be hard on you, for as you say, we have prevented the train from reaching the United States soldiers.

"You can have the oxen and wagon to haul your provisions, your weapons and one mule.

"That is all, so say no more and be off."

Further argument was useless, and under the circumstances the trainmen felt that they had fared better than they had expected and knew that they owed it to Lew Simpson's bold manner of addressing the Danite Chief.

The weapons were all rolled in blankets and placed in the bottom of the wagon, the provisions being packed on top of them to prevent their being used quickly, and the trainmen started on their way to Fort Bridger, all realizing how utterly useless it would be to attempt to recapture their wagons.

It was a sad-faced party of men that pulled out of the camp, the Danites with arms in their hands, silently regarding them.*

---

*Several years ago I accompanied Col. Cody, and a party of foreign and American Army officers on a trip in the saddle through New Mexico, Arizona, Utah, etc., and in the Mormon village of Kanab we met a man who was with Joe Smith at the time he captured the wagon train, and remembered well that Lew Simpson had along with him a "Boy Plainsman"—Will Cody.

As they reached the summit of a distant hill the trainmen halted and looking back saw the Danites taking from the wagons all that they could carry with them, after which they set fire to them.

Many of the wagons were loaded with bacon and hams, and these burned fiercely, while several had ammunition in them, and the explosions that followed put the Danites to flight and sounded like a battle with big guns.

When the wagons and their contents had all gone up in smoke Lew Simpson and his men pushed on to Fort Bridger. Will Cody's mind [was] busy with all he had witnessed and been an actor in.

The boy was to continue to have lessons under the sternest and hardest of teachers—experience.

CHAPTER XXXI.
MORE BITTER EXPERIENCE.

In dogged silence the trainmen pressed on their way, none caring to discuss the inglorious termination of their venture.

It might have been worse, all knew, had the Mormons chosen to take more severe measures with them.

But the Mormons were fighting a war of destruction rather than death, preferring to drive the United States Army out of their country by destroying all their supplies, instead of ambushing and attacking them.

With the Mountain Meadow Massacre and a few other exceptions this was the course they pursued.[54]

At last the trainmen reached Fort Bridger and Lew Simpson found what comfort he could, if any, that his had not been the only train the Mormons had destroyed, two others having shared the same fate, and their men being allowed to go on to the fort.

These three trains, consisting of seventy-five wagons, caused a loss to the soldiers of nearly five hundred thousand pounds of provisions.

It was at once known that unless other trains got through in safety, a winter of suffering for all would follow.

This Mormon and Col. Cody had a long talk together over the capture and other happenings of those stirring times away back in the fifties. —The Author.

Will Cody enjoyed greatly the scenes at the fort, and had little thought of the morrow, though he was sorry to learn that on account of the season being so well advanced the employees of Russell, Majors & Waddell, consisting of nearly four hundred men, would be compelled to remain at Fort Bridger.

So into winter quarters went soldiers and trainmen, and from the first the commissary was known to be in scant condition, though it was hoped that another wagon outfit might be on the way and have better success in reaching the fort.

If it did not there were prospects of much suffering during the winter, and this was not pleasant for even the old rounders[55] to contemplate.

It was now November and a cold winter was anticipated, unless all signs failed.

Fort Bridger was in a prairie, and all fuel had to be hauled a distance of two miles. This was all very well at first, but when the snow began to fly it was severe work for men and cattle.

Then, as no other wagon train had arrived, short rations became a necessity, and the commissary had to soon after fall back upon the oxen for food.

Will was fond of good living, what boy is not, whatever he may develop into in later life.

He missed the "good things" his mother had always sought to have for him, he even found himself longing for the course [sic] fare of the train camps.

But no one heard him complain, and he did his share of the work with the others.

When the cattle had all been butchered, the wood had to be hauled by the men, or carried on their backs from the timberland to the fort, thus adding to the hardships to be endured.

Often did the boy find himself thinking of the cheery wood fire at home, the substantial meals prepared three times a day, the warm bed in his little room with his little brother Charlie for a bed fellow, and wonder if he would ever see the old scenes again, or would starve to death.

"Well, if a little fellow like me can get so hungry, how much more the big men must suffer," was his commentary, and he would take in his belt another hole.

At last the long hard winter passed away and spring came none too soon, for starvation was staring all in the face.

Fortunately Russell, Majors & Waddell had started a large train of supplies to Utah, to push on every day that it was possible to do so, and the result was that before the Mormons believed succor would be started, the welcome wagons were seen coming to the Fort.

How they were received all can imagine, and they were just in time to save many a victim from death by hunger.

The "square meal" that Will Cody ate after the arrival of that train of provisions, he has said was the one in all his life he most enjoyed.

With the spring the civil employees of the Government, along with the teamsters and freighters, started for the Missouri River, and Lew Simpson was in charge, Will of course, accompanying him.

On the way a halt was made at Fort Laramie and there Lew Simpson was placed over two large trains and made Brigade Wagon Master, Will being given work with him, for the man had never forgotten his promise to Mrs. Cody to bring him back in safety to her.

With the train there were some four hundred men, extra hands, all bound to Fort Leavenworth, so no dread of an attack was felt by any one.

Upon reaching Ash Hollow, Simpson decided to follow the North Platte down to its junction with the South Platte, and the two trains were kept some twenty miles apart while on the march and Will was again given the duty of courier to bear orders between them, when anything arose that required a communication to be sent.

One morning Lew Simpson called out to the boy:

"Come, Billy, I am going to the train ahead with George Woods and I wish you to come along too."

Will was only too glad to do so, to escape the slow and tedious march, and rode after the two wagon masters little dreaming that the going was to make that day another important era in his eventful life.

CHAPTER XXXII.
BESIEGED BY INDIANS.

Mounted upon mules and well armed, yet suspecting no trouble, Lew Simpson, Woods and Will Cody rode ahead of the rear train to overtake the one in advance.

They had a twenty-mile ride of it, perhaps a little more, and expected to overtake it by night, remain there in camp, and await the coming up of the rear train about noon the next day, for the two outfits would not seek the same camping place on account of wishing to have plenty of grass for the cattle.

Simpson and his companions had ridden about half the distance, and the Wagon Master had refused about ten minutes before to allow Will to branch off from the trail in search of game, when they suddenly discovered a band of Indians half a mile away, dash out of a clump of timber and charge toward them at full speed.

They were in the midst of a prairie, with no shelter near, and to seek safety by flight mounted upon mules was a questionable expedient.

But Simpson was equal to the occasion, and calling to the other two to dismount he drew a revolver and as rapidly as he could pull trigger fired three shots, not at the Indians however, but the mules.

The act startled Will Cody and then and there he decided that he would never see the old home and loved ones again.

But his companions had no thought for "home and loved ones" just then, or rather were doing that which would give them a chance to see them at another time.

What they were doing was to form a triangular fort with the mules as breastworks.

The animals had dropped dead under Simpson's shots, and dragged into place formed a barrier behind which their riders could take refuge and be fairly well protected.

"Crouch down in here close, Billy, and I guess we can stand 'em off, but if we don't the boys when they come along can see how we died, and can tell your mother I did all I could to save you."

The words touched Will Cody deeply, and he felt that Lew Simpson was indeed a friend to him.

The three were armed with Mississippi yagers, Will having given up his rifle for one some time before, and each had a couple of revolvers and a knife, the customary armament of a Plainsman.

Simpson found time to reload the three chambers of his revolver, which had sounded the mules' death knell, and the Indians were still over a couple of hundred yards distant when he said:

"Now we are ready for them.

"Don't fire Billy, until you have got dead sure aim on your redskin, old fuss and feathers on the white horse; I'll take the one on his right, you the one on his left, Woods."

Will glanced admiringly at Simpson, he was so cool about it, and then surveyed "old fuss and feathers" as he had called the Indian whose war bonnet was that of a chief.

In the band there were all of fifty redskins, had there been less, Simpson would have made a running fight of it back to the train.

They were coming at the full speed of their ponies, yelling like demons, and intended to sweep right over the little band.

"Now, Pards, I'll give the word in a minute—fire!"

The three yagers flashed almost as one, and three saddles were emptied, the chief being one to fall.

This sudden repulse caused the others to wheel their ponies and fly out of range with all speed, where, had they pressed on they might have ridden down their pale face foes.

Will gave a sigh of relief as he saw them stampede, which caused Simpson to say:

"You feel better, Boy Pard, no doubt, but they haven't gone."

"I'm glad to see only three or four of them have rifles," George Woods remarked, for only several bullets had come whistling toward them, while dozens of arrows had.

Will said nothing, but he had shown his nerve, and was ready for another attack, which the others said would soon be made.

Fortunately the first stunning blow made the Indians so cautious that the three fighting for their lives had time to reload their weapons, before they made another charge, which was announced by Lew Simpson calling out:

"Be ready, for here they come again!"

CHAPTER XXXIII.
FIGHTING FOR LIFE.

When Lew Simpson announced to his companions to be ready for a second charge from the Indians, Will Cody drew a long breath, ran his Mississippi yager out over the body of his dead mule, and crouched down as he saw the others do, to take aim and at the same time protect himself as well as he could.

"Have your revolvers ready after you've fired your guns, for they won't turn back so easy this time," said Simpson.

A moment after he called out:

"Fire!"

The guns flashed. The revolvers were seized and opened rapidly, to the amazement of the Indians, who could not understand their rapid firing, as they were not common there in those days, and showers of arrows filled the air, striking in the breastwork of mules and sticking there.

A few shots were fired by the Indians who were armed with rifles, but the revolvers had done the work and once more they were in rapid retreat, leaving a couple of warriors and several ponies dead upon the field.

"Did you see our little bantam rooster, Woods—aint he a game one?" cried Lew Simpson, as he patted Will upon the shoulder.

"You bet he is; but do you think this arrow is poisoned, Lew?" responded George Woods, and he handed to the Chief Wagon Master an arrow he had just drawn out of his shoulder.

Touched at the suffering of a comrade, Will showed more anxiety at the wound than he had at the danger they were in, and having heard stories of poisoned arrows, breathlessly awaited the decision of Simpson, who had taken it and was closely regarding it.

After what seemed an age to the boy, and must have really been so to the wounded man, Simpson said:

"No, it is not poisoned, thank God!"

"We'll load up and then I'll look to your wound, Woods."

"All right, no hurry," was the plucky answer, and with the other, Woods began to reload his weapons.

This most necessary work finished, Simpson looked at the wound, which was deep, but not serious, it appeared, and he dressed it as well as he could, putting a quid of tobacco in it to draw out the poison, if there was any.

The Indians had meanwhile held a council, and not caring to venture another charge, began to circle around the three defenders in single file, protecting themselves by riding on the further side of their ponies, and firing arrows at the little barricade of mule, the three crouching low down for shelter.

"They are making a pin cushion out of my poor mule," said Will, as arrow after arrow struck with a dull thud and remained sticking in the mule.

"We'll drop a couple or more of them, and stop their sport," muttered Lew Simpson and the rifles opened again, with fatal effect in one case and the Indians drew off out of range.

As Simpson said the redskins would not make another charge for some time, the three comrades set to work with knives to strengthen their little fort by digging down as deep as they could and piling the earth up on the mules.

"Ah! They are going to starve us out, for they saw the train go by and think we are left; but they don't know that a second train is following."

This seemed to be the plan of the Indians, for they surrounded the barrier, just out of range, and camped on the prairie, staking their ponies out near them.

Expecting to reach the other train before night, Simpson had brought no provisions along, and they had no water, so felt that it would quickly be a case of starvation, but for the other train.

Hours passed by, and nothing had been heard or seen of the Indians, but a close watch was kept on each side not to be surprised.

Then a breeze sprung up and a bright light was seen.

"The cunning scamps! they are going to set the prairie on fire to burn us out," said Simpson, and then to the great relief of Woods and Will, added:

"The grass won't burn much, it is too short."

But anxiously they watched the flame as it increased in size, and here and there leaped into a dangerous conflagration.

But just where they had halted and turned, at bay the grass was fortunately very short and did not allow the flames sufficient body to feed upon and jump over them.

Still the heat was great and the smoke stifling, and Will had curled himself up under the leg of his mule to keep from smothering, when Lew Simpson cried:

"Now look out for them to come up under cover of the smoke."

At once Will and Woods were all attention, and with their leader they opened fire with a revolver each, and a yell showed that they had done much harm.

Finding that they had not burned out their foes, and could not surprise them, the Indians gave up the attempt and settled calmly down to play a waiting game, an accomplishment in which they certainly excel, as no race of people have more patience, in fact, they seem in this respect to be direct descendants from Job, if inheritance of virtue and vice go for anything in this world.[56]

CHAPTER XXXIV.
WARNED BY A DREAM.

Just as dawn was breaking, Will, who had been overcome with fatigue, was sleeping soundly, and Woods, who had suffered all night with his wound, had at last dropped into a restless sleep, while Lew Simpson's eyes, filled with smoke and tired from long watching, were closed as he leaned his head on his rifle.

What awakened Will Cody he never knew, unless it was a dream that he heard Turk barking and back through his mind in slumber swept bygone memories, and the bay of his faithful dog meant danger.

Again he was back in the old home in Salt Creek Valley, once more his father was in danger, and Turk's loud bark of warning told him that foes were near to once more strike a blow to those he loved.

As the dream flitted through his brain he awoke with a start and looked about him in a dazed way.

He was not at home; he had not heard Turk's bark of warning; all was but a dream; but still foes were near and as he recalled where he was, he looked out over the charred prairie to behold, like spectre form, a number of horsemen riding slowly toward the little fort.

The forms of ponies and riders looked shadowy enough, yet there was substance there for all that.

"Mr. Simpson! Mr. Woods! They are coming!"

At the first sound of the boy's voice Simpson was wide awake, and at a glance took in the situation.

"So they are.

"I was fast asleep on the post of duty, but you are a wide-awake sentinel and have saved us.

"Come, Woods, wake up and we will fire together and show those reds we are still on earth."

The three Mississippi yagers flashed together and the aim of each gun was true, and the Indians were the ones surprised, for they had ridden so near that they believed the defenders had died from wounds or were fast asleep.

The revolvers rattled after the shots of the yagers and failing in a surprise, the Indians broke in a stampede.

But they did not give up, only went off out of range to once more bide their time.

Hungry, tired out, with throats parched for a drink of water, and Woods suffering from his wound, the lot of the little band was a most unhappy one.

"The train will be along in an hour or two," said Lew Simpson.

And the coming of the train was their only hope.

"You kept us from being butchered this morning, Billy, and the train must get us out of this," and Simpson's eyes were cast back over the train with a longing look.

But the hours wore by and noon came with no sign of the coming of the rear train.

What could have happened to it?

Had a large band of Indians corralled it also?

At last the Indians were seen to spring to their feet, those on the trail and several hundred yards away giving the alarm.

"They hear the cracking of the bull whips—the train is coming," cried Simpson.

It was true, for the Indian circle was now wildly excited.

They had not dreamed of another train following the one they had seen.

Then there was mounting in haste and a gathering in a group of the scattered class.

To the ears of those at bay now came the sound of the cracking whips.

No music ever sounded sweeter, and the sounds were as welcome as were the notes of the bagpipes, playing "The Campbells are Coming," to the besieged soldiers in Lucknow.[57]

In a few moments there came into view an assistant wagon boss riding a mule and leading the way; then the spreading horns of the leading oxen and next the white tilts of a "prairie schooner," as the freighting wagons were called.

A few moments more and like a huge serpent of white and brown the long train came crawling over the hill and across the prairie.

The Indians had not waited to tempt the appetite of the mighty serpent, but with a parting charge, demoniacal yells and a shower of arrows, they went tearing away over the prairie to find shelter in the distant timber.

The teamsters had discovered the Indians and ran forward to the relief of the brave defenders of "Fort Mule," as they at once named the spot.

They admired Lew Simpson's ingenuity, praised his pluck and gave three cheers for each member of the garrison.

"You wouldn't have found us alive, boys, if it hadn't been for Billy's dream—it's a long distance to hear a dog bark, from there to Kansas, but the barking of Billy's dog woke him up and saved us."

"Look at the boy now! he's gathering up the arrows, taking the pins out of the cushions, as he called the mules—see! he's but a kid after all, if he can do a man's work."

Three extra cheers were given for Will, who was busy collecting the arrows the Indians had fired at them, to carry home as souvenirs.

―――・∞・―――

CHAPTER XXXV.
A DUTIFUL SON.

The wound of Woods was dressed at once, and he was given a bed in one of the wagons while Will Cody and Simpson ate breakfast, dinner and supper all in one.

The train moved on, leaving the dead Indians for their comrades to come back and bury, and as he rode along on another mule, Will could see that he was regarded as a real hero even by men used to acts of daily heroism.

Each one had something to say to him, and all wanted to hear the story of his dream.

Nothing daunted by the experience of the other attempt to reach the train, Lew Simpson called out, when the train was well on the march again:

"Well, Billy, want to try it again?"

"Oh, yes sir."

"Come along."

Off they started, and as a breakdown of a couple of wagons the day before had delayed the train, the one in the lead had gotten several miles further ahead, so was not overtaken until after dark.

But not an Indian was seen, and the men of the leading train were surprised to hear of the adventure and narrow escape of their Wagon Master and his two companions.

Excepting [sic] to be dogged by a large band of Indians, and having to bring the two trains together for greater safety, and several exciting buffalo hunts, in which Will showed himself as an expert, and won the name of the "Boy Buffalo Killer," nothing of moment happened on the long trail to Leavenworth.

At last, when Leavenworth came into view, Will Cody's heart was full as he felt now soon he would see his mother and sisters and little Charlie.

There was one refrain constantly upon his lips as he rode along:

"Mother, Martha, Julia, Liza, Nellie, May, Charlie and good old Turk will be so glad to see me.

"And won't I be glad too?" and he gave a joyous whistle at the thought.

"I guess I've grown a heap; am more a man than I was; have seen more of the world, and I'll be Big Brother now," he mused, and once his cheery thoughts no shadow felt, no dread of evil to those he loved.

Colonel Majors was one of the first to greet him, and congratulated him upon his fine appearance and improvement, while he told him that Wagon Master Simpson had reported his brave conduct through all the trying scenes they had undergone.

"I have not heard from your home for some weeks, Billy, but your sister Martha has married since you left, came to Leavenworth to live but has returned home.

"Now go and draw your pay, for your mother has not done so, and come back after a vacation and you shall always have work with us, for it is just such boys as you are who grow up to become the great men of our land.

At a Father's Grave

"Under other circumstances I would rather have seen you go to college and get the education you deserve, but I suppose it is best to accept the decrees of destiny, and you will go to the front no matter what your calling in life may be."

Will Cody felt very proud over this little sermon from good Mr. Majors, and went away to the paymasters' quarters to draw his pay.

He had been gone a year; changes had come in that time; his sister Martha had married, left home and returned to the roof-tree[58] once more.

How was his mother and how were his sisters?

The paymaster handed him over his pay in gold, and how proud he felt to be able to carry it home to his mother.

Mounting his mule he did not take the trail directly home, but one leading toward a distant hill.

On that hill was the grave of his father, and the son turned his footsteps thither as a loving duty he owed the dead.

Mature beyond his years, thoughts crowded upon him, as removing his sombrero he stood by his father's grave and remembered all the sufferings he had known.

It was a picture for an artist, as Will Cody stood there with uncovered head, the light of the sun nearing the horizon falling full upon him, his mule, with the precious little bag of gold, standing near and cropping the wild flowers that grew there in the village of the dead.

Thus he stood for some time, his thoughts busy, little dreaming that upon the morrow the very sod beneath his feet would be taken to dig the narrow bed of another dear one who had passed into the dark Shadow Land of the Great Divide.

At last with a sigh he gathered a few wild flowers to bear to his mother, and mounting his patient mule he rode away now on the trail homeward.

It was nearing twilight as he came in sight of his home, and wishing to let them know of his coming, he gave a long, shrill whistle which Mother and sisters and Turk knew so well.

And soon, through the gathering gloom came bounding his faithful dog, and dismounting, Will patted his glossy head as he reared with his paws upon his breast.

But Turk looked cowed, and he uttered low, pitiful whines that seemed to express joy at his young master's return, mingled with some deep sorrow he could not make known by words.

"Turk, you act so strangely—Turk, what is the matter at home?" and with a heart filled with foreboding Will Cody hastened on home to face the sorrow that awaited him.

CHAPTER XXXVI.
THE WANDERER'S RETURN.

The shadow of death rested upon the Cody homestead, and cast a gloom over the return of the Boy Wanderer.

Lying in one of the rooms of the house was the form of the gentle Martha.

Upon her pulse Death had laid its icy hand, stilling its throbbing forever.

Following the dictates of her heart she had left her home a young wife, to return later to the old home to die.

Isaac Cody lay in his grave upon the hill top, Martha had been called away in the full bloom of her young womanhood, Will was far away, perhaps dead, for no one knew then, and surely the cup forced to the widowed mother's lips was full to overflowing with bitterness and under the strain she was slowly breaking down.

That night as the sorrowing family were gathered in the chamber of death, suddenly in the far distance was heard a strange, shrill whistle that had not echoed for a long, long time about the Cody home.

Was it conjured up by fevered fancy or was it real?

Turk the faithful dumb guardian of the household aroused them.

He had loved Martha, and he too was a mourner, lying there near the silent form.

At the first sound of that faraway call, the well known whistle of his young master, he had raised his head in eager attitude, and as the note came to an end he made a bound for the door, and was gone out into the gathering gloom of night.

"My son!" was all that the mother could say.

The whistle and the dog's action had told her of her boy's return.

It was his old familiar signal when nearing home.

On tiptoe to the door went the sisters, then out into the darkness, Julia, the eldest, leading, for there was something to tell the boy wanderer.

Julia must tell him that the joy of his return was clouded by the pall of death resting upon the household.

But Turk had already told him in his dumb way and the boy was in a measure prepared for some sad tidings.

As he dismounted before the door and threw his bridlerein over a peg in the horserack, his sisters met him.

There was no joyous shout, only a silent greeting and then Julia's low voice told the story:

"Oh Will! Martha is dead!"

The blow dealt was a severe one, and the boy stood an instant as though trying to realize all that the words meant that told him his sister Martha was dead.

"And Mother?"

"Is well, and is waiting to see you—come."

His mother was waiting for him, and the meeting Will Cody has never forgotten.

Long into the night they talked and talked, and there was balm to the wounded heart of the boy in placing in his mother's hands the money he had earned.

"There, mother, that will help you out of the troubles you say the claim has given you, and I will make more for you soon."

But there is no need of dwelling upon the scenes of sadness, the dark clouds of sorrow, upon the home, with their silver lining of joy at Will's return.

My province is to tell of the earlier life of my hero, which led him step by step in his ambition to make for himself a name, and in reading of a man who has risen above his fellows, one wishes to know just what has shaped his career from boyhood.

Trifles light as air in early life that would never be taken notice of ordinarily, when one has been crowned with the laurel wreath justly won, are magnified a hundred fold and a little incident is pointed to as the one that led on to fortune and to fame.

Will had been a couple of weeks at home when he decided to again go to school, for awhile at least.

His mother, his sister Martha and the time spent in the little log school house was all the schooling he had thus far received, and his money earned having enabled his mother to be free from worry, by paying off certain small claims threatening trouble against the estate, he yielded to her wishes and once more returned to his studies.

Thus passed the months away, until the boy began to feel that he must again become a moneymaker, did he wish to save his mother from harassing financial cares.

The field of a plainsman was open to him whenever he chose to again venture upon the arduous and dangerous life.

He had grown in "book learning," as the teamsters were wont to call education, he had grown in stature as well, had had experience in aiding his mother in her business and legal troubles, the care of their home and in other purchases, so he felt better equipped for service upon the plains.

So one day Will laid his books carefully away, mounted his horse and once more applied for service with Messrs. Russell, Majors & Waddell.

He was just in the nick of time, and a remark made by Lew Wallace [sic, Simpson], who had been his able teacher, that he was capable, boy though he was, of carrying a train across the Plains, was recalled in his favor, and to his delight he was made assistant under Buck Bomer, a well known master, to go with a train of supplies to the new post of Fort Wallace at Cheyenne Pass.[59]

Returning home he told his mother of his good fortune and the next day farewells were said and he turned his face once more toward the Land of the Setting Sun.

CHAPTER XXXVII.
THE YOUNG TRAPPER.

After what was really an uneventful trip, if important happenings alone are considered, Will Cody returned to Leavenworth and once more went to his home happy as a school boy at being once more able to give his mother substantial pecuniary aid.

He found that her business tact and ability, her energy, self-sacrifice and determined spirit to wipe off every claim against the property his father had left, had met with success beyond his expectations, and there was hope that she might yet be a rich woman, and all through her own exertions and the help he had been able to give her.

Cheered by the prospect, Will was determined to lend still greater help, and believing he could make more money trapping beaver, otter and other fur animals, and being anxious to go on an expedition of that kind, he joined a party of trapper[s] sent out by the Post Trader.

The party set out for the Chugwater and Laramie Rivers, and from the very first it had to fight for existence, the Indians being particularly hostile.

Separated one day from his companions Will met with an adventure which at first threatening the safety of his scalp in the end turned out most fortunately for him.

He was visiting his traps, when suddenly he came upon three Indians, leading their ponies, which were laden down with pelts.

The discovery was mutual, as was also the determination to fight it out then and there.

Dropping his pelts Will Cody threw his rifle to his shoulder, and just there his presence of mind saved him, as well as his quick and deadly aim.

In the twinkle of a second he saw that but one of the three Indians had a gun, and he was the one to aim at, and his rifle was fired before the redskin got his gun to his shoulder.

Down went the Indian and revolver in hand Will dashed forward to face the arrows of the others.

One arrow cut through his hat and the other wounded him in the arm, the first wound he had ever received, and again his presence of mind came to his aid, for he called out, as he waved his hat:

"Come, boys, here they are!"

Wounded by a shot from the revolver one of the Indians turned in flight, his companion quickly following his example, and their retreat was by leaping into the river.

Will Cody waited to see no more, but gathering up the gun of the dead Indian, and seizing the ponies with their heavy packs of pelts, he started off at a trot for camp.

Having had so much trouble with the redskins, and knowing that the two who had escaped would soon bring a force to attack them, the trappers decided to pull up traps and make for Fort Laramie with all haste.

This they did, and Will found himself in possession of a very handsome sum of money when the Post Trader bought from him the pelts he had trapped and captured.

The boy was gratified too when he discovered that he was becoming pretty well known for his pluck and as a young hero of the plains.

Anxious to return home and make known his good luck, he joined two men who were going east on a visit, and, not caring to wait for a train, were willing to risk the dangers of the trail alone.

Buying ponies, and a pack mule for camp outfit, the trio started early one morning for the Missouri.

They had reached the Little Blue River when Will, who was always on the alert for danger, spied a band of Indians hunting on the other side of the river, and about three miles distant.

Warning his companions of their danger they began a retreat, but having been sighted by the Indians a chase began.

Having to cross the stream the redskins thus were left considerably behind, but they made a hot pursuit of it when they did get across, and it looked very dubious at one time for the three fugitives, who were outnumbered ten to one.

But night came on and they were thus enabled to elude their pursuers in the darkness.

Tired by their long race, they at length reached a deep ravine where they decided to camp, and Will made the discovery that a cave was near and so they spread their blankets in its shelter.

Two were to sleep while the third watched, and Will was soon fast asleep, while his companion also off duty, determined to indulge in a smoke.

Filling his pipe he lighted a match, and the yell that he gave as the glare revealed the interior of the cave, awoke Will with a shock and he followed his companion out of the retreat in a hurry.

CHAPTER XXXVIII.
SEIZED WITH THE GOLD FEVER.

The lighted match had revealed to Will's companion in the cave what was to him a horrible discovery, and throwing it down among a lot of leaves, it had instantly ignited them and the boy, awakened by the man's terrified yell, had opened his eyes upon a most ghastly spectacle, for across the further end and not five feet away from the blanket bed was a row of a dozen whitened skeleton forms.

To go to sleep on blankets, spread on a bed of leaves in a comfortable cabin, and with intense darkness around him, and being roused by yelp of fright, behold the subterranean retreat lighted up brightly and find himself facing a dozen skeletons was more than even Will Cody's strong nerves could stand, and with rolling, tumbling, scratching and a mixture of acrobatic feats he got out of the cave.

The cool air and the rain without revived him, and he called out:

"Come back, the cave's on fire and we'll lose our things."

The burning leaves revealed that the cavern was a huge tomb, whether of unfortunate emigrants slain by Indians, or of redskins, there was no man's telling, but there were a score or more of skeleton forms in there, some ranged along the rocky walls in regular order, others scattered about, and the whitened bones proved that they had been there a long, long time.

To drag the blankets and other things out of the cavern was dangerous work, for the leaves were all in flames, and the extra ammunition and weapons of Will and the discoverer of the charred bones were in there.

But dashing boldly in Will seized the things and carried them out, just as the pipe smoker and his companion came back to the scene.

All gazed upon the burning leaves until the flames had nothing more to feed upon, and then Will said:

"We'll get wet out here, and no Indians will come near this spot, so let us go to bed."

"In there?" asked the pipe smoker.

"Yes, why not, for we know what's in there now," Will responded.

"That's just why I want to go."

"Me too, sonny."

With the majority against him, Will yielded, and as the man who had caused the illumination said he would not dare close his eyes for a week, they mounted their horses and left the gruesome spot behind them.

The rain soon after turned into snow and setting into a blizzard they were compelled to halt and camp, even the man who said he would "see skeletons," if he closed his eyes, admitting that it would have been best to remain at the cavern.

But the terrible night at last passed away, and the trail was resumed once more, and after numerous hardships [they] reached Maryville on the Big Blue.

From there on the country was beginning to be settled, so that they reached Leavenworth without encountering any other dangers, or suffering many hardships in spite of the cold weather.

It was in February of 1859 that Will again gladdened the hearts of all at home by putting in an appearance one stormy night, as his mother and sisters were seated about the fire awaiting him.

Turk was there too, for having grown old and rheumatic he was allowed a rug near the hearth, while a younger dog had succeeded him as guardian of the premises.

It did not take Will long to discover that Turk, old as he was, bossed his successor, unmindful that in those days in Kansas the creed of revenge was in vogue.

And alas for Turk the four-legged newcomer lived up to his creed and one day got on the rampage and bit the faithful guardian of the Cody home through many long years.

The behavior of the dog revealed to Will that he was mad, and he quickly ended his career by a shot from his revolver.

But Turk?

Poor dumb friend that he was he seemed to realize that the days of his

Burial of Turk

life were numbered, he would go apart to himself, refuse to enter the house, and at last it dawned upon all that he must be put to death.

The brute must be sacrificed to save human life.

"I cannot, I will not kill him," said Will, turning away from his old friend, while his sisters seemed to feel that one most dearly loved was to be taken from their midst.

Though he shrunk from raising his own hand to end Turk's career, Will still felt that the duty must not be shirked, and so told the hired man to kill him.

"Don't shoot him with any of my weapons, and let me get out of hearing of the shot," he said.

And so poor Turk was killed by the man, and afterward Will and his sisters assembled to give him decent burial.

A coffin was made by Will, who also dug the grave upon the hill in the rear of the house, and there Turk's mortal remains, for the Cody children all decided that he had a soul, were laid to rest, Nellie, at her brother's request, for he always called her the "Little Preacher," sadly repeating a prayer over him.

Rolling a large stone over the grave Will left it as a monument to the ever faithful Turk.

As a good school had now been opened in the neighborhood, taught by a Mr. Denimy.[60] Will decided to attend it, his resolve being a great joy to his mother who was most anxious to have him receive a good education.

So Will went to school and buckled down to hard study through the winter, but when the spring came, the grass began to grow, the trees to bud, Will got the fever on him to once more be on the plains, and joining a party of gold hunters, he started on the long trail to Pike's Peak.

CHAPTER XXXIX.
RUNNING A DEADLY GAUNTLET.

The Pike's Peak gold excitement was at its height when Will Cody started upon the trail in search of the precious metal.[61] He had grown rapidly in height, but his strength had kept apace with his growth, and at fifteen was a handsome athletic youth, daring, impulsive by nature and a favorite with all with whom he came in contact.

Auraria on Cherry Creek, Colorado, was the point of destination of the party leaving Leavenworth, it being near there gold had been found in paying quantities.

It may be of interest to the reader just here to know that "Auraria["] is now the magnificent city of Denver, so named after the then governor of Kansas.

At the time that Will Cody arrived there with the gold fever upon him, Auraria was nothing more than a mining camp, and one beholding it then and today gazing upon Denver could hardly realize that such a transformation could take place within less than two score years.

Pushing up through the Golden Gate, where his mining outfit was purchased, Will went into the mountains to hunt for gold.

But only the lucky few have been able to pick up a fortune in gold by simply hunting for it, and after several months spent in fruitless search, and becoming no richer, my hero came to the conclusion that mining was not his forte, that life on the plains was more to his fancy, and, after innumerable hardships, hopes and disappointments, dangers and sufferings, he abandoned the life of a miner and turned his face eastward once more.

He had others to keep him company, others disappointed in their search for fortune, and they together turned their backs upon the gold fields.

Reaching the Platte river the idea was conceived by Will, who had begun to get a very perfect idea of the western country and its streams, of building a raft on which they could drift down to the Missouri and thus to Leavenworth.

The raft was built, well stocked with provisions, and the party of seven started down stream in great glee.

At noon and at night they tied up along shore, and were congratulating themselves upon the success of their plan, which saved them tramping on foot along the trails, when one day several shots were fired from a clump of bushes on the shore.

The firing begun before the raft was near the bushes, which were on a point, and as quickly as they could seize their guns the men on the raft returned the fire.

Will at once dropped down behind the stores and blankets, for he had learned caution by experience in other dangers, and as he did so half a dozen shots came in quick succession from the point and one of the men fell dead, rolling into the river, while another was slightly wounded.

The others then quickly followed Will Cody's example and with their revolvers and rifles as they were loaded, kept up a fire upon the bushes as the raft floated by the deadly gauntlet.

"They are white men, not Indians," cried one of the party, and presently, as the raft drifted near the point upon which there was a shallow bar, a horseman boldly dashed out whirling his lariat around his head, and urging his horse into the water tried by a skillful throw to send his neuse [sic] over the framework of the brush built over the raft.

But he dropped from his saddle into the river while one of the men on the raft shouted:

"Will Cody fired that shot, and with a revolver too!"

Incensed by the fall of their foolhardy leader those in the bush sprung into view, a dozen or more, and opened a hot fire upon the raft.

But the men had missed being caught by the lasso, and lay low, piling the provisions, bedding and other traps around them to protect them from the bullets.

The raft had now floated out of range, and one of the party said:

"I recognized two of those fellows, and they were in the mines.

Running the Gauntlet

"I guess they thought we had plenty of gold on the raft, and were trying to rob and kill us, and then swim their horses out and tow the raft ashore.["]

This Will Cody afterwards found out was the case, for a drunken man confessed one day at Leavenworth that he had tried to rob a raft on which several miners had been transporting a large sum of gold.

Drifting on with the current the party on the raft, saddened by the loss of one of their number, congratulated themselves that it was no worse and hoped that they would have no more such deadly gauntlets to run.

But vain their hopes, for the next day they were fired upon again from the shore, but this time by Indians, who sent showers of arrows after them, but no bullets.

The man most protected of all was the one who had been wounded the day before, and who was lying down but he alone was the sufferer, as an arrow pierced his throat, killing him instantly.

The shots of the raftsmen drove the Indians to shelter, but as there was heavy timber along the shore at that point they were followed for miles, but however without suffering any harm.

They landed at sunset and their first duty was to bury their dead comrade; and Will Cody has said that it was years before he could get that night burial out of his mind, or cease to think most vividly of the long grave of their comrade on the river bank.

Troubles never come singly, it is said, and so the unfortunate raftsmen found it for after being one week afloat, and running two gauntlets of death, they were caught in an eddy, their raft went to pieces and it was a swim for life to the shore.

CHAPTER XL.
A PONY EXPRESS RIDER.

Fortunate it was that each man on the raft could swim, and so reached the shore, while it was a strange coincidence that the men who knew best the two men who had been killed on the raft, said that they could not swim a stroke.

So it would have been, had they not lost their lives by bullet and arrow, they would have been drowned when the raft went to pieces, for it was every man for himself in that swift current.

All the stores, blankets and the rifles of the men were lost, one of the men having to unbuckle his belt of weapons and let them go as their weight was too great for him to carry.

It was a sorry looking party that reached the shore, but one of the man said that Julesburg was not far distant, and so they set out from there, wet and wretched, but with reason to feel grateful that it had been no worse. Julesburg* happened to be only a few miles distant and it was a great relief to the little party to arrive there.

To his surprise and pleasure Will Cody found there George Chrisman, the chief wagon master under Russell Majors and Waddell, and whom he had often met before.

Mr. Chrisman had just bought out "Old Jules," and was the owner of the ranch, having gone there to become the agent for the Pony Express Line which was just then being started.[62]

---

*Julesburg was a ranch owned by a Frenchman known as "Old Jules."

It afterwards became an important station on the Overland Pony Express and the Stage Trail, and Jules was killed by Alf Slade, a notorious character of the frontier, and of whom Mark Twain speaks in his "Roughing It." —The Author.

He welcomed Will Cody warmly, and said:

"Now, Billy, if you were a few years older here would be your chance to become a Pony Rider, for the pay is big."

Will sighed at the thought he was so young, and Mr. Chrisman went on to say that the company was buying horses and putting them in good running condition, and soon the service would be in perfect condition.

"Mr. Chrisman, don't you think I could stand it?" asked Will eagerly.

"You might if you were a few years older."

"I'm mighty tough for a boy, sir, all that know me say that."

Mr. Chrisman smiled and replied:

"Yes, Billy, so I have heard, but I am glad to have heard also that you are tough only physically and not otherwise, for all give you the name of being a good boy, devoted to your mother and sisters, and a boy who is that can't go far wrong."

"Mr. Chrisman please try me, for I went out to Pike's Peak gold hunting and am going home broke, and I don't want to do that, sir."

"Well, Billy, Lew Simpson said you could stand what a man could, and your comrades told me today that you were the gamest youngster they ever saw, and that you picked that fellow who tried to lasso the raft off with your revolver, so I'll give you a trial, putting you on a short run of forty-five miles a day, with relay stations fifteen miles apart."

"Oh thank you, sir," cried Will, and the next day he rode over his run with one of the men, riding the horses that had been assigned to him.

He was required to make fifteen miles an hour, and change horses every fifteen miles, and after going twice over his run he was broken in for the work.

Soon after the whole line of Pony Express Riders was set in motion, and Will was ready for his ride when the one bearing the express pouches should dash into the Julesburg station.

A short wait, the clatter of rapidly approaching hoofs was heard, and then there came into sight a horse flying along at full speed, and a rider on his back.

Up he dashed, halting suddenly from a full run, Will seized the leather bags, threw them across his saddle, leaped upon his horse and was off like an arrow, followed by a cheer from those gathered about the station.

Along the trail fairly flew the horse, Will keeping him hard at it, and before the hour allowed for the fifteen minutes to the next station was up, he dashed up, leaped upon another animal held ready for him by the stock tender and was away again.

The next station was reached ahead of time, the change made, and when Will Cody drew rein at the end of his forty-five miles he had the satisfaction of knowing that he was twelve minutes ahead of schedule time.

His return trip was made with a few minutes to spare in his favor, and highly elated at his success he sat down and wrote his mother, telling her of his good position, explaining his duties, and admitting that he was greatly fascinated with the life of a Pony Rider, and, as the pay was large, he hoped to be able to stick to it for a long time.

A few weeks had Will been riding Pony Express, and though it was a terribly hard life, as he had to admit to himself, he had no idea of giving it up, and Mr. Chrisman had congratulated him several times upon never having been behind time.

About the stations, or passing through, were often rough characters bound westward to the mines, or going back east in ill humor at their failure to find fortunes, and these men the Pony Riders had to look out for.

It was well known that the Riders often carried large sums of money, valuable packages, and important papers, and characters there were who would not hesitate at taking a life to make what they called a rich haul.

One day Will Cody made the acquaintance of just such a person to dread.

He was flying along half way between stations, when, as he was sweeping through a narrow pass, he was suddenly confronted by a man who covered him with a revolver and called out:

"Halt Boy. I don't want to kill you, but I wants them leather bags you carries."

Will Cody remembered to have seen the man the day before in Julesburg and did not like his face.

He liked it less now, and looking into the muzzle of his revolver he uttered no word but drew the pouches from his saddle and throwing them angrily upon the ground said:

"Take 'em then!"

The man stooped to pick them up, and as he did so the boy's spurs sunk deep into the flanks of his horse, the animal sprung forward with an angry snort, right upon the man, giving him a severe blow that knocked him down, and stumbling, half fell upon him.

But Will recovered him quickly and with his own revolver in hand now turned to face his foe.

CHAPTER XLI.
HOME AGAIN.

To his utter astonishment, when Will Cody turned to face his foe, he saw him lying motionless upon the ground.

He had played a clever and daring ruse to get himself out of a very bad scrape, and expected to knock him over and thus have time to draw his own revolver, wheel his horse and turn the tables on him, thus getting back his saddle bags.

But there was no need to use his revolver for the man lay unconscious.

"Perhaps he's playing possum," muttered Will, but seeing a red gash on his head where the hoof of the horse had struck him, he added:

"I hope he's not dead."

Dismounting, Will approached cautiously, took up his pouches first and threw them across his saddle, after which he laid his hand upon the man's heart.

That was beating, so he disarmed him and with a silk scarf he wore about his neck tied the hands of the man behind him.

"He's got a horse, I know," muttered Will, and a short search found the animal near by.

As he led him back to the spot the man was sitting up looking about him in a confused way.

"Here, get on your horse, for I'll help you, and you've got to ride for it too, for I'm behind time."

The man uttered an oath, but obeyed, and taking the bridle rein of his horse Will started off again at a run.

The man was given over to the stock tender for safe keeping, and when the young Pony Rider returned on his run he took his prisoner with him and delivered him up to Mr. Chrisman, who praised Will highly upon his pluck and cleverness.

While the Pony Rider sought rest, others about Julesburg grouped together, and awakened by loud voices Will came out to find that the Road Agent had been made a victim of frontier justice for the men were stringing him up to a tree.

After three months spent in riding Pony Express, Will begun to realize that Mr. Chrisman was right when he said that fifteen miles an hour on a run would shake any man to pieces, especially one of his age, but he was not thinking about giving it up, at least for a while, when he received a letter from his sister Julia, who had married since he left home, asking him to give up the hard life of pony express riding.

She also told him that his mother was quite sick, and that news at once decided him as to what he should do.

At once he went to Mr. Chrisman, told him of his mother's illness and was promptly released from service, Mr. Chrisman saying:

"I could see that the work was wearing on you, Billy—you are too young for a pony rider, though you certainly have done nobly."

Given a horse by Mr. Chrisman, and with a good outfit, not to speak of a snug sum of money he had earned, Will Cody started along the pony trail on his long ride home.

Without accident or adventure he entered Salt Creek Valley one pleasant afternoon, to find a pleasant surprise for him, his mother having built a large and handsome house on another part of her farm* facing on the Military Road which had been cut through the country.[63]

The great change for the better in Will's appearance was quickly noted by his mother and sisters, for he was rapidly losing his boyish looks and developing into a tall, handsome and manly youth, the very beau ideal of what his little brother Charlie thought such a hero should be.

Will observed too that his sisters were also growing up, his sister Julia had married, and the others would before many years be young ladies.

Then too the country was changing, settlers were coming in rapidly, Leavenworth was advancing to the dignity of a town, a constant stream of humanity was traveling along the Military Road, and Will considered that about the old home was getting too thickly settled for one of his disposition who loved the free life of the prairies and mountains.

---

*Mrs. Cody's new home was known as the Valley Grove House, and was long used as a country inn. It was later destroyed by fire, but stood on the Military Road to Leavenworth, at the foot of what is now known as Cody's Hill. —The Author.

He was glad indeed to find his mother better than he had expected, and as she rapidly recovered, his roving spirit again started him off on an expedition which very nearly cut short his career and would have kept the name of Buffalo Bill from ever being known to the world.

CHAPTER XLII.
VERY NARROW ESCAPE.

It was in November when Will Cody again left home, and he did so to once more try his luck as a trapper.

He decided not to go with a party, some of whom might get into trouble with the Indians, so had for his sole companion in the dangerous venture a young man by the name of Dave Harrington.

The outfit of the two consisted of a covered wagon and yoke of oxen to carry the traps, camp utensils and provisions, and in which they could bring back the furs they secured.

Of course they went well armed, with extra rifles along in case of an accident, and their destination was up the Republican river to the mouth of Prairie Dog Creek, Will having heard that it was a fine beaver country.

They begun trapping near Junction City, Kansas, thence working their way on to the Republican, and from the start found plenty of beavers.

They alternated in driving their oxen, and going ahead, Harrington, being teamster one day while Will acted as scout, going well in advance to pick the trail, scout for danger and find camping grounds.

The next day Harrington would be the scout, and the game they found on the trail well supplied them with food.

One day it would be a buffalo steak, the next venison, then birds, and fish were plentiful in the streams.

They always selected their camp with a view to good protection, and Will would stand guard for half the night, then awaken Harrington who would be on the watch until daylight.

Having seen no Indians as they progressed they begun to feel quite safe, but were too good plainsmen to fail in their watchfulness both day and night.

They were getting rich in beaver skins, and so decided to remain out through the winter, and consequently looked about for the best place in which to pitch their quarters.

It was soon found, a sheltered nook among the rocks and timber, and where in the side of the bank they built their "dug-out," a little hut dug in the earth in the side of a hill, and covered with boughs of trees, dirt and stones.

It had a door, ingeniously made of canvas stretched on poles, and fitting closely.

Across the rear was the bed in one corner, the fireplace and chimney, made of clay and rocks in the other, while there were places to store the provisions and other things.

The wagon had been hauled up before the door, as a storehouse for the pelts, and boughs piled around it aided to shelter the entrance to the dugout, and Will and Harrington congratulated themselves upon their splendid quarters.

The first night they stayed in came their first alarm.

They had made a corral of poles for the oxen, and they were awakened at dawn by a loud bellowing and terrific row among their cattle.

Seizing their rifles they ran out to find a huge bear in the corral, and that he had come for a feast of beef was certain.

The oxen were wild with terror, and one of them was down, showing that he had been hurt in some way.

At once Harrington fired at the bear, he being in advance of Will, and cornered as he was, and wounded, the savage animal turned at bay, rushing upon the man, with gleaming teeth and ferocious growl threatening to tear him to pieces.

Harrington was a cool, brave man, but he sprung backward, drawing his revolver as he did so, but his foot slipped and he fell with the bear almost upon him.

Certain death seemed to stare him in the face, but he rolled over and tried to grasp his revolver, which had fallen from his grasp.

Another moment and David Harrington would have been in the grasp of the infuriated bear, but just then there came a shot from a Mississippi yager, it was aimed well and with a cool nerve, and a large bullet and buckshot, with which the gun was loaded, went crashing into the open mouth and brain of the maddened animal.

Down dropped the bear convulsively tearing up the earth in his death agony, and his head actually fell upon Harrington, who got out of the way as quickly as he could.

A Shot in the Nick of Time

"Billy," and his grasp was like iron as he grasped the boy[']s hand: "You saved my life, and I won't forget it."

It was all he said, but his quivering voice told how deeply he felt.

"It's my first bear," said Will pardonable pride in his tone and look.

Then the two turned to the oxen, and to their deep regret found that one of them had fallen and broken his hip.

There was no help for it and a shot from Harrington's revolver put him out of his misery.

A fire was built, breakfast gotten through with and then Dave Harrington showed Will Cody just how to skin a bear.

CHAPTER XLIII.
A FORTUNATE RECOGNITION.

The winter had not yet fully set in, when one day, chasing a band of elk, Will slipped and fell heavily.

Attempting to rise he suffered great pain in his leg, and calling to Harrington he told him that he believed he had broken his leg.

"Nonsense," said Harrington, and he made a critical examination, for he had once been a medical student, though not a graduate.

"Billy, you are right—your leg is broken," he said with a face that had turned to the hue of death.

"What will we do, Dave?" asked Will with a choking sensation rising in his throat.

"First get to the cabin—I will carry you there."

And he did.

Then he set to work to find just how badly the bone was broken, and was glad to discover that he could set it without a great deal of trouble.

This was done, the leg was securely bound up with splints which Harrington made, and then a pair of crutches were manufactured and Harrington said cheerily:

"I'll tell you what I'll do, Billy."

"Yes, for I can do nothing, Dave, except think.

"I guess you had better shoot me as you did the oxen, Dave."

Harrington laughed but replied:

"The situation is not so bad as that, Billy, but I feel that I ought to go to the nearest settlement and get a team for our wagon, and take you back."

"It's over a hundred miles."

"Yes, but I can make the round trip in twenty days, and you can—"

"No I can't, I can only lie here on my back and wait."

"Don't get blue, Billy, for it won't take me long.

"Fortunately the spring is right at our door, I'll pile plenty of wood up in the cabin, lay in some deer meat, and you can hobble around on your crutches and get along fairly well."

"So I can, Dave, and I'll do it.

"Just put the fighting outfit where I can get it, and I'll be all right.

"Fortunately mother made me bring my books along, so now's the chance to get an education, and if I miss your violin and singing at night the wolves will howl me to sleep; oh yes, I'll get along, never fear."

And so it was arranged that Harrington should go, and after half a dozen handshakes he set out, and Will was left alone.

I leave it to my readers to think what the feelings of the poor boy must have been, left there alone in that little cabin, more than a hundred miles from the settlement, a broken leg and nothing to do but lie there, and, as he had said, think.

Was it any wonder that his emotions choked him when he saw Harrington go, and he was half tempted to hobble to the door and call him back, telling him not to leave him.

He didn't hobble to the door, and though he saw Harrington in the distance driving the ox before him, but he brought his will power to his aid and did not call him back.

The first day he neither ate or looked at a book.

But the next morning he hobbled around and got his breakfast, and then took out his books, which his good mother had urged him to bring.

Studying had never had a great charm for him, but now he found it really a pleasure, and he dived into geography, history and arithmetic with a determination to know it all.

The days went by, the lone boy keeping a strict account of each sunrise and sunset. The wolves did sing for him, as he called their howls, every night, and the winds played mournful dirges about the cabin and in the pines.

It was on the twelfth day after Harrington's departure that Will had fallen to sleep in Africa, for he had been studying about that country, when he was awakened by a touch on his shoulder.

Imagine if you can his sensations when he awoke to find an Indian warrior standing by his side.

It was no dream, as Will Cody at first hoped, no nightmare, but a hideous reality.

There was the warrior, in all his war paint and feathers, showing to the boy's experienced eye that he was on the warpath.

"How," said Will, uttering the usual English salutation of Indians to pale faces, and wondering how it was to be with him.

The reply was in broken English, very broken Will thought, and he asked what he was doing there, and he added that he was going to "kill pale face boy."

Will heard other voices without, and then saw Indian after Indian step into the dugout, and that they intended to kill him he was certain, when just then there entered the chief whom the boy called out to, recognizing him as Rain-in-the-Face, a Sioux chief whom he had met at Fort Laramie and given him some provisions and a red blanket.[64]

The chief looked at the boy and asked in pretty fair English what he was doing there.

Then Will talked as though he was wound up, and as he had never talked before.

He showed his bandaged leg, told how he was trapping, that his pard had gone for help, and asked if he remembered the red blanket and provisions.

Rain-in-the-Face was not like many pale faces, forgetting favors done them at the very time when an opportunity offers them to show a reciprocity of feeling, and so remembered the gift of the provisions and red blanket, and even reminded the boy that he had also given him some ammunition also.

Then Will asked if his young men intended to kill him.

The chief frankly acknowledged that their intention was to kill and scalp him, but as I[65] was a very young man, and had been good to him, he would not allow them to do so, although they were out for scalps.

A compromise was accordingly made, Will's life being spared, in return for which favor, the "young men" took his firearms, ammunition, several blankets and a large share of his provisions, in fact, but for the chief they would have left him to starve to death, and failing in that to starve.

Then they bade him good bye as though parting with a dear friend, and filed out of the cabin, greatly to Will's joy.

That it was the humanity in the heart of the chief that saved him Will well knew.

CHAPTER XLIV.
AGAIN ON THE PONY TRAIL.

Though fond of company and lonely before the Indians arrived, Will saw them go with a degree of pleasure he could not express.

They had spent the day and night with him, had four square meals out of his supplies, showing the courtesy to give him some, one brave remarking in pretty good Indian-English that he had such a small appetite he would not need much food left for him.

That decided Will to stuff himself, and when at last he was left alone, he arose to see the extent of the raid upon his larder.

"If Dave don't get back in ten days I guess I'll starve," was his comment after an investigation.

Two days after the departure of the Indians a snow storm set in.

It proved to be a blizzard and covered the little cabin, completely shutting the boy in it.

But his wood, which Dave Harrington had piled up, lasted well, and he kept a small, but steady fire, stuck to his books, ate his meals with regularity and counted the days before his companion must return.

He knew that the snow would delay Harrington, his provisions were going rapidly, it seemed to him, and then came the thought that his friend might have perished in the storm, perhaps had been killed by the Indians.

As the days passed his thoughts became more and more gloomy, he would go all day without a fire, to save his wood, eat but one meal a day, and his studies no longer had any attraction for him after three weeks had passed and Dave Harrington did not appear.

At last he knew that the end must come, and soon, for the twenty-ninth day had arrived since Harrington's departure.

Wretched and despondent, he was expecting soon to die, when suddenly he heard:

"Whoa! haw there!"

Could he believe his ears? Was it Dave's voice?

Or was it a false hope his fevered fancy called up?

To see if it was true he attempted to give a loud shout.

But his voice failed him. Then he lay there listening, and soon came a step without, then the words, uttered in a doubtful tone:

"Billy, are you there?"

"God bless you, Dave," sobbed the boy.

He could say no more, and Dave Harrington pushed aside the door and stepping within held out his hand.

But Will Cody saw not the hand, his arms went up and were clasped around his comrade's neck, while again he said:

"God bless you, Dave!"

"Why Billy, I've only done my duty, for didn't you save me from the bear.

"Did I go through snow storms to help you, risking life, suffering hardships, and come back with aid to you?"

"Ah no, you have done all for me, Dave."

"Never mind that, but tell me how you have got along?"

"I was here when you left, and here I am; but tell me of your trip, for I know it was a wonderful one."

It was modestly told, of his hardships, and dread of finding his boy comrade dead upon his return; but how he had gotten oxen from a settler and at last made his way back again.

Then he heard Will's story of his marvelous escape from the Indians, whom he had not dreaded as much as the fact that he was to lie there and freeze to death.

"Never mind, Billy, we can stand it until the snow leaves us, and then go."

It was some weeks after Dave's return that they decided to start homeward, Will's leg having nearly healed.

So the traps were gathered in, and with the skins were loaded into the wagon, there being hundreds of them, otter, beaver, wolf, and the bear robe.

Will was given a comfortable place in the wagon, and Dave driving the oxen they pulled out from the little cabin.

On the tenth day out they arrived at the ranch where Dave had gotten the cattle, and the owner was given twenty-five beaver skins for their use, and to carry them onto Junction City, this being equivalent to sixty dollars, or a month's hire of the oxen.[66]

At Junction City they readily sold their wagon, traps and furs for a big price, all except the bear skin, and joining a wagon train bound for Leavenworth, arrived there in the spring of 1860.

Will made Dave Harrington return home with him, and when Mrs. Cody heard all that he had done for her son, she told him that he must remain there as long as he pleased, and come back whenever he needed a home.

Harrington concluded to remain and farm the place during the summer, but alas! for human hopes.

Poor Dave, strong man that he was caught a severe cold that settled upon his lungs, and though nursed devotedly, he died in one week's time, Will clasping his hand as he passed away.

Dave Harrington was laid to rest in the Cody burying ground on Pilot Knob* and his sudden death cast a deep gloom over the household where he was regarded as the dearest of friends.

When the warm days of summer begun to appear Will longed for the cool air of the mountains, and once again started across the plains, going with his old wagon master, Lew Simpson, who was fitting out a train at Atchison, to take supplies to the Overland Stage company, Mr. Russell, of the freighting firm, being one of the proprietors.

Will's intention was to once more ride pony express, and leaving his money with his mother, he secured a letter from Mr. Russell to Alf

---

*Now Cody Hill. —The Author.

Slade,[67] who was the agent of the division extending from Julesburg to Rocky Ridge, with his headquarters at Horseshoe Station, some twenty miles from Fort Laramie.

The outward trip was made with Lew Simpson [and] was devoid of any adventure of importance, and the first man Will met as he dismounted from his horse was Alf Slade.

He read the letter, took his measure at a quick glance and said:

"You are too young for a pony rider—it will kill you."

"I rode three months a year ago on Bill Trotter's division, sir, and I am stronger now."

"Are you the boy rider who Chrisman put on?"

"Yes, sir."

"You'll do.

"I'll try you, and if you weaken I'll give you other work."

The next day Will Cody was assigned to duty from Red Buttes on the North Platte, to Three Crossings on the Sweetwater, a ride of seventy-six miles.

But the "boy pony rider" was not long in making a name for himself there as will be seen.

CHAPTER XLV.
AN INDIAN BATTLE.

Will Cody made his first run through, of seventy-six miles, on the pony express trail on time, and soon after when on another run, he arrived at the end of his route to find that the man who was to have taken the trip out on his arrival, had come in mortally wounded by being fired on by Indians.

This left the station without a rider, and so Will volunteered to carry the express pouches on, a distance of eighty-five miles, through a bad and dangerous country.

But the emergency was great and he started on the trip.

He was determined to make a record on the ride, and reached every relay station on time, and arriving at Rocky Ridge started right back to make his own run out.

Thus he made a wonderful ride of three hundred and twenty-two miles without rest, and on time, riding twenty-one horses in doing so, a record of which he had every reason to be proud.

And this record stands against him today as a wonderful achievement.[68]

Some weeks after making this ride, he was ambushed by a band of Sioux, whom however he escaped from after a very hot chase, as he was splendidly mounted, and used his revolver freely.

Eluding his pursuers he reached the next station. He found the Indians had been there, killed and scalped the stock tender and run off the horses.

Unable to get a remount he rode the same animal on to Pontz's[69] station, a long run for one horse.

Informing the people at Pontz's what had happened, he had a fresh mount and went on and finished his run on time.

In the fall of the year the Indians became more to be feared, killing a couple of the pony riders, then attacking a coach, and the driver and three passengers were slain by them.

They also drove off the horses from several of the stations, killed the stock tenders, and made the trips of the pony riders a most desperate gauntlet to run.

So it was just decided to stop the riders for a few weeks and run the coaches only occasionally, while a force was organized to go out and fight the redskins.

There were stage drivers, stock tenders, pony riders and ranchmen in the force, and the captain was Wild Bill* then driving a stage on that division, and one of the most daring men of the border.[70]

Twenty miles out an Indian trail was found running toward Powder river, and this was followed to where old Fort Reno now stands.

Continuing on the trail was followed to a tributary of the Powder river, known as Crazywoman's fork, where it was seen that the Indians had been joined by another band, and the fresh tracks showed that they were not far ahead.

---

*G. [*sic*, J.] B. Hickok, a noted border man, army scout and guide, who has won a name in the Wild West which will long live in history and romance.

Meeting Will Cody in his younger days Wild Bill became his devoted friend, the friendship ending only when the latter was killed at Deadwood by the cowardly assassin, Jack McCall. Of Wild Bill, William Cody can never say too much, and he loved him as a brother. —The Author.

They were now in the midst of the Indian country, where the redskins had no idea they would be followed, so no guard was kept, and the company under Wild Bill had not been discovered when they got near to their camps.

Awaiting in hiding until dark the attack was made and was a complete surprise.

The surprise was so great indeed that the men rushed through their camp, circled around their own, as well as the horses belonging to the Indians, and while some of the party drove them back on the trail, the others remained and gave battle.

For awhile the fight was a hot one, and Will Cody was in the thickest of it and had his first experience in knowing what a fight with a large band of redskins really was.

Wild Bill handled his men splendidly, and being most of them old Indian fighters, they fought with intelligence and coolness, at last driving the redskins to flight.

After a retreat that was rapid at first, the man went more leisurely and within a week returned to the starting point with all of their recaptured horses and a large number of Indian ponies as well, thus administering a severe blow upon the hostiles. The pony express riders at once resumed duty again, and Will Cody, to whom Alf Slade had taken a great fancy said:

"You are too young for this terrible racket of a pony rider, so I will take you to my headquarters as a supernumerary,[71] riding only when it is necessary, though your pay will be the same."

Flattered though he was, Will did not wish to admit that he did feel the strain, yet went however, and was placed on "waiting orders."

While so serving he started out one day on his express pony to try and kill a bear.

He went to the foothills of Laramie Peak.

The fresh air was a stimulant to brain and body, and mounted on a good horse he felt the full influence of what it was to be a plainsman in that grand country.

Antelope, deer, jack-rabbits, sage-hens were constantly seen, but Will was "looking for a bear."

As he found no bear he camped at noon, and after his dinner resumed his hunt, determined to remain out all night rather than return without his bear.

As dark came on he shot a couple of sage-hens and went into camp for the night, and in a most wild and desolate country.

But Will was accustomed to solitude and did not mind, and was about to start a fire when he heard a horse neigh.

At once he sprung to his horse and threw his blanket over his head to keep him from answering, for he knew Indians might be about.

Leaving his horse staked out he went on a prospecting tour, bear no longer being in his mind, and after a short walk came upon a number of horses feeding in a flat, while across the stream he saw a light, shining from a cabin.

Approaching the spot cautiously, he heard voices, and saw that it was a small dugout, the door being ajar, while within the firelight revealed several men.

A call from Will caused a surprise, but he was invited in, and in he went, though he realized his mistake at once, but knew it would never do to weaken then.

There were eight rough looking men there, and "desperado" was stamped upon the face of each man.

CHAPTER XLVI.
BACK TO OLD SCENES.

Will Cody knew two or three men in the dugout, as discharged teamsters from Lew Simpson's train, and he was confident that he had hit upon the retreat of a band of outlaws who had been infesting the trails, robbing coaches, holding up pony riders and stealing the company horses.

His presence of mind did not desert him, however, and showed no signs of having recognized them, but told how he had left Horseshoe Station on a bear hunt, got lost, saw their fire and came to ask shelter for the night, adding:

"I'll go and get my horse."

"We'll get him," said the leader.

"I don't think you can find him—may I leave my gun here until I come back?"

This seemed to reassure them, and the gun was left, but two of the men went with him after his horse.

To take quick aim and pull trigger was but the work of a second

Will knew that they would kill him, and never allow him to go back and tell of their retreat, so he watched his chance to escape.

One of the men led the horse, the other following Will, who, dropping one of the sage hens he carried called to the man behind to pick it up.

As he stooped to do so, Will dealt him a blow with his revolver that knocked him senseless, and turning he faced the man who had his horse, and who was drawing a weapon from his belt to fire.

To take quick aim and pull trigger was the work of a second, and as the man staggered backward Will caught his bridle rein, leaped into his saddle and rode at a gallop down the creek at the risk of his life, for it was quite dark now.

He saw the men rushing out of the dugout, as they were relieved by the firelight behind them, and he knew that they could make faster time down the steep than he could on horseback, but he had no idea of deserting his horse unless actually compelled to do so.

There was but one place there to where he could ride down, and this his pursuers must know full well, while having been over the ground often before they held another advantage over him.

At last discerning that he must abandon his horse to save himself, he dismounted and gave the animal a hard blow to make him run on down the hill, while he hastily ran off to one side.

He had hardly found a hiding place when he heard them close at hand, and a moment after they ran by, following on after the horse, whose iron shoes rang against the rocks as he kept on down the hill.

As they sped by him they begun to fire at the horse, to try and kill him by a random shot.

Once they had gone by Will left his hiding place, took his bearings, and started out on foot for Horseshoe Station.

It was a long, hard tramp of it, all of twenty-five miles, but he reached there early in the morning, at once reporting what had occurred.

It did not take Alf Slade long to get into the saddle with twenty men following and go on the hunt for the band of outlaws.

Tired out as he was Will Cody went with them, and led the way to the dugout.

But the horses had disappeared, the cabin was deserted, and a fresh grave near told that they had buried their dead comrade, killed by Will, before they had fled.

As they had such a long start, and their trail led toward Denver, Alf Slade gave up pursuit and the party return to Horseshoe, Will completely used up by what he had undergone.

As he had been away from home for a long time now, and the breaking out of the Civil war was drawing pony riders, stock tenders and teamsters into the army, Will decided to also enlist as a soldier.

He accordingly started with a train going to Leavenworth, but on the way met his old friend Wild Bill who was chief wagon-master of a train going to Rolla, Mo[.], for a load of government freight. Wild Bill told Will that he wanted an assistant wagon master, and he accordingly went with him and returned with the supplies to Springfield, Mo.

Before he could return home he got an order to go out upon a horse purchasing expedition for the government, and had no sooner returned from this duty than he was sent to Fort Larned, Kansas, as bearer of military dispatches.

This duty Will gave up to go as guide and scout of an expedition against the Kiowa and Comanche Indians on the Arkansas river.

The command was known as the Ninth Kansas, under Colonel Clark,[72] and Will Cody won the praise of his commander and the admiration of the soldiers by his daring services under most trying circumstances.

He was now of a manly form, tall, powerful in build, and though still young in years no one looked upon him as other than a man capable of doing every duty put upon him.

His mother and sisters had been fearful that he would enter the army and go south, and Mrs. Cody's failing health caused her to urge him to get some service that would keep him near home.

In answer to these letters from home Will joined a command known as the "Red Legged Scouts," commanded by Captain Tuff.[73]

In this service he saw a great deal of hard and dangerous work; but true to the dear ones at the old home, when he learned by letter that his mother had become dangerously ill, he at once gave up his position and hastened to her.

CHAPTER XLVII.
CALLED TO A MOTHER'S DEATHBED.

Many were the changes that had taken place since Will Cody, still a boy in years, had gone out to the far away pony trail to seek service under Alf Slade.

The civil war had broken out, the whole land was aroused, battles had been lost and won, and the long and cruel struggle for mastery had begun.

It was not, however, until the fall of 1863 that William Cody returned to his home, after the longest absence he had yet known, from his mother and sisters.

They could hardly recognize the tall, handsome young man they beheld, as their boy brother of a short time before.

But there he was, a man in size and appearance, stepping across the threshold of manhood almost from boyhood.

But the daring, bronzed face of the young scout, that had never paled before any danger that confronted him, became white, and the lips quivered as he beheld a change in his devoted mother.

She appeared but a wreck of what he had known her, for the insidious disease of consumption[74] had at last caused her brave spirit to break when she could no longer toil for those she loved.

"Julia, I am a soldier now—I have just enlisted"

She greeted her brave son, still a boy to her, with the joy that shone in her eyes at seeing him once more, and said calmly:

"You have come home to see me die, Will, for soon the end will come.

"I wanted you by me in my last hours, and I knew when I bade you come, that you would quickly do so.

"If I had had my way your life would have been different, for you have it in you to make a name for yourself, and, call it a mother's foolish fancy if you will, but a fortune teller, when I was a young girl, told me that I would have a son whose name would be known the wide world over.

"Do you know, Will, I have hugged that belief to my heart, and I feel that you will never disappoint me.

"Fortunately through the aid you so promptly gave, and what I could do, the claims have all been paid off against the estate, and I will leave my children comfortable in this world's goods.

"Your sister Julia will be as a mother to the younger ones, and her husband, Mr. Goodman, will be guardian of the estate for you all.[75]

"I have asked you not to enter the army and go far away from me, for I knew my days were numbered; but when I am gone, if your country needs your services in this bitter, civil strife, which we here in Kansas know the cruelties of, why go as a soldier to uphold her flag."

Thus talked the dying mother to her son, and each word she uttered was dearly treasured by William Cody as the last utterances of the one who was so dear to him.

And so it was that upon 22d of November, 1863, that a good woman, a devoted wife and mother, a true American heroine, passed away with her children about her to cheer her last moments there in the land that had ever been o'erclouded to her, for the hardships, sorrows and sufferings she had known, would have broken a less noble heart and brave spirit long before.

By the side of her husband Mrs. Cody was buried and when the mourners turned from the grave William Cody said firmly:

"I will not return home tonight, for I must go to Leavenworth."

And to Leavenworth he went, but the next day rode out to his home to bid his sisters a long farewell, for he had just enlisted as a soldier in the United States army.

"Julia, I am a soldier now—I have just enlisted," he said as his sister Mrs. Goodman met him at the door.

The regiment he had enlisted in had already been ordered to the front, and the young soldier in his teens still, yet so old in thrilling and sad experience, a veteran in scenes of death and desperate danger, found himself called upon to enter upon a different warfare from any he had ever known.

To follow the career of William F. Cody as a soldier through the Civil war, as a gallant "Boy in Blue,"[76] would require a book alone, and then to still pursue his remarkable life of romance and danger, of shifting scenes in the days when he aided most nobly in making the history of frontier settlement would demand still another book, for as a "Hero of the Plains," he is best known to the world.

Upon the pages of history his name has been indelibly engraven, and the story of the Wild West is the story of William Frederick Cody as one of its principal actors.

From boyhood to manhood I have followed my hero, and when those interested in him seek further to follow his eventful life, they must turn to the pages of history or await other stories told in the biography of his army life and later as one who has been most justly crowned as a true and loyal "Knight in Buckskin."

"LED BY DESTINY"

Or
"A Knight of To-day."
A Story of the Life of
Colonel W. F. Cody—"Buffalo Bill,"
Border Boy, Hunter, Pony Express Rider, Soldier, Chief of Scouts,
Actor, Author and World-Wide Wanderer.

CHAPTER I.
INTRODUCTION.

The Hero of a Novel is always presented to an author's audience in an attractive manner as possible, that he may at once catch the reader's fancy and win an admiration that will hold unto the end.

With the Hero of History his own deeds standing out prominently attract the student and win the applause of admiring throngs, and he does not have to be pictured in fire [*sic*, fine] colors to add to his heroism, for by his works is he known.

A Hero of History may be small of stature, homely, unattractive to the ordinary eye, but be the spark of genius there, that makes the Poet the Painter or the Writer, the courage of the soldier and power to command men, the world will soon bow down to him and he will compel honor and admiration.

It may be true that the evil men do lives after them, the good they have done be interred with their bones;[1] but, if in a man's nature is combined both good and greatness, he will go down into history revered by hero worshipers.

Among the last named I may place my hero, William F. Cody, known the wide world over as "Buffalo Bill," a title gained through the peculiar nomenclature of the Wild West, and a name he has guarded unsullied through a most phenomenal life of half a century, and will send down to future generations one as borne by a typical American of the "times that try men's souls."[2]

Glancing backward through the pages of our country's history, how many names we see of those who rose to fame and greatness, on the field of battle, on the deck of a bravely defended ship, in art, the sciences, statesmanship, inventions and other walks of life, and which Patriotism will ever keep alive in the hearts of Americans.

Washington, Jackson, Taylor, Lincoln, Grant, Sherman, Webster, Clay, Franklin, Fulton, Morse, Irving, Cooper, Longfellow, Poe and hosts of others with Boone, Fremont, Kit Carson, the Pioneers into the Land of the Setting Sun, will never be forgotten, never be blotted from the pages of History, where also will be written the name of William F. Cody—Buffalo Bill.

As those named and many others, have done nobly their part in life and won the laurel wreath for their brows in their separate callings, so has William F. Cody risen to the proud distinction of being one of America's Heroes, and no prouder title could he wear.

Born half a century ago, when all beyond the Ohio was almost a wilderness, nurtured amid scenes where brave men only dare venture, tutored to bear hardships, disappointments, to face death ere he was in his teens, to work, to plan, to think for himself and help in the support of a noble mother and sisters, Will Cody, boy that he was, faced the alternative unflinchingly, and with his eyes fixed upon the star of his Destiny when it rose, followed on after it through storm and sunshine, sorrow and adversity, believing unswervingly in the prophecy that he was born to greatness, that he had been launched upon life's troubled sea for some great good.

From early boyhood he held to this belief, and amidst dangers the greatest, suffering rebuffs and hardships most severe, surrounded by death, and the despair of others, he clung fondly to the belief that he was surely Led by Destiny.

And so I will ask my readers to follow his career in this true story of his fight for fame, from the time that he crossed the threshold of manhood, entered the service of his country as a gallant "Boy in Blue," and fought his way upward, step by step through thrilling scenes of a most checkered life, hunter, pony express rider, trapper, Rocky Mountain driver, guide, scout, Indian fighter, and later, actor, author, traveler, until to-day known and admired the wide world man.

The Author

CHAPTER II.
BOY IN BLUE.

Standing by the side of a newly made grave, his eyes fixed sadly upon it, was a youth, clad in buckskin garb of a plainsman.

His face was darkly bronzed, his hair, worn long, fell in waving masses, upon his broad shoulders, and his attitude though one of utter dejection and sorrow, as he stood with uncovered head and arms folded, was one of natural grace and strikingly picturesque.

Tall, of splendid physique, with a face that was striking in its manly beauty, though stern, determined and courageous, in spite of his being yet in his teens, all about him stamped him as a man among men.

From perilous duty as a pony express rider in the almost untrodden country through which ran the Overland Trail, he had come, in answer to the pleading words of a sister:

"Brother, come home—Mother is dying!"

Hard had he ridden, by day and by night, to reach his home in Kansas, where dwelt all that he held dear upon earth.

He had come to see his mother die, pass away into the Great Beyond and leave behind a vacant chair which none other could fill, none but a mother.

That mother whose indomitable nerve he had inherited, whose love had guided him from boyhood to the threshold of manhood, now lay beneath the mound at his feet, and only her loving memory remained to him, and in the household up the valley.

By her side was another mound, one upon which the grass had grown green with time, and there lay his father, also,

"Sleeping the sleep that knows no waking."

The little burying ground was upon a hill, and the scene about him was one of entrancing beauty, with Salt Creek Valley stretching away upon one side, the Missouri River winding along, and upon its banks the small frontier town of Leavenworth, with the fort of the same name farther in the distance, made up a landscape wondrously attractive, but though ever before gazed upon with rapture by the young plainsman, now it held no charm for him, for his heart was bowed down with grief above the graves of his parents.

The sun sunk nearer and nearer to the horizon, yet still he stood there lost in deepest reverie.

The scenes of death and danger he had passed through, in that valley with his parents, his father's death through the hand of an assassin, his mother's life of toil, of peril and splendid courage, his own boyish deeds of heroism all passed in review before him as he stood there, until at last he felt that the end of all was in the grave.

Suddenly he started and his eyes looked off toward his home up the valley, while aloud he muttered:

"They need me, my sisters in the old home—to me no longer a home now—and I must work for them.

"But my country needs me now this great internal strife, this war of brother against brother.

"Father said that it would come, must come, and now the civil strife has begun, the South has fired upon the Flag, and one side must win, the other lose.

"But can I remain here, spend my days upon the Wild Western Plains, when my country has called for her sons to fight her battles for her?

"No, ah no! the promise I made my mother, not while she lived, to go into the army is canceled by this grave, and from this sacred spot I shall go and enlist as a Boy in Blue, I will become a soldier."

The sun sunk now beneath the horizon, and a look of deepest sorrow passed over his face, his lips quivered as he murmured a farewell to the dead, and turning from the graves walked slowly to where his horse was awaiting him, and mounting rode away in the gathering gloom of coming night.

But it was not toward his home that the head of his horse was turned, but toward Leavenworth.

The day had dawned, the sun had risen before he turned his horse homeward.

He approached slowly the pleasant homestead, located on the Military Road some miles out from Leavenworth, hitched his horse at the rack, and as the door was opened by his sisters they uttered cries of surprise mingled with alarm for he was dressed in the blue uniform of the United States Army.

They knew but too well what that meant—he had enlisted as a soldier.[3]

And that young and handsome Boy in Blue was William F. Cody—Buffalo Bill.

CHAPTER III.
A PERILOUS RIDE.

William Cody's first duty as a soldier was to be sent as a bearer of Military dispatches to Fort Larned, and the very commencement of his army service nearly ended fatally for him.

At that time there were a number of residents in Kansas who had come there from the South, and naturally their sympathies were all with the Confederacy.

As several of these sympathizers intended making their way into the South to join the army there, they were anxious to carry with them any important news of the Northern forces they could gather, and so decided to waylay a courier and capture what military dispatches he had.

As Will Cody, as he was then known about Leavenworth, had been selected to carry the dispatches, it was known that they must be most important, and having a grudge against him on account of his father's well known Free State ideas, these men, five in number decided to hold him up on the trail and take the pouches he bore containing the supposed information that would be most valuable to Southern leaders.

As Will Cody reached a point a mile from Fort Leavenworth, he saw a man waiting for him in the road.

"Ask me no questions, Will, for I won't answer, but keep as clear as you can of the regular trail to Larned, for there are those who intend to ambush you and get those dispatches.

"I don't care for the dispatches, but they will kill you, and I wish to save you.

"There is a creek you have to cross, you will know which it is, as they will be in wait on it at the old herder's camp-ground; but watch the whole trail.

"Goodbye, Will, and luck to you, though I don't like to see that uniform upon you, my feelings being the other way."

With this the man turned and walked away, unheeding Will Cody's call to him to stop.

Recognizing him as a man who had once been in his father's employ and always been friendly with him, he did not doubt what he had told him.

As a Southern man he had evidently gotten news of an intention to ambush him, and though Southern in his feelings he wished to save him for old friendships sake.

On the young soldier rode, and as watchful as a hawk.

He wished to save his dispatches above all things, and he avoided every place where he was likely to be ambushed.

The creek where the herder's camp was he well knew.

He had herded cattle there himself before he was in his teens, and knew the country about it thoroughly.

Away he went at a gallop, and not a tree, a thicket, a mound escaped him, which would afford shelter to his foes.

He did not doubt but that his enemies were men who were going to join the South, and from past experience he had had from boyhood with the men of the Slavery party in Kansas, he knew that they would kill him as they would a dog.

It was growing late in the afternoon as he drew near the herder's camp, a camping place long since deserted.

Knowing the locality as he did, he turned from the trail to strike the creek above the spot, and there cross.

But heavy rains had swollen the stream to an alarming extent, and unable to descend the banks he felt that he must ride down it until he reached the ford, several hundred feet from the old camp.

He argued that as his foes were expecting him from the other direction, they would doubtless be ambushed in the little log cabins, only a few feet from the trail, waiting for him, and he could slip along the bank to the ford and dash in and take his chances in running his horse across, while he had his carbine ready for use.

So down the bank he rode until at last he came in sight of several small log cabins that formed the camp in the distance.

As he did so he rode upon five saddle horses and one pack animal hidden in a thicket on the banks of the creek.

"These horses tell the story—they are there, and it is nip and tuck if I get through," said Will Cody, and he nerved himself for the ordeal.

Keeping as close to the bank as he dared ride, with his carbine across his saddle ready for use, and taking advantage of every tree and bush for concealment, he slowly made his way toward the ford.

Nearer and nearer he drew, and at last the trail was just before him, the ford but a couple of hundred feet away, and he begun to believe he would get by unseen, when a loud voice shouted from the cabin nearest him:

"Thar he goes, boys! right at the ford.

"Kill him!"

With the words the speaker's rifle flashed and five men came running out of the little cabins weapons in hand to take part in the unequal combat.

CHAPTER IV.
A SOLDIER'S SHOT.

Will Cody realized that the time for action had come, and he acted promptly. The words he had heard told him that they meant to kill him.

The shot fired was another convincing argument that they were, while the men rushed out of the cabins, where they had been watching in ambush for him, at once opened fire.

He felt, from the bound his horse gave that more than the spurs driven deep had caused it, that he was wounded, and as he dashed for the ford he wheeled in his saddle, took quick aim at a man who had not yet fired and pulled the trigger.

He saw the man stagger back and fall, and then his horse had reached the ford and plunged in.

The men came running to the banks and fired with their revolvers, while he wheeled in his saddle and returned the shots.

But night was gathering fast, a hundred yards separated him from his foes, and his horse soon gathered footing upon the further shore and he had escaped with his life and had saved his dispatches.

Expecting that he might be pursued, he rode rapidly on, and kept his horse going until he felt that the poor animal could not go a mile further, that he was slowly bleeding to death.

But mile after mile the gallant animal staggered on to suddenly fall to rise no more.

With a sigh for the fate of the poor horse, Will Cody drew off his saddle and bridle, shouldered them, and started on his way afoot through the long and weary night, until he came to a lone ranch where he got a fresh mount.

It is needless to say that his pluck and perseverance won, that he reached Fort Larned in safety, and after a few hours rest there, mounted upon a fresh horse, started with return dispatches for Leavenworth.

Approaching the ford, which had been the scene of the ambush so nearly fatal to him, Will Cody was watchful, though he did not again anticipate trouble there.

He argued that the men who had been bold enough to ambush him, would, when failing in their deadly intention, make all haste to escape Southward from any pursuit he might send after them, especially when they did not doubt but that he had recognized some of them as dwellers about Leavenworth.

Yet he crossed the creek cautiously, his carbine ready for action, and as his horse was going along the trail leading near one of the cabins a faint call reached his ears.

Instantly he halted and listened.

But the call was not repeated, though he distinctly heard low moans coming from within the cabin.

Was it a trick to entrap him?

To get him to enter the cabin?

"Who is there?" he called out sternly.

"Come in! come in! I am dying and need help," answered a low, faint voice.

"Who are you?"

["]Ed Norcross," came the low response.

Will Cody started.

He remembered the one shot he had fired with his carbine, and he thought that he had recognized him as he staggered backward and fell.

"What is the matter with you, Norcross?"

"I was shot, and my comrades deserted me to make their escape.

"Who are you?"

"William Cody."

"Oh Will!"

The cry rang out in a tone of anguish.

Instantly Will Cody had thrown himself from his saddle, hitched his horse and strode boldly into the cabin.

There on the floor lay a young man, several years his senior, and his head was resting upon a blanket.

By his side was a canteen and some food, the first drained of the last drop of water, the latter untouched.

The pallor of death upon the wounded man's face, and his right hand rested upon his heart, where the cruel carbine bullet had cut its way.

Down upon his knees by the side of the dying man William Cody dropped, for he recognized that his shot had laid him low, it was the one he had fired at, had seen stagger backward and fall.

He knew him as one he had known for years, and who had been his companion on many a trail, his friend.

"My poor Ed, how sorry am I to find you thus, and more, to feel that my shot did it."

"Yes Will, but I do not blame you, for we were here to kill you, to get your dispatches.

"I remembered our friendship and wished to save you, so told Nat Ellis to tell you—"

"He warned me."

"I hoped you would take another trail, Will, and I did not fire on you.

"When I was wounded they brought me in here and left me, saying they would send help.

"But they have not done so, but you will stay by me until I die."

His voice was very weak, scarcely above a whisper, and as the minutes went by the pallor on his face increased until at last there crept over it the ashen hue of death.

Crossing the hands upon his breast, closing the cabin door, Will Cody mounted his horse and rode on his way, while from beneath his set teeth came the words:

"And this is war!"

CHAPTER V.
SEEING SERVICE AS A SOLDIER.

When Will Cody returned to the fort, he saw the man who had warned him of his danger, had made known to him the sad end of his friend, asking him to attend to his burial.

The commandant of Fort Leavenworth congratulated him upon his escape, and complimented him upon his plucky ride.

Just as he was beginning to fret under the idle life in camp, he was sent off through the country to buy horses for the government, it being well known what a thorough judge of horseflesh he was.

This work done he asked to be sent with some command as a scout, and received orders soon after that he had been detailed to go with the Ninth Kansas Regiment, of volunteers commanded by Colonel Clark.

He was to go as guide and scout, and the fact that he would again see busy action was a great gratification to the young soldier, for life in a fort did not suit a man of his mettle and ambition.

It was with a feeling of pardonable pride that William Cody, splendidly mounted and armed, rode to the front of the regiment to guide it on its expedition down on the Arkansas River.

The regiment had been ordered to protect the old Santa Fe Trail, between Fort Lyon and Fort Larned, against raids from the Kiowa and Comanche Indians, and arduous and dangerous work they had of it during the summer.[4]

There were several hard fights with the Indians, rough and rapid riding in chase, scouting by day and night, until at last the regiment was relieved, and sent to the Arkansas country and Southwest Missouri, when where many a lively skirmish was had with the bushwhackers, among whom were the famous Younger brothers.[5]

Time and again was Will Cody selected to bear dispatches of great importance to Fort Scott, Fort Gibson, Leavenworth and other posts, and often when on these lonely trails the speed of his horse, his skill as a plainsman and ready nerve saved him from death, the bitter experience of those days fitting him well for the still severer and more important duties of later years.

About this time the Seventh Kansas Regiment, known as "Jennison's Jay-Hawkers,"[6] returned from the war and reorganized as veterans to go at once again to the front.

This is just what William Cody wanted, for he was anxious to be in some of the grand battles that were being fought in the southwest, where thousands were engaged upon both sides.

He had never seen a large battle, and it was his ambition to be in the thick of the fight, to know war as it really was, outside of Indian battles and skirmishes with bushwhackers.

In the Seventh Kansas were many old comrades, brave men—men of the plains whom he wished to be with, and as the regiment was going south he urged several army officers whom he knew well to get him transferred, and by the time orders came to send the Seventh to the front he received his transfer, the colonel being anxious to have a young scout who had already won fame.

The regiment went to the front, and the veterans soon made their worth known, while William Cody was not long in proving his value as a scout and man of action.

Was any dangerous ride to be taken he promptly volunteered for the work, had dispatches to be sent across a bullet storm field "Courier Cody" carried them, and several times his horses were shot under him, but unscathed himself he would continue on foot, undaunted by mishap and peril.

"William Cody, I will get you a commission for your work this day," said the colonel to him, as he dashed up unmarred by the storm of lead he had just passed through, and handed him a dispatch.

"I thank you, sir, but I prefer to remain as I am," and he added in his dry way:

"Men don't want boys to command them, sir."

"Led by Destiny" : 149

In the spring of 1864 the regiment was ordered to Tennessee, arriving in Memphis about the time of General Sturgis' defeat by General Forest [sic].*

Here General A. G. Smith [sic, A. J. Smith] reorganized the army to operate against Forrest, and the regiment in which Will Cody served marched to Tupelo, Mississippi.[7]

In the hard fought battle of Tupelo, when General A. G. Smith defeated the Confederates, William Cody was [sic] honorable mention from his commanding officer for "most conspicuous bravery and valuable services upon the field."

His daring and dash, added to his talent in woodcraft, quick perception in seeing a way out of a difficulty, with his soldierly bearing, utter disregard of himself when arduous and deadly duties were to be performed, won the eye of General Smith, and the young plainsman was ordered to report to headquarters for special service.

Upon reporting as ordered he was detached from his regiment and placed upon special duty as a scout for the command, General Smith remarking to him:

"I am anxious to get certain information of the enemy's movements, and it can only be done by entering the Confederate lines, a thing it takes a man of just your calibre to do."

"You mean in that, I am to go as a spy into the Confederate lines?" said Will Cody quietly.

"Yes, that is just what I do mean, and the chances are that you will be captured and hanged."

"I will take the chances, sir.

"When shall I go, for I am ready now, General," was the prompt and fearless response of the young soldier-scout.

CHAPTER VI.
A CONFEDERATE SPY.

The prompt response of William Cody to General Smith, accepting the perilous duty that he was expected to perform, won at once his commander's esteem and admiration.

---

*The writer being in Forrest's command, Confederate army, opposed William Cody in several battles, notably Tupelo and Corinth. —The Author.

"I am sure, if any man can go through in safety, Cody, you are that man.

"I hear a good account of you from the officers you have served under, and I know of your career on the plains, as Indian fighter, pony express rider and scout, and you are the very one to accomplish intelligently the mission I send you upon, or rather that you volunteer for, as I would order no man upon such work.

"Come here this evening and I will have your instructions ready for you, and in the meantime take these maps and study well the surrounding country."

The maps Will Cody took with him were perfect in their way, giving every road, byway and pass from plantation to plantation.

He had already been on several scouting expeditions about that locality and had thus learned the country from actual observation, which meant a great deal to a man of his experience as a plainsman.

He knew that there had been some Confederate prisoners taken the day before, and though he did not expect they would tell him any direct information, if they knew what he was after, still he believed he could get certain facts from them if he went about it in the right way.

Some days before he had captured a Confederate scout, whom, to his surprise, he recognized as a man who had served with him in one of the overland wagon trains of Runell [sic], Majors and Waddell.

They had been the best of friends in those days, and Nat Golden, for that was his name, owed his life to Will Cody and had never forgotten the favor.

He was from the neighborhood of Holly Springs, Miss., and had run away from home and gone west, but had returned to fight for the South.

"I would rather have captured a whole regiment than you, Nat, for I do not like carrying you in as a prisoner," said Will Cody in his dry way.

"Don't mention it, Will, old fellow, for I must accept the fortunes of war as they come round.

"I was scouting for my brigade and ventured too near your lines and got caught; but I am glad my rifle snapped, as I would have killed you; but as it was I had to surrender to you, and then we recognized each other."

"Say, Nat, if I took you in for what you really are, you'd hang for it mighty quick, so hand over those papers to me, and I'll simply take you in as a prisoner."

The man's face turned very pale, but he asked calmly:

"What do you take me for, Will?"

"A spy."

"Do you think so?"

"I know it."

"Then for the sake of old times let me go."

"I can't do that, but give me up the papers you carry and I will surrender you only as a prisoner I captured."

Nat Golden was silent for a moment and then said:

"Bill Cody, I know when the game is against me as well as any living man, and you have won.

"As much as I would like to get through with the papers I have, and for weeks have risked my life to secure, I would rather lose all than to have killed you.

"I appreciate your position and your kindness, and submit as a prisoner, thanking you that I do not hang as a spy.

"You know me, and know that I am not the man to long remain a prisoner, so I may one day have the chance to return the service you now do me."

With this he took from an inside pocket in his undershirt, a square, thin package of papers.

Buffalo Bill saw that they contained most valuable information of the Union forces, positions and expected movements, with other material of a like nature that would have put the Confederates in possession of facts of estimable value to them.

"Nat, I shall take them, and it is your secret and mine; but I am just tickled to death you didn't get through with them.

"I see that you have a Confederate uniform outside of your blue one, so I'll get you to take the latter off, for that alone would hang you as a spy."

The blue uniform was discarded, the spy having just gone to the spot where he had hidden his gray suit upon entering the Union lines, and drawn it on, believing that he was safe, when suddenly Will Cody had ridden upon him.

As a simple prisoner then Nat Golden had been taken in, and his captor kept his papers and his secret.

Knowing that the prisoners lately taken were from the same locality, William Cody felt that they must know Nat Golden, and so with the permit from the General he went to interview them.

He looked them over carefully with his searching eye, picked out those he deemed it best to interview, and then asked:

"Does any one of you know a Confederate scout by the name of Nat Golden?"

Several answered promptly in the affirmative[.]

"I wish to speak to you," and Will Cody led one of the men aside, saying abruptly:

"Is Golden your friend?"

"Indeed he is."

"He has been captured as a spy and you know that means death," were the words that startled the Confederate prisoner.

CHAPTER VII.
STRATEGY.

The prisoner looked pained at the news given him by Will Cody, and while his lip quivered said:

"Poor Nat."

"What do you know of him?"

"Nothing, if you expect to get information to make it worse for him than it is."

"I asked you what you knew of his life!"

"Well, he was born in Mississippi, his father being a planter; but he preferred guns and horses to books, and ran away from home, when his father sent him on to college, and went west.

"When the war broke out he returned and entered the army, and I believe he made money in mining then."

"That is all you know?"

"About all."

"What is his position in the Confederate Army?"

"He is a scout, though he could have been a captain in General Lorning's[8] staff, but refused it, preferring to scout."

"You do not wish to see him hang?"

"Do you really think we Southerners are as black as your Northern newspapers paint us—

"You as a soldier ought to know."

Will Cody smiled at the indignant response of the Confederate soldier, and replied:

"I know Golden even better than you do, for we were together a couple of years upon the plains, and I have often had him tell me of his Mississippi home.

"There is a debt of a life between us, and I do not wish to have harm befall him, so desire to aid him, and do all in my power for him, so wish you to help me."

"How can I, prisoner that I am?"

"I wish you to look over this map with me, tell me just when I am right and wrong, for I intend to make my way to the headquarters of the Confederate general, upon a special mission, and if I can get Nat Golden out of trouble I shall do so."

Said as it was there was much to imply a false statement to the Confederate prisoner and yet Will Cody had kept strictly within the bounds of truth. All through his life he had shunned a liar more than he would a foe, and has prided himself, as he expressed it, that "he was not built with a split tongue."

In telling the prisoner that there was "a debt of a life between Golden and himself," he did not say which one of them owed the debt to the other.

He now saw a chance, by using strategy, to get information of value to him from the prisoners, and he went to work in a most ingenious way to do so.

One after another he called the prisoners, he had picked out, apart from the others, which had about the same conversation with those who knew Nat Golden, and thus verified the maps he had and positions of the Confederates.

This done he went at once to General Smith and said:

"I have reason, sir, to know that a Union spy has gotten maps and full details of the Confederate lines as they now exist, and though in honor bound not to give my authority, I will vouch for the truth of it, General Smith, and report it to you so that you can be on your guard."[9]

General Smith regarded the young soldier scout attentively and replied:

"As you say you are in honor bound, Cody, to keep secret the source of your information, I must respect it, and shall at once send word to the commanders changing the whole order of the situation as it now exists.

"Have you reviewed those maps?"

"Yes, sir, and verified them."

"How so?"

"From Confederate prisoners, sir, whom I interviewed separately, telling them a ghost story to unloosen their tongues."

"You are going the right way to work, Scout Cody.

"When will you start upon this mission you have volunteered for?"

"Tonight, sir, for I am all ready now, and have my uniform."

"What uniform?"

"A rebel gray, sir."

"Ah, yes, you are going to change your flag."

"Not my flag, sir, but my colors, from the blue to the gray; but my principles are as unchangeable as the leopard's spots."

"Well said, Cody.

"Now, let me give you your instructions of just what you are to accomplish, as far as lies in your power, though of course you are to be governed by circumstances as to what you can and cannot do.

"Caution, nerve, wit and pluck alone can serve you, and you have your share of each, and I rely upon you fully."

"Thank you, sir."

Then General Smith went over the instructions he had prepared for the daring scout, and for an hour they were thus engaged.

Then William Cody saluted and was leaving the tent when the General said warmly, as he extended his hand:

"Good-bye, Cody, and success attend you through all."

Another hour and William Cody was mounted upon his horse and riding toward the Confederate lines, having taken his life in his hands to serve his country.

CHAPTER VIII.
THE UNION SPY.

Buffalo Bill carried at the cantle of his saddle a little roll that might be the cause of his death.

It was a Confederate uniform, and he had purchased it in "sections" from the prisoners, a hat here, a pair of pants there and a coat from another.

He had rehearsed well the part he was to play within the Confederate lines, and had names, localities, and all on the end of his tongue if cornered.

After passing the last Confederate outpost he halted and made a transfer of uniforms.

That is he put the Confederate uniform on over the blue, having selected his suit of gray from larger men for that very purpose.

Making a few other minor changes, he surveyed himself as well as he could in the moonlight, and saw that there had been a complete metamorphosis, a Union soldier had outwardly been changed into a Confederate soldier, and he must be most particular to see that he could prove himself just what he appeared to be, a cavalryman of Dixie.

His hair worn rather long, his darkly bronzed face and general appearance might well cause him to be mistaken for a follower of the "Bonnie Blue Flag."[10]

It was just dawn when he began to approach the position of the first Confederate outpost.

He did not wish to be fired upon from ambush, and so rode along in a somewhat noisy way, trying to hum Dixie; but not having been blessed with a talent for music, in fact being decidedly wanting in that respect he seemed to realize that he was not making a success of the song.

My hero has a pleasant voice in conversation, a ringing, commanding voice in the field, but the man or woman who would attest that he can sing are themselves lacking in a musical ear.

"I must stop this or some rebel will shoot me for murdering Dixie," he muttered with a sense of his imperfection of voice and tune of song.

"Halt! Who comes there?" rang out in stern tones ahead of him.

"I knew it; that song roused them," he muttered, and to this day he attests that Dixie saved his life, for he says they would have shot him without challenge, had they not heard the words, if not the tune of "Way down South in Dixie."

"Friend," he answered promptly.

He had taken the boldest way of carrying his plan into execution, not sneaking into the Confederate lines like a thief in the night, but going in fearlessly in the guise of a soldier of the South.

"Dismount, friend, advance and give the countersign," came the order.

He obeyed as far as dismounting was concerned and advancing, calling out:

"I can dismount, pard, and advance, but I can't give the countersign as I do not know it, being just out of the Yankee lines."

"Ah! a deserter?"

"Not much, and glad to get back into Dixie.

"Better take me to headquarters, I reckon, as the General might wish to see me."

Will Cody prided himself upon two "ten strikes" as he said, one in having said "Yankee," and again using the "reckon" of the South instead of the "guess" of the North.

He saw in the dim light that he had struck a picket post, for there were five Confederates in the group he walked up to, and their horses were hitched a short distance in the rear.

"Are you a Confederate soldier?"

"Not exactly."

"What are you doing with that uniform on then?"

"I thought it would keep me from being shot in entering the Confederate lines."

"And it did, so far, but give an account of yourself."

"I wish to see General Forrest who commands here, I believe."

"Two of you men disarm him and carry him back to headquarters, reporting how we captured him," said a man wearing corporal's stripes and who was in command of the outpost.

William Cody felt that he was in for it then, but he had made the venture and did not shrink from it.

Day had dawned, and as he rode to the rear, a Confederate cavalryman upon each side of him, he kept his eyes open to all that he saw.

He beheld other lines of outposts, each stronger than the outer one, and after riding several miles the Confederate camps began to appear, the soldier[s] looking at him with curiosity at seeing a man in gray uniform a prisoner.

"Is he a deserter, boys?"

"Have you got a spy, then?"

"What has he been up to?"

Such were the questions asked, and to which no answers were given by his two guards who, however, seemed to feel their importance in having a man in charge about whom nothing was known.

At last the headquarters camp appeared in view, and William Cody was led into the presence of the daring and darling Confederate cavalry general, N. B. Forrest.

CHAPTER IX.
A CLEVER RUSE.

"A man came into our lines, sir, but the corporal sent us to guard him to your quarters, General."

So said one of the two men who had William Cody in charge, addressing a tall, well formed man in gray uniform bearing the rank of Confederate Major General upon his collar.

He had a stern face, piercing dark eyes and a rather sad expression rested upon his countenance, while he wore a goatee and moustache.

It was General N. B. Forrest, a man who had risen from a private to high rank through his indomitable pluck and military genius; a man who had he been a West Point graduate, would have proven himself the greatest military chieftain the war produced, either North or South, for he was a born leader of men, a natural commander.

"Well, sir, who and what are you?" asked Forrest in his abrupt manner.

"May I speak to you alone, sir?" asked William Cody saluting politely.

"Yes, come with me," and the General unhesitatingly led the way to his tent.

"Now, what have you to say?"

"You send Nat Golden into the Union lines, sir?"

"I know of the man, a scout in my command—what of him?"

"He was captured several days ago, sir, and being an old friend of his I secured the papers and maps he had with him, and which would have hanged him, as you well know, sir, had they fallen into the hands of others."

"Where are they?"

"I brought them with me, sir, and will give them to you," and Will Cody began to take from their hiding place the papers which Golden, the Confederate spy, had turned over to him.

"Did no one else than yourself suspect Golden?"

"No, General, he was turned over as an ordinary prisoner and sent to Memphis with others."

"And just what are you?"

"I have never enlisted in the Confederate army, sir, but being Golden's friend saved him, and brought you the papers he risked his life to obtain, and I think I can render better service, General, by going to and fro, for I would never be suspected by the Union soldiers."

"Then you are a valuable man, and I shall need you.

"These are most important papers you bring, and two days ago would have been invaluable, but certain changes are now taking place with the troops which prevent our acting upon them.

"Do you know what these papers are?"

"Perfectly, sir, for I studied them well to be able to report them to you in case I was forced to destroy them."

"That was right.

"You look like the very man for this work, though rather young."

"What is your name?"

"Frederick Williams, sir," and the young scout gave his first two names with the addition of an s on William.[11]

"I am sorry Golden got captured. He was doubtless returning to our lines when it happened, but am glad he was not suspected of being a spy.

"He was not one of my men, but sent to me for special work, and from what I have heard of him[, he] has often been a prisoner before, but always manages to escape, and I hope he will this time.

"As for you I can soon find work for you so you can remain about headquarters until I call on you."

"I wear a Union uniform on beneath this gray one, and would like to change it."

"I will send you to mess with my couriers, and you will be made fairly comfortable; but how did you get out of the Union lines?"

"I am so situated, sir, that I can get the countersign and have full freedom.

"That was why I was able to save Nat Golden.

"See here, sir, is a freedom pass from General A. G. Smith."

The General took the slip of paper and read:

"The bearer, Frederick Williams, has full liberty to pass through the lines."

It was signed by General Smith, and officially stamped.

"You can serve me well, I see.

"Now, I will look over these papers," and calling an orderly General Forrest ordered him to conduct "Mr. Williams" to the courier's camp and tell the sergeant to make him comfortable there.

Will Cody gave a sigh of relief as he got out of range of the searching eyes of General Forrest, and soon after found himself in the company of the sergeant commanding the couriers, and a gentleman whom he has since met and become most friendly with, the two having often talked over the venture of the daring soldier sent as a spy into the Confederate lines.

"So far my ruse goes.

"It was a lucky capture I made when I caught Nat Golden, lucky for him as well as for myself," he muttered as he went into a tent to take off his blue uniform.

CHAPTER X.
A VERY CLOSE CALL.

As the days passed away and no call came from General Forrest for his services, Will Cody began to grow weary.

Allowed the freedom of the camps he had roamed about and picked up much information.

Other news he had gotten from the Sergeant and his couriers, and still more he had gleaned here and there.

He had jotted down valuable notes, drawn maps and these papers were hidden away at a certain point beyond the camps.

At last he began to fret, as he hoped the General would call upon him, and then he would be safely passed through the Confederate lines, without having to run the gauntlet.

He would also doubtless learn much from the General before going.

But no call came to him to go to headquarters, so he decided he would seek an interview with General Forrest, and tell him that it would be best for him to return into the Union lines if only to show himself.

So toward headquarters he wended his way to suddenly stop short, while fearless as he was he knew that his face had changed color at what he saw.

There standing before the General's tent, talking with the assistant adjutant general was none other than Nat Golden, the Confederate spy.

It did not take Will Cody long to act, for he knew that his life hung by a thread.

Instantly he turned and made his way back to the couriers' camp, and going into the tent where he slept, he found no one there to his great delight.

It took him just three minutes to draw off the gray uniform, draw on his blue once more and put the gray on over that.

Then he slipped away to where his horse was kept, bridled and saddled him and rode off in a direction that would keep him well out of sight of headquarters.

Glancing back he saw that thus far no one suspected his flight, or at least no one was yet in pursuit.

He did not doubt but that Nat Golden would try to save him, if he could; but with it suddenly sprung upon him by General Forrest that he had received his papers by the hand of his friend, Frederick Williams, he must betray the friend without thinking of the consequences to him.

To the delight of William Cody, he had time to secure the valuable papers he had hidden away, and as he approached the outpost where he had come into the lines he smiled and uttered:

"Fate is good to me, for the same sergeant is on Duty, I am glad to see."

He wrote up to the outpost and saluting politely said:

"Sergeant, direct me how to find the outposts to the left, as I have instructions for them, and when an aide de camp comes up tell him which way I have gone."

The sergeant had seen Will Cody at headquarters; he knew how he had been received by the General, and he believed him to be all right, and saluting politely, directed him along the outer line of picket posts.

Hardly had Will Cody ridden fifty yards when he glanced back and saw a party of horsemen coming at a gallop, and at their head was an officer and Nat Golden riding by his side.

Instantly he urged his horse into a gallop, wheeled into a bit of timber near, and then driving spurs deep went on like the wind, to suddenly dash upon half a dozen Confederate cavalrymen, having as prisoners two Union soldiers.

CHAPTER XI.
A FRIENDLY MEETING.

The remarkable nerve and presence of mind of Will Cody was never more fitly shown than when he dashed upon the six Confederate cavalrymen with the two Union soldiers as prisoners.

The latter were also cavalrymen, but disarmed and dejected looking, and in the supposed Confederate soldier thus coming upon them they saw no hope of rescue.

"Ho, men, a Union spy is escaping, so scatter each way and head him off, and I will guard your prisoners.

"Quick, for he must not get away!"

The stern command and what was said, coming from the lips of one they supposed was an officer, set the cavalrymen in quick motion, and they darted right and left to head off the spy, leaving their prisoners, as they soon learned to their cost, in very dangerous hands.

Hardly had they gone a dozen rods, when Will Cody cried:

"Come with me, men, for I am the Union spy, and we must ride for our lives!"

Their faces at once beamed with joy, and wheeling their horses they drove spurs deep and the three went bounding away together.

"They have discovered the cheat, and there come others in the pursuit.

"We must ride for it, men!" cried Will Cody, as he saw two of the cavalrymen turn at their flight, and remain in mute astonishment, while Nat Golden and his party dashed into sight a few hundred yards away.

Then it became a race for life, and the cavalrymen who had been so duped and lost their prisoners, wheeled in pursuit, firing as they did so.

The bullets flew about the fugitives, and one of the rescued men was slightly wounded in the hip, and Will Cody's horse got a bullet in his neck.

But on they rode, keeping well in advance of their pursuers, and though Will Cody's horse was fleet and fresh, and he could have distanced his companions, he kept well back with them, determined not to desert them unless compelled to do so.

To them, if retaken, it meant imprisonment until, exchanged, to him, a spy, it was certain death, and he recalled, as he rode along, the piercing eyes of General Forrest, and his stern, sad face, and knew he need expect no mercy there.

Then too it flashed across him that as Nat Golden had been captured as a spy and escaped, he wished to show him that he could do the same.

The running fire of the pursuers was kept up, though without doing more harm, until the Union outposts, feeling the prisoners were escaping, rallied their reserves and came to the rescue.

A few more minutes and Will Cody breathed a sigh of relief as he dashed into the midst of the rallying Boys in Blue, and wheeling his horse he was about to join in the skirmish that followed, when he recalled the important papers he carried, and also that he wore a Confederate uniform.

To slip the gray suit off was quick work, and then he rode rapidly on to headquarters, accompanied by the two rescued prisoners, and soon stood in the presence of General A. G. Smith.

Having heard his story the general warmly congratulated the brave soldier upon his valuable services and his escape, as [sic, and] also the release of the two prisoners, and then a council of war called to decide upon what movements should be made upon the information secured by the spy who had risked an ignominious death to serve his country.

In the movements that followed the council of war William Cody did not participate, for his colonel had made a request for him to be returned to the regiment as it had been ordered to Memphis on special service.

It was upon his arrival in Memphis that Will Cody learned how Nat Golden and a number of other Confederate prisoners had daringly made their escape, his old pard the plainsman being the leader, and both had regained their own lines.

It may be as well to mention here that a dozen years ago, when Colonel Cody was playing the "Knight of the Plains,"[12] a melodrama written for the famous scout by the author of this biography, he met there Nat Golden, now a Mississippi planter, and the two old friends, one time foes, and again united under one flag, talked through the long hours of the night over the thrilling days of the war, and Mr. Golden said to me:

"I never once dreamed that Cody was the spy, until after I had told General Forrest that I had sent no one through with my papers.

"Then the order came to arrest Frederick Williams, and too late the truth flashed upon me, and glad was I to find that he had escaped."

CHAPTER XII.
MEETING WITH WILD BILL.[13]

It is a noticeable fact that nearly every frontier character of fame is a native of the West, there seeming to be something in the air to inoculate them as children with a love of adventure. Wild Bill was no exception, for as James Butler Hickok he was born in LaSalle County, Illinois, on May 27th, 1837. The family consisted of four boys and two girls, all of whom are now living save James—Wild Bill—as he is best known. Always fond of firearms, horses and adventure, and as a premium was offered on the scalp of wolves at fourteen years of age the boy won a name as the "Wolf Killer."

At eighteen James Hickok went to Kansas, and when years after he met William Cody, then a boy, and befriended him the two became pards for life.

Though called a desperado, Wild Bill never deserved the name, for he was a tender-hearted, generous fellow, brave as a lion, one of the deadest shots that ever roamed the prairies, and took life only when compelled to do so in the discharge of duty or in self-defense. As a scout, a soldier and a spy during the civil war, and in numerous other capacities in which he served, Wild Bill won fame. In General G. A. Custer's[14] "Life on the Plains," is the following tribute to Wild Bill:

"Among the white scouts were some of the most noted of their class. The most prominent man among them was Wild Bill, whose highly varied career was made the subject of an illustrated sketch in one of the popular monthly periodicals a few years ago.[15] Wild Bill was a strange character, just the one which a novelist might gloat over. He was a plainsman in every sense of the word yet unlike any other of his class. In person he was about six feet one in height, straight as the straightest of the warriors whose implacable foe he was; broad shoulders, well-formed chest and limbs, and a face strikingly handsome; a sharp, clear, blue eye, which stared you straight in the face when in conversation; a finely-shaped nose, inclined to be aquiline; a well-turned mouth, with lips only partially concealed by a handsome mustache. His hair and complexion were those of a perfect blonde. The former was worn in uncut ringlets falling carelessly over his powerfully formed shoulders. Add to this figure a costume blending the immaculate neatness of the dandy with the extravagant taste and style of the frontiersman, and you have Wild Bill, then and now the most famous scout on the plains.

"Whether on foot or on horseback, he was one of the most perfect types of physical manhood I ever saw. Of his courage there could be no question; it has been brought to the test on too many occasions to admit of a doubt. His skill in the use of the rifle and pistol was unerring; while his deportment was exactly the opposite of what might be expected of a man of his surroundings. It was entirely free from all bluster and bravado. He never spoke of himself unless requested to do so. His conversation, strange to say, never bordered either on the vulgar or blasphemous. His influence among the frontiersmen was unbounded, his word was law; and many are the personal quarrels and disturbances which he has checked among his comrades by his simple announcement that 'this has gone far enough,' if need be followed by the ominous warning that when persisted in or renewed the quarreler 'must settle with me.' Wild Bill is anything but a quarrelsome man; yet no one but himself can enumerate the many conflicts in which he has been engaged, and which almost invariably resulted in the death of his adversary. I have a personal knowledge of at least half a dozen men whom he has at various times killed, one of these being a member of my command.[16] Others have been severely wounded, yet he always escaped unhurt. On the plains every man openly carried his belt with its invariable appendages, knife and revolver, often two of the latter. Wild Bill always carried two handsome ivory-handled revolvers of the large size; he was never seen without them. Where this is the common custom, brawls or personal difficulties are seldom if ever settled by blows. The quarrel is not from a word to a blow, but from a word to the revolver, and he who can draw and fire first is the best man. No civil law reaches him; none is applied for. In fact there is no longer recognized beyond the frontier [besides] that of 'might makes right.' Should death result from the quarrel, as it usually does, no coroner's jury is impaneled to learn the cause of death, and the survivor is not arrested. But instead of these old-fashioned proceedings, a meeting of the citizens takes place, the survivor is requested to be present when the circumstances of the homicide are inquired into, and the unfailing verdict of 'justifiable,' 'self-defense,' etc., is pronounced, and the law stands vindicated. That justice is often deprived of a victim there is not a doubt. Yet in all of the many affairs of this kind in which Wild Bill has performed a part, and which have come to my knowledge, there is not a single instance in which the verdict of twelve fair-minded men would not be pronounced in his favor.

"That the even tenor of his way continues to be disturbed by little events of this description may be inferred from an item which has been floating lately through the columns of the press, and which states that 'the funeral of "Jim Bludso," who was killed the other day by Wild Bill took place to-day.' It then adds: 'The funeral expenses were borne by Wild Bill!'[17] What could be more thoughtful than this? Not only to send a fellow mortal out of the world, but to pay the expenses of the transit!"

Wild Bill was murdered in Deadwood, in the Black Hills, August 2d, 1876, by Jack McCall, a desperado, who was afterwards tried and hanged for his crime. —The Author.

When the Seventh Kansas arrived in Memphis its stay there was of short duration, for it was almost immediately ordered to Cape Girardeau, in Missouri, to meet a Confederate force under General Price, who was then making a raid into the State.[18]

Hurried to the front the Seventh Kansas joined the forces opposing Price, and Will Cody was again assigned to special scouting service, his talents in that kind of work having shown his value to a commanding officer in the field.

It had been a new experience for the young plainsman, this going into battle upon a large scale where thousands of soldiers on each side were struggling for victory, and all he saw he was determined to profit by, studying the science of war with great diligence, and trying to solve the mysteries of certain maneuvres that at first could not be accounted for.

He saw how thoroughly the handling of troops in the field was a game of chess on a large scale, a play of one general to checkmate the other.

Then the young scout realized how thoroughly the commander in the field must rely upon his scouts for news of the movements of foe, and how exact these same scouts should be in all the information they gave, and he determined to risk much to unearth the enemy's plans and yet take in only such news as he could vouch for as being exact, and this resolve governed him through all his after years, and made him the famous scout he is today, respected and endorsed by every commander under whom he served without a single exception, from Generals Sherman and Sheridan down to General N. A. Miles commanding in the last Indian campaign,[19] where the services of William F. Cody were most conspicuous.*

Will Cody had seen enough of scouts carrying in false reports, guessing at the movements of the foe instead of discovering really what was being done though at great personal risk, and he knew that only now and then could a man sent out for information be implicitly relied upon.

He was therefore determined that he would risk much to get news, and carry in only such information he had discovered to be true.

The first large fight with General Price, after the Seventh Kansas regiment joined the Union army in Missouri was the Battle of Pilot Knob,[20] and from that time on for two months followed severe skirmishes almost daily, in many of which Will Cody was engaged, and in which the opportunity was given him of discovering most effectually just what war really was.

As it is not my intention to deal with movements and incidents of the war which are matters of history, excepting so far as concerns the part played in them by my hero, I will now more particularly dwell upon his personal acts that stand out in bold relief in his checkered life.

Still devoting himself to the duties of a scout from headquarters, with a little spying work thrown in when necessary, he rode out one day to try and gather some news of just what General Price was doing, for the

---

*In this campaign referred to[,] William Cody served not only as Chief of Scouts, but also as Brigadier General of Nebraska National Guard. —The Author.

Confederate general was known to be a very able commander, foxy and sudden in his movements, keeping the Union commander constantly on the qui vive[21] as to what he would do next.

As a compromise in his work to both armies, so as to serve the one and take advantage of the circumstances in the Confederate lines when necessary, Will Cody wore a semi-uniform of gray jeans of Missouri manufacture that might pass well for "Rebel Gray," and also be within bounds for a Missouri soldier.

Pushing out from the camps one day he rode along ready to take advantage of any discovery he might make to favor his cause, or defend himself if he happened upon a foe.

Coming to a farm house on the road, he saw a horse saddled and bridled and hitched to the rack just outside of the gate.

The house had a military look, and it was for Will Cody to be cautious as he knew, for he was just as likely to run upon a Southern scout there as a Northern one, in fact the chances were in favor of the former.

But he rode on to the house, dismounted and hitching his horse to the rack, was about to ascend to the piazza when he was startled by the words:

"Well, Billy, how are you?"

With the utterance of the words there appeared in the doorway a tall form clad in the uniform of a Confederate captain.

Though at first startled, and at once on guard, Will Cody recognized the one he thus met and stepping quickly upon the piazza cried earnestly:

"Wild Bill! my dear old pard and in a Confederate uniform?"

The man glanced behind him, and then answered in a low tone:

"As you appear to be, Billy."

"Yes, I am scouting."[22]

"And I am a spy in the Confederate lines," was the calm rejoinder of Wild Bill.

CHAPTER XIII.
THE TWO SCOUTS.

When Will Cody had first met the man he then saw in the Missouri farm house, in the uniform of a Confederate captain of cavalry, it had been years before when he was a mere boy in the overland freighting train of Russell, Majors and Waddell.

Then Will Cody was barely in his teens, Wild Bill was the wagon-master of the outfit to which he was attached and had one day promptly taken his part in an affair when a bully had imposed on him.[23]

From that day the two had been devoted friends, though one was a man the other a boy, and Will Cody soon discovered the true worth of his defender.

Returning from a long overland journey Wild Bill had gone home with the youth, and Mrs. Cody and her daughters had done all in their power to make him enjoy a visit, and often afterward had he gone to the Cody home where he was ever most welcome.

At another time Will Cody had been thrown with Wild Bill when the latter was captain of pony express riders on the overland trail,[24] and my hero one of the pony riders.

Now the two met again when in the service of their country, and both on special duty for their commanding officers in the movements going on in Missouri.

Of course the meeting between the two former plainsmen was a joy to both, for many a time side by side had they roughed it together, risked life side by side and the same blanket had covered them when on the lone trail.

They had met in St. Louis soon after Will had enlisted, and each knew that the other was a soldier of the Union and true as steel to the Flag.

Now, the one in the Confederate uniform, the other in a suit that might be taken for the gray of a Southern soldier, they met again on the Dead Line, as it were, between the two armies. But neither for an instant doubted the other, and Will Cody knew at once that Wild Bill was just what he represented himself, a Union spy in the Southern lines.

"You are taking big chances with your neck, Bill, in that uniform," said Will Cody in a low tone.

Wild Bill laughed and replied:

"I have heard an old saying, Billy, that the pot can't call the kettle black."

"Oh! this jeans [sic] will go for a Missouri farmer."

"Yes, or a Union soldier playing hayseed."[25]

"But you are in a Confederate officer's uniform, rank and all."

"Led by Destiny" : 169

"Yes, it goes best where I have been.

"You see I am Captain James Hickok of Texas, ordered to General Marmaduke's Division with dispatches, which said dispatches fell into my hands through a duel I fought on the road with the bearer who was killed.[26]

"I am mighty glad to see you, Billy my boy, for I was on my way toward our lines to carry certain letters and papers to General McNiel [sic];[27] but now as I have met you I will turn them over to you and return to gather further important information I know I can get."

"You are a trump, Wild Bill, and this is a fortunate meeting, for I was just out on an expedition to see what news I could obtain regarding the movements of General Price."

"I will tell you all that I know, Billy, so we will have a talk after awhile, for I am waiting for these good people to get me some dinner, and you can share it with me."

This Will Cody was more than anxious to do, for being a soldier he [was] willing to eat at any time.

So having "learned the ropes," as it were, about the house, Wild Bill went back to tell the good housewife that he had met an old friend, and not to be afraid of preparing a most substantial spread for both of them, as he recalled that his young friend had an appetite like a grizzly bear.

While the extra allowance was being prepared the two friends walked out to where their horses were and Wild Bill took out of an inner pocket of package of letters and said:

"These I wish you to give to General McNeil, whose scout I am, and tell him that I am getting so much valuable information of the forces and movements of the Confederates that I shall return and remain some days longer."

"And when will I meet you again, Bill?"

"Quien sabe,[28] Billy.

"It may be before long, perhaps never until we meet across the Great Divide."

"Do be careful of yourself, Bill."

Wild Bill laughed and said:

"You are the kind of preacher, Billy, who never practices what he preaches; but I am careful, and yet when the time comes to hand in my chips I won't whine; but do you be careful of yourself, for you are younger than I am by a number of years, and I can never go beyond what I now am, though with you it is different for I do believe what the old fortune teller told your dear mother, and she often spoke of it to me with the firm belief in the prophecy, that you were destined to win a great name some day, that you were led by Destiny as it were.

"Yes, Billy, I believe there is a great future before you," and Wild Bill spoke with an impressiveness of manner that could not but leave its stamp upon Will Cody, for never has he forgotten the words his friend then uttered, when the lives of the two were hanging by a thread, as it were, meeting as they did so strangely within the Confederate lines.

CHAPTER XIV.
A SELF-CONSTITUTED DEFENDER.

Throwing off suddenly the mood that was upon him, Wild Bill begun to give Will Cody personal explanations of the movements of the Confederate forces, and all other data which he deemed would be of use and interest.

Will listened most attentively to all, making notes here and there, and had just finished doing so when they were called in to eat the meal prepared for them.

The woman had a kindly face, and telling them that she had a son in the Confederate Army asked them if they knew him, giving his name.

Neither remembered having heard of him, and while they ate the chicken, hot biscuit, potatoes and coffee provided for them, they listened to her talk, hoping to glean some information that would be of service to them.

Among other things she told them was that her son and a nephew were coming home that night, to remain several days, though she would have to keep them in hiding while there.

Both of the Union scouts saw their chance to make a capture and Will Cody glanced at Wild Bill who quietly shook his head, and while the confiding woman went for some more coffee, he hurriedly said:

"It would never do, Billy."

"No for I can understand just how my poor mother would have felt to have seen me carried a prisoner from home, perhaps killed if I resisted."

Having finished eating, Wild Bill took out some "greenbacks" to pay for what they had, but the woman firmly refused to accept anything, and said:

"If you were Yankees I could charge you sir, but while I have anything left Confederate soldiers, poor fellows, are welcome to it."

Soon after the two friends mounted their horses and with a firm grasp of the hand in farewell each rode his separate way, Wild Bill returning to the Confederate quarters to again risk death as a spy, while Will Cody hastened back with the valuable dispatches to General McNiel.

Returning to his own command Will Cody sought General McNiel at his headquarters and made known to him his meeting with Wild Bill, and handed over the letters and papers which had been given to him.

He also told the General all that Wild Bill had personally told him, and how he had returned to General Marmaduke's camp for more information.

"Wild Bill is too reckless, and the next we hear of him will be that he has been hanged as a spy.

"But you have brought most valuable information from him, Scout Cody, such as will prove of much use to us, and you show daring in going into the enemy's lines as you did.

"I may call upon you later."

So said General McNeil, and he did call upon Will Cody only a few days after, when the Army was on the move, sending him well to the front of the advance guard to reconnoitre.

Riding on ahead alone, and having neglected to fill his canteen, Will Cody determined to venture to a handsome mansion back from the road and get a drink of water.

There was also belief in his mind that he might pick up a bit of information there.

So turning in at the gate he approached the house slowly up the long avenue of trees.

As he drew rein before the house a lady stepped out upon the piazza, followed by two young and very pretty girls.

The appearance of the three ladies revealed to Will Cody that they were gentle folks and not of the ordinary farming class about there.

He raised his hat politely and asked if he could go around to the well and quench his thirst.

Both the elderly and the younger ladies showed by their faces that they were much alarmed by seeing a Union soldier appear before them and the former said:

"Certainly you can get what you ask for, but I have heard that your army is on the march this way and then, I suppose, we will lose everything."

Finding that the ladies were all alone, that there were no men about the premises, and being hospitably asked to come in and have some breakfast, Will Cody felt for the mother and her daughters, as he knew that when the army came along the stragglers would ransack the mansion, confiscating everything they could carry off with them.

So he decided that he would take it upon himself to protect them, and at the same time, as the mistress of the home had shown evident knowledge of the coming of the Union forces, he felt that she must be posted upon the movements of the Confederates, and he might glean from her valuable information.

He knew that the marching force would encamp a few miles beyond, and then he could overtake them, for in reconnoitering he was allowed to act according to his own judgement.

Having thus determined he said:

"There are lawless men in an army, Madam, that do rob homes, and I will remain and protect you from those who may come here."

And in thus offering himself as a defender to helpless women, Will Cody did not dream how near he was coming to signing his death warrant.

CHAPTER XV.
ON GUARD.

Will Cody greatly enjoyed the substantial and tempting late breakfast set before him by the good lady of the house, and talked glibly of the movements of the army, hoping to bring her out and thus glean some information.

But the mother and daughter, though hospitable toward him, were yet inclined to be a little suspicious, at any rate they did not commit themselves.

They admitted being in sympathy with the South, and that they had kindred most near to them who were in the Confederate army, while on their part they seemed most anxious to draw out the "young and handsome Yankee," and glean what information they could.

Thus was it a case of diamond cut diamond between the young scout and the mother with her two handsome daughters.

Having finished his breakfast at a late and very fashionable hour, Will Cody led his horse around to the rear of the mansion and fed him there, while, rifle in hand he took up his position in the parlor to await the coming of the first soldiers, whom he was very sure would pounce only too quickly upon all they could secure, for invariably an army on the march is merciless, especially in an enemy's country.

Will had an eye to feminine beauty of face and form and has ever been as courtly as a knight of old to the fair sex, and toward foes he would make no exception.

He had been struck by the calm repose and fine face of the lady of the mansion, recalling vividly to his mind his own, brave, dear mother under circumstances when she had had to protect her home and children, and all of his sympathy went out to the Southern woman in distress and danger.

The beauty of the two daughters won his admiration, and seeing a piano he asked one of them if she would not play for him, for he loved music, though, as I have said, he could never give vent to the music within him.

"Yes, I play—would you like to hear Dixie?" asked the girl with a sly twinkle in her eyes.

"Yes indeed," he answered pleasantly.

"As you are so generous then I will first play you Yankee Doodle."

"No, play Dixie first, and then Yankee Doodle to kinder take the edge off the other."

The girls laughed and seating herself at the piano one of them played Dixie, and in a very brilliant manner.

Instantly her mother appeared at the door with a reproachful look, and said:

"My daughter, it would be more courteous to play one of the Northern national airs, rather than a Southern piece."

"Pardon me, Madam, but I requested Dixie," said Will.

"And then Yankee Doodle to kinder take the edge off of Dixie," laughed the musician.

So Yankee Doodle followed Dixie, and then the two sisters sung a duet for the young scout, a ballad known as, "Those Dark Eyes."

The way they cast shy glances at Will's "dark eyes," made him feel that if he did escape capture from Confederate soldiers, it would not surprise him, or pain him, if he became the prisoner of one of those southern beauties, and he begun to rather like the self-imposed duty of guarding the rebel household.

After some time the mother again appeared at the door and announced that a number of horsemen were in sight.

Quickly Will Cody took up his position at the window and said:

"It is the advance guard—they will not come in, but others will soon follow."

It was just as he said, the advance guard rode by, and soon after a cavalry regiment and a battery of light artillery followed.

Then came General McNeil and his staff, his escort close up, and the different regiments, batteries and wagon-trains passed along in a long, continuous line until the ladies felt that they were looking upon an enormous army, so easy is it to be deceived by the numbers of marching soldiers.

The house set back several hundred yards from the highway, and it was not until half the column had passed, and the rear begun to straggle, that men got out from under the eyes of their officer and begun to straggle into the grounds.

First came a squad of a dozen, and there was delight in their faces at what they expected to find in the fine house.

But suddenly out upon the piazza stepped Will Cody, and his clear voice rang as he called out:

"Halt!

"You cannot enter here!"

"And why can't we?" asked a soldier.

"It is against orders."

"Who says so?"

"I say so—halt! if any man attempts to enter this house I will shoot him dead!" came the sternly uttered words of the Northern protector of a Southern home.

CHAPTER XVI.
IN DEADLY PERIL.

At the stern threat of the young sentry, the would-be marauders shrunk back.

Several of them recognized Will Cody as a special scout at headquarters, and they did not doubt for an instant but that the general had placed him there for some reason to guard the mansion and its inmates.

So, after a whispered consultation among themselves they asked if they could get some water.

"Your canteens are full, and you must go.

"Quick! be off men, or I will fire a signal for aid," said Will as he feared the men, if they got to the rear of the premises, would do some harm and get beyond his control.

In a surly way they moved off, one of them making some remarks about "the general protecting rebels he knew."

It was not long before another group of soldiers came in sight, having crossed the fields below.

There were quite a number of them and they came along in a noisy way, as though bent on mischief.

"Please go and play Yankee Doodle to help me out with this lot," said Will to the young lady who had played for him.

Instantly came her answer, while her eyes flashed:

"No, I will not play it under force, though I did for you as you were kind to us."

"You've got true grit," said Will admiringly, and he continued:

"Go in then and sing, you and your sister, that pretty song about Dark Eyes, while I tackle these fellows, for I'll make them believe you have officers for company.["]

They obeyed, and carbine in hand, Will paced to and fro, and again halted the coming soldiers.

As they appeared in an ugly mood, he said sternly:

"Now be off men, for I know my orders and shall obey them.

"March, or I'll call the colonel out to you!"

The words were uttered in a way that sent conviction that the "colonel" was in the house, and the duet which the two girls were singing, though with quivering voices from alarm, added to the belief, and the men turned away.

And so it was with a third and a fourth party, the daring sentry still stood his ground until at last but two men rode up, and Will Cody recognized in them real stragglers and hangers-on of the army, a very ugly element to deal with.

But his firm stand, aided by the music in the parlor, sent the men on their way, when, had they not believed officers were within doors, and Will was alone, they would not have hesitated to try conclusions with him.

"I'll stay a little while longer, for there may yet be a straggler or two, and then I will hate to leave you unprotected," he said.

The mother had stood by the door, concealed, but listening to all that had been said and done.

She saw the sentry's bold stand in their behalf, and when at last he uttered the words above written, she grasped his hand in both her own and said:

"God bless you, my dear young friend, for friend you have proven yourself to me and mine.

"Come, my daughters, and thank this Northern soldier for all that he has done for us."

"It was only my duty—true men don't war on women," said Will, blushing under the praise bestowed upon him for his pluck and cleverness, for it seemed as though all three could not say too much.

They were perfectly well aware that he had acted wholly without orders, upon his own responsibility, and were therefore the more grateful, and regarded him as a true hero.

As the command had taken hours in passing they insisted upon his having dinner with them before leaving, and they urgently set about preparing it for him.

Always ready to eat a good meal, Will had not the stomach to refuse, and when it was ready he sat down and enjoyed it immensely.

He had just risen from the table, and was preparing to take his departure, when suddenly through two of the doors and an open window were thrust three double-barreled shotguns.

Three faces ran along the sights, three fingers were upon the triggers, and with no time to draw a weapon, or the shadow of a chance for his life should he do so, Will Cody felt nearer to death for a moment that ever before in his eventful career.

But suddenly between him and the threatening guns sprang the brave mother and her two daughters, for they too saw as he had, that his life hung by a thread.

CHAPTER XVII.
THE BLUE AND THE GRAY.

The dignified, kind-faced mistress of the household, and her two brave daughters, took in the situation at once.

They saw the three men, the leveled guns and felt the danger their gallant protector was in.

With one accord they had sprung to shield him, and in a voice that thrilled the mother cried:

"My husband! my sons! You must not harm this man.

"Lower your guns at once!"

Instinctively the men obeyed.

There was that in the look and voice of the woman that commanded instant obedience.

They saw in their home a Federal soldier, and supposed he was there for evil rather than good.

But they lowered their guns and one by one they came into the room.

They were the father and brothers of the young ladies, and were Confederate soldiers, who, fearing trouble at home as the Federal forces were moving in that direction they had returned to protect as best they could those they loved, and also glean what information they could that would be of service to their commander.

One of the young men had been scouting that morning and reported the coming of the Union army, and at once the three had gone into hiding near the home, compelled to leave the three ladies alone.

They had seen the Union horsemen ride up to their house in squads, and at last had decided to venture home, and discovering Will Cody's presence regarded him only as a bitter foe.

Supposing that others were there they had acted promptly, and thus had the life of the young scout been nearly forfeited through his kind act.

Quickly the mother told her husband and sons of all that the brave Northern soldier had done, and stepping forward with extended hand, while his voice trembled with emotion the father said:

"I thank God my wife and girls acted so promptly, for I would not have harmed one who has thus befriended them for a fortune.

"Boys, give him your hand, for he has been your friend, and if he does wear the blue and you have the gray, blood is thicker than water and he is our honored guest."

The two young men at once came forward and offered their hands, which Will took in his hearty way and with the remark: "I'd rather have you for friends any day than for foes, but you have cast your lot with the South and I as a Northerner am fighting for the Union.

"We are all right now, but tomorrow we may be shooting at each other, though I'd never pull the trigger on you if I recognized you."

The manly appearance, handsome face and bonhomie manner of the Northern soldier quite won the heart of the Southerners, and they urged him to remain longer, but he said that he must at once depart, as he had taken it upon himself to stay behind and added in his dry way:

"I must get on and see just where you rebels are, and what you are up to, as we do not wish to ride into a trap, you know.

"You couldn't tell me could you?"

All laughed heartily at Will Cody's dry way of asking the Confederate for information, and one of the boys said:

"I reckon we could tell you, and we would like to return the favor done us, only we won't."

"You canceled that by not pulling the trigger on me; but I must be off.

"My name is William F. Cody, I am from Leavenworth, Kansas, have been on the Plains about all my life, and now a Union soldier scout, and if the fortunes of war go against you, look me up."

The mother now came forward with a warm robe the girls had made and a few articles of wear, while the daughters had filled a bag with choice provisions from the storeroom and insisted that he should take them.

He could not refuse and one of the boys having led his horse around, he bade all goodbye, then turned and taking off his hat said in a low, respectful tone:

"You remind me so much of my dear, dead mother—will you kiss me goodbye?"

She did so and from her lips came the low words:

"God bless you, my brave boy."

With a bound he was in the saddle and away, all standing upon the piazza and watching his departure.*

But suddenly as they watched there rose up before him and upon either side, a score of Confederate soldiers with carbines leveled and all heard the loud command:

"Halt, or you are a dead man!"

CHAPTER XVIII.
A RACE FOR LIFE.

William Cody rode away from the Southern home with the consciousness of having done only his duty and having saved from pillage the home of a Confederate soldier.

He recalled vividly how his own home had been pillaged during the Kansas war, his father hunted to death and his mother and sisters were made to suffer by foes and marauders.

But he did not believe in the war of retaliation against the innocent, his was not a revengeful nature, and he would not see the innocents suffer for the guilty and so he had acted from principle and a stern sense of duty, and his conscience repaid him for the act.

Upon each side of the avenue leading to the gate, the trees grew thick, and there was a hedge, and yet he did not look for danger lurking there.

---

*Twenty years after, when the writer was with Colonel Cody in Missouri, and was starring in a frontier play, a gentleman called and asked to see him.

He was one of the sons of the lady he had protected, and making his identity known, the man of the Blue and the man of the Gray had a long talk together.

The father was dead, killed during the war, as had also been his brother, and the mother had died only a few years before, while his two sisters were married and living in distant states.

He also was married and his family occupied a box at the theatre that night and went away much impressed with the great scout, their father's friend of war times. —The Author.

He had nearly reached the gate, and he remembered that it was so hard to open that he would have to dismount to do so, when suddenly he saw forms in gray leaping up from hiding places all about him, and heard the stern command to halt.

His first impulse was resistance, his next escape, but a glance showed him that either meant death, so in the wild western way he raised his hands above his head and said in his cool way:

"I pass—play your hand."

"Hold there! harm not that man on your life."

The words were uttered in a voice that was distinctly heard, and there came running like deer toward the scene the father and his two sons.

The officers commanding the captors of Will Cody paused as they advanced upon him, and awaited the coming of the three men running from the mansion.

"Ho, Silbey, that man goes free, for he guarded our home from pillage while the Yankee army went by.

"He is our friend."

"That alters the case, captain; but we saw him go there early this morning and decided to capture him, as one of my scouts reported that he had not left, and we supposed he was a spy," said the Confederate Lieutenant.

"Nothing of the kind, for we owe everything to him; he must go free at once, and send one escort with him in case others of our men have fallen in behind the Yankee column and may fire on him."

"No sir, I will not ask that, for you have already returned the service I rendered you," said Will.

"But I will.

"Send an escort, Sibley [sic], until he gets up with his column."

And so Will Cody enjoyed the strange sensation of being escorted by Confederates, and yet not being a prisoner.

The wisdom of the order given the Confederate Lieutenant, Will soon recognized, as other soldiers in gray were come up with. [sic]

But his escort protected him until he knew that his own forces were not far ahead, and bidding them good-bye he dashed on and soon came up with the Union army in camp.

But his horse had been well rested and fed, he had also been well cared for, so he rode to the front and brought in information of the Confederate movements in their front which the general complimented him upon obtaining, so he felt that he had made up for his half day at the Confederate home.

From that day the movements of both Union and Confederate forces were rapid and of moment.

General Price and his army were crowded toward Kansas City, in the vicinity of which place they were met by a force of United States troops in Kansas.

Thus checked, General Price begun the skillful and memorable retreat back into Kansas.

Will Cody, with thousands of others, while both armies were drawn up in line of battle near Fort Scott, Kansas, here witnessed the most thrilling scene, and one in which the young soldier-scout felt himself particularly interested in.

In plain view two men were seen rapidly leaving the Confederate lines, and making a dash with all the speed of their horses toward the Union forces.

At first their intention did not seem to be realized either by Confederates or Federals, but then an alarm was given and shot after shot was fired upon the flying horsemen.

When nearing United States lines one of them fell dead from his horse under the Confederate fire, but the other kept on and Will Cody went out with the regiment hastily ordered to meet him and check the pursuers of the daring fugitive.

As he drew nearer to him, though he was dressed in a uniform of a Confederate officer, Will Cody recognized him and shouted:

"It is Wild Bill, the Union scout!"

CHAPTER XIX.
A PLEASING EPISODE.

As Wild Bill dashed up to the Kansas Regiment that had gone to his support, he was given a raising cheer, for the words of Will Cody had told who he was, and his daring escape deservedly won their admiration.

"Ho Billy, you there?" he cried.

"Yes, and had given you up for dead long ago."

"No, I am all right now, but take me at once to General Pleasanton's[29] headquarters, for I have valuable information for him."

They soon arrived there and General McNiel was also at headquarters, the two officers welcoming Wild Bill warmly, and congratulating him upon his daring escape.

Wild Bill at once told them that though General Price was making a bold showing in their front the rear of the army was then crossing a stream difficult to ford, four miles from Fort Scott, and an attack made then must bring victory.

He also stated that he had been suspected of being a spy for several days and was being closely watched, but could not escape before.

At last, as he was sure that he and his fellow scout, who had been killed, were going to be arrested, and that meant certain death, they mounted their horses and made the desperate dash for liberty, in which he had been successful, his companion had been killed.

Upon the information given him by Wild Bill, General Pleasanton at once ordered an advance upon the Confederate lines.

The charge was in a measure successful, but night checked the fighting, and doubtless saved the Confederate army, for had Wild Bill been able to escape earlier in the day General Price would have met with a signal defeat.

Price retreated south of the Arkansas River where the pursuit was given up, and in all that march and series of skirmishes, Will Cody and Wild Bill scouted together.

Upon the return of his regiment from the pursuit of General Price, Will Cody, to his surprise, and at first to his regret, was ordered on detached service at Military Headquarters at St. Louis.

It seemed that his lucky star still guided him, in leading him to St. Louis, for it was there that he met in a romantic way the lady who is now his wife.

It was his custom to exercise his horses, and show his fine horsemanship every afternoon when not on duty in the suburbs of St. Louis, and on several occasions had he met and particularly noticed a striking looking young girl also riding.

Her face, form and perfect seat in the saddle attracted him and he tried to discover who she was, but in vain, until one afternoon fortune favored him.

He was just going out upon his ride, when he heard shouts ahead and beheld a horse coming madly along the highway toward him.

Upon his back was a rider, and it was the young lady in whom he had become so deeply interested.

But he saw and realized her danger, for the bit in her horse's mouth had broken and she was at the mercy of the now maddened animal, for, splendid rider though she was, she had no control of him.

Will Cody knew that on ahead she would soon come to the paved streets of the city and meet innumerable vehicles, and the horse was liable to fall or dash into some of the carriages or wagons.

Quickly his mind was made up, his horse wheeled about, put at a full run, and as the runaway animal came near he was ready for him.

A glance backward showed that the young lady retained her presence of mind, but was deadly pale, seeming to know what her fate might be.

Another moment with a touch of the spurs Will Cody was along side of the runaway, his lariat, which he never went without, was noosed over the head of the animal, and gradually as it began to choke him he slackened his pace and was brought to a standstill.

"Take my bridle, Miss, for I can ride with my lariat," he said, raising his hat politely.

But this she would not hear to, and a bit of rawhide thongs was quickly made by Will Cody, who at once offered himself as an escort to see her home in safety.

The offer was accepted, for the young girl felt unnerved somewhat after her danger was over, and she led the way to a pleasant little home in the city, where she presented her gallant rescuer to her family.[30]

The young lady was Miss Louise Frederici, now, as Mrs. William F. Cody, the mistress of an elegant mansion in North Platte, Nebraska, the home of Colonel Cody.

CHAPTER XX.
WILL CODY LOSES HIS HEART.

Stationed at Army Headquarters in St. Louis, where he could make love to lovely Louise Frederici, Will Cody found more delightful occupation than in being in the field with a large force, or on detached service scouting for guerrillas.

From the afternoon he first saw Miss Frederici he was interested in her, and when he was so fortunate as to render a great service, perhaps save her life in the wild runaway her horse was making, he fell desperately in love with her and was too frank natured and innocent of the ways of the world in society to hide what he felt.

With a gay season in the city, the theatre, entertainments and various invitations out, a young and handsome soldier had every chance to enjoy himself after all the dangers and hardships he had known.

A city paper had not been long in finding out that there was a hero in town, and he was at once found by an interviewer.

But Will Cody would not talk, though naturally proud of many of his own deeds he would not tell them to the world, and he was too modest to speak of his part.

But reporters are not easily "bluffed," and he went on the hunt of someone who knew the retiring young soldier-scout and found him in Wild Bill, another most modest man about his own deeds, but very communicative in speaking of the record of a friend.

From Wild Bill he learned much of Will Cody's early career, and the next day it was laid before the readers of the paper.

Not since he had seen his name in print, as the "Youngest Indian fighter on the plains," where at eleven years of age he had killed his first Indian, had Will Cody believed himself the hero that article made him, and he was actually ashamed to face his friends after one of them had brought him a paper.

"That will make you solid with the old man, Billy," said Wild Bill, who made reply when Will Cody asked:

"I wonder who could have told that tenderfoot all that trash about me?"

"Why isn't it all true?"

"In point of fact, yes; but if I was all that guy makes me out I ought to be in command of the army.

"Why I have not got money enough to buy land to bury the dead Indians he has made me kill, and you know, Wild Bill, I never drew trigger on white man or redskin except in the discharge of duty."

"I know that Billy but these reporters are the kind who paint the lily to improve it and never get things exactly as they are, and he just piled it on to make a lion of you."

"I'll make an example of him, if I cross his trail—why I'm ashamed to be seen."

"Nonsense, for it has made you a hero, and that pretty black-eyed girl."

"She'll cut my acquaintance certain."

"Wait and see, for women love men for the dangers they have known, at least I have read that in poetry somewhere."

But Will Cody would not leave his quarters until duty sent him forth, and then he found that he was indeed an object of admiration if not awe.

As a "feeler" to see how Miss Frederici had taken the article upon his "heroism," he sent her a bouquet of choicest flowers and promptly came a note of thanks and a request that he should call that evening and meet some friends.

"She's got too many friends," muttered Will as he recalled how many rivals there were in the field against him and he added:

"If the old man don't shoot me for a desperado, after that article, I shall be surprised—I wish I could take that newspaper liar with me, and I'd show him how I could dodge a bullet behind him."

But Will Cody went to the Frederici home to meet the "friends" referred to in the note and he blushed like a school girl when he was complimented upon his last career.

Instead of going for his "gun," the master of the house received him so cordially that he was emboldened soon after, won by the kind treatment of the maiden he now deeply loved, to ask for her heart and hand.

CHAPTER XXI.
HOME AGAIN.

With the hope of gaining a prize [illegible] is coveted, worth more to him than a colonel's commission, Will Cody returned to duty with a better feeling for the unfortunate "pen pusher" who had aroused his ire.

But with a promise from the lady he loved, that some day in the future she would become his wife, he asked to be again sent to the front, for he felt that as much as he wished to be near her, she would think more of him if he was in active service with an army in the field.

Knowing his worth as a Dispatch Bearer the General ordered him on courier duty where the danger of getting through was great, from one command to the other.

There he was engaged when the war ended and he received an "honorable discharge" at St. Louis,[31] where he again saw Miss Frederici, and the two talked over plans for the future.

But Will Cody was too anxious to place himself upon a firm financial basis, that would enable him to marry to remain in St. Louis, though he would gladly have done so.

He felt that his first duty was to his sisters, and he would return to his old home and visit them, after which he must enter upon work that would pay him well.

So to Leavenworth he went, and securing a horse he started for the old homestead, the scene of so many stirring incidents in his own life.

But if he owed a duty to the living, he felt that there was one due to the dead, and he turned his horse toward the burying ground where rested the ashes of his loved father and mother, a sweet sister and little brother.

He would first go to the resting place of the loved dead, as had been his wont in returning home from his expeditions and then to greet his sisters.

To the hill then he went and from there turned his steps homeward.

On the Military road he was sweeping along at a gallop until the house came in sight.

The flood of memories swept over him, and he recalled their first dwelling place in Kansas, the little cabin, then enlarged to quite a pretentious residence, and now the handsome mansion ahead of him.

His father had worked hard to establish himself in Kansas, and his mother had nobly aided him, and when her husband had passed away she but nerved herself the harder to bear the weight that bowed her down and in the end had triumphed, though she had broken down upon the pressure.

There was satisfaction in Will Cody's heart as he rode along, to feel that he had helped while in boyhood, youth and manhood to save the home and had worked hard and risked life to earn money to give to his mother.

So the thoughts crowded upon him as he drew nearer and nearer to the house.

His sisters knew that the war had ended, that the tattered "Bonnie Blue Flag was forever furled," and that their brother, who had borne well his part in the fierce struggle would soon be home, and they had planned how he would remain there and take charge of the house and farm.

But they did not know him when they so planned.

Nearer and nearer the home he drew, and forgetting the years that had gone by, he checked himself as he was about to do as in the long ago, whistle to call his faithful old dog Turk, that ever came with a glad bark of welcome to greet him.

Poor Turk lay in the grave Will had dug for him upon the hill overlooking Salt Creek Valley.

Hitching his horse to the rack he approached the house, his hand was upon the door, when suddenly it was thrown open and his sister Nellie sprung forward to greet him with a glad cry upon her lips.

The cry rang through the house, Will's own call was heard and in another moment his sisters were there to welcome the soldier back from the war.

"And we read what the papers said of you Will, and—"

"Oh Lord!" groaned Will, and Nellie paused, while May asked innocently:

"Don't you think, Will, the account was a little overdrawn?"

Will had learned a few choice expressions in the army and he felt like giving vent to them then and there, but wisely refrained and thought them over in connection with the St. Louis repartee.

But he was home again and he was happy, though his thoughts would linger upon the vacant chairs.

Then he told of Louise Frederici, and instead of being jealous of her, his sisters all welcomed her as a new member of the family. Julia—now Mrs. G. T. [sic] Goodman of North Platte—remarking in a low tone: "Now Will will stay at home."

CHAPTER XXII.
PURSUED BY INDIANS.

The prophesy of his sister Julia that Will would stay at home, was not fulfilled, for he fretted to be at work, and after a short stay at the old home he accepted an offer to drive a dove [sic] of horses from Leavenworth to Fort Kearney, the pay for which would be large.

So bidding good-bye to all at home he started out at once to lay the basis of his fortunes, with the fair maiden in St. Louis being a strong incentive to guide and urge him on.

He arrived safely at Fort Kearney, without "loosing [sic] a hoof" as the drovers expressed it, and there met his old friend Bill Trotter.

"Say, Billy you are quite the man I want," cried Bill Trotter upon nearing him.

"What can I do for you, Bill?" Will Cody asked.

"You know I am Division Stage Agent out here, and as some of the drivers have been picked off of late by Indians, as outlaws pretending to be redskins, for since the war there is a mighty large lawless element about, I find it hard to get a man who can handle the reins well and at the same time will take the chances of being killed.

"Now you are one who will take chances and I know how you can handle the ribbons, while you know the country well."

Will Cody did not snap at the offer as Bill Trotter had expected he would do.

He did not wish to drive stage, but to get work more congenial to him, and had thought of offering as scout at the Fort.

Bill Trotter saw that he hesitated and said: "I am authorized to offer big money, Billy, to the right man, though I do not name the sum if I can get them to go for less.

"Now it's different with you, and I'll give you the limit," and leaning forward he whispered the sum into Will Cody's ear.

It was so much more than he had expected, proved such a good chance to get a hug[e] sum laid by quickly, to place with what driving out the string of horses to Kearney had paid him, that he said promptly:

"I will drive, Bill."

"Good! now I feel O.K."

"When shall I begin?"

"From now."

"I'm ready now," and Will Cody only took into consideration the large pay he was to receive, never once thinking of the dangerous gauntlet he had to run to earn it.

Will started out the next morning with his coach, handling [sic, hand-ing] the reins over his six horses with a skill that showed he was an expert in driving, and once more had he begun life upon the plains.

His "run" was from Fort Kearney to Plum Creek, the stage trail running near the spot where he had had his first Indian fight when he was a boy, nearly a dozen years before.

It was a long, desolate and lonely trail, and the weather was bleak and cold, but he did not flinch from the hardships and kept a bright lookout for the dangers that might beset their [*sic*, his] way.

Learning at Plum Creek one day that prowling bands of Indians were about, he kept a bright lookout for them, and was rewarded by discovering a number skulking along through a fringe of willows bordering a small stream, to try and get in and head him off.

There were several passengers in the coach and he instantly called out to them to hold hard and get their weapons ready, as they were to have a race for life with Indians.

Then he "laid the silk" upon his horses and started for the ford, to reach it ahead of the Indians and make a stern chase of it.

He did reach the creek, gave his horses time for a few swallows of water, and then once more put them at their speed.

As he came out upon the plains he saw that he had fully five hundred yards lead of the redskins, and that his having been on the watch saved him, as otherwise they would have headed him off.

There were at least forty Indians in the band and they were lashing their ponies in full pursuit.

But the coach horses were running well, and though the stage swayed and rocked all was holding well and Will Cody could see that though the Indians were gaining, it was but slowly, and he hoped to reach the relay station, and with the aid of the two stock tenders there, stand them off, for he placed little dependence in his passengers who had already poked their revolvers out of the windows and fired at random.

As the station was still some distance away, and the Indians begun to draw near, Will Cody halted suddenly, took up his rifle and with quick aim sent a bullet back at them.

He had fired at the chief, and as he saw him topple from the saddle he sent his team on once more at full speed.

The lesson taught the Indians had been taken to heart by them, and they hung back, some of them remaining behind, a sure proof that their old chief had been either killed or wounded.

Hearing the fire the stock tenders dashed out to the succor of the coach, and Will Cody smiled as one of the passengers shouted:

"We fired on them, men, and drove them back."

Whatever the cause for their giving up the pursuit, they did so, and the coach rolled into Kearney without further adventure.

CHAPTER XXIII.
A CASE OF PREVENTION.

Many congratulations were showered upon Will Cody for his escape from the Indians, for it had been feared that he had been killed, with all his passengers, and troops had already been sent out to scour the country for the prowling bands.

No other adventure of note occurred to my hero while on the stage trail until the last of January, and what then happened I will relate.

All through the winter he had stuck to his dreary and perilous task, happy in the thought that he was adding each month to the money he had laid aside as the corner stone of his fortune.

Through blizzards of blinding snow and sleet, through rain and darkness he held on his way, and though no dangers had threatened of late he was ever on the alert to guard against a foe.

"Keep a bright lookout this run, Billy, for you carry a youug [sic] fortune in money, and it may be that some spy has already found it out," said Bill Trotter one day when he was starting.

"All right, sir, I'll save it if I can," was Will Cody's reply, and mounting his box he gathered up his reins and waited for the word to go.

He had not liked the looks of two of his passengers, the only ones he had, and keeping his eye on them he discovered that they were talking in low tones together, one of them constantly leaning his head out of the window to watch him.

Instantly he made up his mind as to his course, and if wrong he would take the consequences.

He did not intend to be shot in the back and have his assassins get the treasure he was carrying.

So halting on the trail, as though to fix his harness, he asked the men to look for a rope inside the coach, and as they handed it to him, he suddenly covered them with his revolver and called out:

"Hands up!

"You may be all right, but I doubt it, and I am going to be on the safe side and keep you from doing any harm."

Resistance was in vain, and the men were forced to submit to being tied, Will Cody the more convinced that they were road agents from the fact that one of them whispered to the other:

"It's all up with our game, Dave, but ther Cap'n will set us free and git it."

Will Cody pretended not to hear what was said, but it was a warning of more danger ahead.

The first relay station was not far away, so he drove rapidly on there and turned his prisoners over to the stock tenders to keep until his return, when he would take them back to Kearney with him and report what he had done.

With a fresh team he drove on his way once more, wondering just what those whispered words meant:

"It's all up with our game, Dave, but ther Cap'n will set us free and git it."

"Now that means in my opinion," mused Will Cody, "that the two have confederates in their intention to rob the coach, and had arranged to get it all for themselves, and I thwarted them.

"Then they felt that I would carry them on to Plum Creek and their comrades would hold me up, set them free and get the treasure.

"I may be wrong, but that is just how it looks to me, and if I am right there is trouble ahead for me sure.

"How to avoid it is the next question."

On his way he drove, lost in deepest reverie, until his face lighted up as an idea suddenly flashed upon him.

He was not one to plot long before his clever mind found a way out of a bad scrape.

Coming to a halt he took the mail and everything of volume he carried, along with his own watch and other valuables, and cutting open the box cushion he put all into it, so as to have it appear natural, throwing the straw away, and sewing up the cut again with a harness needle and thread he carried with him.

This done he again started his team ahead and drove on with a look on his face as though he had lost his last friend.

"I know where they will hold me up, if I am right in thinking they will.

"They'll be in the willows where the Indians so nearly headed me off last November."

That Will Cody was right in his prognostication was proven, for as he approached the growth of willows, growing thick on either side of the ford, several men with rifles leveled suddenly stepped into view, and one of them called out:

"We want what you carry, Cody.

"Resist, and you are a dead man!"

CHAPTER XXIV.
NERVE WHEN NEEDED.

When he saw the men step out from among the willows, and heard the threatening words of the leader, Will Cody was not in the least surprised.

It was just what he had feared would happen and had prepared for accordingly, as best he could.

Putting his foot upon the brake and at the same time drawing rein he brought his team to a halt and coolly asked:

"Well, what is it you are after?"

"We know that you carry a lot of the boodle and we are going to have it."

"You can't get blood out of a turnip, pard."

"What do you mean?" asked the leader of the outlaws in an angry tone.

"Did you expect your pards who took passage with me would leave anything?"

It was a random shot, uttered only on suspicion, but hit the target, for the leader called out:

"Ha! did they get to Kearney in time?"

"Yes, came through on the coach, and left with me, but showed their cloven hoof[32] mighty soon after."

"And what did they do?" anxiously asked the leader, coming closer, while his two comrades also peered forward.

"Just look through the old coach and see what they did—you're welcome to what you can find," and Will Cody gave a deep sigh as he patted his empty pockets.

With an oath the leader shouted out:

"They have tricked us and have run off with the booty themselves."

"Say, Cody, did they hold you up and rob you and the coach?"

"I know when the game is dead against me, pard, so I passed—

"Can't I borrow a gun, for this is no trail to travel unarmed."

"Where is your strongbox?"

Will Cody drew it out and revealed its emptiness.

A groan came in chorus from the men.

"Where was it they robbed you?"

"Some dozen miles back where you will find some straw in the trail."

"Did they have horses to meet them?"

"When I last saw them they were on foot."

Another curse and then the words:

"We must catch them, men."

Paying no more heed to the coach they ran for the willows and soon after dashed out on horseback back on the trail.

With a smile Will Cody drove on, and his horses were pushed hard on that run, for he did not wish to be overtaken, should the outlaws decide to return and search him.

But he got through to Plum Creek and safety and gave up the treasure he had saved by cleverness and nerve.

Expecting trouble upon his return he was on the look out for it, but he reached the spot where he had thrown the straw out of his cushion without seeing anyone.

The tracks of the outlaws' horses he saw there, and then they led away to the right as though some clue had been found by which to track the fugitive robbers, as they supposed them to be.

Arriving at the station Will Cody found that the stock herders had safely guarded his prisoners, and though it was risky work for him he determined to take them on with him.

He knew if the other three outlaws were on the trail and should halt him and discover how he had tricked them, his life would be worth precious little.

But, as was his wont, trusting in his Lucky Star "he took the chances."

By going on without the prisoners, if held up, they would not be in evidence against him, and he knew that his commandant of the fort would send out a guard after them.

But Will Cody loved to "play with fire" as it were, and with his prisoners in the coach and securely bound, he started upon the trail to Kearney.

As good fortune would have it he went through in safety, and Bill Trotter warmly wrung his hand when he told him of the ruse he had played to get the treasure through.

"Those two fellows ought to hang on your testimony, Billy, but I doubt if they will.

"They'll be sent back to some Eastern jail to rest up and get fat, and then be turned loose to do more damage," said the division agent, who added:

"A letter came for you in the last mail from the East."

Will Cody hastily took the letter to his quarters to read.

It was from St. Louis and when he had finished reading it he said:

"Yes, I will give up this rough life and go home."

CHAPTER XXV.
BECOMING A BENEDICT.

When Will Cody handed in his resignation to the division agent, it was with the greatest reluctance that it was accepted, Bill Trotter remarking that he had hoped he would remain all the summer.

The young stage driver said:

"It is just this way Mr. Trotter, I came West to make some money so that I could get married, and through your kindness I have gotten big pay and saved every dollar I did not need for actual expenses.

"I had a letter today, the one you gave me, from the lady I hope to marry and she urges me to give up this rough life, as she puts it, and return East and seek some other calling, and I intend to do so, just as soon as you get a man to put in my place, for of course I would not leave you in the lurch."

In due time a man was found and Will Cody started Eastward, going by stage and carrying a draft for a snug sum that he had to his credit.

He had written to Miss Frederici that he had obeyed her urgent request to give up a rough life, and having saved up a fair sum of money, he was carrying to St. Louis to claim the fulfillment of her promise to become his wife, as soon as he had first gone to his home in Kansas and arranged for their new home.

He further begged her to set a day when the marriage should take place and he would be on hand in ample time.

Having made his arrangements in Kansas, according to his wishes, Will Cody set out for St. Louis, the wedding day having been set for March 6th, 1866.

He was cordially received by the parents of the expectant bride, and she also gave him a welcome that repaid him for all he passed through in his struggle to get the means to make a Benedict of himself.[33]

The sixth of March came around none too soon for the happy young plainsman, and the wedding ceremony was performed at the residence of the bride's parents and before a large number of invited friends.

It is not my desire to compliment my hero or his wife, these long years after the consummation of that happy event, but wishing to be exact as an authentic biographer I must say that all reports agree in saying that no handsomer man or maiden ever stood up together than William F. Cody and his bride.

It had been arranged that they should depart for their home soon after the ceremony, and Will Cody had already engaged passage upon a Missouri River steamboat to go that way to Leavenworth.

A large party of friends went with the bride's parents to see them off on their voyage through life together, and many a fervent wish for happiness and a Godspeed was sent after them as the steamboat swung away from the wharf boat and started upon her trip, which was to prove a most eventful one to the young couple.

The boat had not gone many miles when Will Cody could not but see that he was an object of interest to a number of excursionists who were on board, and an interest that was showing itself in decided rudeness.

Entering into conversation with the gentleman who formed one of a party from Indiana, and who were en route to Kansas to settle there, Will asked him if he noticed the looks and comments made upon him by the excursionists.

"Yes, I have noticed it and was just about to speak to you about it," was the answer.

"May I ask if you know the cause, for my wife was so annoyed by their actions she retired to her stateroom," Will remarked.

"They appear to have no love for you."

"For what reason, as I do not recall having met any of them before."

"Frankly, Mr. Cody, I will tell you that they are a party from Lexington, Missouri, and they say that some of them recognize you as having been one of the Kansas Jayhawkers, one of what they called Jennison's Bushwhackers,["] replied the gentleman.

Without changing color Will Cody said to the Indianian:

"Yes, I am a Kansan, and am not ashamed of it.

"I was a soldier during the war and a scout in the Union Army.

"Also, I may add, I was in Kansas during the Border Ruffian War, as it was called, in 1856, though I was very young then, and now knowing who I am, doubtless explains the rude behavior of these people," and Will Cody went on to explain to the Indianian just what those early days in Kansas were, and how his own family had cruelly suffered under the persecution of bitter foes.

CHAPTER XXVI.
A FATEFUL BRIDAL TOUR.

When night came on the Missouri party got up a dance, but neither Will Cody or the Indianians who had appeared friendly to him, were invited to join them.

Seeing that the young bride seemed nervous and anxious, the Indianians determined to also get up a dance and Will Cody entered heartily into it, engaging the negro barber who played the violin, and a couple of waiters with their guitars.

This made excellent music and the "rival dancers" kept tripping the light fantastic as long as the Missourians saw fit to do so.

The next day the party of excursionists still maintained their rude behavior toward Will Cody, who at his wife's pleading took no notice of what was really meant for insults.

In the afternoon the steamer landed at a lonely place on the river, where there was no other habitation than a cabin for the keeper of the woodyard.

As the roustabouts were about to make the boat fast to "wood up," the men of the Missourian party gathered excitedly on the guards and just then up dashed a band of twenty horsemen all of them armed and yelling like mad.

Believing that his boat was to be attacked the Captain hastily called to the roustabouts to come aboard, something they needed no second invitation to do as the horsemen begun firing at them, while their leader dashed close up to the shore and called out:

"Where is that Kansas Jayhawker, for we have come for him.

"Come, men, follow me aboard and we will soon take him!"

The intention was good to do so, but the boat was already backing off under a full head of steam, dragging her huge gang planks along through the water, the negro crew too frightened to drag them aboard.

Shots were fired and yells of disappointment filled the woods, but the boat had gained a position of safety and pushed on up the river.

All this while Will Cody stood ready for a fight to the death.

He had gotten his revolvers from his state room and stood at the head of the steps to dispute the coming of his foes, for all had heard the cry of one of the men:

"We know you, Bill Cody."

But there were others there to protect the young plainsman, though at the time he knew nothing of it.

There were a party of old soldiers, half a dozen in number, and they had quickly rallied, determined to take a hand in the unequal conflict, while the men of the Indiana emigrants were also determined to stand by the gallant young scout.

And the young bride: She had not flinched under the ordeal, and when her husband had left the stateroom, telling her to remain there, she had followed, carrying along a new rifle he had been presented with while in St. Louis, thus proving herself well worthy to be a frontiersman's wife.

It was afterwards ascertained that some of the Missourians on the boat had been bushwhackers themselves, and recognizing Will Cody they had telegraphed ahead from a landing, telling them where the boat would stop to take on wood, and telling them to be there to take off "Bill Cody the scout."

Had the party gotten on board a fierce fight would have followed, and if not captured Will Cody would doubtless have been killed in spite of the battle for life that he would have made.

After the failure of the party on board to carry out their plot, they kept very quiet until they landed at Lexington to the great delight of the young wife.

Observing how his young wife grieved over the way these people had treated him, and realizing how she must feel, going into a new country with a husband whom men sought to kill, Will Cody decided to prove to her that he was not wholly friendless, that if he did have foes, the result of the bitterness still lingering in many breasts after the war, he also could boast of those who were glad to call him their friend.

When the boat reached Kansas City, therefore, Will telegraphed several friends in Leavenworth that he would arrive that evening with his wife.

Had the young plainsman gone on a personal "round up" of his friends in Leavenworth, he could not have been more successful in getting a crowd of good people to refute by their welcome that he was not the bad man the bushwhackers had painted him.

CHAPTER XXVII.
LANDLORD CODY.

If William Cody's young bride had been grieved by the treatment her husband had received on the trip on the Missouri steamer, all remembrance of it faded away under the grand reception given them upon their arrival in Leavenworth.

Driven to the home of his sister Eliza, who had married Mr. George Myers, a well known citizen of Leavenworth, Will Cody found that he numbered friends by the score, and in the reception tendered them the fair Louise found that her husband was a hero indeed and the lion of the hour, though he was unspoiled by flattery and most modest withal.

With a dread in her heart that Will might soon return to his adventurous life upon the plains, Mrs. Cody won from him a promise that he would seek some other calling where he was not daily in deadly peril.

Looking about for that other "calling," Will Cody suddenly conceived the idea that he would make the first-class "mine host,"[34] or in other words keep a hotel.

Forgetting that it has been said that a man must be gifted with certain virtues that fall to the lot of a few, to properly run a hotel, Will decided to make the venture.[35]

Perhaps he was prompted in this decision by a longing to dwell once more amid the scenes of his boyhood, to live under the same roof that had sheltered his loved mother and sisters, for the place in Salt Creek Valley once owned by Mrs. Cody was for rent.

It had been purchased by Doctor J. J. Crook, late a surgeon of the Seventh Kansas, was on the Military Road, delightfully situated, was large, comfortable and just the place for an inn.

So Will rented the commodious mansion, called it the "Golden Rule House," and put on the airs of a full-fledged landlord.

He looked rather young to "run a hotel," but inquires [sic] among the "oldest inhabitants" failed to find one who would assert that the table was not just what it should be, the rooms neat and comfortable and the landlord most popular.

If the truth must be told, Will's popularity as a landlord was too great, for he gave too many meals free, and a man without money always knew that the Golden Rule House was the very place for him to put up.

Applying the "Golden Rule" to too many, worked against himself to the detriment of profits, and the hotel did not prove the gigantic financial success its young landlord proudly hoped it would.

But the fever was upon my hero to again seek the life on the plains he had loved so well, and having an advantageous offer to sell out the Golden Rule House, he began the difficult task of convincing his wife that he was not built to run a hotel, but was a success as a Plainsman.

With regret Mrs. Cody yielded to his wishes to once more turn his face toward the land of the setting sun, and saw him depart with sorrow and forebodings of evil to again make a trial for fame and fortune in the old life he had led.

Settling up his affairs of disposing of the Golden Rule House, he turned over to his wife all his worldly goods, left her in a comfortable home and once more well mounted, armed and equipped turned his face westward.

Knowing that Saline, Kansas, was then the terminal of the track of the Kansas Pacific Railroad,[36] Will Cody made that his destination, hoping to find some profitable employment there.

On the way he went via Junction City, and there to his great delight, ran across his old and tried friend, Wild Bill.

The meeting was one of mutual pleasure, and Wild Bill told Will Cody that he was just the man of all others whom he wished to see adding:

"I have been thinking much of you of late, Bill, and intended writing to your old home to see if I could find you."

"Anything particular, Bill?"

"Well, I think so, and you will too, if you are of the same way of thinking as you used to be, that is, if marrying has not spoiled you."

"No indeed, it has made me more of a man, Bill, and I am out on a still hunt now hoping to find a way of making a fortune for my good wife.

"Do you know where there are any fortunes lying round loose that I can pick up?"

"Wish I did, Billy."

"But I can tell you where you can make a good living to begin with."

"I am your man."

"I am scouting for the Government, and am stationed at Fort Ellsworth,* and I happen to know that the Commandant is in need of good men as scouts, and you are just the man for the work, as I will vouch for, and the pay is fairly good.[37]

"Where are you going from here?"

"To Ellsworth."

"I'll go with you."

"Good! and you will go on duty at once, I am sure," answered Wild Bill.

So the two friends left Junction City together, and upon arriving at Fort Ellsworth Buffalo Bill found all to be just as Wild Bill had represented.

---

*Afterwards called Fort Harker. —The Author.

CHAPTER XXVIII.
ON SCOUTING DUTY.

Introduced by a man of Wild Bill's reputation, upon applying for a position as an army scout, Will Cody was flatteringly told by the commandant of Fort Ellsworth that he knew of his record, and was at once assigned to duty.

The country was by no means new to him, and he had to scout between Forts Ellsworth and Fletcher.

He had not been long on scouting duty before he showed that neither marrying or keeping a hotel had caused him to lose his nerve or cunning, two most requisite things for a scout to possess, and he soon won favor with his commanders, and the admiration of his comrades by his bold and clever work.

During the winter of 1866–67, he continued scouting duty and was at Fort Fletcher in the spring of 1867 when General Custer arrived there to accompany General Hancock[38] on an Indian expedition, many of the noted commanders of the Civil war having dropped back to their rank in the regular army and doing gallant service against redskins, as they had in fighting the men of the South.

At Fort Fletcher there it was that Will Cody first met the daring dashing Custer, the hero of a hundred battles, and formed for him a friendship that ended only with the death of the general at the head of the brave three hundred who fell with him fighting Sitting Bull[39] and his thousands of warriors.

While Will Cody was at Fletcher, the Post was drowned out by heavy floods of Big Creek, on which it stood.

As the water rose above the fortifications, it rendered them unfit for occupancy, so the fort was abandoned by the Government and a new fort founded, Fort Hayes[40] some distance to the westward, and located on the South Fork of [B]ig Creek.

Going with the forces to Fort Hayes, Will Cody still continued on scouting duty, his pay enabling [him] to send a snug sum home to his wife each month, while the services he rendered added more and more to his fame as a thorough Plainsman.

While returning to the fort one day from an extended scout Will Cody came upon Indian "signs" that told him that the hostiles were abroad in considerable force, and he was hastening to the fort to give the news when he discovered that they were on the trail between him and the Hayes.

Hardly had he made this discovery when he heard the sound of approaching hoofs, and he prepared for a fight or a footrace, when there dashed into view General Custer with only ten men as an escort, he having come up from Fort Ellsworth.

Riding up to the General he saluted, told him of his discovery, and that they could only reach Hayes by making a flank movement and a rapid ride of it.

"Our horses are tired scout, but lead the way," was the terse reply of General Custer.

With a salute Will Cody wheeled, put spurs to his horse and was off in a sweeping gallop, the General keeping close up and the small escort following and not at all liking the precarious situation in which they had found themselves, but thanking their lucky stars that they had met Scout Cody.

Without seeing a redskin, on the trail the scout led him, General Custer reached the fort in safety to discover, by the reports brought in by others that his escape had been a narrow one, for what would not the Indians had given to have captured or killed the "Blonde-haired Chieftain."

General Custer was on his way to Fort Larned, sixty miles distant and he wanted a guide at Hayes to take him across the country.

He also asked if Scout Cody could not be assigned to the duty, a request the commanding officer was pleased to grant, while he remarked:

"He is the very man I intended to send with you as guide, general, for you must take no more chances than are necessary, and Cody knows this country like a book and also just what to do in an emergency."

So Will Cody was ordered to report to General Custer for instructions, and was told by him to be ready early next morning as he wished to ride through to Fort Larned in one day.

When he reported in the early morning, Scout Cody was mounted upon a large mouse-colored mule, an animal he was much attached to.

Upon coming out to mount and observing the mule General Custer said:

"See here, Cody I am a fast rider and wish to go through as quickly as possible and I don't think that mule of yours can set the pace."

Will smiled and replied:

"Don't fear for my mule, general, he'll get there.

"That mule's a good one, and when you get to Larned we'll be with you."

The general laughed but said no more, and mounting the start was made.

CHAPTER XXIX.
A RIDE WITH CUSTER.

As they started upon the trail General Custer, always quick, anxious to get ahead, and untiring, rode at a pace, that kept William Cody constantly tickling the flanks of his mule with his spurs.

At one time the General shoved him so hard he begun to think he had made a mistake in riding the mule.

But, catching a gleam in the eye of Custer, he saw that he was crowding the mule to worry him into an acknowledgement of his error in having selected one of the long eared kind for such a ride.

At once he decided that the laugh should not be upon him.

He knew the great endurance of the animal he rode, and that he could if he would, make much better time and stick to it.

Cody also was aware that the pace the General forced him to go was a killing one for the horses and he smiled grimly as he looked at his mule and muttered:

"You'll get there, old long ears."

Fifteen miles had been gone over, and the ambitious, spirited thoroughbred General Custer was mounted upon still pulled hard on the bit, while the horses of the troopers kept up without waning.

Then the Guide said quietly:

"I think we can go a little faster, General."

"If your mule can stand it, Cody, go ahead," was the answer.

To the surprise of the General and his escort the mule began to draw ahead, he had gotten his second wind, and encouraged by the spurs of his rider, he set the pace after crossing the river and reaching the sound [sic] hills, where the traveling was heavy, which soon begun to tell on the horses, even the General's thoroughbred.

He had gotten warmed up to his work and the scout did not have to encourage him by a touch of the "persuaders."[41]

Half the distance to Fort Larned being passed General Custer called for rest and lunch, principally the latter, for he saw that all the animals needed [it], except the mule.

The scout, as they were preparing to mount again could not resist asking:

[Line omitted from the *Duluth Press* article.][42]

"Cody, you have a much better vehicle there than I thought you had, and I wish to add that his rider knows what he is about, for you are a fine guide, going by instinct, as the Indian does, seemingly, rather than by trails and landmarks."

William Cody was proud of this praise from a man like General Custer, appreciating it more from him than he would from any other Indian fighting officer on the Plains just then.

It was just four o'clock when the scout rode into Fort Larned, the General a short distance behind, but with a very tired horse, and the escort stretched out in a long string over a mile back, with animals that were used up for the day.

"Cody, that quadruped of yours is good for a return trip," said the general as he rode on to headquarters, and added:

"You brought me straight as the crow flies across the country, independent of trails, and I shall have need of your services again.

"If you are out of work at any time report to me and I'll fix you."

Knowing that his services were needed at Hays, and General Custer intending to remain for some time at Fort Larned, the scout, after having rested his mule and himself for a couple of hours, started on the return trail.

Night fell soon after he left the fort, but he had not forgotten that on his "way to" Larned, he had attracted General Custer's attention to signs of Indians about, the trail of a small band of mounted braves.

On his return he was careful not to run upon the band in the darkness, and was going cautiously along when a light in the distance suddenly flashed upon him.

At once he halted, but saw no more of it.

Riding back a few paces he beheld it again.

Then he lost sight of it once more.

He at once put on his thinking cap and decided that the light was visible only through some narrow space, so returning to the spot from whence he could see it, he dismounted, hitched his mule and made his way on foot straight toward it.

He went thus for half a mile to find himself in a pass between two sand hills.

The pass led into a little hollow, and there encamped in it about a small fire was a large band of Indians.

Their ponies were in the background, and the scout felt confident that in the pass lurked an Indian sentinel somewhere that he must be careful not to run upon.

But he knew that his duty demanded that he obtain an estimate of the number of Indians there, better than he could by the glimpse he had of them through the pass, and he was preparing to gain a position from whence to do so, when his mule gave forth a bray unequaled by any calliope the scout had ever heard on a Missouri steamboat.

CHAPTER XXX.
A MULE'S TALE OF WOE.

The wild, discordant note, of what the soldiers in the Civil war were wont to call a "Jersey canary bird," was a positive startler to William Cody, just as he had determined to slowly reconnoitre the Indian camp.

The bray of a mule is not musical at any time of the year, day or night, but to be sprung upon the solitudes of nature far from the habitation of man, in the depths of the wilderness, and in the drear [sic] hour of midnight was positively ear splitting and heart-rending.

If William Cody did not utter a damn with a great big D, his early training certainly had a firm hold upon him.

That he thought it, with all the "trimmings" I have reason to believe, and it was well perhaps that he did not get hold of just then what the general had called facetiously his "behicle" [sic].

As it was the scout had time to see that the bray of the mule acted like an electric shock upon the Indians, and as they sprung to their feet and hunted cover, throwing something on the fire to smother it, his experienced eye revealed to him a good guess at the number of hostiles.

It revealed another thing also, that he had been within twenty feet of an Indian sentinel, who was beyond doubt asleep on his post, for he leaped to his feet and sped into the valley like a deer.

Had the scout gone in that direction, as his intention had been, he would have fallen upon the redskin and that would have made him "tired," to use a slang expression.

Without awaiting to see the result, the scout made a run of it, straight for his mule.

As he saw again the cayotes [sic], birds and redskins were startled by the mule's bray, and it was repeated at intervals like minute guns at sea, as though belched forth as signals of distress.

And such indeed the high pressure notes were, for as William Cody drew near, running as lightly as a deer, he heard voices, and knew that the mule had fallen into the hands of the Philistines.[43]

That the two Indians did not see him, or hear him, was owing to the antics of the mule.

The animal had been captured in the timber and appropriated by the two redskins, and refusing to be comforted he tugged back on the reins and showed the firmness for which his kind have a record.

While hanging back with energy he brayed with fervor, and the two braves had their hands more than full in their attempt to lead him.

Then the scout recognized that his mule had been signaling to him, that it was his "tale of wo" [sic] that had accompanied the bray and that he had no desire to change masters.

The Indians were both mounted, but tug as they would they could not move the mule. [T]he "vehicle was stalled," and like Balaam's ass he would not move.[44]

Quickly the scout took a hand in the affair and a shot from his rifle emptied one of the saddles, while the second redskin dropped the mule's bridle rein and went off like a bow from an arrow [sic, arrow from a bow].

But the mule stood firm and greeted the appearance of the scout with a bay [sic] that had a ring of laughter and triumph in it.

With a bound the scout was in his saddle, just as an arrow cut into his coat from the Indian whom he had fired upon, and who lay wounded upon the ground.

But the scout did not return the fire, he would not fire upon a man when down, but with a word to his mule went flying away through the timber, while the shouts of Indians coming in pursuit echoed in his ears.

"Now, good mule, show your good qualities, and Custer is your name," cried the scout, and "Custer," from joy at his recapture, delight at his new name, and the prospect of food and rest on arriving at Fort Larned did show his good qualities, for he ran along like a racer, and as untiringly as a buffalo.

Not able to see their foe in the darkness the Indians scattered and pursued for a short distance and then gave up the chase, as the wounded redskin doubtless informed them that there was but one man to fear, and that the sound they had heard was simply the bray of a mule and not the warning notes of Gabriel's horn.[45]

CHAPTER XXXI.
BLACK BOYS IN BLUE.

Upon his arrival at Fort Hays, though it was before dawn, William Cody reported to the Commandant the safe arrival of General Custer at Larned, and the discovery he had made upon his return, with the important part the mule had played in saving him.

"I am sure the redskins are on the warpath, sir, for they are in full war paint, as I saw by the firelight, and I estimated them as being a couple of hundred in number, and fear we shall hear of them raiding some place soon," said William Cody.

"I shall order a force out in the morning, Cody, and if you are not too badly used up on your long ride, I should like to have you go as a scout of the expedition, and take your mule along if you wish," and the Colonel smiled.

"I'd like to go, thank you, sir, but I will leave the mule, for it don't do to go after Indians with the brass band accompaniment, sir."

"You are right.

"Go and get what rest you can, for the command will start in about four hours."

The scout hastened to his quarters, and, after caring for General Custer's namesake as he deserved, turned in and was at once lost to the world in dreamland.

He had just four hours rest, then a good breakfast, and mounting his best horse reported for duty to Major Arms [sic, Armes][46] of the Tenth Calvary [sic], who was to command the expedition.

The force was well mounted and armed, consisting of one Troop of Cavalry, colored, and a howitzer, also manned by negro soldiers.[47]

Just as the command was waiting for orders to move, a courier arrived in great haste bringing news that a band of Indians had raided the Kansas Pacific Railroad that was being built, killing six of the workmen, wounding others and running off over a hundred mules and horses, besides capturing a lot of commissary stores.

At once orders were given to Major Ames to depart and to push ahead with all speed in pursuit of the raiding redskins.

The Major was a hard rider, a severe disciplinarian, a daring fighter and a good soldier, and what he could stand he felt that his men must.

So he said:

"Go to the front, Cody, and as you heard where the Indians had struck the railroad, you are about the best judge where to head them off and I leave all to you until we strike them.

"Set the pace and a good one, for we must not have it said that we were slow in getting there."

With these instructions William Cody set a good pace, for he knew just what Major Ames wanted, and the negro soldiers were kept on the move with little rest until nightfall when they went into camp.

They were in the saddle again before dawn, and heeding no trails, the scout led them straight across country following his own ideas of where he would strike the Indians.

That morning they discovered a large band of Indians, upon the opposite side of the Saline River, showing how exact had been the scout's calculations as to where he would head them off.

They were about a mile distant, and had discovered the soldiers almost as quickly as the scout had seen them, and, confident in their numbers, came charging down upon them.

Not to show weakness, in the face of great odds, for the Indians far outnumbered his force, Major Ames placed his howitzer upon a rise, left a guard of twenty men with it, and then, crossing the river with the remainder of his command he met the Indians in their charge.

They had barely crossed the stream, when a terrific yelling was heard in their rear, and he at once realized that he had gotten between two fires, that there was another band of Indians besides the one now charging upon them.

"They are charging the gun, sir, and the negro soldiers are deserting it," cried the scout, and Major Ames saw that his Black Boys in Blue were really flying from the gun and hastening on after him.

"They have got the gun, sir," said William Cody, as he saw that the redskins had reached the cannon and were howling and dancing about it with commingled triumph and dread, for they did not know that it might prove a boomerang upon them, not understanding just what a "wheel gun" was, and half expecting to hear it "thunder" destruction upon them.

At once Major Ames, wheeled his troops and charged across the river to recapture the gun, the black soldiers, with

"Redskins to the right of them,
Redskins to the left of them,"

seeming strangely somber and silent.

But the gun was retaken, though not until the Indians had overturned it and broken the carriage, rendering it useless, and as the Indians were swarming down upon him, and his black troops were growing dangerously near a panic, Major Ames saw that to save a stampede he must beat back the redskins and then retreat.

The Indians came on with a rush and Major Ames, his officers and William Cody did all in their power to calm the Black Boys in Blue, and the charge was met in a way that sent the hostiles reeling back to shelter.

But instead of being cheered by the driving back of the Indians the negro troops were demoralized by the killing of six of their number and wounding of many more, Major Ames himself receiving a wound, while beating the redskins, the retreat was at once ordered, for the contest was too unequal.

It was with remarkable alacrity and eagerness that the negro soldiers obeyed the command to retreat, for with their faces toward the fort and their backs turned upon the foe they felt that instead of a fight it would be a race, and just then that was what they felt they could excel in.

CHAPTER XXXII.
HE OWNS THE TOWN.

In his retreat from the field Major Ames was in the position of Napoleon at Waterloo[48] for he wished night or reinforcements to come—he got the latter.

William Cody was ordered to the front to guide the way, and the colored troops wanted him to make better time, the same as he had in going to find the Indians, but the scout well knew that too fast time would lead into a run and a run into a stampede, and he held the crowding soldiers in check with a little good advice, backed up by his well-known way of doing just what he said he would.

So thus held back, and with Major Ames and his officers in the rear fighting off the pursuing redskins, the retreat was made in good order until night came on and checked the advance of the hostiles.

It was a hard, bitter ride of suffering that night with dead and wounded encumbering them, the scout leading straight as the crow flies through the darkness, the horses and men worn out, and the Black Boys in Blue looking constantly for Indians to ambush them on the way.

But at last, just at dawn, a beacon of hope beamed out ahead and the exhausted command arrived at Fort Hays, able only to boast of having found the Indians and escaped from them.

Major Ames was suffering from his wound, but was full of grit, and felt that had he commanded other troops he could have rendered a better account of his expedition, while one of the colored soldiers remarked:

"I don't want to foller that Scout Cody no more, fer he finds Injuns too easy ter please me.

"Why he know'd just whar ter jump 'em, on'y we was de ones as got jumped.

"I tinks I like handlin' a hoe better dan a gun, and drivin' a mule ter ridin' a hoss, leastwise in war times wid red Injuns."

This was about the sentiment of all the sable command.

But there was trouble still in store for the soldiers, for a threatened disease at the fort had broken out malignantly the day before, and already were five or six dying daily.

It was the cholera,[49] and the dread disease was making greater ravages in the ranks than the Indians ever had.

"Led by Destiny" : 211

But the Indians were by far the most feared by the Black Troops, and every one of them was ready to volunteer as a nurse to a cholera patient, rather than take the saddle on the trail of the redskins.[50]

Some days after the return of the disastrous expedition to Fort Hays William Cody was sent off on a special ride with dispatches for Fort Harker.

One of a group of colored soldiers who saw him ride off at twilight on his long and dangerous ride said:

"I wud'nt go on dat expedition fer money, no I wud'nt."

"De red Injuns will git dat fool white man's scalp yit afore he dies."

But William Cody laughed at the prediction and held on his way, reaching Fort Harker and delivering his dispatches in safety.

While detained at the fort he visited the new settlement of Ellsworth, three miles from Hawker [sic], and there met a man by the name of William Rose who had a contract from the Kansas Pacific Railroad for grading near Fort Hays.

He had come to Ellsworth to purchase stock, as what he had had been run off by Indians.

Mr. Rose told the scout that he had some intention of laying out a "farm" on the west side of Big Creek, near the fort, and asked him for his views regarding the enterprise.

The answer was that he thought it was a "big thing," and Mr. Rose at once proposed taking the young scout into partnership with him.

As it takes two to make a bargain, and the two were there and both of them of the same opinion, the plan was soon arranged to buy out the town, build a store and saloon there and then wait for events to shape themselves.

Though he had sent a generous sum each month to his wife, whose letters were ever a bright era in his eventful life, William Cody had also managed to lay aside for a rainy day some money in the Paymaster's hands, and with this he bought such articles as were needed in a frontier store, hired an engineer to survey the site and stake it off in lots, put up the cabins and then gave it the classical name of Rome, perhaps with the hope that all roads must lead there.

Just to encourage settlers, Messrs. Rose & Cody, proprietors of the "town," donated lots to anyone who would build upon them, but it was a case where "skimmed milk masquerades as cream,"[51] for they kept the best ones to sell.

Rome soon threatened to be another Eternal City, from the way it grew, in fact might have deserved the name of Infernal City, as there was a saloon and gambling dive for every cabin otherwise occupied.

Within a month there were two hundred cabins there, and the delighted proprietors saw that "Rome had begun to howl."

A hotel was full blast within another month, half a dozen stores, blacksmith shops and the saloons keeping pace with all other improvements, while the citizens already begun to put on airs.

As deaths occurred with remarkable regularity from "gun shot fever" a graveyard was "incorporated" and Rose & Cody owners at large of Rome already begun to loom up as prospective millionaires.

One day Rome had a visitor in the person of Doctor W. E. Webb.

He was a good looking, pleasant-spoken gentleman who went to the store of Rose & Cody, and said he had come to ask if they did not wish a partner in their enterprise.

"No, a partner was just what they did not want."

Then he told how he was "locating" towns for the Kansas Pacific Railroad, and as Rome was already thriving, he wanted them to give the company a show.

But they said that they had the only good site for a town in that neighborhood and the railroad must come that way.

"Then I must start another town near you," said Doctor Webb.

He was told to first start himself and then the town.

CHAPTER XXXIII.
THE FALL OF ROME.

In speaking today of his venture in founding a town, William Cody says he made the mistake of his life, in refusing to take in a railroad as third partner in the enterprise.

Having the power to do so Dr. Webb located another town within sight of Rome and named it Hays City.

He also gave the citizens of Rome to understand that Hays City's greatness would be assured, for there the railroad would run, its shops be established, and in fact the place would become the great metropolis of Kansas in time, only he did not mention the time, fortunately for his reputation as a prophet.

The result of all this was that Rose & Cody saw a perfect stampede from Rome to Hays City.

Those who had built stores, saloons and homes in Rome carted them over to Hays City to set them up again.

Rome fell, and the two proprietors of the deserted village sat in front of their store one bright summer morning and looking with grim humor upon the demolition of the last building save their own.

"Pard, we'll move too," said William Cody.

"Where, Bill?"

"Well, we'll get out of Rome and go and complete our contract for grading that five miles of road westward of Big Creek for the Kansas Pacific."

"All right, Bill, we'll do it; but what will we do with Rome?"

"We'll leave it right where it is, for nobody will steal it, rest assured," and taking the hopeful side of the case once more William Cody continued:

"You see, they may not be able to get the water they wish in Hay's [sic] City and be glad to come this way after all."

"May be so: but what will you do with your wife and child[?]"

A short while before the fall of Rome—Kansas—Mrs. Cody had come on to visit her husband, bringing with her a little miniature of herself in the form of a baby girl, which the grandfather had named Arta.[52]

He had fitted up a cabin near the store for them, and once more his wife thought he would be willing as a heavy landowner and prospective millionaire, to give up the life of a scout and settle down.

But the downfall of Rome caused him to feel that he must almost begin life over anew, and that he might not give any cause to his wife for worry, he thought it would be a good idea for her to go to St. Louis on a visit, carrying Arta, who had been born in Leavenworth, to show to her parents and friends there.

So Will Cody said, in response to the question of Mr. Rose: "I'll tell you what I'll do, I'll send them to St. Louis."

"A good idea, Bill, for though your wife adopts herself to circumstances, this wild country is no place for her."

So Mrs. Cody and little Arta were driven to the nearest station by the ex-millionaire on their way to St. Louis, and then he returned to settle down to hard work once more.

Just to see how matters were going in Hays City he went over on a visit and was warmly welcomed by Dr. Webb, whom he later liked very much as a fine fellow, in spite of his having brought him down by one fell blow from prospective riches to a poor contractor.

While carrying on his Railroad grading contract William Cody devoted much of his time to buffalo hunting, and Doctor Webb was only too glad to be the companion of the scout, for whom he had really formed a strong attachment.

The hunting was not done merely for pleasure on the part of the hunter, but to procure meat for the laborers in his employ, Mr. Rose superintending the work.

On one occasion while out on a buffalo hunt, accompanied by Dr. Webb, the two met with an adventure that very nearly cost the lives of both.

Doctor Webb was mounted upon a beautiful bay which he had brought from the East, and a very fleet animal of much endurance while my hero rode his own splendid buffalo hunting horse which he had named Brigham.

When about ten miles from Hays City the hunter scout saw a band of Indians riding rapidly to get between them and the town, and he at once pointed them out to the Doctor.

"It is a race, Doctor, to prevent them from heading us off.

"Come!"

With the command the two let their horses out at full speed, for they saw that they had a mile to ride, while the Indians had one third less that distance.

Over the plains the two horses ran side by side, the Indians heading for the same point, and lashing their ponies hard to reach there first, thus cutting the hunters off, and forcing them away from the town and between themselves and another band that appeared in sight.

It was a hard, close race, but the two white men passed the line ahead of the redskins by a hundred yards, and continuing on received their scattering fire unhurt.

Failing to entrap or kill their foes the redskins vented their disappointment and hatred in wild yells and rode off towards the Saline River.

On the ride back Doctor Webb said:

"See here, Cody, as I made Rome 'howl,' I wish you and Rose to accept a couple of lots each from me in Hays City and make that your home."

The scout thanked the doctor for his generous offer, but told him that just then he had about as much land as he cared to own, in fact a "city site to sell."[53]

CHAPTER XXXIV.
BETTER THAN HE LOOKED.

As horses were needed in camp one day, William Cody treated his splendid horse Brigham to a suit of harness and attached him to a scraper to aid in grading.

But Brigham considered himself insulted, in being forced to work thus, and was resenting the indignity tooth and hoof, when one of the men called out that there was a herd of buffalo in sight.

Meat had been scarce in camp of late, and anxious to kill and bring in a few buffaloes the scout called out to one of the men to hitch two horses to a wagon and follow him.

Brigham was instantly stripped of his harness, the scout seized his rifle—an improved breech-loading needle gun he had named Lucretia Borgia[54]—and springing upon his horse without a saddle was off in the buffalo chase.

He had gone but a short distance when he saw appear over a rise a party of five officers.

They proved to be a party of new arrivals at the fort, and had left there to kill a few buffalo, as they had also sighted the herd.

The scout quickly took in their ranks, from their shoulder straps, one being a captain and the other lieutenants, and though being unknown to any of the five, he concluded to be of assistance to them in the hunt.

"Ho, my friend, are you after those buffaloes?"

"Yes sir, for we are short of meat in camp and I thought I'd give them a try."

They scanned Brigham, who was a great deal better man that he looked, gazed at the blind bridle,[55] no saddle, the scout's general make-up, just as he had come from work, and supposing him a greenhorn the Captain asked:

"Do you expect to catch those buffaloes on that gastric[56] steed[?]"

The scout replied that he hoped to, by pushing hard on the reins.

"You'll never do it, for it takes a fast horse and a good hunter to kill buffalo."

The scout put on a look as though he had been caught stealing the whole herd and asked innocently:

"Can I go along with you, sir, and see you kill them[?]"

"Yes, come along with us, for we are going only for the sport of it, and all we wish is the tongues and a tenderloin or two, and you can have the balance."

"Thank you, sir," was the reply and the party rode on until they again came in sight of the buffaloes.

There were eleven of them, and about half a mile distant.

Away dashed the five officers, as though they had a sure thing of bagging the whole lot; but the scout had already noticed that the buffaloes were making for the creek for water, and understanding thoroughly the nature of the animal he was well aware that it would be very difficult to turn them from their direct course.

He therefore started for the creek to head them off, the officers riding more directly toward the herd.

The officers were soon sighted by the buffalo, who quickened their pace, while Cody, having gone off obliquely had them pass him at a rush, and not a hundred yards away, their pursuers being some distance in the rear.

Then the man who had already made a name as a buffalo hunter decided to show those officers that he was not altogether a tenderfoot, and he took the blind bridle off Brigham who at once understood that he was out for buffalo.

One of the best trained buffalo hunting horses on the plains Brigham jumped to his work at tremendous speed, and was soon alongside of the animal furthest in the rear.

Then old "Lucretia Borgia" was brought into play by the great hunter and the buffalo fell dead.

Then Brigham overtook the next, and the next, until twelve shots had been fired by William Cody and the eleven buffalo lay dead on the plain in a long string.

Springing to the ground as the officers came up, not one of them had had a shot, while Brigham stood patiently by, William Cody saluted politely and said:

"Gentlemen, permit me to present you with all the tongues and tenderloins you wish from these buffaloes."

The officers were utterly astounded, and the captain, whose name was Graham, said:

"Say, who and what are you?"

"My name is William Cody, sir."

"By Jove, you are Bill Cody the scout I saw at Fort Harker—I didn't recognize you before," cried Lieutenant Thompson[57] and he presented the Buffalo Hunter to the other officers, all of whom were from the Tenth Cavalry.

Captain Graham then remarked:

"That horse of yours is a goer and a stayer, Cody, much better than he looks.

"In fact you and your horse both did us up beautifully, but we forgive you for what we saw you do, for I did not believe a man without a saddle or bridle could kill a herd of buffalo on one run—if there had been a hundred you'd have gotten them all.["]

CHAPTER XXXV.
LEADING A HOT CHASE.

Any feeling the officers might have had at losing their buffalo killing was compensated for in seeing the achievement of William Cody as a hunter, and Captain Graham and the others were struck with his modest assertion that Brigham did the work, he simply having to pull the trigger when the well trained horse placed him alongside of each animal, which he did with the human appreciation of the situation, as the scout had no bridle rein to guide him with.

The scout also explained how Brigham would not leave a buffalo if he did not fall at the first fire.

The wagon coming up which the scout had ordered a workman to follow him with, he skillfully butchered his meat, presenting the tongues and tenderloins to the officers, with whom he rode to the fort, Captain Graham telling him that he was to be stationed at Hays to be sent on scouting expeditions and wished to secure his services.

Although very busy with his grading William Cody was too fond of the life of a scout to refuse, and he accordingly promised Captain Graham that he would go with him when he wished him to do so, adding:

"It may be sooner than you think, Captain, for I have seen signs of Indians about and know that they are threatening mischief."

That he was right was proven that very night, as the redskins raided the camps and run off a number of horses.

At once the scout sprung upon Brigham, ready for action, and rode over to Fort Hays reporting the raid.

Captain Graham and Lieutenant Emrich[58] one of the buffalo hunters that did not get a shot, were at once ordered out, with one hundred colored cavalrymen to pursue and capture the horses if possible.

This particular troop of black skins had never been on a trail after red skins, but led by white skins thought that they could, as a colored sergeant remarked:

"Jes' eat dem Injuns up."

The scout felt a little dubious, remembering the experience of Major Ames, but picked up the trail and followed it, though none too rapidly for the eager black boys which Captain Graham, a brave, impetuous and fine officer, said:

"Don't let it be another buffalo hunt, Cody, for I wish to give my colored troopers a show."

"They'll get a chance, sir," was the reply, and the scout soon after discovered that the Indians had camped at the Saline river only long enough to feed and water their animals, then pushing on toward the Solomon.

Once they were beyond the Saline they made no effort to cover up their trail, and so the scout led on at a rapid pace, but none too fast for the black braves who were pursuing the red ones.

Upon drawing near to the column the scout reported that he was sure the Indians had camped there, and were not looking for pursuit to be pushed so far, and advised Captain Graham to go into camp for rest and supper while he went on alone and found out just where they were.

In about two hours he returned and reported to Captain Graham that he had found their camp, they had the stolen horses with them, and numbered about two hundred braves.

The scout also reported that he could lead the troops almost upon the camp, and thus drive them down into a bend of the river and:

"Wipe dem from off of de yarth," as a corpoal [sic] said.

It was agreed to wait until the moon rose, and then the march begun.

But one of the black warriors, either from a desire to be humane and let the Indians be warned to get out of their way, or be the first man to fire a gun, fired off his carbine before the force was within half a mile of where the scout wished to lead them, and the result was a perfect stampede.

The Indians at once sprung for their horses and escaped, while the colored troops wishing to scare them into going faster, blazed away as though they were resisting a charge.

Captain Graham swore by nabe, Lieutenant Emmick came in on the chorus in the same strain, and William Cody, though deeply chagrined enjoyed the fun.

"Follow me!" shouted the Captain, anxious to catch up with the redskins.

The sudden charge set the colored troopers going pell-mell, the horses of some of them ran off, and fearing that they would be scattered worse than the tribes of Israel[59] the Captain ordered the bugler to sound the recall.

It was daylight before some of the colored warriors found their way back to camp, and then Captain Graham told the scout to again prick [sic] up the redskins['] trail and he would follow them.

But that wild charge of the "Black Brigade" ha[d] given the redskins a scare that kept them going, and having only a day's rations along, the return was ordered, for the horses were also nearly used up.

As for the black trooper who had put the redskins to flight and spoiled all, Captain Graham made him dismount and walk back to the fort as a punishment.

William Cody as they neared the fort and Captain Graham rode up and joined him, said:

"There is no man I would rather follow than you, Captain, but whatever fighting the colored troops may have done in the civil war, out here fighting Indians they don't seem to make a success of it, and I may add that very few white soldiers are fitted for warfare against the redskins."

"You are right, Cody, the Indian does cause terror to colored troops, and a command of white soldiers must be long on the frontier before they understand fighting redskins."

Upon his return to Fort Hays William Cody found a most important communication awaiting him, one that stamped him ever after with the name of "Buffalo Bill."

CHAPTER XXXVI.
WINNING THE NAME OF BUFFALO BILL.

The communication which William Cody found awaiting him, upon his return from the unsuccessful pursuit of the Indians with Captain Graham, was a letter from the Messrs. Goddard Brothers, the contractors who boarded the hands working on the Kansas Pacific road.

The railroad was being pushed ahead with great rapidity, and twelve hundred men were employed in the work.

As the Indians were giving considerable trouble it was no easy task to obtain meat with which to feed a small army of workmen, and buffalo hunters were engaged to furnish fresh meat for the employees, it being equal to stall-fed beef.

Having heard of William Cody's skill as a buffalo hunter, they made the offer to engage him to hunt for them, and on account of dangerous and hard work involved they agreed to pay him five hundred dollars a month.[60]

For this sum he was to furnish twelve buffaloes a day, which as only the hindquarters and hump, with the tongue of each animal were taken, made a large supply of meat, causing a ride of many miles in search of game, the butchering and especially looking out that he didn't lose his scalp, as the redskins swarmed through the country.

The hunter also had to look out for the man that drove the wagon that followed him to carry back the meat, and so after all the pay was none too large.

Leaving Mr. Rose, his partner, to complete his grading contract, William Cody begun his career as a professional buffalo hunter.

As a boy he had won the title of Buffalo Billy for his skill in killing the great prairie monarchs, but now he was to make what had formerly been sport, a business.

Entering upon his duties he faithfully did his share of the work, and was not very long in making a name as a famous buffalo hunter, for he entered into the work as he always did with everything he undertook, with energy, skill and determination to carry it through.

In this hard and dangerous work passed a year and a half of William Cody's life, and pushing ahead with the advance workers on the railroad, exposed to the greatest hardships, often having to fight for his life, or a race for it from Indians, he never once gave up the contract, and was known all along the trail as "Buffalo Bill."

That he deserved the title will be frankly acknowledged when I state that in the year and a half he was engaged as a buffalo hunter by the Kansas Pacific Railroad he killed four thousand, two hundred and eighty buffaloes (4,280) for he kept a strict tally and never once left the camps without fresh meat.[61]

It was during this time that William Cody also won that just title of "Champion buffalo killer of the plains," as he entered into a match with the man who was said to be his superior in that kind of work.

That man was Billy Comstock, a noted scout, guide and interpreter, a life-long plainsman with a fine record.

He was chief of scouts at Fort Wallace, Kansas, and the officers who knew him and Cody as well, arranged a match between the two men.

The hunt was to be for one day of eight hours beginning at 8 a.m. and ending at 4 p.m.

The purse was to be five hundred dollars and the man who killed the greatest number of buffaloes was to be the winner, and no shots allowed save on horseback.

The hunting ground was some score of miles from Sheridan, Kansas, and a number of officers, soldiers, frontiersmen and railroad hands were there to witness the two giants battle for victory.

There was besides, an excursion party of ladies and gentlemen from St. Louis to witness the match, it having been advertised that a train would be run to the buffalo country to witness it, and having written his wife to come, William Cody was delighted to find that she had done so, and had brought little Arta along also, the latter then developing into a very beautiful little girl of two years.

The buffaloes were very plentiful, and it was agreed that both hunters should enter the same herd at the same time and kill at will, referees being appointed to follow each man and keep count of the number slain.

The onlookers came in the rear in wagons and on horseback, keeping out of sight until the hunters dashed into the herd.

William Cody was mounted upon Brigham, than [sic] which no better buffalo horse ever wore saddle, and carried his needle gun "Lucretia Borgia," calibre 50.

Comstock was mounted upon his favorite buffalo horse, and carried a Henry rifle of large calibre, and a very rapid fire gun.

At last the herd was sighted, and it was a large one.

The two hunters rode [side] by side and their referees followed close in their rear, also well mounted.

When near enough word was given to go ahead and the two champions made a dash for the herd Comstock on the left, Cody on the right.

CHAPTER XXXVII.
THE CHAMPION.

As is their wont, when chased by more than one hunter, the herd divided as they saw the two horsemen after them one bunch going to the right, the other to the left.

Comstock took the bunch to the left, his referees following, while Cody spurred for the herd on the right, with his referees keeping well up.

"Buffalo Bill," as I must now call him, had a talent in killing buffalo, and it was to get them circling, by riding at the head of the herd and killing their leaders.

This he did and he soon got them running round and round in a circle, and in his run he killed thirty-eight, dropping them fairly close together.

Comstock meanwhile riding at the rear of the herd drove them before him and in his run brought down twenty-three, strung out over three miles of prairie.

The Excursionists from St. Louis coming up set out their lunch, with wines, and it was while enjoying it that another herd of buffaloes was sighted.

It proved to be a small bunch of cows and calves, quicker however in their movements than the bulls, and dashing in among them the two hunters scored on their run eighteen for Cody, fourteen for Comstock.

Pushing ahead another herd was discovered and Buffalo Bill, with the score standing fifty-six to thirty-seven, daringly pulled the bridle and saddle off his horse, and once more the two hunters dashed forward to bring down their big game.

In spite of having no bridle on his horse, or saddle either, Buffalo Bill turned the herd and in full sight of the large crowd brought down thirteen buffaloes, finishing the third run with sixty-nine to his credit.

Comstock came in on this run with forty-six all told as his score, thus losing the match to Buffalo Bill who won by a large margin.*

Billy Comstock and his backers gracefully yielded the palm to Buffalo Bill as the "Champion buffalo hunter of the plains."†

This match made the name of Buffalo Bill famous the country over.

The name of Buffalo Bill became a Trade Mark, as it were to William Cody, and today is known throughout the wide world, while in all that he has passed through it has been the open sesame to success.

As scout he became well known, then his past daring deeds being told in the papers, and his services appreciated even by the military were also acknowledged by the public to be of a most valuable nature.

When he had won such fame that he became the hero of border verse and romances, the name of Buffalo Bill was used in fiction more than that of any other living man, and always, I may say, with the foundation of truth for what was said of him.

Brought before the public through his deeds and romances written of him, Buffalo Bill was induced to go upon the stage and live over the

---

*The heads of the buffaloes thus slain were dressed and mounted by the Kansas Pacific Co., and were sent about the country as an advertisement, and some are still preserved in ticket offices and hotels. —The Author.

†Billy Comstock was killed some time after near Big Spring Station, Kansas, by Indians who pretended friendship for him and a scout by the name of Grover who was with him. Grover, though severely wounded, made his escape, while poor Comstock was killed and scalped. —The Author.

scenes of his life on the plains before the footlights, and here also he won success.[62]

Prevailed upon to write of the scenes he knew so well he drifted into authorship, and his romances have sold enormously, for there was the brand of truth upon them.[63]

So has the Kansas boy made the name of Buffalo Bill famous, and the dreams of his youthful years have been realized and upon everything he has undertaken, led by the destiny he firmly believes that has shaped his life, he has put the stamp of success.

Remaining a short time on the frontier with her husband, after the buffalo slaying match with Comstock, the young wife and little Arta again returned to Leavenworth, for the duties of the husband and father kept him constantly in the saddle and away from his cabin home, and he realized how lonely it must be for his loved ones there in that drear [sic] land.

As for Mrs. Cody she had come to realize that she could not stem the tide of destiny that bore her husband onward in the adventurous cause he had chosen in which to make a name.

He was a born frontiersman, and other callings held no attraction for him so yielding to the inevitable she bade him continue on in the path he had chosen to follow, lead where it might, and once more she turned her face toward civilization, leaving him to the bivouac of the plains.

CHAPTER XXXVIII.
SCALP HUNTERS.

Some little time after his match with Comstock, Buffalo Bill met with an adventure that very nearly ended his career then and there.

He had ridden over to the valley of Smoky Hill river, where game was plentiful, and giving Brigham a rest was gazing upon the beautiful scenery, for the beauties of nature have always won his ardent admiration, when a band of thirty Indians came dashing out of a covert directly for him.

Realizing that his only chance of escape was to make a run for it, he mounted Brigham and started upon his race for life.

But he had given his horse a hard ride in going over, and he saw that he was tired while he also discovered that the Indians were exceedingly well mounted.

After a run of three miles the Indians had closed up the gap considerably, at least nine of them had, for they were bunched together while the others were strung out in the rear according to the speed of their horses.

Then one on the spotted horse, a chief by his war bonnet begun to come on more rapidly than the others, and, armed with a rifle he sent a bullet after the flying scout that came dangerously close to his head.

As the chief had opened the ball, Buffalo Bill accepted the gauge of battle, wheeled Brigham, raised his rifle and covered the gaily painted redskin.

"It's his trade, and I won't do it."

"The horse is what I fear most," he muttered, and lowering the muzzle of his rifle a few inches he pulled the trigger.

Down went the spotted horse and his rider had a bad fall, while Buffalo Bill sped on again.

But the others now spurred more madly on, and a brave springing from his saddle as they came up with the chief gave him his horse, and a good one.

Brigham did his best, but the horses of the redskins were fresh and they steadily gained, the chief again forged to the front.

Riding in a bee-line to the point where the railroad ended, and where two companies of soldiers were stationed as a guard, protecting the workmen, Buffalo Bill hoped to reach within hail and there make a stand, for Brigham was steadily failing.

A fringe of timber on a creek appeared ahead and as the scout drew nearer to it he saw that there were friends there, for some men were out with a wagon gathering wood for the camps, and they saw him coming and determined to go to his rescue.

"Keep hidden and we'll give them a surprise," he shouted, and this they did, the scout springing off of Brigham as soon as he got in the shelter of the timber.

Suspecting no aid, and believing that their foe had continued on his flight, the chief led his braves on with a rush, until they were met by four rifle shots from the timber, and three saddles were emptied and one pony fell.

The chief had fallen by the bullet of the scout, who called out, as the others fled and his rescuers were preparing to fire again:

"Let them go, pards, for they are no longer dangerous."

As he turned to look after Brigham hoofs were heard and Captain Nolan[64] of the Tenth Cavalry dashed up, having been scouting in the timber and hearing the shots rode at full speed to the scene.

"I want you, Cody.

"One of you men give your horse to Scout Cody," called out Captain Nolan, and leaving Brigham to be cared for by the dismounted soldier Buffalo Bill took his horse and rode to the front to lead the chase after the Indians.

The soldiers' horses were fresh, those of the Indians tired, and in the running fight that followed for a dozen miles eight braves fell.

Then Captain Nolan started back to camp, and upon arriving there the scout was glad to see Brigham quietly grazing and none the worse for his hard run that saved his master's life.

But Buffalo Bill having failed to get his supply of buffalo meat, mounted a fresh horse, and accompanied by a man by the name [of Scotty], who drove the wagon and helped him butcher the meat, started out again to supply the commissary.

He was successful in finding a herd and having killed fifteen buffaloes they secured what they needed, placed it in the wagon and started for camp, as night would soon be coming on.

They had arrived within half a dozen miles of camp when they saw some two score Indians appear over a rise and make for them.

Well mounted as he was Buffalo Bill could have made his escape, but would not leave Scotty, so he at once decided to act for the safety of both.

To think with Buffalo Bill was to act, and he at once sprung from his saddle, the mules were unhitched and tied to the wagon, the buffalo meat was thrown out and piled around the wheels as a breastwork, and then the two men crept into the little fort to fight it out.

CHAPTER XXXIX.
A SIGNAL OF DISTRESS.

Buffalo Bill and Scotty, calm and determined, stood at bay, or rather lay at bay beneath the wagon, protected by the buffalo meat.

The wagon had been driven over a buffalo wallow[65] which gave that much better protection and the two mules and horses had been fastened so securely that they could not break away and if killed would be that much better protection to the two men.

Scotty had perfect confidence in his companion, relying wholly upon him to extricate them both from their dangerous situation.

Too often had Buffalo Bill been in like danger to be moved by it now, and his only thought was to make a good fight for it.

Hardly had they become comfortably located when the Indians came charging down upon the little fort with yells that were terrible to hear and firing as they came.

The two mules and horse struggled to get away, but were quickly killed by the fire, while the defenders waited until their foes came well up and then opened with their rifles and an extra gun the scout always had taken along in the wagon.

Their revolvers were thus brought into play and the galling fire caused the redskins to halt in their charge and begin to ride around the wagon.

With their animals slain and night near at hand, Buffalo Bill knew that their foes were in sufficient number to get the best of them if help did not come, and he determined to put into practice an expedient he had agreed upon, in case of just such trouble as they were in, with the officers, soldiers and workmen.

This was to build a signal fire, seeing the smoke by which their friends would learn of their trouble and send aid.

So he lighted a newspaper he had in his pocket, threw it out upon the prairie grass, and a dense smoke ascended as the fire spread.

The Indians seemed to think that the firing had ignited the grass, and still kept peppering away from windward, driven by the burning grass from the other direction.

They were promptly replied to, and now and then a shot told upon a brave.

The signal fire was seen in the camps, a relief party at once started out, and just at sunset came in sight where all but five Indians took to flight, those five remaining to be registered under the name of good Indians, as General Sherman always designated dead Indians.[66]

Horses were hitched to the wagon and the meat was carried to camp, a trifle heavier for the arrows and bullets shot into it.

The Kansas Pacific Road having pushed out as far as Sheridan, it was decided by the company not to build it any further just then, and Buffalo Bill found himself like Othello, with his occupation as buffalo hunter gone.[67]

But he at once determined upon a field in which he could render better service, and that was more congenial to his taste, that of scout.

The Indians had become so troublesome that a general war was threatening all along the western borders, and General Sheridan had come in person to direct troops in putting it down.

The General had taken up his quarters at Fort Hays, and Buffalo Bill at once reported for duty as a military scout.

He was told to report within a given time at Fort Larned, to Captain Dangerfield [sic] Parker,[68] commandant, and this allowed of his first going to Leavenworth where he wished to secure a little home for his wife so that his family would be comfortable.

As many officers wanted to buy Brigham, as a noted buffalo hunter, the horse was put up to raffle off, at the suggestion of several, all thus had an equal chance.

There were ten chances at thirty dollars each, and the grand old horse was won by Mr. Ike Bonham, a gentleman from Wyandotte, Kansas, and I may as well state here that his owner entered him in a running race for a purse of $250.

Many of Mr. Bonham's friends laughed at what they call his "dizzy steed," entered for a four mile race, and, as I have made known, Brigham was no beauty; but far better than he looked.

When the races started, and there were a number of them several led Brigham for a mile or more; but then the old buffalo hunter warmed up to his work and when they had gone three miles he was the guide, and his rider then let him out and rode to the hotel, the end of the race in Wyandotte, a quarter of a mile ahead of the nearest horse to him.

Then the news went around that the horse was "Brigham, William Cody the scout's great buffalo hunter."

With his old equine comrade in good hands Buffalo Bill went to Leavenworth, settled his family in a comfortable home, and then started for Fort Larned, where he reported for duty to Captain Dangerfield Parker as guide and scout of the fort, where nearly all of the Kansas scouts were then making their headquarters under Dick Curtis, a noted frontiersman and interpreter.

CHAPTER XL.
A STORY WYLL [SIC] TOLD.

At Fort Larned General Hazen[69] had his Headquarters, though the fort was only garrisoned by one troop of cavalry and two companies of Indians [sic, infantry].

There were camped near the fort when Buffalo Bill reached there, some three hundred lodges of Indians of the Kiowa and Comanche natives, under the leadership of such chiefs as Satanta,[70] Lone Wolf, Kicking Bird, Satauk, Sitamore and others whose names afterward became well-known for their stubborn fight against the whites.

These Indians, though not then hostile, were in a very uneasy frame of mind, and General Hazen was doing all in his power to pacify them.

Upon his arrival at Larned Buffalo Bill was at once appointed General Hazen's special scout.

Desirous of going to Fort Harker, General Hazen told Buffalo Bill he wished him to accompany him as far as Fort Zaroli,[71] thirty miles away, when he was to then return to Larned to keep a watchful eye upon the Kiowas and Comanches.

The trip was to be made under escort of a six mule wagon and twenty infantry soldiers, the General, his aide and Cody alone being mustered.

Zaroli was reached in safety, and thinking an escort no longer necessary General Hazen dismissed his escort to return the next day to Larned.

But telling the Sergeant he would return at once Buffalo Bill mounted his mule and started.

He had reached Paunee [sic] Rock, half way to Larned, when half a hundred Indians suddenly dashed around him with every showing of friendship.

One of them held out his hand, and when the scout took it he held it fast, others seized his other arm, grasped his reins, took his revolvers, and one dealt him a stunning blow upon the head.

Seeing that they were the Indians from about Larned, and in full war paint, he knew that they had started upon the warpath and that he was their first victim.

Collecting his thoughts after the severe blow on his head, he looked about him and saw a large village of Indians moving along upon the other side of the river, and he knew that they had left Larned and were out for scalps.

Just then a party of chiefs on horseback came up, and recognizing Satanta Buffalo Bill asked him why his young man had thus treated him, when he had gone off with the big chief—General Hazen—to drive up a herd of whoa-haws* intended for his, Satanta's people.

The bait was quickly swallowed by the cunning chief, who asked if their [sic] were any soldiers with the whoa-haws.

Of course there were.

Then Satanta wished to know where they were, and Buffalo Bill told him he would go and tell the soldiers where his people were so they could bring in the cattle to them.

The veteran truth dodger then told the scout he was sorry his young men had made merry at his expense, that they were only testing his bravery, and it was all a joke.

The joke was not visible to the scout, but as they gave back his weapons he rode off to "fetch the cattle," telling Satanta that the soldiers might fire on them as hostiles if his young men went with him, and muttering sotto voce:

"I am something of a liar myself when necessity demands it."

So off he rode, but he saw that band of "funny young men," followed at a safe distance, so he gained the shelter of the river bank and then put his mule at full speed.

He was discovered when the young jokers reached the river, and a hot pursuit was begun.

Thus it was kept up as far as the crossing of Pauhee [sic] Fork, when the Indians in the lead, were not a quarter of a mile in the rear of the scout.

But the fort was only two miles away and soon after some soldiers were spied in a covered wagon, and hailing them, Buffalo Bill found a scout comrade, Denver Jim with them, and they at once rallied to his rescue.

With Denver Jim and the soldiers in ambush it became the same old story of a sharp fight and the retreat of the Indians leaving several of their number on the field.

---

*The name the Indians call cattle. —The Author.

The firing was heard at Fort Larned, the bugle sounded the alarms, the drums beat, and when Buffalo Bill and those with him made their appearance the post was ready for battle, it being supposed that Satanta and his people were returning to make an attack upon the post.

It seems that as soon as General Hazen had left that morning Chief Satanta drove over from his village to the post in style in an ambulance[72] presented to him by the government, threatened Captain Parker, and said that his eight hundred warriors could capture the post.

Captain Parker told him to try it, and the chief sold his ambulance to the post trader, bought whiskey, from men every [sic] ready to sell it to the Indians, in violation of both civil and military law, and with his braves made a hostile demonstration.

But his Dutch courage,[73] inspired by the whiskey, was not sufficient to cause him to attempt to take the fort, and he went off with his whole village, making threats, and later met Buffalo Bill, as has been seen, upon the return trail, and was quelled by the scout's plausible tale about the "whoa-haws."

CHAPTER XLI.
A NIGHT RIDE.

On their retreat from the Post the Indians had killed some woodchoppers a short distance away, and thus it was that Buffalo Bill's proverbial good luck did not direct him, for the soldiers with Scout Denver Jim had gone after the bodies of the slain men and were returning when they rallied to his support.

At the fort all was excitement, for Captain Parker realized fully his weakness, though he had maintained such a bold front, and he was trying to get a volunteer to take dispatches to General Sheridan, informing him of the condition of affairs, when Buffalo Bill reported to him, told him what he had passed through and as Dick Curtis reported that none of his men cared to make the ride by night to Fort Hays, he at once said:

"I will go, Captain Parker."

"But Cody, you have just had a long hard ride, that blow on your head has an ugly look, and the storm is coming up, while there are Indians encamped on Walnut Creek between here and Hays, as Dick Curtis reports and I do not wish to have you take the chances, when it is not your place to do so, being under General Hazen's special orders."

"All right, Captain, I am not thirsting for any more riding and fighting to-night, but will go if you can get no one else."

No one else would go, and Buffalo Bill after half an hour's rest, reported himself as ready for the ride.

Mounted upon the best horse in the fort Buffalo Bill started on his long ride of sixty-five miles, at night and through a country full of hostile Indians.

The darkness he did not mind, for he knew the country well, but fearing that his horse might fall into a gopher hole in [sic] took the wise precaution of attaching one end of the lariat to his bit the other about his wrist, so as not to be left on foot by the animal running away from him should he fall.

That he had acted wisely was proven by his horse going down into a prairie-dog hole before he had gone half a dozen miles.

Nearing Walnut Creek he had to pick his way, as the country was seamed with ravines, and it was so dark he could see but a short distance ahead of him.

Upon drawing near the creek his horse suddenly halted, for he had gone directly into a herd of horses, which started off in alarm.

Instantly recognizing that they were Indian ponies, he was getting out of a bad scrape as rapidly as possible, when he heard a dog bark, and that aroused the Indians who were guarding the herd, though he [sic] had evidently been asleep.

Putting his horse into a run he turned up the creek and left danger far behind him, and after going several miles halted, took out his pocket compass, lighted a match and got his bearing exactly.

Now and then he started up a herd that proved, to his delight, either buffalo, deer, or antelope, but as he progressed, he began to ride more cautiously, fearing to run upon another band of Indians.

Crossing Smoky Hill river he rode to the northward, struck the old Santa Fe trail, and just as reveille was sounding rode into Fort Hays.

Colonel Moore aide to the general, told Buffalo Bill he would give the dispatches to General Sheridan when he got up but the scout said that they were important, must be delivered at once and that he would give them in person, and his firmness gained immediate admission for him.

General Sheridan was in bed, but called out:

"Hallo, Cody, is that you?"

The dispatches were handed over and quickly read, and then the general questioned Buffalo Bill as to where General Hazen had gone and all about the breaking out into hostilities of the Kiowas and Comanches.

"Bill, you have had two hard rides of it, and some close calls, but somehow, catlike you light on your feet every time.

"Go and get some breakfast and rest, and then report to me."

Going over to Hays City, the place which had squelched Rome, Buffalo Bill went to the Perry House and had breakfast, meeting with many old friends; but after a nap of two hours he returned to the fort in time to discover that General Sheridan had offered a couple of hundred dollars to any scout who would carry dispatches through to Fort Dodge, ninety-five miles away.

As three scouts had just been killed bearing dispatches out of Hays, no one jumped at the offer made, and reporting to Sheridan Buffalo Bill said quietly:

"General, I will carry those dispatches through to Dodge, or at least as far as the Indians will allow me to go."

"I do not like to ask you, Cody, after your recent hard ride, but it is most important that these dispatches should go through."

"I am ready for the try, sir."

"Good for you, Cody.

"Get ready then, for the sooner the better, and take the best horse you can find."

Within an hour Buffalo Bill was on the trail to Fort Dodge, bearing the important dispatches, with night coming on as he crossed the Smoky Hill River.

CHAPTER XLII.
A MEMORABLE RIDE.

When he started for his long night ride of ninety-five miles, from Fort Hays to Fort Dodge, bearing the important dispatches General Sheridan had entrusted to him, Buffalo Bill knew that the chances were ten to one against him.

He spared his horse by riding slow, so that he should have reserve force in case of a ride for life, and had reached Lawlog Croning on the Pounce Fork [sic, Saw-Log Crossing on the Pawnee Fork], seventy miles from Hays without seeing an Indian.

It was nearing daylight, and having been told that a troop of colored soldiers were stationed there, from the past experience he had had with the Black Cavalrymen, he expected they would fire upon him before calling a halt, and not caring to die any death so inglorious, he shouted out:

"Don't shoot!

"Scout from Hays with dispatches!"

The sentinel obeyed and entering the lines the scout delivered a letter to Major Cox, the officer in command, from General Sheridan, got a fresh horse and some breakfast, and before sunrise was again on his way to Dodge, where he arrived at nine o'clock.

Delivering the dispatches to the commanding officer, [who] also complimented him upon his splendid achievement, Buffalo Bill went off to the quarters of John Austin, the chief of scouts at Fort Dodge, and took a much needed rest.

Austin told him the fort had been surrounded by Indians for days, and some men had been killed, while horses and cattle had been run off, and added that how he had gotten through he could not understand.

He also told him that the hostiles were very thick on the Arkansas river, between Dodge and Larned, the latter post being sixty-five miles away.

As the commandant had dispatches for Larned, Austin could find none of his men to bear them, and again Buffalo Bill came to the front as a volunteer, modestly remarking:

"Larned is my fort, you know, and as I wish to return there, I will take the dispatches."

"If you can stand the trip, Cody, after all you have undergone, you can go," said the commandant.

"All I desire, sir, is a good horse."

"But we have not a decent horse here, though some fine government mules, and you can take your pick."

Buffalo Bill made a grimace when a mule was mentioned, but did take his pick and started.

Halting at Coon Creek, he dismounted to get a drink of water, when his mule suddenly swung back, kicked loose and started in the wagon trail to Larned, instead of back to Dodge as the scout had anticipated would be his course.

Buffalo Bill followed in after the mule, truly in a frame of mind that few cannot describe.

Mile after mile that mule browsed on ahead, just beyond reach, and coaxing "good mule," and loving terms had no more effect than did epithets liberally expressed when patience ceased longer to be a virtue.

It was thirty-five miles from Coon Creek to Larned, and Buffalo Bill began to think prospects were good to walk the whole way, unless the Indians varied the monotony by capturing the mule and shooting him, a prospect that seemed most likely of consummation.

So on through the night continued the pedestrian watch, man against mule, and fortunate it was for the scout, and the mule, that Indians keep quiet at night.

Just as day was breaking, they, Cody and the mule, descried the lights of Larned in the valley, four miles away, and as the sunrise gun was fired the one in advance answered the morning salute to the orb of day with a ringing bray.

That was too much for his pard on the long night[']s tramp, it was the last ounce that broke the camel's back, so to speak, and throwing his rifle to a level the scout said:

"Laughing at me, eh?" and his finger touched the trigger.

With the report the mule saw, or felt, his mistake and with a vicious kick gave up his muleship's ghost then and there.

"I'd really like to feel sorry, Mr. Mule, but it isn't in me after all I've gone through the past forty-eight hours," said Buffalo Bill, and stripping his saddle and bridle off of the mule he limped on toward the fort, his feet blistered, his eyes half closed with dreariness and every bone and sinew aching.

The shot alarmed the fort, but Buffalo Bill told them that he had seen no Indians, only killed a government mule, and delivered his dispatches to Captain Parker he was soon fast asleep.

During the day General Hazen returned under escort from Fort Harker, and having dispatches to send it through to General Sheridan, Buffalo Bill, elated over his great ride, and seeing that he was making a record over the other scouts, at once offered to bear them to Fort Hays.

Leaving on a good horse, for he declined General Hazen's offer of a government mule, he made the ride through without incident and at daylight again aroused General Sheridan in his headquarters at Hays.

"Cody, are you trying to kill yourself," asked General Sheridan when he heard the scout's report, and added:

"Your services shall not soon be forgotten, for let me see, you rode from Larned to Zarob and back, sixty-five miles in twelve hours, was captured by Satanta's practical jokers and escaped, then from Larned to Hays, sixty-five miles by night, and in the next twenty-four hours from Hays to Dodge, ninety-five miles, and in the following night thirty miles on the hurricane deck of a mule, thirty-five miles on foot—but the least said of that the better—and now come in here after a night ride from Larned of sixty-five miles, in all, as I figure it three hundred and fifty-five miles in fifty-eight hours, it is simply wonderful, Cody, wonderful, and will never be forgotten for pluck and endurance."

And General Sheridan was right, for he might have added that the average was once six miles an hour, making in the night, over all wild land, following no trails, except the one the mule led the way, and with the whole country swarming with hostile Indians whom he had to be ever on the alert for.

Truly a memorable ride.

CHAPTER XLIII.
APPOINTED CHIEF OF SCOUTS.

This most memorable and remarkable ride of Buffalo Bill won for him deserved promotion from General Sheridan himself.

"You need not report to General Hazen, Cody, as I intend to appoint you to a higher position.

"The Fifth Cavalry, one of the finest regiments in the army is on its way to this department, and I intend to send it upon a special expedition.

"Now I intend to appoint you as guide and chief of scouts to the Fifth."

Thanking General Sheridan warmly for the honor done him, Buffalo Bill asked him as to where the command was going, as he wished to find out if he knew the country. "It is going on an expedition against the Dog

Soldier Indians* Cody, who are infesting the Republican River country and need looking after badly."

Soon after the Fifth Cavalry—the "Gallant Fighting Fifth," as it has been called, than which there is no more famous regiment in the service, and which has been the nursery of scores of brave and able officers—arrived at Fort Hays.

General Sheridan himself presented Buffalo Bill to Colonel William Royal, who commanded the regiment, and a gallant officer and a genial gentleman.[74]

As General Sheridan was anxious to punish the Indians who had been fighting General Forsyth,[75] the regiment was pushing on to the front with all speed, Buffalo Bill riding out at its head, proud, and justly so, of his new position of guide and chief of scouts to see such a splendid command.

Treated with courtesy by all the officers, he was invited by Major Brouse[76] and Captain Sweetman to join their men which he did, and his clever way of telling a story, his wit, brilliant repartee, outside his record as a plainsman, made him a universal favorite and today he is achieved and respected by all the officers of the Fifth.

The other scouts under Buffalo Bill's command, had a mess[77] of their own and a dashing, daring band of fellows they were, rough riders, hard fighters, dead shots and skillful trailers, while they were all sound good comrades.

As the regiment was strung out over the prairie, Buffalo Bill from an eminence ahead looked back over it, with its hundreds of troopers, seventy-five six mule wagons, ambulances and pack mules, and felt that it would make a record for himself on the expedition that would still more add to its fame.

With a brush now and then with the scouting bands of Indians and a buffalo, or antelope hunt, the command pushed on its way averaging on the march about thirty miles a day.

---

*The Dog Soldier Indians were a band of Cheyennes and unruly, turbulent members of other tribes, who would not enter into any treaty, or keep a treaty if they made one, and who had always refused to go upon a reservation. They were a warlike body of well-built, daring and restless braves and were determined to hold possession of the country in the vicinity of the Republican and Solomon Rivers. They were called "Dog Soldiers" because they were principally Cheyenne—a name derived from the French chien, a dog. —The Author.

Camping early one afternoon on the South Fork of the Solomon river, Colonel Royal asked his chief of scouts to go out and bring in game for the boys.

"All right, sir, please send after me a couple of wagons for the game," was the reply.

"I'll send after the game when you have killed it, Cody."

Buffalo Bill made no reply, but rode out of camp, soon found a herd of buffaloes, rounded them up and headed straight for camp, beginning to ride alongside and bringing them down as he neared the encampment.

There were seven buffaloes in the herd, and the last one was killed right in the camp as he was charging wild through it, threatening a stampede of the mules and horses.

Colonel Royal and the other officers saw the whole hunt, and the former said with some show of anger:

"What does this mean, Cody?"

"I was making the buffaloes bring themselves into camp, sir, so that you would not have to send out the wagons," was the reply.

The colonel smiled and turned away, while his officers all enjoyed scout's wit, as some of them had heard him ask for the wagons and get a refusal.

After a three days march the command arrived on Beaver Creek, where it went into camp, and Buffalo Bill reporting Indians about a strict watch was kept, but in spite of it a dash was made by the redskins who killed two soldiers and ran off sixty horses belonging to H. troop.

Major Brown with three companies was at once sent in pursuit, pushing ahead of the command, with Buffalo Bill guiding.

But they could not overtake the red horse thieves and the whole command camped on the Saline River to await supplies.

With the supplies came a new commander for the regiment, General E. A. Carr who had ranked Colonel Royal, being the senior manager of the Fifth.[78]

General Carr having an idea as to where to locate the Indians, told Buffalo Bill to guide him to Elephant Rock on Beaver Creek and there a large trail was found and followed.

Upon some bluffs ahead the Indians were discovered in considerable force, and going into line of battle General Carr attacked them.

The Indians had evidently been surprised by a larger force than they had expected, and they fought desperately, to give their village a chance to escape, and being some eight hundred warriors strong it became quite a battle and a number were killed and wounded.

But the regiment dislodged them from the cliffs and night being near at hand the soldiers went into camp.

While at supper with Major Brown, Captain Sweetman and Lieutenant Bache, a bullet fired from the bluffs struck a plate upon the little folding table, breaking it, at which Buffalo Bill coolly remarked:

"That's what I call a crack shot."[79]

CHAPTER XLIV.
AN UNEXPECTED SHOT.

At daylight the next morning the command was in the saddle in pursuit of the Indians.

The camp of the Indians, when surprised the day before, was soon found, and Buffalo Bill reported that they were in larger force than the general had supposed, having fully five hundred tepees.

Pushing on, Buffalo Bill rapidly followed the trail, and soon after came up with the retreating Indians.

The chiefs sent the village on in its retreat, and turned back with their fighting braves to give battle.

They set fire to the grass in front of the soldiers and upon either side, but the regiment kept [on], and all through the rest of the day a running fight was kept up, the redskins trying every device and cunning trick to throw their pursuers off the track.

At last Buffalo Bill sent one of his scouts back to General Carr with word that the Indians were scattering to put the soldiers at fault, for which was their main trail it was hard to tell.

Night again put an end to the pursuit, and the command went into camp; but with the first peep of light the pursuers were again in the saddle, and it was found that during the night the scattered bands had united, and once more a scout was sent back with the information that the Indians were making a complete circle in their retreat, and were back near the point where they had first been discovered.

Pushing them hard Buffalo Bill reported that the warriors were again in battle away ahead, and once more a fight was made, the Indians being put to flight by the boys in blue, who drove them on until night once more checked pursuit.

And so it continued, until the Indians, driven too hard, were forced to scatter in earnest, and by traveling night and day thus divided, gained a long lead of their pursuers.

Confident that he had given them a most wholesome fight, that would drive them out of the Republican river country, north across the Union Pacific railroad, General Carr returned to the Republican and camped there.

Pushing on toward the Beaver the next day, General Carr rode ahead to where Buffalo Bill was guiding, well in advance of the command, and asked how far it was to water.

"About eight miles, general."

"There are men in command and who say they know this country and that the Beavers are dry at this season and you will find no water."

"They don't know, general, that is all, for where we will strike the Beaver there are immense beaver dams, which we can cross on and where there will be plenty of water."

"Go ahead then, only remember, I don't like dry camps."*

About seven miles from where the general had overtaken his chief of scouts, a little stream hidden in the hills was found, and the water was excellent and there was grass and wood in plenty.

The stream was only eight or nine miles long, as had Buffalo Bill reported that it had no name, General Carr took out his map and wrote it down as "Cody Creek," while he said to Major Brown:

"That man knows what he is about, and those who knew this country so well and said he was going wrong, have to admit that they were vastly mistaken."

Leading the command that morning, Buffalo Bill reached Beaver Creek after a short ride, when suddenly, without wavering, there came two shots from ambush.

One bullet cut close by his ear, the other pierced the head of his horse which fell dead under him.

---

*A camp without water for men or stock. —The Author.

"Led by Destiny"

Catching on his feet, Buffalo Bill dropped down behind his dead horse and was ready to meet his foes shot for shot.

CHAPTER XLV.
CAMPAIGNING IN THE WINTER.

The shot that had killed Buffalo Bill's horse was totally unexpected just then, and had the aim of the red skin at him been as true as the one who had fired at the animal, then and there would the career of William F. Cody have ended.

He would never have known what killed him.

But he was still under the guidance of his "Lucky Star," and the Indians found in their front instead of a dead man, one very much alive and at bay.

To run back to the command on foot and give the alarm was the chief of scout[']s first thought; but he quickly changed his mind and determined to await the coming up of the regiment, hoping thus to give the Indians a surprise.

Having come to the conclusion that the scout was alone, and, as they hoped, wounded, the Indians decided to surround him, and they were carrying out this intention by crossing the creek, when suddenly the advance guard came into view, and away they fled at full speed.

General Carr at once ordered I Company to go in pursuit, Buffalo Bill on a fresh mount scouting on ahead.

After a running fight of several miles their camp was found and a hot fight followed, in which the Indians lost several braves killed and the soldiers captured a number of horses and half a dozen lodges.

Camping upon the Beaver, the command crossing on the beaver dam as Buffalo Bill said, daily there followed skirmishes with the Indians, until, supplies running short, the regiment returned to Fort Wallace, after a three days march.

While waiting for orders, Buffalo Bill was engaged in buffalo hunting, and one day when out with several officers the party were attacked by half a hundred Indians, who were beaten off after a very severe fight, one of the officers being wounded and several horses killed.

Returning to camp with their buffalo meat General Carr complimented them highly upon their good fight and added:

"You were fortunate to have Cody along."

General Sheridan received orders for a winter campaign into the Canadian River country, General Carr marched at once to Fort Lyon, Colorado, to fit out for the expedition.

Arriving at Fort Lyon it was found that General Penrose[80] had left that post a short while before with three hundred men, carrying no wagons, but only pack mules with supplies.

Here Buffalo Bill learned that his old comrade, Wild Bill was guide and scout for General Penrose, and he was glad to know that General Carr intended to at once follow with supplies and overtake him as soon as possible.

As it was most important not to lose the trail of General* Penrose, Buffalo Bill with four of his scouts was ordered on ahead, while the command was getting ready for the march, and were told to leave their way well marked.

In a blinding snow-storm Buffalo Bill and his four comrades started, after scouting up and down Cimarson [sic, Cimarron River] found one of General Penrose's camping places.

Having found what he had started out for, Buffalo Bill left his men in camp and rode back to bring up the command.

He found General Carr anxiously awaiting news for him, as he was fearful for the safety of General Penrose.

The next morning the command pulled out, and a terrible march the men had of it, the teamsters often having to shovel their way through the snowdrifts.

Going on ahead from Penrose's camp, Buffalo Bill found that he had kept on the west side of the Cimarson, and the country was too rough to follow with wagons, so General Carr followed Buffalo Bill's advice to take the east side of the stream.

After a ride of some miles they came to a bluff, looking down into a beautiful valley and General Carr at once looked at Buffalo Bill and said:

"This checks us."

"No, General, we'll get down all right."

---

*I here give the officers the titles they held by courtesy, as having held such ranks in the Civil War, but dropped back to their rank in the regular army after the war— [illegible], becoming again captains, majors and colonels, where they had been generals. —The Author.

"The men can dismount and scramble down with their horses, but how about the wagons, Cody?"

"I'll see to them, sir."

"I certainly shall be glad to have you do so," was the answer with a quizzical smile.

The wagons had come up and the drivers all asserted that they could go no further. Buffalo Bill ordered the mess wagons first had the mules unhitched, the wheels were all locked, then the wheel mules[81] alone attached, and with ropes held by men in the rear the start was made and successfully made.

An hour after every wagon had been landed in the valley without a single accident, General Carr remarking:

"Well done, Cody.

"I had forgotten that you were once boss of a wagon outfit across the plains."

By this clever descent of what was considered by officers and men an impassable mountain, it was soon after discovered that they had accomplished in one day what had taken General Penrose seven to make even with his pack mules and no wagons, for, marching on a high plateau he had come to a bluff on the other side of the river which he could not descend and so had to retrace his way and take another trail.

CHAPTER XLVI.
TO THE RESCUE OF COMRADES.

While encamped down in this valley the command enjoyed a better hunt than going after Indians, for the whole country was alive with wild turkeys.

In fact they did not have to hunt for them, for three hundred soldiers went on a round-up after the turkeys, got them into a grove of timber and in short while half a thousand "birds" were bagged for food, and delicious food to[o] it proved to be, a dish in anticipation of Thanksgiving and Christmas.

The camp was most appropriately named "Camp Turkey," and Buffalo Bill was given the credit for procuring the feast, as he had led the command down into the valley.

For several days after the men were treated to the luxury of roast turkey, boiled turkey, spitted turkey, fried turkey, in fact turkey ad libittun [sic].[82]

Striking the Penrose trail it was followed toward the Canadian River, and not an Indian was seen for days.

Riding well in advance of the command one day, along San Francisco Creek, Buffalo Bill was startled by suddenly hearing his name called, and to his utter amazement beheld across the stream nothing less than a negro.

He was hiding in the willows, and called out:

"Glory ter gracious! its Massa Buf'ler Bull!"

Then to some one not visible he continued:

"Come out, for its Massa Buf'ler Bill."

Then came the earnest query:

"Massa Bill has yer got any hard tack[83] wittals wid yer?"

Recognizing the man as one of the Tenth Colored Cavalry, Buffalo Bill told him that the wagons would soon be along and he could get something better than "hard tack."

"Dat's de bestest news I has heard for sixteen long days, Massa Bill."

By this time two other negro soldiers appeared out of the willows.

They had deserted the command of General Penrose, which was in a starving condition, and were trying to make their way back to Fort Lyon.

Buffalo Bill tried to find out just where General Penrose was, but as they did not know where they were themselves the half starved fellows could not tell.

When Buffalo Bill took his "find" before General Carr, the latter at once ordered Major Brown to take two companies of cavalry and fifty pack mules with supplies and hasten to the relief of General Penrose and his command.

It was on the third day after leaving the main command, that Buffalo Bill, riding well in the lead, beheld the camp they were looking for, on the Palladora [sic, Paloduro] Creek.

Cheers greeted the arrival of the relief party from the half starved soldiers, and the gallant rescuers answered with cheer after cheer in return at having found them.

The camp presented a most pitiful sight indeed, and the men were slowly starving to death.

Over two hundred horses and mules had died from starvation and fatigue and the men were suffering greatly.

General Penrose, fearing that General Carr would not find him, had sent back a company of the Seventh Cavalry to Fort Lyon for supplies, but nothing had been heard of it thus far.

The rations brought to the starving men by Major Brown were the means of saving many lives, for they came none too soon, and Buffalo Bill had the satisfaction that he had well done his part in the rescue.

One of the first men whom Buffalo Bill saw in the camp whom he recognized, was Wild Bill, his friend tried and true, and that night the two talked for hours as they sat around the camp fire.

As a well marked trail had been left by the rescue party, General Carr came rapidly on; and upon the arrival of the command the late comers knew that Buffalo Bill had led Major Brown none too rapidly to the scene of suffering and death.

Being the senior of General Penrose in rank, General Carr took command of the combined forces, and unloading the wagons sent them back to Lyon for more supplies.

He then picked out five hundred of the best men and horses, and taking along a pack train, started south for an expedition to the Canadian River, the rest of the force remaining in camp.

With this expedition Buffalo Bill went also and he was glad to have his pard, Wild Bill, accompany him.

CHAPTER XLVII.
TRAILING OUTLAWS.

General Carr struck the south fork of the Canadian River, or Rio Colorado as it is also called, near an old adobe fort, where Kit Carson had once had a battle with the Indians.[84]

Going into camp there, General Carr sent for his chief of scouts and said:

"Cody, I wish to send some dispatches to Camp Supply, to be sent from there to Sheridan."

"I will take them, sir."

"No, it is a ride of two hundred miles, intensely cold, and I wish you here: but do you go and select the man to carry them."

Buffalo Bill found it rather a difficult task to find scouts who cared to make the ride, but Wild Bill volunteered, and then a half breed known as Little Glory,[85] and three other men said they would accompany him and the dispatches were accordingly started on their way.

Thus the days passed in scouting along the Canadian until Wild Bill and his men returned, Buffalo Bill meanwhile keeping the troops supplied with Buffalo meat, killing about twenty a day.

As no Indians in force had been seen, General Carr decided to return to Fort Lyon, and arrived at that post in March of '69, when orders came for the command to recruit for thirty days and then go to the Department of the Platte.

Thus ended a most severe winter campaign.

Granted a leave of absence by General Carr, Buffalo Bill rode one hundred and forty miles to Sheridan, the nearest railroad station and took the train for St. Louis to visit his family, and a pleasant visit it was too, to the hardy scout after all the dangers and hardships of the winter.

Returning to Fort Lyon he was cordially greeted by General Carr who said:

"I am glad you have returned, Bill, for you are wanted."

"A number of valuable horses, besides stock belonging to the Government, have been systematically stolen for weeks."

"I'll start out in the morning, General, and see what I can do to catch the thieves," was the answer.

The next morning, with three of his scouts he started upon the trail, picked it up, and found the places where the stolen animals had been hidden in the timber until they could get together a large number.

But from there the trail had been most cleverly concealed, and not caring to lose time in a search, Buffalo Bill told his men that they would ride to a point miles from there and make a complete circuit, thus crossing the trail at a place where no effort had been made to cover it up.

This plan was successful for the trail was discovered and followed toward Denver, where the animals were evidently being taken to be sold.

Entering Denver Buffalo Bill and his men at once took up a position to watch for the thieves and the stolen animals.

They had not long to wait, for a man came in, whom Buffalo Bill recognized as an old government hand, and he was riding an animal stolen from Lieutenant Forbish,[86] and leading another bearing the brand of U.S.

The man put the stolen animals up at auction, and just then Buffalo Bill stepped through the crowd and arrested him, showing the auctioneer his badge as a United States Secret Service officer.

The other scouts now came up, and the man, whose name was Williams, was taken away from Denver, and believing he was going to be hanged, he confessed that his partner in guilt was another government hand by the name of Bill Bevins, and was at the cabin with the rest of the stolen animals some miles from where they were then.

Guiding the party there Bill Bevins[87] was surprised and covered by Buffalo [Bill] before he could draw a weapon, and there were found their saddles, rifles and complete outfit, with all of the other stolen animals.

Tying the prisoners upon their horses, the party started for Fort Lyon, but, camping at night, when allowed to make himself comfortable, Bill Bevins suddenly made a bound for liberty just before day, and bounded away in the darkness, losing one shoe however in doing so.

At dawn Buffalo Bill followed him on horseback, trailing him easily through the snow, and though the country was full of prickly pears, which lacerated his shoeless foot, Bevins made a run of eighteen miles, leaving one red footprint at every step.

Overtaken at last, Buffalo Bill's sympathy was aroused for the game outlaw, and telling him to mount his horse he thus took him to camp while he walked.

General Carr complimented the chief of scouts on his successful expedition, and sent the prisoners to Boggs Ranch, where they were turned over to the civil authorities and jailed, to remain only a short while however, as Bevins made his escape and developed into a Road Agent Chief in the Black Hills,[88] from whence he sent word to Buffalo Bill that if he ever crossed his path he would kill him.

But the man was captured later on, and is now serving a life sentence in the State's Prison of Nebraska.

Shortly after Buffalo Bill's return to Fort Lyon the Fifth Cavalry received marching orders, and started on the trail for Fort McPherson, Nebraska, a post in sight of the present elegant home of the chief of scouts.

CHAPTER XLVIII.
A COMBAT AT CLOSE QUARTERS.

It was while the Fifth Cavalry was encamped upon the North Fork of the Beaver, that Buffalo Bill rode off alone on a scout, for he had told the general that he felt sure Indians were about, though in what numbers he could not determine without investigation.

He had gone about three miles from camp when he struck decided "sign," and he was not long in discovering that there were heavy trails on each side of the creek, where a large force of redskins had passed along.

His experienced eye told him that there were at least four hundred lodges, which meant about three thousand souls, counting braves, squaws and children.

Back to camp rode the scout and made his report, and ten minutes after he was guiding Lieutenant Ward[89] and a dozen troopers out on the Indian trail.

Seeing by their many camps that they were hunting on the way, and consequently marching slowly, Lieut. Ward and Buffalo Bill left their horses with the men, gained a point of observation on foot, and some three miles distant beheld thousands of ponies grazing up on the prairie, and a large Indian village in plain view.

They also saw coming in from another direction, a large number of mounted Indians, their ponies loaded heavily with buffalo meat.

A quick retreat was made to the men, Lieutenant Ward wrote a note to General Carr and dispatched it by the corporal, whom he ordered to ride back on the trail with full speed, while they would lie concealed until the command came up.

He had been gone but a few minutes when shots were heard, and back into view he dashed, pursued by half a dozen Indians.

"This is a bad break—the whole Indian village will now know soldiers are about," and the lieutenant ordered a charge to rescue the soldiers.

"I'll take the note, sir," said Buffalo Bill.

The lieutenant gladly handed it to him, and he was off in an instant, to soon after rush upon another band of Indians, returning to their village with buffalo meat.

Instantly the scout opened fire upon them, and in the confusion created by his bold act, which tumbled a brave from his saddle, he got around them and was away for the command, the Indians, throwing the buffalo meat off their ponies starting in full pursuit, to be quickly distanced however, as their horses were tired out from hunting.

In less than an hour the note was in General Carr's hands, "Boots and saddles["][90] sang out through the camp, and with two companies left as a guard to the train, all the rest were on a rapid trot for the Indian village.

On the way, Lieutenant Ward was met with one horse wounded, for he had had a brush with the band that had pursued the scout, killing one of their number.

A few miles further on Buffalo Bill, who was well ahead, sent back word that several hundred mounted warriors were advancing from their village to give battle.

General Carr being anxious to strike a severe blow at their village ordered a charge to break through their lines and keep straight on.

But this clever move was frustrated by a daredevil lieutenant by the name of Schinosky,[91] who charged to the left with his company, was surrounded by an overwhelming force of Indians and the recall had to be given to rescue the foolhardy officer and his men, which was accomplished, not until, however, his company had lost severely.

This delay enabled other warriors to press forward from the villages which was rapidly packing up and moving off.

With the increased force of Indians the regiment had hard fighting of it to hold its own and as the two companies had not appeared, according to orders following with the wagon train, General Carr was fearful that it had been surrounded, and night being at hand a retreat was ordered up the creek to meet it.

It was after dark when the train was met and the regiment then went into camp, but were astir before dawn, once more in the saddle and advancing to the attack.

But not an Indian was to be seen, for during the day they had:
"Folded their tents like the Arabs,
And as silently stolen away."[92]

Buffalo Bill had left camp, however, in the night, with several of his scouts, and one of them was met returning with word to General Carr that the Indians were retreating toward the Republican, had broken camp at dark, so have a night[']s start of the command while they were in larger force than they had appeared the day before, as he had found another village deserted further on.

Pushing on to the Republican, General Carr decided to send his wagon train direct to Fort McPherson, and to push ahead with his regiment with several days provisions.

The next day Buffalo Bill reported a force of warriors ahead and the advance guard soon engaged and begun to drive them and captured their hastily deserted lodges and many horses, while along their trail all kinds of Indian furniture and outfits had been thrown away in their rapid flight.

As the Indians practiced their old ruse of scattering, a halt was called, their belongings were gathered up and burned and their ponies caught, while, being determined to still press on, General Carr dispatched Buffalo Bill to Fort Kearney, sixty miles distant to procure supplies.

CHAPTER XLIX.
MAJOR NORTH'S PAWNEE INDIAN SOLDIERS.

Buffalo Bill returned from Kearney with supplies, but the Indians had so scattered that General Carr decided to go onto Fort McPherson and out for another expeditions [sic].

Fort McPherson thus became the headquarters of the Fifth Cavalry and remained so for some time, and it was while scouting around that post that the famous plainsman settled upon the spot which he was to make his future home.

Riding over the prairies one day, guiding a command of soldiers, he crossed the North Platte River, just above the North Platte, and gazing over the beautiful landscape of rolling prairie, rivers and distance bluffs, he said to the officer with him[:]

"Right here I am going to pitch my lodge some day, for though a wild land now, this inviting prospect will, before many years, lure settlers to it and these prairies will be dotted with comfortable homes."*

---

*How true the prophecy was may be seen when I state that on the spot where William Cody then stood, now stands his homestead, surrounded by thousands of acres and dotted with the finest of blooded cattle, while fields of grain can be seen upon every side. The place is known as "Scout's Rest Ranch" and passengers on the Union

It was while at Fort McPherson that the Fifth Cavalry was re-enforced by Major Frank North,* and his three companies of Pawnee Indian scouts, a very welcome addition to the command.[93]

General Carr having recommended Buffalo Bill for promotion, for his past valuable services, General Augur,[94] in command of the department, appointed him chief of scouts for the department of the Platte, a position that gave him far better pay and far more authority.

It was amusing to see the Pawnee scouts in uniforms, or rather in and out of it, for some of them wore a suit, with a war bonnet on their heads.

Others had on the regulation hat, adorned with eagle feathers, and a coat, but no pants, only a breech clout.

A few had boots, no pants and an overcoat, and were bareheaded.

But for all this grotesque dress, equal to Mark Twain's converted Sandwich Islanders,[95] they drilled well, obeyed orders and fought desperately.

They were well mounted, good shots, proud of being United States soldiers, and were devoted to their White Chief, Frank North.

As he was to be stationed for some time at Fort McPherson, and many of the officers had their families there, Chief of Scouts Cody sent for his wife and child to join him there, his sister Nellie† accompanying them.

Upon arrival they found that a pleasant cabin had been prepared for them and a warm welcome awaited them from all.

While guiding the command on an expedition along the Republican,

---

Pacific Railroad look with great interest upon the "home of Buffalo Bill" as they are whirled by. A couple of miles distant lies the beautiful and thriving city of North Platte, situated between the North and South Platte Rivers, and across the former on the ruins of what was once Fort McPherson. Behold through what strange paths and devious ways Destiny leads us in a short life time. —The Author.

*The celebrated Pawnee Indian scouts commanded by Major Frank North. His officers were Captain Lute North, brother of the Major, Captain Cushing, his brother-in-law, Captain Morse, and Lieutenants Beecher Matthews and Kislandberry. The Pawnee scouts had made quite a reputation for themselves as they had performed brave and valuable services in fighting against the Sioux, whose bitter enemies they were. Major North was a splendid type of the plainsman, brave, courteous and generous hearted, up to his death he was the devoted friend of Buffalo Bill.

Miss North, the "Star" of "A Farmer's Daughter" company is the daughter of Major North, and has a brilliant future before her as an actress. —The Author.

†Now Mrs. Hugh A. Wetmore, partner of Col. Cody in the Duluth Press. —The Author.

shots were heard one day at the mule corral and a herder dashed into camp with an arrow sticking in his back.

Springing upon his horse without a saddle Buffalo Bill was quickly upon the scene to find the Pawnee scouts before him, for waiting no orders from officers, they had gone to the spot, and the raiding Sioux were amazed to see their life-long foes the Pawnees coming after them.

They did not know the Pawnees were with the command and even well aware that it took regular soldiers sometime to turn out, so they were thwarted by their old foes, who gave chase, Buffalo Bill leading and being splendidly mounted.

But well mounted though he was the scout was surprised to see a Pawnee riding a large "buckskin" horse, shoot rapidly by him and go to the front.

"I want that horse," he muttered, and after chasing the Sioux for miles, and killing several of them, the return to camp was made and Buffalo Bill asked Major North about "that buckskin horse."

It proved to be a government horse, and Buffalo Bill, by making presents to the Pawnee scout arranged a trade of horses, though not as his own, as his too was U.S. property.

The animal proved to be another "Brigham" in speed and endurance and was named by the scout "Buckskin Joe."

That he was a splendid animal may be known when I say that Buffalo Bill rode him for four years, and he was the horse that the Grand Duke Alexis of Russia rode on his famous buffalo hunt with the scout.*

As this chase after the Sioux was the first time the Pawnee scouts had seen Buffalo Bill in a fight, they became more interested in him after that, and their regard and respect was greatly increased when they later on, in a buffalo hunt, saw him in one run bring down thirty-six of the prairie monarchs in less than half a mile chase.

They at once named him the "Buffalo Killer," for an Indian, even the best hunters, seldom ever could kill more than four or five buffaloes in a run, and Buffalo Bill had slain thirty-six with thirty-eight shots.

From that day, the scout was held in awe by the Pawnees and looked upon as a great white chief.

---

*This horse was sold by the government in 1872 and bought by Dave Perry of North Platte, who presented him to Buffalo Bill, who owned him until he [the horse] died in 1879. —The Author.

CHAPTER L.
A SHOT IN LONG RANGE.

While encamped upon the Republican under Colonel Royal, with three troops of Cavalry and Major North's Pawnee scouts, a number of warriors were seen coming toward the command and were at once supposed to be Sioux.

But Buffalo Bill reported, as they were singing, that they were Pawnees, and had been in a battle.

The Pawnees in camp also begun to sing and yell, and when the other approached it was seen that they were bearing several dead and wounded with them, and they reported that they had been in a fight with a band of Sioux who were following a large trail, evidently of their own people.

General Carr at once started in pursuit, and upon coming to where they had encamped, the print of a woman's shoe was found by Buffalo Bill, and this told the sad story that they must have white captives.[96]

All was greater anxiety now to overtake them, and Buffalo Bill was sent ahead with a dozen Pawnee scouts, to keep some ten miles in advance of the command and report when the Indians camped.

After an hour's ride he found the village in the Sand Hills of the South Platte, and word was at once sent back, and the command soon came up. Buffalo Bill having reconnoitred well meanwhile being able to lead the Indians close up to the Sioux camp without being seen.

Then saddle girths were tightened, the men ordered into columns for a charge.

"Sound the charge, Bugler," ordered the general; but the Bugler was so excited he could not sound a note, and became more so when again given the order:

"Sound the charge!"

Realizing the intense excitement of the man, Captain Hays[97] the quartermaster, spurred forward, seized the bugle and blew the "charge," after which he threw the bugle away and was now in the front.

The Sioux were just bringing their horses into camp, preparatory to moving on, when they were surprised by the rush of the cavalry upon them.

Some mounted and fled, others sought safety on foot on a flight to the sandhills, and the troopers and Pawnee scouts charged through the village spreading death upon all sides.

The pursuit was continued for sometime, when the Indians, like quails, scattered, and then the command went into camp upon the South Platte.

The next morning the pursuit was continued by companies, to better follow the scattered trails, and it was not long before Buffalo Bill reported that the Indians had not only re-united ahead, but other forces had joined them, so that scouts were sent to the different troops to also unite, as it was hazardous to be separated longer.

The advance company had already been sighted by the Indians, and six hundred Sioux warriors charged and drove them into corral, and standing at bay a desperate fight followed, the troops, however, heading them off with heavy loss, though a number of soldiers and horses were wounded.

They then pretended to draw off, but Buffalo Bill saw through their plot, and as they had left only a small band under a chief to keep watch, and they kept riding round and round the besieged troop, the scout decided to go out and attempt to bring down their leader.

Creeping out of the ravine he reached its head, several hundred yards away, and when the chief led his band once more around the circle Buffalo Bill stepped out on the prairie and fired.

The distance was all of four hundred yards, but the chief fell dead from his saddle, and his horse ran right toward the soldiers, one of whom caught him and presented him to the scout upon his return.

The chief bore the name of Fall Bull [sic, Tall Bull],[98] one of the bravest and most able leaders the Sioux had, and his loss caused them to retreat, thus releasing the troop from its siege in the ravine.

Some days after this occurrence General Carr had another engagement with the Indians, in which their village, three hundred warriors, hundreds of ponies and a number of women and children were captured, among them several white captives that were with them.

Among the captured squaws was the wife of the chief Fall Bull, and she seemed proud that her husband, a great leader of his people, had been killed by the great white Prairie Chief, a name that Buffalo Bill was well known by, and he had been readily recognized by the warriors who saw him fire that fatal shot at such long range.

General Carr having thus punished and dispersed the Indians, went into barracks at Fort Sedgwick, when soon after news came that the Sioux were raiding the Union Pacific road, and Buffalo Bill was ordered there to go out with a battalion of the Fifth under Major Brown.

CHAPTER LI.
LED BY DESTINY.

To follow the career of William F. Cody step by step, would be to write a history of the struggle of civilization against savagery.

It would show that he was easily a King of Pioneers, daily risking his life to beat back savage foe before the onward march of empire.

Finding the gallant little armies under able and daring leaders, scouting night and day hand in hand with death as it were, to keep the brave soldiers from being entrapped by the cunning Sioux, fighting fearlessly when a battle occurred, but ever merciful to a fallen foe, William Cody went on winning the laurels that he wears with honor today, went on in the grand fight that made it possible for the mighty west to become what it is today.

Many people, sitting in the safety of their homes in the east were wont to cry out against the driving of the Indians from their hunting grounds with sword and bullet, and say that it must be done by missionary work, by prayer, preaching and peaceful endeavor.

But had not their ancestors gained their foot-hold here by fighting back the Indians, and is not the savage nation doomed to fall before the one of civilization?

Has it not been proven in all uncivilized lands, especially among our own redmen, that powder, lead and steel are the best missionaries in dealing with savages?

There are a few of our military leaders who can be pointed to as having been cruel to the Indians, though it is an acknowledged fact that one must "fight the devil with fire,"[99] and the cruelties of the redskins, to all foes, to women and children the same as men, are well-known.

It has not been the military that ill-treated the Indians, but that demoralized class of whites ever to be found ready to strike a blow against law and order, and to make capital out of the misfortunes of Indians, those who would sell liquor and arms to the redskins with which to keep up the fight against all settlers, renegades to their own race whose vile deeds have reflected upon good men and true.

With this little sermon for those who, in their ignorance of facts and mistaken judgment, carp at the army and such men as Buffalo Bill and other bold explorers and pioneers of the wild west, I will return to my story of a man's heroism in the trying scenes that make him stand out prominently as a "Knight of To-day," a true Cavalier in Buckskin, winning his spurs in the saddle and at close quarters with desperate foes, the brave, subtle, and in many cases the chivalrous sons of the plains.

It was when Buffalo Bill reported to Major Brown at Fort McPherson, to go on an expedition after the red skins who had raided O'Fallon station on the Union Pacific, that he was told that they were to be accompanied on the scout by quite a noted personage who was better known under his nom de plume of "Ned Buntline"[100] than by his real name.*

"He has come out to get acquainted with you, Cody, to use you as a hero in the novel," said Major Brown.

Buffalo Bill fairly blushed at the suggestion of being made the hero of a novel—he had gotten bravely over that diffidence on that ground since, being the hero of several hundred romances published in half a dozen tongues.

"Now wouldn't I look pretty in a novel?" was the scout's sarcastic comment, to which Major Brown replied:

"If they pictured you as you are, Bill, I rather think you would."

The scout doffed his sombrero in courteous acknowledgment of the

---

*Colonel E. B.[sic, Z.] C. Judson was a sailor, soldier and author, and in each calling won fame. He begun writing sixty years ago when very young, and his novels of love, adventure and the sea were much read, and made a hit.

Col. Judson was a naval officer, serving with distinction during the war both on sea and land. In his later years he wrote much for New York publishers, and it was to get data for a story of Buffalo Bill that carried him out to McPherson to meet the noted Plainsman. The first novel written of Buffalo Bill was from the pen of Ned Buntline, and made a sensation. He also wrote several others of him in connection with Wild Bill and Texas Jack. Ned Buntline also wrote the Border Drama in which Buffalo Bill made his debut as an actor, thus laying the foundation for the great fortune William Cody has amassed. Col. Judson died some years ago at his home in New York State. —The Author.

compliment, but before he could reply a gentleman entered the quarters, and the major whispered:

"Speak of an angel, Bill, you know."

"Or speak of the devil and his imps will appear," muttered the scout, who was not pleased at the thought of being "written up."

With one of his quick glances Buffalo Bill took in the author, soldier, sailor and man in particular.

He saw a rather stoutly built gentleman in an undress [sic] military coat and black slouch cavalry hat.

Upon his left breast were pinned a number of badges and medals, which caused the scout to mentally observe: "I could pick any one of them with my revolvers at thirty paces."

His face was bronzed, rugged, stern, determined yet kindly, and as he came forward he walked with a cane and limped slightly.

The major presented the two men and Ned Buntline looking the scout squarely in the face, while he still held his hand in an iron grip, said bluntly:

"Now I've seen you face to face."

"William Cody, I believe all that men have said of you."

"We will be friends, and as Major Brown has said I may accompany him on this scout, we will get better acquainted, see if we don't."

Thus the scout and the author, Ned Buntline met, and, later the career of Buffalo Bill, though still clinging as it ever will, to the wild life of the west, begun slowly to shape itself into another channel to further bring out the character and resources of this man of Destiny.

CHAPTER LII.
FIGHTING AGAINST ODDS.

Pulling out of McPherson for O'Fallon's station, Buffalo Bill guiding rapidly, the South Platte river swollen by recent rains had to be crossed by swimming the horses.

Finding that the Indians had a start of two days the command returned to McPherson, while Ned Buntline went on to Fort Ledgewick [sic, Sedgwick] with Buffalo Bill whose guest he was.

Another expedition Buffalo Bill made under Colonel Royal, General

Carr having gone east on leave, and it was a hard ride and chase of a large Indian village across the North Platte and toward the Niohara [*sic*, Niobrara] river.

While scouting in the Niohara country the Pawnee Indian scouts brought into camp one night some very large bones which the surgeons of the command pronounced human bones.

As Buffalo Bill spoke the Pawnee tongue well he explained to the officers the interesting legend the Indians attached to these human bones of enormous size, and which may be of interest to give here.

The Indians claimed that the bones they had found were those of a person belonging to a race of people who a long time ago lived in this country; that there was once a race of men on the earth whose size was about three times that of an ordinary man, and they were so swift and powerful that they could run alongside of a buffalo, and taking the animal in one arm could tear off the leg and eat the meat as they walked. These giants denied the existence of a Great Spirit, and when they heard the thunder or saw the lightning they laughed at it and said they were greater than either. This so displeased the Great Spirit that he caused a great rain storm to come, and the water kept rising higher and higher so that it drove those proud and conceited giants from the low grounds to the hills, and thence to the mountains, but at last even the mountain tops were submerged, and then those mammoth men were all drowned. After the flood had subsided, the Great Spirit came to the conclusion that he had made man too large and powerful, and that he would therefore correct the mistake by creating a race of men of smaller size and less strength. This is the reason, say the Indians, that modern men are small and not like the giants of old, and they claim that this story is a matter of Indian history, which has been handed down among them from time immemorial.

As they had no wagons with them at the time this large and heavy bone was found the command was obliged to leave it in camp and it was never again found.

Fort McPherson had been placed under command of General Emory,[101] who was commandant of the District of the Republican, and it was a very delightful post for headquarters.

Game was plentiful, a few buffalo, deer, elk and antelope, and Buffalo Bill led many a hunting expedition out from the post, among them being two parties of English gentlemen.

A novel horse race was also indulged in between Buffalo Bill, on his Indian horse Tall Bull and a racer of Captain Spaulding's company of the Second Cavalry.

In this race Buffalo Bill during the run of a mile, was to ride Tall Bull without saddle or bridle, and dismount and mount while running, eight times.

The race was won by Buffalo Bill on, and off, Tall Bull, I may say.

Several days after this novel race the scout horse Powder Face was run off by Indians, along with a number of other animals, and the feature of the pursuit was that when the cavalry, under Lieutenant Thomas, came up with the Indians, Buffalo Bill surprised them and in making their escape two warriors springing upon one horse were both killed by one bullet.

The scout fired at them at short range, seeing but one Indian, and was amazed at beholding two braves fall from the back of the horse.

In this pursuit the little command had gone without rations, and after recapturing the horses returned to Fort McPherson after a ride of one hundred and thirty miles in two days without food, and the whole party received most complimentary mention in a special order, while Buffalo Bill's double shot was the talk of the camp and set down as his having killed "two (red)birds with one stone."

General Duncan,[102] a hale, blunt old soldier, taking an expedition out on the warpath after Indians, Buffalo Bill went along as chief of scouts, the Pawnees under Major North accompanying him.

General Duncan had his own way of conducting a campaign, and he saw no reason why Pawnee scouts should not call out the hour as did the white sentinels, thus:

"Post number one, nine o'clock, and all's well!" This was all very well in a fort, and for soldiers who could speak English, but this last accomplishment the Pawnees did not possess to any extraordinary extent.

But General Duncan insisted that they should be taught, and therefore the Pawnees who had their regular turns at standing upon guard, were ordered to call the hour the same as the white soldiers.

Major North explained to them that when the man on post next to them should call out the hour, they must call it also as nearly like him as possible.

It was very amusing to hear them do this. They would try to remember what the other man had said on the post next to them. For instance a white soldier would call out: "Post No. 1, half-past nine o'clock, all is well!" The Indian standing next to him knew he was bound to say something in English, and he would sing out as best he could, lose his grip on the English the white sentinel had spoken, and put in the best he knew of the white man's language in place of it, and perpetrate something like this:

"Poss number—five cents—one o'clock—damn—I don't care!"

As there [sic] calls were so perfectly ridiculous, and the officers gathered to hear them, some of the young lieutenants slyly teaching the Pawnees some choice English to express themselves in, General Duncan was only too glad to countermand his own orders.

While proceeding up Prairie Dog Creek, near the scene where years ago Buffalo Bill as a boy had so nearly lost his life, by breaking his leg and having to wait long weeks alone in a dug-out, while his devoted friend, Dave Harrington, went for aid, the scout again very nearly terminated his career.

He had ridden on in advance with Major North, when they were charged upon by half a hundred Indians, and brought to bay their deadly aim and rapid firing of their revolvers at close quarters alone holding their red foes in check until assistance arrived from the command, and the game fight the two plainsmen had made was the admiration of officers and soldiers alike.

When Buffalo Bill returned to the fort he was greeted by the pleasant news that his wife had given birth to a son.

The naming of this little son was a matter of interest to all at McPherson, his father desiring to name him Elmo Judson, after Ned Buntline, but Major Brown won the day with the name he proposed—that of Kit Carson Cody.

CHAPTER LIII.
MY HERO BECOMES A JUSTICE OF THE PEACE.

"A stern chase"[103] on land as on sea, is proverbially a long one, and so a squadron of the Fifth found in pursuing another Indian village in retreat.

Buffalo Bill had with him on this expedition a scout who knew the country perfectly and the Indians equally as well.

He was an odd genius, hailing originally from Virginia, but had cast off the old love for the new, in other words had become so attached to a wild life that he took unto himself an Indian wife, the sister of a prominent chief, and who had saved his life a la Pocahontas.[104]

In the village of the Indians he had a family of young pale-face redskins, and seemed much attached to his squaw wife and children.

His name was John Y. Nelson, shortened into Jack Nelson, though he was just as well known by his Indian appellation of Cha-sha-cha-o-po-ge-o, which being interpreted means Red-Willow-Fill-the-Pipe.*

In pursuing the Indians Buffalo Bill found Jack Nelson an able ally, and the scout was one who was not above learning a lesson from anyone.

The second day of the stern chase after the Indian village, Buffalo Bill and Jack Nelson were well in advance, and came across an aged squaw who had been left by her people to die upon the prairie upon the plea that self defense is the first law of nature and she retarded their flight.

The Indians had built for her a wicky-up† and left her blankets and some food enough as they thought to last her on the easterly trail she had to follow to the Happy Hunting Grounds.

John Nelson recognized the old squaw as a relative of his wife, and having a talk with her she told him that they were pursuing the band of Pawnee Killer, a big chief, and they had lately killed a party of nine surveyors under Captain Buck,[105] at the place she named on Beaver Creek.

Driving these Indians across the Platte the command returned to Fort McPherson carrying the old squaw with them, thus treating her more humanely than had her own people, and she was cared for at the fort until her death.‡

---

*John Nelson was one of the scouts whom Buffalo Bill introduced to civilization on the stage and in his Wild West show. —The Author.

†A little lodge of brush the Indians leave their aged and infirm thus when in flight.

‡Later it may be mentioned herein Royal Buck, son of the slain surveyor came to McPherson, and went out under Buffalo Bill's guidance and an escort of cavalry to secure the remains of his father and those killed with him.

The skeletons only were found and decently interred at the mine of [illegible]. —The Author.

A number of petty crimes having been committed at the fort, among the civilian contingent, and no way to punish the offenders, General Emory had the county commissioners appoint Buffalo Bill justice of the peace, although he told the general that he knew no more about law that a mule did about singing.[106]

He was appointed however and up went his sign in a conspicuous place, reading:

WILLIAM F. CODY,

JUSTICE OF THE PEACE.

His first case was to prevent a stranger from carrying a horse out of the country, the owner of the animal coming to ask the scout-justice for a writ of replevin.[107]

He took down "Lucretia Borgia" and said:

"Come on."

The owner of the horse followed in dumb amazement at the "squire's" way of issuing a replevin, and followed.

The man and the horse were found and the justice covered the former with "Lucretia Borgia" and said:

"I want you and that steed."

"Take the horse but I have no time to go."

"I'll try this case right here, and as I know the facts of the case you are to give up the horse and pay the costs right here."

"What are the costs?" asked the man.

"Just twenty dollars."

The man counted the money, was given some advice gratis, about being more particular in the future about getting hold of the right horse, and was told to go, which he did without further trouble.

"That's what I call justice and law," said the owner of the horse, though perhaps the one who had lost the case would not have agreed with him.

I may add here that the Scout-justice settled all cares upon the basis of justice without perhaps studying up the law, until General Emory thought it best to have an assistant justice in the person of Lieutenant Burr Reilly of the Fifth Cavalry.

An important demand made upon the services of "Justice Buffalo Bill" at McPherson was to tie a marriage knot.

"Led by Destiny" : 263

Lieut. Reilly was away and could not be consulted, and so the scout had to depend upon his own resources.

The more he thought it over the more he became lost in uncertainty, and was tempted to get up an "Indian scare" and start at once upon the trail.

But reflection showed that he had not better do that.

So he spent hours trying to find some officer who had a bible to lend him, and at last found one, but it was a gambler at the fort who was the owner.

Obeying the injunction to "search the Scriptures,"[108] he did so diligently, but found nothing to help him out, and muttered:

"I could follow a jack-rabbit's trail easier," muttered the justice and then he turned to the only book in his library the statutes of Nebraska.

But he did not find anything there and as a messenger came up for him to say that the bride and bridegroom were waiting he broke out into a cold sweat, buckled his belt of arms and started.

He grew weak kneed as he saw the crowds gathered at the cabin of the bride, a buxom widow who was to marry a sergeant at the fort, and muttered to himself:

"I'd rather tackle a nest of grizzlies—tomorrow I'll resign.["]

CHAPTER LIV.
SPORT IN THE WILD WEST.

There have been a few situations in which William F. Cody has been placed that he has not had the presence of mind, or cleverness, to extricate himself; but when he had to marry the sergeant to the widow at Fort McPherson he felt that for once he had gotten beyond his depth and could find no straw even to grasp for aid.

He looked upon the large assembly of soldiers, and guests of both sexes there, for Fort McPherson had a large following about it, and in all that crowd he saw not one upon whom he could call for aid.

The soldiers had seen him time and again in a position where his word was law, when upon him hung their lives, and he was always cool and determined.

But now he felt, as he has since said he never felt but at one other time in his life, and that was when he faced an audience in a crowded theatre, when he was the star of the play.[109]

"Stand before me!" he roared, and the sergeant and bride-elect obeyed in that they faced him, for they were already standing up.

He asked the sergeant his name, then the bride;

"Mrs. Bridget Maloney, yer honor."

"In the eyes of the law you are Miss, for your being a widow don't count before this court.

"I'll call you plain Bridget—no, I cannot call you plain, for you are a very good-looking woman—sergeant, you have shown that you have good taste, whatever Mrs. Mallory, as I intend to make her, may have done," and the justice was plainly searching for the "trail" which he must strike into to properly go through the ceremony.

Suddenly recalling the words that had been asked him at his own marriage, he brightened up and said:

"See here, sergeant, I want to ask you if you will take this fair woman, ex-wife of Patrick Maloney, deceased—I suppose he is dead, Widow—"

"Yis, yer honor."

"Amen! May he rest in peace—as I was saying, sergeant, do you take this woman to love, to share your pay and be your loving wife so long as you both can agree?"

"It's what I will do, yer Honor."

"Spoken like a man.

"And do you, Bridget, take this man, the sergeant here, to be your husband, with no thought of the man that's gone to the Happy Hunting Grounds, or elsewhere, with no comparisons with the bygone Maloney, so long as you live[?]"

"Indeed I will, yer honor."

"Heaven bless you both, and remember all here present, that whoever the Lord hath joined together, with the aid of Buffalo Bill, let no man, or woman either, put asunder."

After the ceremony there was a feast, and "his Honor" was complimented upon the "eloquent" manner in which he had tied the two loving hearts together, but later discovered that a number of officers had stood outside the cabin and heard the whole service, as performed "according to Cody."

During the summer of 1871 Professor Marsh,[110] of Yale College, with a large party of students, came out to Fort McPherson on a search for fossils.

The professor had heard of the huge human bone found by the Pawnee scouts, and wished to find it, but as Buffalo Bill was ordered off on an Indian trail Major North accompanied the fossil hunters.

Though the party failed to find that big bone, they returned to the fort loaded down with all kinds of things to be treasured by the scientists.

As McPherson was in the very heart of a fine game country, though surrounded by hostile Indians, a number of adventurous huntsmen came out to bag big game, and in September, '71, General Sheridan brought a number of friends out for a grand game round up.

The party consisted of General Sheridan, Lawrence R. Jerome, James Gordon Bennett, of the New York Herald; Leonard W. Jerome, Carroll Livingston, Major J. G. Hecksher [sic, Heckscher], General Fitzhugh, General H. E. Davies, Captain M. Edward Rogers, Colonel J. Schuyler Crosby, Samuel Johnson, General Anson Stager, of the Western Union Telegraph Company; Charles Wilson, editor of the Chicago Evening Journal; General Rucker, Quartermaster-General, and Dr. Asch—the last two named being of General Sheridan's staff.[111] They were met at the station by General Emory and Major Brown with a cavalry company as escort and a sufficient number of vehicles to carry the distinguished visitors and their baggage.

A brisk drive of less than two hours over a hard and smooth road brought them to the fort, where they found the garrison, consisting of five companies of the Fifth Cavalry, under the command of General Carr, out on parade awaiting their arrival. The band played some martial music, and the cavalry passed very handsomely in review before General Sheridan. The guests were then most hospitably received, and assigned to comfortable quarters.

Lieutenant Hayes [sic, Hays], the quartermaster of the expedition, arranged everything for the comfort of the party. One hundred cavalry under command of Major Brown were detailed as an escort. A train of sixteen wagons was provided to carry the baggage, supplies, and forage for the trip; and beside these there were three four-horse ambulances in which the guns were carried, and in which members of the party who became weary of the saddle might ride and rest. At General Sheridan's request Buffalo Bill was to go as guide and scout in the big hunt.

The entire party greatly enjoyed the hunt, and secured buffalo, elk and antelope, while they took much interest in the villages of the prairie dogs, sometimes several miles in extent.*

The hunters on their return, a short distance beyond the dog town, discovered a settlement of white men, who proved to be the Clifford brothers, Arthur Ruff, Dick Seymour, and John Nelson. Each of them had a squaw wife and numerous halfbreed children, living in tents of buffalo skins. They owned a herd of horses and mules and a few cattle, and had cultivated a small piece of land. Their principal occupation was hunting, and they had a large number of buffalo hides, which they had tanned in the Indian manner.

When the party at last returned to McPherson they one and all pronounced Buffalo Bill a "mighty hunter," for he had certainly shown them game in abundance, and they had killed buffaloes, elk, deer, antelope, wild turkeys, teal ducks, rabbits, raccoons, prairie dogs and coyotes galore.†

Upon his return from this hunt Buffalo Bill again started out with General Carr and some friends, it being a scout after Indians and buffalo hunting combined.

CHAPTER LV.
THE DUKE ALEXIS HUNT.

In the latter part of 1871 the Grand Duke Alexis of Bunia [sic, Russia],[112] visited the United States, and as he was an all round good fellow, barring

---

*These animals are found throughout the plains, living together in a sort of society; their numberless burrows in their "towns" adjoin each other, so that great care is necessary in riding through these places, as the ground is so undermined as often to fall in under the weight of a horse. Around the entrance to their holes the ground is piled up almost a foot high; on these little elevations the prairie dogs sit upon their hind legs, chattering to each other and observing whatever passes on the plains. They will permit a person to approach quite near, but when they have viewed him closely, they dive into their dens with wonderful quickness. They are difficult to kill, and if hit generally succeed in crawling underground before they can be captured. Rattlesnakes and small owls are generally found in great numbers in the prairie dog towns, and live in the same holes with the dogs on friendly terms. Prairie dogs are found to be very palatable eating. —The Author.

†A little volume of the scout was written by General Davies, and entitled "Ten Days on the Plains." —The Author.

his inherited title "by the grace of God," every effort was made by Americans having his entertainment in charge to give a royal good time in this republican country.

Feasting, balls and city amusements he could have at home, and he was given a surfeit of them in the east, but the wild west of America he knew only by report, and he longed to become better acquainted with life on the plains.

The Duke had been a great traveler, had hunted big and savage game in eastern lands and was a crack shot and perfect sportsman.

He spoke English well, had a staff of good comrades with him, and all were anxious to accept General Sheridan's invitation to a hunt in the Wild West.

Avant couriers were sent to Fort McPherson to prepare the way, and General Sheridan had ordered that Buffalo Bill should find a good camp ground on the Red Willow Creek, and find out where game was most plentiful.

He was also to find old Spotted Tail,[113] chief of the Sioux Indians, then enjoying patched up peace with the whites, and induce the great chieftain to come to the Alexis camp, accompanied by a hundred of his leading chiefs and warriors, to make the acquaintance of the Grand Duke.

The general wished Buffalo Bill to notify Spotted Tail that he wished him to get a grand war dance for the entertainment of the Duke, and to have some of his best buffalo hunters along to show how the Indians killed their game.

The journey to Spotted Tail's village Buffalo Bill found by no means a pleasant one, for the weather was very cold, and then too, though Spotted Tail was friendly to the whites just then, many of his young man were not and the scout took big chances in going alone a hundred and fifty miles to the Sioux village.

To better insure his safety, after discovering the village, Buffalo Bill entered it by night, wrapping a blanket about him and making his way to the headquarter tepee of the Indian General.

The chief recognized him the moment he appeared before him, and treated him cordially, there being present a white man who was Spotted Tail's agent, a man who had lived much among the Sioux, and whose name was Todd Randall.[114]

Stating his business, Buffalo Bill told Spotted Tail he would greatly please General Sheridan if he would meet him at the old Government Crossing of the Red Willow, in "ten sleeps" from that night, to welcome the Big Chief from across the great water.

Spotted Tail seemed pleased at the honor done him, and said he would select those who were to accompany him, and would be at the Red Willow on time.

He then congratulated the scout upon his cunning way of getting into his village, as many of his young man would have wished to kill him, had they seen him, and with the hospitality of a "fine old country gentleman," bade a squaw to get his supper, and called a brave to care for his horse.

That night Buffalo Bill slept in the Chief's tepee, and the next morning when the villagers were assembled they were asked if they knew the scout.

From the numerous replies Buffalo Bill saw that he had a very large acquaintance, scores of warriors answering:

"It is Pa-e-has-ka the Prairie Chief."*

Telling his people that he was the friend of Pa-e-has-ka, Spotted Tail said they must treat him as such, but Buffalo Bill read in the looks of many a longing for his scalp lock.

But he had to take the chances of losing it and started upon his return for the camp on the Red Willow, arriving in safety, to find Captain Egan of the Second Cavalry there preparing for the entertainment of the Grand Duke, his suite,[115] the other guests, and Spotted Tail and his following, who were to be most generously dealt with.

Upon January 12, '72, the Grand Duke and party arrived by special train at North Platte, and an escort of cavalry and Buffalo Bill were in waiting.

Presented to the Duke by General Sheridan, Buffalo Bill was much pleased with the Prince of Russia, and before the hunt was over the two became fast friends.

General Custer also formed one of the party and he and the Grand Duke seemed to be congenial spirits.

True to his promise old Spotted Tail and his people came to the camp, and the Duke had an opportunity of seeing just what the American In-

---

*Long Hair, the Sioux name for the scout. —The Author.

dian was, and he showed much interest in them, while when Two Lance, a chief, in hunting buffalo sent an arrow clean through a large bull running at full speed, he marveled greatly as did the others of the party, for it was an accomplishment which Two Lance alone could do.

Guided by Buffalo Bill the Duke was enabled to kill a number of buffaloes,[116] and he was so pleased with his hunt.

On the return to the train General Sheridan and the Duke rode together in an open carriage drawn by six cavalry horses, and as Buffalo Bill was to drive the General told the scout to give his highness an exhibition of how he could drive a coach and six over the Rocky Mountains.

The scout obeyed too literally, the General and the Duke having hard work holding themselves in the vehicle, when the spirited team was put at a run down into the valley of the Medicine Creek, a distance of three miles and made in about seven minutes.

Though without any accident the ride was made, the Grand Duke when asked how he enjoyed it, frankly confessed that he would rather return to Russia via Alaska, swim Bering straits and then home all the way on a mule, than take another such ride, which went to show that he had fun enough for one outing.

Upon arriving at North Platte the Duke invited Buffalo Bill to his car, presented him with several valuable souvenirs of his hunt, thanked him most warmly for his kindness and invited him to visit him if he ever crossed the seas.

CHAPTER LVI.
IN A MIMIC ROLE.

From North Platte, after bidding the Duke Alexis good-bye, Buffalo Bill accompanied General Ord,[117] then commander of the department of the Platte, over to McPherson in his ambulance.

On the way the General tendered the scout a commission as an officer in the regular army, an honor that was courteously yet firmly declined.

As General Sheridan had urged upon the scout to accept the many invitations he had received, to go east, he decided at last to do so.

Obtaining a thirty days leave of absence, Buffalo Bill took the train for Chicago, where he became the guest of General Sheridan, and spent several days most delightfully in what he was pleased to call "a swallow-tail expedition among the pale faces."

From Chicago Buffalo Bill took the "trail" to New York, having every honor shown him on the way.

Arriving in the great Metropolis he was cordially welcomed by those who had known him upon the plains, among them being Mr. James Gordon Bennett of the Herald, and Leonard N. Jerome who treated him most royally, as did his friend Ned Brinkline [sic, Buntline] who could not do too much for the noted plainsmen who at once became a "lion" in society.

One evening, with Ned Buntline and others, he attended the theater when Jack Studley was playing the part of Buffalo Bill in a play dramatized from Buntline's story of the scout published in the New York Weekly.[118]

The audience at once called for the "real hero, Buffalo Bill," and he was led out upon the stage and presented to them, retreating however as quickly as he could do so into what he called, "one of the canyons of the stage."

The manager then and there offered him Five Hundred Dollars[119] a week to play "Buffalo Bill" himself, but the offer was declined with thanks.

After a visit to General Henry R. Guss, an uncle living in Westchester, Penn., Buffalo Bill turned his face once more toward the Land of the Setting Sun, much pleased with his visit east, and wholly unspoiled by the flattery showered upon him, as was shown by his at once taking the saddle again as "Cody the Scout" to go out upon an expedition after Indians who had raided the McPherson railroad station, killed three men and run off a number of horses.

Upon this trail Buffalo Bill went with the Third Cavalry and had as an ally Texas Jack* a scout upon whom he knew he could thoroughly rely.[120]

The trail started upon was a difficult one to follow, but Buffalo Bill mastered it, and after two days hard riding, being far ahead of the command with Texas Jack and a few other scouts, they came up with and had a brush with thirteen braves killing two of them.

---

*Texas Jack, J. B. Omohundro, a [T]exas ranger in the Confederate Army, later a scout in the Northwest and a brave, dashing fellow, the boon companion of Buffalo Bill and Wild Bill, and later associated with William Cody in his first dramatic venture. Texas Jack died some years ago in Leadville. —The Author.

But the Indians rushed in to close quarters, and in the hot fight that followed Buffalo Bill killed two of them with his revolvers, but was wounded himself in the head, while his horse also received a severe wound.

One of the scouts had been killed, Buffalo Bill and his horse wounded, and the Indians lost six out of their band of thirteen, but took to flight when the soldiers appeared in the distance coming to the rescue.

And so the scouts after the hostiles continued, Buffalo Bill steadily adding to his reputation as a great scout, guide and Indian fighter, under the different commanding officers with whom he served, until his name became known the land over.

In the fall of 1872, it may be interesting to know, on account of his name having been in all the American papers as the plucky owner of the [yacht] Valkyrie, the Earl of Dunraven[121] came to McPherson, bearing a letter from General Sheridan to Buffalo Bill, asking him to guide him and others on an elk hunt.

As Buffalo Bill was recalled from that hunt before it ended, he left Texas Jack in his place, and that scout afterwards accompanied the Earl upon several expeditions on the prairies and in the Rocky Mountains, and I may here remark that the Earl of Dunraven, whom the writer also met on the plains is a most congenial hunting companion, a splendid sportsman, utterly fearless and a gentleman whom it is an honor to have the friendship of.

Upon his return from a long scout in 1872, Buffalo Bill was surprised, and somewhat abashed to find that some of his friends had made him their candidate for the Twenty-sixth District in the Nebraska Legislature.

The District was largely Republican, he was, and is, a Democrat, and he felt that it was a forlorn hope to run.

But he was in the hands of his friends, made the run, with no effort of his own however, and was elected,[122] thus winning the title of "Honorable" so long used before his name before it was supplanted by the, to him, better united [sic, suited] one of Colonel, which rank he attained in the Nebraska National Guard, though today it is Brigadier General William F. Cody.

As Ned Buntline had conceived the idea that Buffalo Bill would make a great hit upon the stage, he continually wrote to him to come east and make his fortune as a dramatic star.

At last Buffalo Bill decided to make the venture, though with many misgivings, and he accordingly sent his family to St. Louis on a visit, and taking Texas Jack on the trail with him started for Chicago to join Buntline.

Mark Twain cannot tell a story more humorously than does Buffalo Bill tell of that first venture, the writing of the play, study of his part, stage fright before an audience that packed the house, and awaking the next morning to find that the "Scouts of the Plains"[123]—the name of the play—was an immense success.

In the "Indian killing scenes," Buffalo Bill asserts that both Texas Jack and himself were at home, a great success, slaying the "supers,"[124] made up as Indians, in one act, to have them bob up serenely in the next to be killed over again.

Thus was the Rubicon passed, and Buffalo Bill saw there was no backing out then, he had become an actor, living over upon the stage the stirring scenes of his life, yet, with a stern sense of duty to the dwellers upon the far frontier, letting it be known to the commanding officers, whom he had served so long and faithfully, that the unreal would be dropped for the real the moment that they called him to come.

"HONORS EASY"

Or
Trailing Toward Sunset:
A Biography of the Later Years of
Colonel W. F. Cody—"Buffalo Bill"

Note—"Honors Easy" is the third and last of the Biographical Series of Col. W. F. Cody, the first being "A Man of the West," the second, "Led by Destiny," which follow the noted Plainsman from earliest boyhood to the present day, through all his eventful and phenomenal career. —The Author.

CHAPTER I.
A MAN AMONG MEN.

How phenomenal is the nature of a man, who, born in the "Land of the Setting Sun," reared amid scenes of hardship and danger, becoming a hero when a boy, devoting the earliest years of his teens to the support of his mother and sisters, step by step climbed to fortune and fame, unaided save by his own pluck and determination. The uniform of an army officer, the full dress of a society man, and the picturesque costumes of the footlights, William F. Cody Buffalo Bill wore with the same ease and grace that he did his leggings of buckskin, hunting shirt and sombrero.

Having now passed the half century post of age, William Cody is wearing all the honors he has won with modesty, and has faced the trail towards sunset with the same firm front that has marked each deed of his early life.

In writing a biography of such a man it has been my desire to bring him before my readers from earliest boyhood up to the present time, from the barefoot boy to the man full of honors won, and who, approaching the closing years of life can look back over his checkered career without fear and without reproach.

A hero before he entered his teens, he has always seemed to feel that destiny was leading him on to some great end, and his whole career has been marked by a determined purpose to carry out that fate whatever it might be.

Born at a time when indeed the wild west was a wilderness, and a Land of Death to the bold pioneers who invaded it, he has seen in his short life—for half a century is but a few years after all—the prairies, plains and mountains he trod in earlier years, become peopled with millions of inhabitants, and grand cities spring up upon the scenes of the early bivouac, and magnificent homes built on many a field of desperate battle with the redskins.

It was the fame won in those early days as pony express rider, stage driver, guide, scout and Indian fighter, that made the name of Buffalo Bill known throughout the world. It gave to that name a fame that was recognized by Ned Buntline—Col. E. Z. C. Judson, soldier and author when he wrote his first story "The Great Plainsman," a romance founded upon strangest and sternest facts.

It has been said by many that:

"Ned Buntline made Buffalo Bill."

Heroes are born, not made, and circumstances bring them out of obscurity, and cause them to show what is in them.

William Cody began to make a history for himself when but twelve years of age, and it was when his name was spoken around every camp fire upon the frontier that Col. Judson found in him a hero for stories of the West, and hence made a pilgrimage to the Plains to see what manner of man he was.

He found him not one whit over estimated, indeed that the half had not been told of the daring army scout and Indian fighter, and returning to the east he wrote for Street & Smith's new weekly story paper, the novel that created such a great sensation, its chief merit being that it made a hero of a real personage, whose deeds were then the talk of every border bivouac.

The success of this story called for a second one, and a third, from the same facile pen that had charmed so many with its romances of both sea and land, but is now stilled forever, as the hand that held it, and bravely wielded the sword as well, is folded in the sleep of eternity.

With such a man for a hero as William Cody, Ned Buntline had the material for his romances, for the claim to heroism has been well-founded.

Upon the romantic career of Buffalo Bill, the writer of this biography, following the example set by Ned Buntline, and knowing the hero when he was fighting for fame, has written many a border tale "founded on fact," but he is now telling the story of his hero's life as it was and not as painted in the glowing tints of fiction.

It was that same fame won on the lone trail, in the dreary march, in battle, and in the death struggle, that afterwards led William Cody to the East, to portray upon the dramatic stage the mimic scenes of his life in the wild west, the tragedies of an eventful career, and here again Ned Buntline was the author of the scout's first play, bringing into it, with Buffalo Bill, his border pards, "Wild Bill" James B. Hickok, and "Texas Jack"—John B. Omohundro, men of the Buckskin who have gone on their last trail across the "Great Divide."

Making a pronounced success as a writer, William Cody was sought after by publishers, for stories founded on facts in his eventful life, and being a good storyteller around the camp fire, he was tempted to become one with the pen as well as the tongue. Thus it was that he drifted into authorship, his first story, a short sketch, having been taken down in short hand as he told it years ago to the writer of this biography.

His second sketch was written by himself, and an amusing part of it was, that when asked why he did not use capitals and punctuation marks, his reply was: "Life is too short to make big letters where little ones will do, and if the readers cannot catch their breath without my having to jot down all those little marks for them, they will have to lose it, that's all."

Later, however, when orders began to flow in, with big prices offered, Mr. Cody realized that the "little marks," and the difference between the small and big letters, as he put it, meant a great deal, and he settled down to hard study, his school days having ended very early in his teens. As he determined to learn from books as he had from signs on the plains, he was not long in becoming master of a fair education and a fine reader of human nature, and a close observer of all he sees, he is to day a man of most universal information. None except several most intimate friends, knew how hard he studied, and that no cadet at West Point ever "boned" his lessons with more energy and determination to learn is a fact I can vouch for.

Within less than a year after receiving his first order for literary work, Mr. Cody sent in a clean manuscript, well written, the story well told, and with as few errors from first to last as many a college student would have been guilty of.

As no money, offered by theatrical managers, could tempt him to go out of the field as an actor, that he knew perfectly, the field of the Wild West, so no inducement of publishers could make him write of other than the scenes of his buckskin days.

Thoroughly familiar with army life, with the geography of the West, with the game of the Rocky Mountains and Plains, with its wild animals, he was well fitted to write of such as one who well knew, but themes outside of that he would not touch upon.

Once, when sending a border story to a publisher, Mr. Cody wrote as follows:

"I am very sorry to have had to lie so in this story, but I believe it is the fashion of a novelist to do that—in fact that is the romance of it I am told.

"I have made my hero slay more Philistines—I mean Indians—in one war trail, than I ever was forced to slay in my life; but I am told that one must do this to interest the reader, as the more blood and thunder[1] there is in a novel the more it is liked.

"If you think my hero used his revolver, rifle and bowie knife too freely with the red skins, you can cut out a fatal shot or two wherever you deem best, and charge it to fiction.

"Let me state, however, that the scenes are all real, the fiction is founded upon facts, and I have tried to keep as near the truth as it was possible for a pen, liar to do."

The publishers brought this story out as written, and in spite of the author's remarks regarding the number of Indians slain in the romance in comparison to other border stories written by writers who pretend to know much of the wild west, there was very little killing done.

In his romances, which are intended to be as true to life as possible, he takes typical characters of the western country: the mining camps, the wagon trains, and the denizens generally of a border settlement.

These characters are handled with a master hand; brought into romance just as they are in reality, save for exaggeration demanded by sensational literature.

Having been forced into authorship as he was into acting, William Cody looked about him for other fields to conquer, that is, if he was to be an actor at all, he preferred to be one with the surroundings of the plains about him.

So it was that he evolved through his fertile and energetic brain, the idea of the "Wild West Exhibition," which was first produced in Omaha, Nebraska.

CHAPTER II.
THE FIRST THEATRICAL VENTURE.

Between the time William Cody's debut as an actor in theatres, and his appearance before the public as the Chief of the Wild West Exhibition, years elapsed, so, as a faithful recorder of facts, I must speak more on the subject of his dramatic career.

The "Scouts of the Plains," the melodrama written for him by Ned Buntline, had in it leading parts for two prairie pards, "Wild Bill" and "Texas Jack," two men also closely connected with frontier history.[2]

Never caring to take a trail alone when he could travel in good company, Buffalo Bill had written West for the two plainsmen to come East—Chicago was far East then—and join him in an important enterprise he had on foot.

He dared not tell them what that enterprise was, as he knew full well that they would "stampede."

Willing to follow Buffalo Bill's lead the two pards went to Chicago and the "Three of a kind" met in the Palmer House one morning, where the two late arrivals were presented to Col. Judson—"Ned Buntline."[3]

Just how to explain matters to his two pards Buffalo Bill did not know, and that he was greatly embarrassed having to do so may be seen from the manner in which he opened the subject, for he began with:

"Don't shoot me, pards, but I've enlisted you for the most tangled trail of your lives.

"I'm awful sorry, as you will be, but it couldn't be helped, you know, for we must follow our destiny, lead where it may, and this gentleman here, a distinguished writer, as you know, has decided what we are to do.

"He will drill us, coach us he calls it and—well I'll just let him explain for I see that you are getting ready to slay me if I keep on."

Wild Bill and Texas Jack were worried.

What had their devoted friend gotten them into, they wondered.

But Ned Buntline was a man equal to any occasion, awake to any emergency.

He looked with delight upon the newly arrived scouts.

Not so handsome as Buffalo Bill, they were yet fine specimens of manhood, and their long hair set off faces that would command admiration and respect anywhere, while in physique, though of different build, they were all that could be desired.

As intelligence showed in their faces, Ned Buntline was assured that he could make actors of them, while the "records" they had would make a hit anywhere.

Ned Buntline was a man with quiet dignity, one who made his presence felt, and the two new comers saw in him a man to command their esteem.

In his quiet way then he began to unfold his plot, and was listened to with deepest attention by all, Buffalo Bill watching eagerly the effect of his words upon Wild Bill and Texas Jack.

They listened with deepest attention, now and then glancing at each other, as though to question:

"What has pard Bill gotten us into?"

When they looked toward Buffalo Bill his face was a study for an artist.

He looked the picture of indifference, seeming to take all as a matter of fact too trifling to consider.

At last Ned Buntline's story was told, the plot unfolded, and he continued with:

"Now, boys, you know it all.

"You are to go upon the stage and act just as you have upon the plains,

Buffalo Bill Cody, courtesy of Buffalo Bill Museum and Grave, Golden, CO

only I'll teach you a few words to say at the proper time, and I'll furnish you with the Indians to kill—mock Indians you know—whom I can get for 25 cents a night.["]

"Do you mean that men in Chicago are so anxious to get out of town they will let us kill them for 25 cents?" asked Wild Bill, while Texas Jack added:

"You'll pay them in advance I suppose, so they can chip in and buy liquor to get drunk on?"

Ned Buntline explained that it must be "mock killing," as well as "mock Indians," and soon let the scouts into the secrets of "supers" and how they were used.

As Buntline himself was to take a part in the play of an old hunter, which he looked without being made up for the occasion, Wild Bill and Texas Jack were at last led into a promise to become actors, especially as they were to make a tour of the country as such.

"You must know, Pard Buntline, that if the Indians get on the rampage while we are East, this contract don't hold a little bit, for we'll be needed with the army," said Buffalo Bill and his two pards agreed with him.

"All right, boys, that goes into the contract, and if you are called back into the army to fight redskins I'll go with you."

This reply of Buntline's got for him a cheer that stampeded the chambermaids off the floor of the hotel where their rooms were.

But the contract was made and Ned Buntline at once began to write his play, a feat he accomplished in four days as can be vouched for.[4]

The "parts" were written, a company engaged, with some fifty "supers" to play Indian and be killed, printing was gotten out, advertisements put in all the papers stating that:

"Buffalo Bill and his brother scouts would appear in an Indian melo-drama, entitled: 'The Scouts of the Plains' at the Amphitheatre," etc. etc.

Their "parts" were given to the scouts who looked at them as they might at the Chinese alphabet, when told they had to learn them, picking up their lines as they got their cue.

For a while Ned Buntline feared they would strike the trail for the far West; but by dint of encouragement, persuasion and patient teaching he at last felt that he would make a success of his undertaking.

CHAPTER III.
IN A NEW ROLE.

Instead of six months which Texas Jack had first decided it would take him to learn the lines he was to speak in the play of the Scouts of the Plains, he was but half as many days committing them to memory, and Buffalo Bill rejoiced in the fact that he also knew his part perfectly. Whether they could speak them before a large audience was a question that bothered the scouts, especially as Ned Buntline had hinted to them that actors were frequently taken with a stage fright which rendered them incapable to utter a word.

"But we are not actors," had been Buffalo Bill's argument.

When the night came for the performance Ned Buntline corraled the scouts in his room and said:

"For the Lord sake, boys, don't weaken now."

Had it not been for Buffalo Bill just then, there is no doubt but that Wild Bill and Texas Jack would have taken a fast train to the West, and it would have been a miracle to have ever gotten them East again.

"Stick to it boys, for pard Ned here says that it is the turning point of our lives, and will lead us on to fortune and to fame," said Buffalo Bill.

"A fortune is just what I am after, I've been poor too long, and I'll give the wheel a turn to see what luck I will have on this deal," said Wild Bill,[5] and the faint reply came from Texas Jack:

"I'm with you pard."

The rehearsals had hardly been a great success, but still there was some hope that the play would pass off reasonably well, as all the actors and actresses engaged to support the scouts were well up in their profession.[6]

Going to the theatre the scouts donned their buckskin suits, the costume in which they were to appear, and Ned Buntline, in his frontier garb, looked more than ever like a thorough frontiersman.

As the time came for the curtain to go up, there was more nervousness shown in that group of scouts than they had ever been guilty of in the face of the deadliest danger.

They would look through the holes in the curtains and see the people gazing toward the stage, and this made them more and more uncomfortable.

At length the curtain rose, and they nerved themselves to the task before them, and stepped out to make their first bow before the public over the footlights.

Ned Buntline in the part of "Cale Durg" gave the cue to Buffalo Bill to speak his lines, but the tongue of the scout clove to the roof of his mouth, and he uttered not a word.

All the lines which he had known perfectly, faded from his memory, and he was in professional parlance "completely stuck."

But Buntline was equal to the occasion, and asked in an easy way:

"Where have you been, Bill, and what kept you so long?"

At that moment the eyes of Buffalo Bill fell upon a gentleman from Chicago seated in a box surrounded by his friends, one whom he had met upon the plains, and guided in a grand hunt.

He knew him as a popular man, and that he was widely known in Chicago, so he replied to Buntline's question:

"I have been out on a hunt with Milligan."

This caused immediate applause, for the whole hunt had been written up in the Chicago papers, at the time of its occurrence, and many a joke had been told of Milligan's scare by the Indians.

The audience cheered and applauded, and this gave Buffalo Bill confidence at once that he could go through the play, if he could only remember his lines.

Buntline saw the situation, and said immediately:

"Well, Bill, tell us about Milligan's hunt."

At once at his ease, Buffalo Bill proceeded to relate in detail and in his inimitable style, the particulars of the hunt, and succeeded in making it very amusing for he was frequently interrupted by rounds of applause at Milligan's expense.

If he began to weaken Buntline would chip in with some word to give him a fresh start, and in this way a quarter of an hour went by without the distinguished scout uttering a single word of his part.

The prompter who stood in the wings, attempted to prompt him, but it did no good, it was not the lines of the play that Buffalo Bill wanted just then, and he continued to "chip in" on anything he thought of.

Being an Indian drama, the Scouts of the Plains had at least fifty supers dressed up as Indians, and when it came to "shooting scenes" the three scouts were decidedly at home, and blazed away with a skill and rapidity that fairly paralyzed the audience, and sent the mock Indians down upon the stage at every shot.

Finally when the curtain dropped, except the line spoken by Buntline and the real actors and actresses of the play, not a word of the lines had been uttered by the scouts.

Financially the play made a success that opening night.

There was no backing out after that and the scouts felt that they must go on, for they could see that Buntline had been right in his prophecy that it would lead them on to fortune at least, if not to fame.

The criticisms that appeared in the Chicago papers the following morning were simply funny.

They gave the scouts a far better send off than the men in Buckskin had expected, for the critics didn't once attempt to criticize them as actors.

As the acting of the professionals had been good they gave them the credit they deserved, but Buntline was made the butt of much amusement by the reporters, who stated that the author had said he had written the play in four days, and the question was asked:

"What had he been doing all that time?"

Another paper stated that the play could be played from the middle both ways, or begun at the end and played backward with equal success.

Another paper stated that Buntline as "Cale Durg," was killed in the second act, and that there were regrets in the audience that he had not met his end in the first act, especially as he had taken the opportunity to ring in a temperance lecture whenever he had the opportunity to speak.

That the play was a financial success can be better shown by stating that a number of managers at once wrote asking to take full charge of the company, others to purchase partnership in the enterprise.

For what they were as scouts of the plains in realty [sic], Buffalo Bill and his pards received full credit, the audience all recognizing in them real heroes, men who had passed through scenes of deadly danger, and who had faced death a hundred times in the defense of others.

The following week the [S]couts of the Plains played at De Bar's Opera House, in St. Louis, to a tremendous business, and the week after in Cincinnati where the theatre was so crowded every night that as many people were turned away as gained admission to the house.

"*Honors Easy*" : 285

So it went on with equal success and triumph in all the large cities of the country, offers of engagements being made by all managers of the leading theatres.

Having become easy in their lines, and no longer abashed at looking at an audience in the face over the footlights the scouts aided all in their power in making the play a complete success, artistically.

As an evidence of the financial success of Ned Buntline's venture with the men in buckskin, I may mention that the gross receipts at the Boston theatre for one week was $16,200 and at Niblo's Garden, New York, the house was crowded to its utmost capacity, the amount realized on the week being nearly $20,000.[7]

In not a single city where the scouts appeared was there a seat to be had after the rise of the curtain.

In many of the places visited, Buffalo Bill became a social lion, being received by the first people, who vied with each other in showing him courtesy and kindness.

This remarkable tour closed on 16th of June, 1873,[8] and it decided Buffalo Bill in going upon the road the following year, and being his own manager.

Longing to get back upon the plains, the scouts started westward after a short visit in New York city, and arrived at Fort McPherson, Nebraska, where Buffalo Bill at once entered upon his duties as Chief of Scouts of the Department of the Platte.

After a few months of service on the plains Buffalo Bill again went to the east and organized a theatrical company for the season of '73–'74, Wild Bill and Texas Jack being brother scouts in the enterprise.

But Wild Bill had seen enough of the east and longed to return to the plains.

As he could not get leave to go, Wild Bill determined to get discharged, and to do this he got into the habit of firing his blank cartridges so close to the legs of the supers, who were playing dead Indians, that he was wont to bring them to life again with wild yells.

The supers of course were not to blame, and Buffalo Bill finding expostulations with his pard were useless, put the blame where it was due and told Wild Bill that he must either quit resurrecting the dead Indians or leave the company.

No more was said at that time, but when the curtain arose again Buffalo Bill suddenly discovered Wild Bill sitting in the front row in the orchestra, where he seemed to be greatly enjoying the play.

With a comrade of many a long trail, Buffalo Bill could not be angry, and that night after the performance was over he tried to persuade Wild Bill to return to the company, but in vain.

He, therefore, made him up a purse and bade him goodbye, a longing coming over him as he saw his friend depart for the plains, to accompany him, for the old love was strong within his heart.

CHAPTER IV.
THE RETURN TO THE PLAINS.

After playing a most successful season, Texas Jack remaining with him throughout, Buffalo Bill closed the company in Boston on May 13th, 1874.[9]

The two comrades of the plains were longing to don their working buckskins in earnest and once more, rifle in hand, be in the saddle.

The luxuries and pleasures of the east with all the admiration they had won there, the success they had conquered, could not wean them from their old love, a life in the Wild West.

The love of the prairies, the mountains, the bivouac and long trail, the solitude of mighty Nature was too deeply bred in the bone of the scouts to remain amid scenes so widely different from what they had been accustomed to.

While in New York, preparing to start west, Buffalo Bill met an English gentleman by the name of Medley.

He was from London, a man of large wealth, and being a great hunter in foreign lands he had come to America for a hunt on the plains, and was most anxious to secure the services of the great scout as a guide.

The liberal pay offered—one thousand dollars a month and expenses—decided Buffalo Bill in making up his mind to accompany the Englishman, especially when the latter told him that it was not to be a mere pleasure excursion but that he wished to rough it in every sense of the word.

To the hunting grounds of Nebraska they went then, the start being from North Platte, then a village, and a very different place from the handsome city of today.

I need here merely to say that the hunt was a most enjoyable one, and Mr. Medley was more than pleased with his experience of wild life on the western plains, while he won the scout's admiration by proving himself a fine hunter, and when in camp was always ready to do his share of the work, of carrying wood and water, looking after the fire and attending to the horses.

Having escorted Mr. Medley to the railroad, Buffalo Bill found orders awaiting him to report to Colonel Mills,[10] who was going on an extended scout to the Powder River.

The command started from Rawlings [sic, Rawlins] Wyoming, with Buffalo Bill as Chief of Scouts, while he had as able allies two prominent bordermen, Tom Surr [sic, Sun] and Bony Ernest.

On this expedition Buffalo Bill felt he was going home, so to speak, for he was upon the scene of his pony riding and stage driving days, where he met with many a thrilling adventure as the reader will recall.

Arriving in the Indian country Colonel Mills left his two companies of infantry to guard his supply camp, and with seven troops of cavalry went on a rapid scout, surprising Little Wolf's band of Arapahoes and driving them back into the agencies.

The chief of scouts then guided the command along the Powder River, Crazy Woman's Fork and Clear Fork, then westward through the mountains into the Wind River country.

After several months spent on this expedition, in which much valuable service was done, the command returned to Rawlings, and the winter season approaching Buffalo Bill once more left the real life on the plains for the mimic, returning east to re-organize his dramatic company for the tour of 1874–75.

As Texas Jack was in the Yellowstone country, hunting with the Earl of Dunraven, of now unfortunate yachting fame,[11] Buffalo Bill, as he expressed it, "had to play a lone hand" as an actor, as far as comrades in buckskin were concerned.

But be it known that he had, with the same energy, determination and intelligence with which he had entered upon any duty, accomplished wonders in a dramatic way.

He had become thoroughly accustomed to the various workings of the stage, and had mastered the intricacies of managing as well, understanding the "front of the house" as he did the stage.

Swinging around the circle of the principal cities Buffalo Bill found that he was the same tremendous "drawing card" as before, and he was nearing the fulfillment of Ned Buntline's prophecy of "fame and fortune."

But he still had a longing to accomplish more than he had yet done, he wished to play in a drama of more pretensions than the opening piece, and put it upon the stage in the very finest style as regards scenic effects and artistic support.

To this end he did not remain long on the plains after his season closed, but moved his family to Rochester, and begun preparations for his next venture, in which Texas Jack was to be again his ally.

The season opened brilliantly, and all was going artistically when just before the curtain rose one night at Springfield, Massachusetts, April 20th, 1876, William Cody received a telegram that sent the blood surging through heart and brain.

It was from his temporary home in Rochester, and told him that his only son, the idol of the family, little Kit Carson Cody was lying at the point of death.

Since his mother's death William Cody had never received a severer blow; but he was outwardly calm, whatever he inwardly felt, and calling his manager—John M. Burke[12]—he told him the sad news, and said that he would play the first act himself, and then he, Burke, must make the proper excuses to the audience and take his part for the rest of the performance.

This was done, Buffalo Bill playing through the first act without faltering, and then catching the train for Rochester, while John Burke, a fine actor and man of much experience, assumed the role of the great scout.

Arriving at Rochester the next morning William Cody the loving father, found little Kit still alive, and bending over the tiny counterpart of himself, he saw that he was known, for the small hands were raised and clasped about the neck of the strong man whose idol was to be taken from him, for, burning up with scarlet fever there was no hope for the little boy.

All day long the strong man, with a touch as tender as a woman, sat by the dying boy, waiting with a loving mother and wife for the end to come.

At last the feeble breath floated away and little Kit Carson Cody, of whom his father and mother had such hope for after years, had faded out of sight.

"He is dead," said the father and he turned to comfort the loving wife, who so deeply felt the blow that had fallen upon her in the death of her only son—poor little Kit, cut off in the brightness of his boyhood years.

CHAPTER V.
A SCOUT ONCE MORE.

It was with a very sad heart that William Cody bade his wife and daughters, Arta and Ora [sic, Orra] goodbye, after Little Kit had been laid to rest in Mount Hope Cemetery, Rochester, and returned to his life on the stage once more.

Those who knew him best saw that a shadow had fallen upon his life which time alone could drive away, for he is a man of deepest feelings devoted to his family and home life and a little vacant chair would forever remain in his memory.

Not long after his return to his Theatrical company the scout received a letter from Colonel Mills giving him a hint that there was trouble enough on the frontier for his services to be of great value just then.

Though he was playing to crowded houses nightly, and money was filling his pockets, Buffalo Bill was not so much of an actor that he could refuse to go to the front when he deemed his comrades in arms needed his aid.

So he at once decided to close his season and leave for the west, cancelling all dates, and paying his company liberally.

This was in the very early spring of the Centennial year, 1876, later to be known as the "Custer Year," for the loss of the gallant General Custer and his men of the Seventh Cavalry is still fresh in the memory of the people.

It was Buffalo Bill's intention to go as Chief of Scouts with General Crook, intending to overtake him in the Powder River country.[13]

Upon reaching Chicago, however, he was ordered to join General Carr, who had written asking to have him sent to the Fifth Cavalry, Cody's old command then on the march from Arizona to join Crook.

Arriving at Cheyenne Buffalo Bill found the Fifth Cavalry encamped there, and the welcome he received from the gallant Regiment told how glad officers and men were to see him.

He was at once appointed guide and Chief of Scouts, and the next morning the command pulled out for Fort Laramie, where General Sheridan had halted on his way to the Red Cloud Agency.

Buffalo Bill was at once sent with Gen. Sheridan on his ride to Red Cloud and after returning in safety to Laramie, scouting operations were begun by the Fifth Cavalry on the South Fork of the Cheyenne and about the Black Hills, and a number of engagements were had with the Indians.

General Carr being relieved of the command by General Wesley Merritt,[14] who had lately been promoted, the Fifth Cavalry was kept constantly busy, and soon drove the Indians out of that section of the country.

The valuable services of the regiment in this campaign of hardship and hard fighting I can well vouch for, as I had accompanied the expedition as the guest of the Chief of Scouts.

For weeks under the burning sun the Fifth scouted over a large portion of Wyoming, and weary and out of rations the command went into camp on War Bonnet Creek, and sent back to Fort Laramie for the much needed supplies.

In returning with these stores chief Cody, who had accompanied the wagon train, dashed into camp exclaiming:

"Custer and the Seventh Cavalry have been wiped out of existence!"[15]

It was indeed but too true.

While the Fifth was upon the tranquil War Bonnet the Little Big Horn was rolling away, its bosom crimsoned with the life-blood of the men of the Seventh.

Without delay the Fifth took up the march to join Crook who had lately been giving a rather stiff fight on the Rosebud, and was then awaiting the arrival of his favorite regiment.

As day after day the command moved along through that broad expanse of unexplored country it was little wonder that the men gave expression to their rapturous delight at the beauty and grandeur of the magnificent and varying scenery. The towering Big Horn mountains, upon whose tops the snow was plainly discernible, smiled down upon the command in seeming pity as the column, sweltering beneath the hot July sun, moved along but a short distance from their base.

"What a perfect Paradise!" said an officer when camp was made upon Goose Creek.

The bluest sapphire have envied the tint of the clear cold water wherein danced the largest "speckled beauties" that ever delighted a Nimrod.[16] Sulphur and other mineral springs, that in the East would have been utilized years before for their medicinal qualities, were from time to time passed, as the trail led along through picturesque canyons, over broad flowering mesas, rich with the nutritious Buffalo grass, and across fertile valleys luxuriant in the only vegetation that they had ever known.

A veteran officer turned in his saddle and said:

"After we are all dead this will be the grandest stock range under the heavens."

Little did he think his prophecy would be fulfilled within three years; but so it proved. That expedition opened up the country to the adventurous few, those brave, deserving Argonauts, that formed the nucleus of the communities now scattered throughout that delightful section. And no fairer land, no more delicious climate, no more invigorating air, no more gorgeous sunsets can be found in these United States.

The Big Horn Basin, like the valley of Jehoshaphat,[17] may truly be said to be "God's own country."

―――⧖―――

CHAPTER VI.
A LONG RANGE DEATH SHOT.

After a brief and much needed rest on the banks of the Yellowstone, the Fifth Cavalry moved out with Fort Lincoln as its objective point. This plan was unfortunately changed later.

"Across the Bad Lands to the Black Hills"[18] was the watchword.

This probably was the most disastrous and useless march ever made by United States troops. The ten days supplies which would have sufficed to enable the command to reach Lincoln, were soon exhausted; the poor animals perished in their tracks, worn out and starved.

Many of those in better condition were killed and eaten by the command. The situation was such that even now it is not pleasant to contemplate by those who were on that memorable march.

It was at this junction that a party of men were picked from the Third cavalry with a view to finding one of the settlements in the Black Hills, and sending out supplies to the destitute command.

This little party, sixty strong, started forth, and upon that very evening they came upon an Indian village, a remnant of those engaged in the Custer massacre. At dawn the village was attacked, some Indians were killed and a large pony herd was captured.

Word was sent back to the main command, and by noon it was upon the scene. The Indians that escaped, and a large number of others who joined them, tarried upon the mountainsides watching movements of the troops and every now and again giving excellent exhibitions of their marksmanship.

Some few Indians, who had been unable to make their escape, had taken refuge in a narrow ravine, or ditch, from which it proved difficult to dislodge them. It was while engaged in taking a desperate chance to accomplish this that poor white "Buffalo Chips"[19] the faithful friend of Buffalo Bill met his death.

By afternoon the mountain sides were alive with the enemy, who from undercover at a safe distance stampeded our herds and send bullets into our midst. There was one Indian, arrayed in a flowing War-Bonnet and mounted upon a spirited white pony, who seemed to take special delight in exposing himself, as a target for the rifles of the soldiers.

A little neck of the valley extended in a "V" shape between two large bluffs, and across this space, from one side to the other, this Indian repeatedly dashed. He did not appear to be over three hundred yards distant, and he would fire at the command as he galloped across the space. The fire was returned, but the bullets of the soldiers failed to hit the tantalizing human target. To my certain knowledge one entire troop of cavalry fired several rounds of their best ammunition at this daring foe, but without effect.

He succeeded, however, in killing several of the men and wounding others.

It was when this fusillade was at its height that William Cody, with a smile lighting up his handsome face, mounted upon his huge roan, dashed up.

"What are you all shooting at?" he cried.

"I haven't been able to find any game."

"At that Indian yonder, who can carry more lead than a type foundry," answered a young subaltern, as he sent another shot after the flying redskin.

Intensely interested, Cody for a while watched this exchange of bullets; then, at a signal, his roan sprang forward on a run.

Reaching a little knoll, he stopped, and a moment later, the Indian, for about the thirtieth time started to make his run, which his confidence now prompted him to regard as unattended by danger. As he reached the centre of the space, and from under the neck of his running pony fired at the command, his own little white animal that had served him so well was seen to fall and lie motionless upon the ground.

As the Indian sprang up, apparently from beneath the dead pony, and attempted to escape, another puff rose from the muzzle of the rifle, leveled by the rider of the roan, who was visible to all, the little knoll forming a pedestal for the superb equestrian statue above. With a piercing yell of wrath and pain the Indian sprang into the air, then fell never to rise again. An eye as true as his, a hand more steady had this time directed at him the leaden messenger on its errand of death.

Instantly the friends of the dead warrior rushed from their hiding places to recover the dead body of their comrade, believing that if they failed in this, he would never enjoy the blessings of the Happy Hunting grounds. But active as they were, the roan and his rider were before them. It was a perilous undertaking—but was Cody ever deterred by danger?

The cheer that greeted his daring act made the mountains echo and reecho again, and the chief of scouts became more than ever a hero.

CHAPTER VII.
THE FIRST SCALP FOR CUSTER.

It is a well known fact that the Sioux Indians, for several years before the Custer massacre, were regularly supplied with the very best firearms and ammunition by the agencies of Grand River, Standing Rock, Fort Berthold, and others.

During the campaign of '76, even after the band of heroes under Custer's lead in the valley of the Shadow of Death, these same Indians received hundreds of Remington, Winchester and other make of rifles, with the very best ammunition that was manufactured.

Powder, lead and primers[20] were also supplied them in some mysterious way, also small arms and ammunition therefore.

Is it any wonder then that the Sioux were able to resist the soldiers, and by their great quantities of firearms attracted to them all of the dissatisfied warriors of the Cheyennes and other Indian tribes of the Northwest?

Sitting Bull was acknowledged by all of the Indians as having the elements of a great chief. One whose superior qualities had never been equaled by chief of any other tribe.

His strategy, cunning, intelligence, cruel and uncompromising nature, with his powers of leadership were known to all, and having decided to participate in a war against the whites, he chose his position and his chiefs with wonderful judgment, and selected a vantage point from which he could retreat to the "Bad Lands," and keep his supply source open by feigning friendship with the Canadian French.

Some years before he had professed conversion to Christianity under the preaching of a noted priest,[21] and this now stood him in good stead with the same French people, and it was doubtless for this reason that he pretended to be converted.

War against the Sioux under Sitting Bull was brought on by the combined causes of the outrages in the Black Hills, and Sitting Bull's intensely hostile attitude. Hence it was decided to send out large forces of troops to meet him.

One force was to move from the North under General Terry, another from the East under General Gibbon,[22] and a third from the South under General Crook, the latter from Fort Fetterman, and these movements were to be simultaneous, the junction between them being intended to be somewhere near the head waters of the Yellowstone river.

It is well known that the command did not start at the same time, but there is no need of discussing here, where the blame belonged.

Much of the trouble in the Powder River fight, was caused by the assertion attributed to General Crook, that instead of their [sic] being between 1,500 to 20,000 hostile Indians in the Black Hills and Big Horn Country, as reported, they numbered instead about 2,000, and it was upon this assumption that this expedition was prepared. The allied forces of General[s] Terry, Gibbon and Custer did not number more than 2,700 men while they were opposed by fully 17,000 warriors, every one of whom was armed with the latest pattern of repeating rifles.

Custer's force numbered in all 28 officers, 747 men of the Seventh cavalry; 8 officers, 135 men in the Sixth and Seventeenth infantry; two officers and 32 men in charge of Gatling battery, and 45 enlisted scouts, in all less than 1000 men.[23]

On the march of the separate commands to hem in Sitting Bull, no instructions were given as to the rate at which they should march, and Custer always noted for his rapid movements made ninety miles the first three days. Discovering the Indians in large numbers he divided his regiment into three battalions, one of which he placed under Col. Benteen, another under Major Reno and the third he led himself. Major Reno coming upon the hostiles overestimated their strength, and believing he was to be surrounded, at once commenced a retreat, while Benteen coming up to the support of Reno also took alarm, and got out as quickly as possible without striking a severe blow at the Indians.

Both Benteen and Reno were trying to keep a way open for their retreat, while their impetuous leader, Custer, coming in sight of the Indian village at once determined to charge into it. Before doing so Custer sent a courier to the two commander[s] of the other battalions with the following dispatch:

"Big village; be quick, send on the packs."

Instead of obeying these explicit orders from Custer both Colonel Benteen and Major Reno stood aloof and allowed the gallant Custer and his brave men to rush alone upon the Indian village like an avalanche.

The Indians swarmed down to meet the heroic band, and in numbers that threatened to overwhelm them at once.

Down the valley swept that torrent of Indian humanity, and Custer and his heroic followers formed a hollow square, intending to try and thus make a retreat and hold their own until the rest of the regiment should come up.

How longingly this heroic band fighting against fate, yearned for Reno and Benteen can well be imagined, but thinking that they might soon come, each man cheered his comrade and fought on, piling up heaps of slain about their feet.

As time passed on and no aid came in sight the survivors knew that they must fight to the bitter end. As comrade after comrade fell, the Indians came nearer and nearer upon them, filling the air with their demoniacal yells of:

"Hi-yi-yip-yah-yah-hi-yah."

It was an uneven struggle, and death was the destiny of the Boys in Blue, and like the brave men they were, Custer and his comrades in arms met their fate on this ensanguined field.

I have given this account of the Custer fight as it was told soon after the fateful affair, and made known how it was that Custer came to attack the Sioux village, and how and why he did so.

Soon as the news of Custer's death reached the separate commands, every one of the soldiers swore to avenge him and the heroes who had perished with him. As the whole of the Sioux and Cheyenne tribes were then on the warpath it was certain that a very severe campaign was in prospective.

Word had been sent to the Fifth Cavalry, just prior to the receipt of the news of the death of Custer, that 800 Cheyenne warriors had left the Red Cloud agency to join Sitting Bull's forces in the "Big Horn" country, and, notwithstanding his orders to proceed immediately to join General Crook, General Merritt assumed the responsibility of intercepting these Cheyennes, and preventing them from carrying out their intention.

Selecting half a thousand of his best men and horses, he made a forced march back to War Bonnet Creek, and William Cody was sent ahead on a scout, to discover whether the Indians had yet crossed the stream or not.

On his way the chief of scouts discovered a band of Cheyennes coming rapidly from the South, and he immediately hurried back to the command with the news.

Ordering his man to mount the general kept them out of sight, and with Buffalo Bill and several aids [sic] went on a tour of observation to the summit of a hill not far distant.

From there the Indians were seen coming directly towards them. As they were looking at these Indians a small band of warriors were seen to separate themselves from the main body and dash over in the direction from which the regiment had come the night before, and the field glass of the chief scouts soon discovered two soldiers, evidently carrying dispatches, pushing along the trail.

The Indians had discovered these couriers and had determined to intercept them, and to save them was the question.

Cody asked the general to let him take his scouts and go to the rescue, and the reply was:

"All right, Cody, do so if you can."

Riding back to the command, William Cody picked out a dozen of his men, and returned with them to the point of observation, when General Merritt called out:

"Now for it, Cody."[24]

The two couriers were now several hundred yards from where General Merritt stood, and the Indians were following them about half that distance beyond.

With a call to his men Buffalo Bill dashed to the rescue directly between the Indians, and coming into sight of them a running fight begun, in which they killed three of the band, while the rest rode off towards the main body which had now come in plain right [sic] and halted.

By this time the scouts were half a mile from General Merritt's position, and the Indians turning upon them, another lively skirmish took place.

One of the Indians was handsomely decorated and wore the war bonnet of a great chief. As he came nearer he called out in his own tongue:

"Me know you Pa-he-has-ka! Come fight."*

Buffalo Bill was not the man to refuse such a challenge, and at once separated from the midst of his scouts, advanced toward the Indian.

The chief also rode towards Buffalo Bill, both riding at the full speed of their horses.

Neither the Indian chief or the chief of scouts fired a shot until within thirty yards of each other. The immediate band of Indians and the company of scouts standing off and viewing the remarkable duel, which was taking place before them.

The Indian was the first to fire and Buffalo Bill's horse fell heavily, but not from being shot as he had trod in a gopher hole. Catching nimbly upon his feet Buffalo Bill fired almost instantly and the animal ridden by the Indian fell dead in his tracks.

Both of the combatants were now on foot and in fighting trim.

Again they fired upon each other and simultaneously. The bullet of the redskin missed its mark, while the bullet of the scout struck the In-

---

*The name given the scout by the Sioux, and meaning "Long Hair."

dian chief squarely in the breast, bringing him to his knees. Before he had fairly reached the ground Buffalo Bill was upon him knife in hand, and buried the weapon to the hilt in his heart, while with another quick movement he tore off his war bonnet and scalped him.

From beginning to end the duel had occupied hardly a minute of time, and yet the Indians were now wild with rage and charged down to avenge their chief by cutting the scout off from his command and capturing him.

General Merritt had witnessed the duel from the hill, where he and the officers with him were standing, and realized the full danger into which the scout had gotten himself.

At once he ordered to the rescue company "K" and the order came none too quickly, for a large number of Indians were almost upon Cody, who dismounted as he was had [sic] stood in his ground to make a brave fight of it, one to the death if need be.

As the soldiers now came dashing up the Indians were checked in their charge, and swinging the war-bonnet and scalp about his head, Buffalo Bill shouted in ringing tones:

"The first scalp for Custer."

CHAPTER VIII.
CHASING THE REDSKINS.

The duel of Buffalo Bill and the great Indian chief, who was afterward discovered to be no less a person than Yellow Hand,[25] a prominent leader of the Cheyennes, prevented General Merritt from carrying out his intention to ambush the party of redskins on the march.

Determined, however, to strike a blow the General at once ordered the whole regiment to charge down upon the Indians, who made a stand determined to resist the soldiers to the very last.

It was however, of no use, for 800 Indians to attempt to drive back the Fifth regiment when in a charge, and their lines were broken badly and immediately a rapid retreat began.

The retreat of the redskins was towards the Red Cloud agency and forced by the Fifth, they kept up a rapid pace for a distance of twenty-five miles, being pushed so hard that they were obliged to abandon their loose horses, all their camp outfit and everything else possible in their endeavor to escape the soldiers who were glad and anxious to avenge Custer and his men.

When the Indians were driven into the agency, the Fifth cavalry followed quickly, not deterred by the fear of having to encounter thousands of others who might be at that point.

General Merritt was not certain whether other agency Indians had determined to follow the example of the Cheyennes and also go upon the war trail, but that made no difference to him and the men of the Fifth. They were in a fighting mood and would have faced any number of hostiles at that time to avenge Custer.

Night came on as the regiment rode into the agency, and faced the thousands of Indians collected together, but the latter had been cowed by their rapid retreat, and showed no disposition to make an attack upon the troops. It was while there that Buffalo Bill learned who it was that he had killed in his duel, and discovered that Yellow Hand was the son of old Cut Nose, a head chief of the Cheyennes.

Of course as Chief Cut Nose was at the agency, Buffalo Bill expected trouble from having killed his son, but the old chief was a warrior through and through, and when he learned who it was who had slain his son in the duel fought in the sight of so many, both Indians and soldiers, he sent a messenger to Cody offering four ponies if he would turn over to him the war bonnet of Yellow Hand, with his ornaments and other accoutrements.

Had he followed his own inclinations, Buffalo Bill would have given to Chief Cut Nose the souvenirs taken from his son, even to the scalp, but many of the officers of the Fifth urged against his doing so, as it is a well known fact that an Indian is not considered dead until he is scalped, and many felt certain that a great deal more would have to be done in killing hostiles, if they expected to avenge Custer and his men.

The night was spent at the agency, and then the command pulled out to join General Crook, who had camped near Cloud Peak in the "Big Horn" mountains, to await the arrival of the Fifth Cavalry before starting out on another expedition against the Sioux, who were reported to be somewhere near the head of the Little Big Horn river.

A rapid march was made to reach Crook's camp, and the Fifth arrived there on August 3d. Here Buffalo Bill was congratulated by many of his old friends and new, upon his daring duel with Yellow Hand the Cheyenne chief, and for the first time the chief of scouts met General Crook, as also, a half breed guide of whom he had heard much but never before crossed the path of, and whose name was Frank Girard.[26]

This scout, Frank Girard had lived for over six years in the village of which Sitting Bull was a chief, and knew him thoroughly, as also the country through which they would now have to march, so was a most valuable man to have along with the command.

A halt of only one day was made here on Goose Creek, and then the troops pulled out for the Tongue River, leaving the wagons under guard in Corral.

The march led to the Rosebud where an Indian trail was struck leading down the stream. This trail Buffalo Bill reported to be at least three days old, and indicated that the force of Indians that had passed along there was not less than seven thousand.

For several days the command pushed on rapidly, but Buffalo Bill reported that they were not gaining on the Indians, who were evidently making the same marches that the soldiers were.

On the fifth morning of the march, Buffalo Bill rode a long distance ahead of the command, at least a dozen miles, and while scanning the country far and wide with his field glass, he discovered a large cloud of dust rising miles down the stream.

Watching closely he noticed a party of men marching towards him, whom he at first supposed to be Indians, the party of which they were in search, but in a short while he discovered that they were soldiers.

Calling to a scout who accompanied him, Buffalo Bill at once sent back word to General Crook of his discovery, and hardly had his messenger gone before he observed a band of Indians on the opposite side of the creek, and another band directly in front of him.

Seeing these two bands of Indians led him to believe that he was mistaken in his belief that the forces in front were soldiers, but he soon saw that they were forming into line in a way that soldiers only would do, and he knew that it must be General Terry's command, and that the Indians in front of him could be none other than the redskins scouts who were known to be with Terry, and they must have mistaken him for a Sioux, for he saw them flying back towards the troopers and shouting in their own tongue:

"Honors Easy" : 301

"The Sioux, the Sioux!"

Alarmed by the report of his own scouts, General Terry, doubtless with the idea of another Custer massacre in his mind, at once prepared for action, forming a line across the Rosebud and ordering up his artillery ready to open fire.

These maneuvers Buffalo Bill watched from his position on the hill with considerable amusement at the manner in which he alone was sending a small army into line of battle.

After watching the situation, for a while, the Scout galloped down towards the soldiers waving his hat and Colonel Weir of the Seventh cavalry recognizing him advanced to meet him, calling out as he did so:

"Boys here comes Buffalo Bill, give him the cheer he deserves."

Three rousing cheers were at once given for the Chief of Scouts, and it was repeated all along the line.

Col. Weir then led Cody to where General Terry was and presented him to him, and there was great relief felt at his finding that the dust seen by the Indian scouts had been caused not by redskins but by General Crook's advancing soldiers.

At the request of General Terry, Buffalo Bill returned with him to meet General Crook, and that night both commands went into camp upon the Rosebud. As General Terry had his wagon train with him, and everything to make life comfortable, a pleasant evening was spent by Crook's men, who presented a great contrast to the soldiers of Terry's command, who were all in such fine form.

General Crook's cooking utensils consisted of a quart cup, in which he made his coffee, and a stick upon which he broiled his bacon.

Comparing the two commands Buffalo Bill came to the conclusion that General Crook had gone out in the right manner to fight Indians, for to keep up with redskins on a retreat, one must travel in light marching order, and not be attended by wagon trains and baggage.

That night the Fifth Infantry was ordered by General Terry to return by forced marches to the Yellow Stone [sic] and proceed down the river by steamboat to the mouth of the Powder river, where the Indians could be intercepted in case they should attempt to cross.

The forced march of thirty-five miles was made by General Mills[27] and a splendid march it was for an infantry regiment through a mountainous country.

Still pressing on the Indian trail it turned in the direction of the Black Hills, General Crook now being in command of the consolidated forces.

Supplies being nearly out the trail had to be abandoned, and the troops kept on down the Powder river to the junction of the Yellow Stone where General Mills was met, and he reported that no Indians had as yet crossed the stream.

Several days after the arrival of the command at this point, several steam boats arrived with large quantities of supplies, and the soldiers were correspondingly happy.

It was while camping on the Yellow Stone at the mouth of the Powder River that Buffalo Bill had orders to go with Louis Richard a half breed scout, to join General Mills on a scouting expedition on the Steamer "Far West," down the Yellow Stone river.

The two scouts were to ride on top of the pilot house of the steamer, and keep a sharp lookout on both sides of the river, to see if there were any trails showing that Indians had crossed the stream.

The novel idea of scouting on a steamboat pleased Buffalo Bill greatly, and he was anxious to go, anticipating a pleasure trip, it being so different from an expedition on foot or on horseback. So he reported promptly to the General, who had with him five companies of his infantry regiment.

The first thing the scouts were asked by General Mills was:

"Where are your horses"?

This was a surprise as they had not expected to do much riding on the deck of a steamboat, but General Mills told them they would need them before they got back, and, therefore, they went after their animals, and brought them onboard.

The steamer was then sent booming down the Yellow Stone river, the scouts at their posts of duty on top of the pilot house.

CHAPTER IX.
SCOUTING ON A STEAMBOAT.

Scouting on a steamboat was a novelty even to William Cody, who from boyhood had been a scout.

The steamer Far West was commanded by a man who thoroughly

knew his business, Captain Grant Marsh, who was, taken altogether, a very remarkable character.[28]

It was Captain Marsh, who transported the wounded men after the battle of the Little Big Horn, to Fort Abraham Lincoln on the Missouri river, at which time he made the fastest steamboat run on record. A successful and experienced pilot, who handled his boat with remarkable dexterity, the men under him were as thoroughly disciplined as soldiers of the regular army. With a full head of steam on, the Far West went flying down the river, past islands, over sand bars, and around bends, running at a rate that was most exhilarating. Standing upon the top of the pilot house Buffalo Bill and Louis Richard kept their eyes fixed upon the shores to look for Indian trails.

Observing as he thought in the distance a number of Indian horses grazing, Buffalo Bill reported it to General Mills, and the captain of the steamer was at once asked if he could land the boat and let the two scouts go ashore. Captain Marsh replied:

"Yes sir I can land her in there and take her out on the prairie if I only had a heavy dew. She will go anywhere."

A landing was made and Buffalo Bill went ashore, supported by two companies of infantry. Mounting his horse, the chief of scouts pushed as rapidly as possible towards the spot where he had seen the supposed Indians, and upon drawing nearer found it was a false alarm, as the objects he had mistaken for horses proved to be Indian graves.

There were quite a number of graves there, and they showed that they were of braves recently killed in some battle. A return to the steamer was then made, and the Far West continued down the Yellowstone to Glendive Creek, where Colonel Rice[29] and his company of the Fifth infantry were found.

On the day previous to our arrival, Col. Rice reported that he had had a battle with a party of Indians, several of whom he had killed at long range with his Rodman cannon.[30]

The Far West was to remain at Glendive over night, and being anxious to send dispatches back to General Terry at once, reporting what had been done, General Mills asked Buffalo Bill to be the bearer of them. Buffalo Bill promptly signified his willingness, and taking the dispatches he started upon his seventy-five mile night ride through the Bad Lands of the Yellowstone. Without particular adventure, but after a hard ride, the scout rode into Gen. Terry's camp early in the morning, and delivered his dispatches, for which he was highly complimented by the commanding officer.

As the prospect for much more Indian fighting seemed slight, Buffalo Bill decided that he would leave the command and return to the East, to once more reorganize his dramatic combination, intending to place upon the stage a new drama written specially for him, based upon the Sioux war. As the Sioux uprising had excited the greatest interest in the East, Buffalo Bill was farsighted enough to know that a melo-drama based upon the scenes then enacted in the West, would draw crowded houses, and for this reason was anxious to return, and open with his company.[31]

Receiving his discharge from the commander in chief, he started down the river on the steamer Yellowstone bound for Fort Beauford.

The steamer upon which Buffalo Bill had embarked had gone only a short distance down the river, when another boat was discovered coming up and aboard of which was Gen. Whistler[32] and other troops bound for Terry's command. Signaling each other, the boats made a landing, and the first person who greeted Buffalo Bill's eyes upon the other steamer was his old partner and scout, as well as comrade, Texas Jack, who was at that time bearing dispatches from the New York Herald.

Learning from Buffalo Bill that Gen. Terry had left the Yellowstone, Gen. Whistler asked him to be the bearer of important dispatches from Gen. Sheridan, telling him he would soon overtake Terry's command, and as an extra inducement he offered him his own thoroughbred horse, which he had with him on the boat.

Buffalo Bill at once consented to go, and was soon mounted upon the General's thoroughbred speeding over the rough mountainous country towards Powder River. In a few hours he overtook the command of General Terry, and delivered his dispatches, but he was forced to have to report to Gen. Whistler that the thoroughbred was not the kind of a horse for that rough work as he was utterly exhausted by the journey.

After reading the dispatches Gen. Terry asked Cody if he would carry a letter back to Gen. Whistler, and this he consented to do. Captain Smith,[33] aide-de-camp of General Terry's command, gave him his horse for the trip.

The horse loaned to him by Captain Smith proved to be a fine animal, and Cody rode him over forty miles through the Bad Lands in four hours, and reached Gen. Whistler's command near the steamboat at one o'clock at night. During his absence the Indians had made their appearance in the vicinity and several skirmishes had been had with them by the troops.

Reading the dispatches Gen. Whistler turn to Buffalo Bill and said:

"Cody, it is very necessary that I send information to Gen. Terry concerning the Indians who have been skirmishing about here all day. Not a man of the command can I induce to go, and so I must once more call on you. It is asking a great deal I know, after your long ride of eighty miles, but you know the urgency of the case and you are a man that can always be called upon a time of need."

"Get your dispatches ready General, and I will start at once," was Buffalo Bill's reply.

Mounting Captain Smith's horse, which he had ridden from Gen. Terry's command, Buffalo Bill struck out for Terry's camp once more. It was just two o'clock at night when he left the camp and six hours after he rode up to Gen. Terry's headquarters, just as the command was about to start on a march.

In this ride, partly by night and over a very wild country, William Cody had made the distance of one hundred and twenty miles in just twenty-two hours, a truly remarkable feat for both horse and rider.

CHAPTER X.
BUFFALO BILL BECOMES A CATTLE KING.

After reading the dispatches brought him Gen. Terry halted his command and rode on accompanied by Cody and overtook Gen. Crook, and a council of war was held between the two officers, the result of which was that Crook's command moved on in the direction they had been marching; while Terry's men marched back to the Yellowstone, and crossed the river on steamboats.

At the request of General Terry Buffalo Bill remained with the command to accompany him as a scout in the direction of the Dry Fork of the Missouri, where it was expected they would strike a large number of Indians.

The march from the Yellowstone was made in the night, as the General wished to get into the hills without being discovered by Indian scouts, and consequently Buffalo Bill had no rest, other than he could obtain on the way.

A march of several days brought the command to the buffalo ranch where fresh signs of Indians were discovered, they having been killing buffalos. Gen. Terry at once called upon Buffalo Bill to carry dispatches back to Col. Rice who was still encamped at the mouth of Glendive Creek on the Yellowstone, eighty miles from where they then were.

Buffalo Bill took the dispatches and struck off in a storm of blackness and a drizzling rain, through a country with which he was entirely unacquainted.

After traveling throughout the night, he halted at daylight in a secluded spot at the head of the ravine where there was a bunch of ash trees, and he concluded to remain there until night, not daring to cross the wide prairies in the bright glare of day.

Unsaddling his horse he ate a breakfast of bacon and hard tack, and then lay down to sleep, using his saddle for a pillow. How long he slept he did not know, but he was awakened by a roaring sound. He knew what it meant. He seized his gun and at the same time led his horse into the bushes. Then climbing up a steep bank of the hill he looked over into the prairie beyond and saw a large herd of buffalo, being rapidly pursued by a band of some thirty Indians.

As the herd fled before the Indians buffalo after buffalo would drop, as they were killed by the redskins. For several hours Buffalo Bill watched the Indians as they cut up the meat, packing it on their ponies. Finishing this work they rode off in the direction from which they had come, and which happened to be the one in which Buffalo Bill wished to travel; this told him that their camp must be lying between him and the Glendive Creek.

Waiting until nightfall, he resumed his journey, making a detour to avoid the Indians, and without seeing a hostile, he rode into Col. Rice's camp just at daylight.

Upon his arrival Buffalo Bill found that Col. Rice had been fighting Indians every day since he had been camped at that point, and he was anxious to advise General Terry of this fact, so scout Cody was once more requested to be the bearer of dispatches back again.

After a short rest Buffalo Bill started off again to look for Gen. Terry, but it was not until the third day that he overtook him at the head of Deer Creek, and on his way to Col. Rice's camp.

Finding that the General was not going in the right direction to reach the camp, Buffalo Bill so informed him, and was at once placed at the head of the command as guide.

Having returned once more to Glendive, Buffalo Bill bade goodbye to his comrades and took passage on the steamer "Far West" down the Missouri. Leaving the steamer at Bismarck he proceeded by rail to Rochester, New York, where his family were then living, and while there he arranged with a manager of an opera house to open his dramatic season in that city.

A new play was dramatized, from a novel written by the author of this biography, and a criticism of it on its first night from a Rochester paper is too good to be left untold.

It was said the play had no head or tail, and to begin with one act would be just as entertaining as to begin with another, while a number of newspaper critics went crazy trying to follow the plot.

The play, however, served a good purpose, because, for some reason the entertainment pleased the people, and made for the "Star" a great deal of money.

During the tour Buffalo Bill played through the Eastern, Western and Middle States, and everywhere to crowded houses, continuing his season upon the Pacific Coast, where he met a most enthusiastic reception and added largely to his bank account. Leaving San Francisco, Buffalo Bill made a circuit of interior towns and closed the season in Nevada, at Virginia City.[34]

Returning to his home in North Platte Buffalo Bill went into the cattle business with an old frontier friend and comrade, Major Frank North, commander of the Pawnee Scouts in the United States Army. They established their ranch in the South Fork of the Dismal River, some seventy-five miles to the north of North Platte, Nebraska.

Leaving Maj. North to manage the cattle ranch Buffalo Bill proceeded to the Red Cloud agency and secured a number of Sioux Indians whom he intended to introduce into this theatrical tour of 77–78.

Another play had been written for this season by Major A. S. Burt, an officer in the United States army, which was entitled "May Cody," or

"Lost and Won," being named after his sister, and founded upon incidents of the Mormon war.

This play proved a great success, both artistically and financially and the season was one of the most profitable that he had known.

When a scout at Fort McPherson, Buffalo Bill had taken a great fancy to the country around there and had made up his mind that some day he would have a home at North Platte, Nebraska. After the close of his season in '78, he went to the then village of North Platte, and a home was built for a family residence, Mrs. Cody personally superintending everything in its construction.

After the close of his season Buffalo Bill returned to North Platte to join his wife and children in their beautiful home, where the latch string always hung on the outside to all of his old comrades.

Thus it was that Buffalo Bill became an extensive land owner and rancher, and saw fortune within his grasp, for already was he becoming known as one of the cattle kings of Nebraska.

Of his later years the general public has been kept well informed. Everyone knows of his successful tour of the old world and his reception among royalty. Although getting well along in years, Col. Cody is still one of the most active men in the world.[35] His capacity for business seems unlimited and his executive ability is something marvelous. Aside from managing the Wild West Show, which, by the way, is the largest show in the world, and is making a tour of the United States, Col. Cody is president of the largest irrigation enterprise in the world; president of a townsite company; president of two transportation companies; president of one hotel company; publisher of a newspaper, Buffalo Bill's Press, issued at Duluth, Minn.; has several farms and ranches to manage, and every day he has to entertain several hundred guests, besides take a part in every performance of the Wild West Show.

He has had honors showered upon him and he wears them easy. He has had success unbounded, but he has earned it. In spite of his busy life and his many cares he always has a moment for all and a word of cheer to extend.

APPENDIX:
PRENTISS INGRAHAM'S BUFFALO BILL NOVELS

Published by Beadle and Adams:
Buffalo Bill's Clean Sweep, synopsis:
Don Junipe y Morada's blacksmith is found dead. Buffalo Bill and his pards suspect the killer is "Silvernail," a rogue who raids ranchers unless they pay him tribute. Pursuing the villain, they find animals and vegetation killed by a poisonous gas, then they are chased by Yaquis Indians. If the Yaqui leader would lead them to Silvernail's trail, Cody promises to not take him captive. "I am Pa-e-has-ka . . . I never break my word." On the way, they encounter a giant black horse whose rider has no head. "'Holy salamanders!' ejaculated Wild Bill. 'That was no Injun.'" Pawnee Bill eventually finds Silvernail and throws his bowie knife at him. Pursued by Buffalo Bill and cohorts, Silvernail falls off his horse, dead.
Buffalo Bill, the Buckskin King
Bison Bill, the Prince of the Reins
Adventures of Buffalo Bill from Boyhood to Manhood, synopsis:
Many stories Ingraham related in his biography of Cody evolved from this novel: Mr. Cody's Free State speech and subsequent attack, Billy's crush on schoolmate Mollie Hyatt, his work for wagon-train masters Frank McCarthy and Lew Simpson. Ingraham elaborates on the night Simpson, George Woods and Billy used yagers to fight off Indians, Billy's broken leg and his encounter with Rain-in-the-Face, and his subsequent military duty. Ingraham writes that Cody married Louisa at "farmer Frederici's home," then won Comstock's challenge as best buffalo slayer. He allows Cody to tell his own story of becoming an actor and, in 1876, how he avenged Custer's death by killing Yellow Hair. The reports of Cody's "perilous adventures . . . tinged with romance, and seeming fiction, will go down to posterity as true border history."
The Pony Express Rider
The League of Three

Buffalo Bill's Grip
Buffalo Bill's Bonanza
Buffalo Bill's Swoop
Buffalo Bill's Secret Service Trail
Buffalo Bill's Big Four
Buffalo Bill's Double
Buffalo Bill's Brand
Buffalo Bill's Boys in Blue
Butterfly Billy, the Pony Rider Detective
Butterfly Billy's Man Hunt
Buffalo Bill's Buckskin Braves
The Three Bills—Buffalo Bill, Wild Bill, and Band-box Bill
Buffalo Bill's Secret Ally
Buffalo Bill's Peerless Pard
Buffalo Bill's League
Buffalo Bill and the Surgeon-Scout
Buffalo Bill's Quandary
Buffalo Bill's Blind Trail
Buffalo Bill's Buckskin Brotherhood
Buffalo Bill Baffled
Buffalo Bill's Scout Shadowers
Buffalo Bill's on the War Path
Buffalo Bill's Body-guard
Buffalo Bill's Beagles
Buffalo Bill and His Merry Men
Buffalo Bill's Blind
Buffalo Bill's Flush Hand
Buffalo Bill's Mascot
Buffalo Bill's Sweepstake
Buffalo Bill's Spy-shadower
Buffalo Bill's Dead Shot
Buffalo Bill's Winning Hand
Buffalo Bill's Death-knell
Buffalo Bill's Red Trail
Buffalo Bill's Volunteer Vigilantes
Montebello, the Gold King
Buffalo Bill's Sharp-shooters

Buffalo Bill's Life Raffle
Buffalo Bill's Red-skin Ruse
Buffalo Bill's Double Dilemma
Buffalo Bill's Royal Flush
Buffalo Bill's Death-charm
Buffalo Bill's Marked Bullet
Buffalo Bill's Crack-shot Pard
Buffalo Bill's Road-agent Round-up
Buffalo Bill's Boy Mascot
Buffalo Bill's Lone Hand
Buffalo Bill's Tough Tussle
Buffalo Bill's Snap-shot
Buffalo Bill's Grim Guard
Buffalo Bill's Life-stake
Buffalo Bill's Mazeppa-chase
Buffalo Bill's Decoy
Buffalo Bill's Rough Riders
Buffalo Bills Death-deal
Buffalo Bill's Rush-ride
Buffalo Bill's Rifle-shots
Buffalo Bill's Dead-shot Dragoon
Buffalo Bill's Fighting Five
Buffalo Bill's Lasso-throwers
Buffalo Bill's Bluff
Buffalo Bill's Secret Six
Buffalo Bill's Drop
Buffalo Bill's Decoy Boys
Buffalo Bill's Black Pard
Buffalo Bill's Sure-shots
Buffalo Bill's Block Game
Buffalo Bill's Texan
Buffalo Bill in Arizona
Buffalo Bill at Bay
Buffalo Bill's Blue Belt Brigade
Buffalo Bill's Invincibles
Buffalo Bill in Disguise
Buffalo Bill's Pony Patrol

Buffalo Bill's Relentless Trail
Buffalo Bill's Daring Deed
Buffalo Bill's Trump Card
Buffalo Bill's Pledge

Prentiss Ingraham's novels published by Street & Smith were listed on the front pages of each novel. Many more titles were collected under the umbrella of "The Buffalo Bill Stories." Titles by "the author of *Buffalo Bill*" have been credited to Ingraham by modern editors.

Buffalo Bill, the Border King
Buffalo Bill's Raid
Buffalo Bill's Bravery
Buffalo Bill's Trump Card
Buffalo Bill's Pledge
Buffalo Bill's Vengeance
Buffalo Bill's Iron Grip, sample:

When they realized that the old fort was unoccupied, that those they had expected to find there were not visible, Buffalo Bill and Lieutenant Ames, in their anxiety, rode forward at a gallop.

For once the scout forgot his caution in his desire to find out why their friends were not there, and not until they dashed into the stockade gate did Buffalo Bill realize his mistake and cry out:

"That time I did very wrong, for suppose an ambush had been waiting for us here."

"You are right, Bill, and it would not have surprised me had there been; but neither of us thought of that in our desire to know why the Mildmay party had not arrived."

"They are not here, lieutenant."

"No."

"And have not been."

"Are you sure?"

"Oh, yes, for they would have left some sign for us had they been."

"They have been delayed."

"By Indians, doubtless; but I hope they have been able to stand them off."

"Well, they may get in to-night; but should they not do so?"

"We can do but one thing."

"And what is that?"

"Go on the hunt for them."

Buffalo Bill's Capture
Buffalo Bill's Danger Line
Buffalo Bill's Comrades
Buffalo Bill's Reckoning
Buffalo Bill's Warning
Buffalo Bill at Bay
Buffalo Bill's Buckskin Pards
Buffalo Bill's Brand
Buffalo Bill's Honor
Buffalo Bill's Phantom Hunt
Buffalo Bill's Fight with Fire
Buffalo Bill's Danite Trail
Buffalo Bill's Ranch Riders
Buffalo Bill's Death Trail
Buffalo Bill's Trackers
Buffalo Bill's Mid-air Flight
Buffalo Bill, Ambassador
Buffalo Bill's Air Voyage
Buffalo Bill's Secret Mission
Buffalo Bill's Long Trail
Buffalo Bill against Odds
Buffalo Bill's Hot Chase
Buffalo Bill's Redskin Ally
Buffalo Bill's Treasure Trove
Buffalo Bill's Hidden Foes
Buffalo Bill's Crack Shot
Buffalo Bill's Close Call
Buffalo Bill's Double Surprise
Buffalo Bill's Ambush

Buffalo Bill's Outlaw Hunt, synopsis: When the ruby Montezuma's Eye goes missing from the Mexican palace, Governor Mendoza hires Cody to recover it. Could the thief be the governor's daughter? Mendoza is certain she "could not do such a thing, unless she was insane. 'There is no insanity in the family?'" Buffalo Bill asks. He attempts to find the girl and the jewel, suspecting both are in the hands of an outlaw nicknamed Wild Ox. Buffalo Bill's courage is evident when he plans on going alone. "Your plan imperils your life!" cried Mendoza. "I realized that well enough, when I began to think it over. Yet I am willing to take the risk," says Cody. Besides confronting a gang of notorious outlaws and a member of the governor's household who aids their escape, Cody clashes with Chiricahua Apaches and Pueblo Indians.

Buffalo Bill's Border Duel
Buffalo Bill's Bid for Fame
Buffalo Bill's Triumph
Buffalo Bill's Spy Trailer
Buffalo Bill's Death Call
Buffalo Bill's Body Guard
Buffalo Bill's Still Hunt
Buffalo Bill and the Doomed Dozen
Buffalo Bill's Prairie Scout
Buffalo Bill's Traitor Guide
Buffalo Bill's Bonanza
Buffalo Bill's Swoop
Buffalo Bill and the Gold King
Buffalo Bill, Deadshot
Buffalo Bill's Buckskin Bravos
Buffalo Bill's Big Four
Buffalo Bill's One-armed Pard
Buffalo Bill's Race for Life
Buffalo Bill's Return
Buffalo Bill's Conquest, sample:

"Dart Deering, you must do me a great favor."

"If it's to give up my life for you, Buffalo Bill, I'll do it."

"Thanks, old pard; but I ask that of no man."

"Yet you are ever ready to sacrifice yourself for others."

"I take chances, yes, but always with the hope or belief I will pull through all right."

"And you do, whether from your proverbial luck, for 'Buffalo Bill's luck' is famous, or from skill, nerve, and daring, or all combined, I do not know; but you do it, Bill, as well I know."

Buffalo Bill to the Rescue
Buffalo's Bill's Beautiful Foe

Buffalo Bill's Perilous Task
Buffalo Bill's Queer Find
Buffalo Bill's Blind Lead
Buffalo Bill's Resolution
Buffalo Bill, the Avenger
Buffalo Bill's Pledged Pard
Buffalo Bill's Weird Warning
Buffalo Bill's Wild Ride
Buffalo Bill's Redskin Stampede
Buffalo Bill's Mine Mystery
Buffalo Bill's Gold Hunt
Buffalo Bill's Daring Dash
Buffalo Bill on Hand
Buffalo Bill's Alliance
Buffalo Bill's Relentless Foe
Buffalo Bill's Midnight Ride
Buffalo Bill's Chivalry
Buffalo Bill's Girl Pard
Buffalo Bill's Private War
Buffalo Bill's Diamond Mine
Buffalo Bill's Big Contract
Buffalo Bill's Woman Foe
Buffalo Bill's Ruse
Buffalo Bill's Pursuit
Buffalo Bill's Hidden Gold
Buffalo Bill in Mid-air
Buffalo Bill's Queer Mission
Buffalo Bill's Verdict
Buffalo Bill's Ordeal
Buffalo Bill's Camp Fires
Buffalo Bill's Iron Nerve
Buffalo Bill's Rival
Buffalo Bill's Lone Hand
Buffalo Bill's Sacrifice
Buffalo Bill's Thunderbolt
Buffalo Bill's Black Fortune
Buffalo Bill's Wild Work

Buffalo Bill's Yellow Trail
Buffalo Bill's Treasure Train
Buffalo Bill's Bowie Duel
Buffalo Bill's Mystery Man
Buffalo Bill's Bold Play
Buffalo Bill, Peacemaker
Buffalo Bill's Big Surprise
Buffalo Bill's Barricade
Buffalo Bill's Test
Buffalo Bill's Powwow
Buffalo Bill's Stern Justice
Buffalo Bill's Mysterious Friend
Buffalo Bill and the Boomers
Buffalo Bill's Panther Fight
Buffalo Bill and the Overland Mail
Buffalo Bill on the Deadwood Trail
Buffalo Bill in Apache Land
Buffalo Bill's Blindfold Duel
Buffalo Bill and the Lone Camper, synopsis:
Indians have kidnapped Doc Miner. Aided by a black guide, Buffalo Bill and Pawnee Bill rescue him. The men head to the saloon where a man hawks items to the crowd. Following the conman, the two Bills run into Indians to whom Cody reiterates his philosophy: "Indians be good, and Pa-e-has-ka will be friend. Indians bad, and Pa-e-has-ka fight them." When Buffalo Bill is recalled to Fort McPherson, he encounters the wagon train of Mr. Markham who is unknowingly being guided off-course by the scoundrel Kio Carl. After Cody points him in the right direction, Miss Markham observes that, "How different he [Buffalo Bill] is from what I had pictured him, when reading romances of his strange deeds upon the border. He seemed to me, as the writers pen-painted him, a giant and ferocious being whose hands and clothing must be covered with the blood of his foes. But we find him an elegant gentleman, courtly, and as handsome as a picture."
Buffalo Bill's Merry War
Buffalo Bill's Star Play
Buffalo Bill's War Cry
Buffalo Bill on Black Panther's Trail

Buffalo Bill's Slim Chance
Buffalo Bill Besieged
Buffalo Bill's Bandit Round-up
Buffalo Bill's Surprise Party
Buffalo Bill's Lightning Raid
Buffalo Bill in Mexico
Buffalo Bill's Trader Foe
Buffalo Bill's Tireless Chase
Buffalo Bill's Boy Bugler
Buffalo Bill's Sure Guess
Buffalo Bill's Record Jump
Buffalo Bill in the Land of Dread
Buffalo Bill's Tangled Clue
Buffalo Bill's Wolf Skin
Buffalo Bill's Twice Four Puzzle
Buffalo Bill and the Devil Bird
Buffalo Bill and the Indian's Mascot
Buffalo Bill Entrapped
Buffalo Bill's Totem Trail
Buffalo Bill at Fort Challis
Buffalo Bill's Determination
Buffalo Bill's Battle Axe
Buffalo Bill's Game with Fate
Buffalo Bill's Comanche Raid
Buffalo Bill's Aerial Island
Buffalo Bill's Lucky Shot
Buffalo Bill's Sioux Friends
Buffalo Bill's Supreme Test
Buffalo Bill's Boldest Strike
Buffalo Bill and the Red Hand
Buffalo Bill's Dance with Death
Buffalo Bill's Running Fight
Buffalo Bill in Harness, synopsis:

Three stories comprise the novel. First, Buffalo Bill and Nick Wharton join Wild Bill in a fight against cattle thieves.

Grant Millman and Glen Wilmes are ready to duel for Hellgate Mine, a "magician's cave, a source of fabulous wealth." A gang of toughs follows them, but they are saved from ambush by Buffalo Bill. When Indians attack, Clellie, Glen's sister, mysteriously disappears. When Wild Bill and Nick Wharton arrive and have the situation explained to them, "Like all border men of that time, Wild Bill deferred to Mr. Cody in all cases where sound judgment was needed. A brave and sometimes reckless Indian fighter, Buffalo Bill still had a reputation for coolness and correct thinking which made him a much-sought man on the plains and in the mountains." They eventually find Clellie in the mine, but also more Indians, Glen's evil uncle, and a pile of dynamite.

On his way to join the army at Tucson, Cody is diverted by the opportunity to earn a $5,000 reward for the murderer of Lon Becker. He may be Salsido, a rich Mexican. Before he's done, Buffalo Bill gets involved with a sacred mountain lion, a kidnapped girl, Sioux Indians, the voice of the Great Spirit, a near lynching, and a stabbing. "'Hurrah! . . . it's Buffalo Bill!' . . . the Indians turned in fear at the very sound of the name."

Buffalo Bill Corralled
Buffalo Bill's Waif of the West
Buffalo Bill's Wizard Pard
Buffalo Bill and Hawkeye
Buffalo Bill and Grizzly Dan
Buffalo Bill's Ghost Play
Buffalo Bill's Lost Prisoner
Buffalo Bill and the Klan of Kau
Buffalo Bill's Crow Scouts
Buffalo Bill's Lassoed Spectre
Buffalo Bill and the Wanderers
Buffalo Bill and the White Queen
Buffalo Bill's Yellow Guardian
Buffalo Bill's Double "B" Brand
Buffalo Bill's Dangerous Duty
Buffalo Bill and the Talking Statue
Buffalo Bill between Two Fires
Buffalo Bill and the Giant Apache
Buffalo Bill's Best Bet
Buffalo Bill's Blockhouse Siege
Buffalo Bill's Fight for Right

Buffalo Bill's Sad Tidings
Buffalo Bill and "Lucky" Benson
Buffalo Bill among the Sioux
Buffalo Bill's Mystery Box
Buffalo Bill's Worst Tangle
Buffalo Bill's Clean Sweep
Buffalo Bill's Texas Tangle
Buffalo Bill and the Nihilists
Buffalo Bill's Emigrant Trail
Buffalo Bill at Close Quarters
Buffalo Bill and the Cattle Thieves
Buffalo Bill at Cimaroon Bar
Buffalo Bill's Ingenuity
Buffalo Bill on a Cold Trail
Buffalo Bill's Red Hot Totem
Buffalo Bill under a War Cloud
Buffalo Bill and the Prophet
Buffalo Bill and the Red Renegade
Buffalo Bill's Mailed Fist
Buffalo Bill's Round Up
Buffalo Bill's Death Message
Buffalo Bill's Redskin Disguise
Buffalo Bill, the Whirlwind
Buffalo Bill in Death Valley
Buffalo Bill and the Magic Button
Buffalo Bill's Friend in Need
Buffalo Bill with General Custer
Buffalo Bill's Timely Meeting
Buffalo Bill and the Skeleton Scout
Buffalo Bill's Flag of Truce

NOTES

INTRODUCTION

1. David McCullough, *The American Spirit: Who We Are and What We Stand For* (New York: Simon & Schuster, 2017), xiii.

2. Charles Rankin, Western Writers of America panel discussion, June 20, 2018.

3. *Buffalo Bill Cody, A Man of the West* (Lawrence: University Press of Kansas, 2019), part 1, chap. III; hereafter Ingraham, *Buffalo Bill Cody*.

4. James B. Lloyd, ed., *Lives of Mississippi Authors, 1817–1967* (Jackson: University Press of Mississippi, 2009), 252.

5. (Challis, ID) *Silver Messenger*, October 20, 1903.

6. (New York) *Evening Telegram*, April 20, 1901; Chandra Manning, *Civil War History* 52, no. 2 (June 2006): 174–175.

7. (Saratoga Springs) *Daily Saratogian*, February 18, 1885.

8. *Evening Telegram*, April 20, 1901.

9. J. Edward Leithead, "Colonel Prentiss Ingraham," *Roundup* 32, no. 1 (January 1964): 2; *Buffalo (NY) Courier*, September 25, 1904.

10. (St. Louis) *Republic*, May 30, 1903.

11. Prentiss Ingraham, "The Classic Dime Novel and Its Gradual Disappearance," *New York Herald*, February 3, 1901; *Brooklyn Daily Eagle*, January 19, 1930.

12. Ingraham, *Buffalo Bill Cody*, part 3, chap. I.

13. Richard Slotkin, *Regeneration through Violence: The Mythology of the American Frontier, 1600–1860* (Middleton, CT: Wesleyan University Press), 5; (Terre Haute, IN) *Daily Express*, October 10, 1873.

14. Albert Johannsen, *The House of Beadle and Adams and Its Dime and Nickel Novels*, 2 vols. (Norman: University of Oklahoma Press, 1950), 2: 157–158.

15. Johannsen, *The House of Beadle and Adams*, 156; Lloyd, *Lives of Mississippi Authors*, 253.

16. A. C. Chase, "Colonel Prentiss Ingraham: His Life and Work," *Bob Taylor's Magazine* 2, no. 6 (March 1906): 697; *Evening Telegram*, April 20, 1901.

17. (Marshalltown, IA) *Evening Times-Republican*, August 19, 1904.

18. Ingraham, "The Classic Dime Novel"; *St. Paul Sunday Globe*, May 4, 1884.

19. (New York) *Morning Telegraph*, May 17, 1903.

20. Ingraham, *Buffalo Bill Cody*, part 3, chap. V.

21. *Evening Telegram*, Apr. 20, 1901.

22. Sandra K. Sagala, *Buffalo Bill on Stage* (Albuquerque: University of New Mexico Press, 2008), 213, 218, 220.

23. McCracken Research Library, Buffalo Bill Center of the West, MS6.0053a-b, letters dated September 9, 1879, August 17, 1880; *Omaha Daily Bee*, Monday, April [illegible], 1884.

24. Sandra K. Sagala, "Nate Salsbury's *Black America:* Its Origin and Programs," *Points West* (Fall/Winter 2018: 10–15; Spring 2019).

25. Cody to Salsbury, October 6, 1899, Yale Collection of American Literature MSS 17 box 1 f. 11; Don Russell, *The Lives and Legends of Buffalo Bill* (Norman: University of Oklahoma Press, 1979), 284; *Duluth Press*, August 3, 1895.

26. *Duluth Press*, June 8, 1895; Buffalo Bill Center of the West, Cody, WY, MS6 box 13 folder 13; Paul Lundgren, *Area Women in History*, http://www.paullundgren.com/journalism-area-woman-helen-cody-wetmore.cfm, accessed September 24, 2014.

27. Buffalo Bill Center of the West, Cody, WY, MS6 box 13 folder 13.

28. George Duby, ed. *A History of a Private Life: Passions of the Renaissance* (New York: Belknap Press, 1989), 103.

29. *Duluth Press*, May 30, 1896.

30. http://codyarchive.org/texts/wfc.bks00014.html, chapter 30; Nellie Snyder Yost, *Buffalo Bill: His Family, Friends, Fame, Failures, and Fortunes* (Chicago: Swallow Press, 1979), 311–312; Stella Adelyne Foote, *Letters from Buffalo Bill* (Billings, MT: Foote Publishing, 1954), 66.

31. George Jenks, "Dime Novel Makers," *Bookman* 20 (October 1904): 112.

32. James W. Cook, *The Arts of Deception* (Cambridge, MA: Harvard University Press, 2001), 3, 17.

33. Ingraham, *Buffalo Bill Cody*, part 1, chap. XLIII.

34. Prentiss Ingraham, *Adventures of Buffalo Bill from Boyhood to Manhood* (New York: Beadle and Adams, 1881), 2.

35. William F. Cody, *The Life of Hon. William F. Cody Known as Buffalo Bill* (Hartford, CT: Frank E. Bliss, 1979; rept. ed. Frank Christianson [Lincoln: University of Nebraska Press, 2011]), 419, hereafter, Cody, *Life*; Ingraham, *Buffalo Bill Cody*, part 3, chap. IX.

36. Cody, *Life*, 263.

37. Ibid., 321.

38. Ibid., 152.

39. Ingraham, *Buffalo Bill Cody*, part 2, chap. XLV.

40. Cody, *Life*, 97; Ingraham, *Buffalo Bill Cody*, part 1, chap. XXXIV.

41. Ingraham, *Buffalo Bill Cody*, part 1, chap. XXXIX; Barbara Leaming, *Orson Welles: A Biography* (New York: Viking Penguin, 1985), 3.

42. Ingraham, *Buffalo Bill Cody*, part 2, chap. LIII.

43. Ingraham, *Buffalo Bill Cody*, part 2, chap. LI.

44. Paul Lundgren, "Buffalo Bill Cody, His Little Sister Helen, and Their Connection to Duluth," https://www.perfectduluthday.com/2012/03/31/buffalo-bill-cody

-his-little-sister-helen-and-their-connection-to-duluth, accessed February 15, 2017; *Philadelphia Inquirer*, October 6, 1895; Russell, *The Lives and Legends*, 279.

45. Paul Reddin, *Wild West Shows* (Urbana: University of Illinois Press, 1999), 145.

46. *Chicago Tribune*, August 18, 1904.

PART I: "A MAN OF THE WEST"

1. This introductory piece was originally a footnote but is here included in the text for clarity.

2. The family moved from there in 1854 when Bill was six years old.

3. Isaac Cody (1811–1857).

4. LeClaire is situated fifteen miles northwest of Davenport.

5. Samuel Cody (1841–1853).

6. Elijah Cody.

7. Cody does not mention Turk in his autobiography; his sisters Julia and Helen introduce the pet in their biographies of their brother.

8. Shakespeare, *Hamlet*, act 5, scene 2.

9. Alexander Pope in his mid-eighteenth century "Essay on Man" wrote, "Lo, the poor Indian! whose untutored mind sees God in clouds. . . ." By the mid-nineteenth century, "Lo" became, in the popular press, the Indian content in his innocence and ignorance as he walked the woods.

10. With the 1830 Indian Removal Act, the Kickapoo and other tribes east of the Mississippi were forced to cede their lands and move westward.

11. The fort was established as the eastern terminus of the Oregon and Santa Fe trails. Its purposes, and those of most western forts, were to protect Americans heading west and to maintain peace among various Indian tribes.

12. Hegira, or migration, customarily refers to the prophet Mohammed's flight from Mecca to Medina to escape danger in 622 A.D. and marks the beginning of the Muslim era. By the mid-eighteenth century, it came to mean any arduous journey.

13. Salt Creek Valley, Kansas, lies near the confluence of Plum Creek and Salt Creek.

14. Writing "Westward the star of empire takes its way," John Quincy Adams misquoted George Berkeley, whose poem on patriotism reads "Westward the course of empire takes its way."

15. Highwaymen were a constant threat to prairie travelers and to those settled near the forts.

16. Weeds.

17. The Enabling Act of Kansas Territory and the Kansas-Nebraska Act of 1854 created two new territories and allowed the settlers to determine their stance on slavery.

18. Prior to 1854, non-Indian Kansas settlers were mostly soldiers stationed at the forts and missionaries hoping to convert the tribes.

19. Signal.

20. The battle over slavery led to the Bleeding Kansas or Border Wars.

21. M. Pierce Rively.

22. Nearly two hundred men attended Kansas territory's first squatters' meeting on June 10, 1854, during which slave owners were advised to bring their slaves to Kansas as soon as possible.

23. Charles Dunn, an employee of Elijah Cody.

24. Broom.

25. In the Kansas wars, both pro- and anti-slavery proponents engaged in deadly guerrilla skirmishes, often killing innocent townspeople.

26. Powerful politician James H. Lane (1814–1866) was a zealous abolitionist.

27. At Hickory Point, Kansas, Lane led his forces against pro-slavers in September 1856. Lacking firepower against the well-fortified defenders, he retreated, but reinforcements from Lawrence surrounded the town and killed one pro-slavery man.

28. Grasshopper Falls in Jefferson County, Kansas, is now known as Valley Falls.

29. Isaac Cody served on the Kansas legislature's Ways and Means Committee and Accounts Committee. Andrew H. Reeder (1807–1864), a pro-slaver, was Kansas Territory's first governor.

30. Comanche were possibly the first plains Indians to adopt the horse for hunting and war.

31. The title page of Majors's book lists a preface by Cody with editing by Ingraham, who may also have been a ghostwriter. In Cody's autobiography, he met with William Russell. The freighting firm of Russell, Majors, and Waddell hauled military supplies west from the Missouri River.

32. Twenty-five dollars in 1856 equals about $704 in today's value. Not until 1899 did several states institute child labor laws, so children frequently worked on farms, as house servants, or in mines or factories.

33. The nickname of Helen Cody.

34. A school paid for by the citizens of the community.

35. Charles Dickens used the phrase in *Great Expectations* (1860), perhaps first finding it in James Thomson's poem "Spring" (1726).

36. Buttercup sings, "I mixed those children up" in Gilbert and Sullivan's 1878 opera *H.M.S. Pinafore*.

37. In Cody's autobiography, he called her Mary Hyatt; in his 1881 story, Ingraham named her Mollie Hyatt.

38. John R. Willis (1837–?) years later became a judge in Poinsett County, Arkansas.

39. Like most military forts, Kearny supplied Overland Trail travelers and outfitted military units for Indian campaigns. Ingraham misspells the name throughout.

40. Ingraham's first version in a Beadle novel has Cody leaping into a cottonwood tree to escape the stampede, then jumping onto a bull's back to ride him out.

41. Alexander Majors (1814–1900).

42. When Pres. James Buchanan appointed a territorial governor for Utah's Mormon settlers over the protestations of Brigham Young, Gen. William S. Harney

(1800–1899) and Col. Albert S. Johnston (1803–1862) led military troops charged with federal control. The resulting "Utah War" lasted May 1857–July 1858.

43. Charles Whitney Cody (1855-1864).

44. Helen Cody Wetmore wrote that a $1,000 claim was levied against the estate for lumber and supplies. If allowed, the family would be homeless, but it was settled in the Codys' favor when the bookkeeper, Mr. Barnhart, testified that the bills had been paid.

45. A popular pre–Civil War muzzle-loading hunting rifle carrying a ball and two buckshot.

46. A low wall quickly put up as a battle defense.

47. Angels ordered Lot and his family to leave Sodom and not look back. His wife did and was turned into a pillar of salt. (Genesis 19:26)

48. The Republican flows from Colorado through Kansas and Nebraska.

49. About $1,100 in current value.

50. In Cody's autobiography, Mrs. Cody appeals to Mr. Russell.

51. Despite some schooling, Cody could not yet sign his name but made his mark, a cross.

52. In the Battle of Ash Hollow (September 2–3, 1855), Gen. Harney's command killed over one hundred Indians and destroyed their village in retaliation for the Sioux massacre of Lt. John Grattan's troops near Fort Laramie. Grattan initiated the original confrontation over the killing of a cow.

53. Beginning in 1838, a short-lived covert society, the Danites, engaged in vigilantism to avenge Mormon persecution and intimidate dissenters. Mormonism founder Joseph Smith (1805–1844) died before Cody was born. Maj. Lot Smith likely is referenced here.

54. In September 1857, Danites and Paiute Indians slaughtered 120 non-Mormon emigrants headed for California from Arkansas. Mormon leader John D. Lee was executed by firing squad twenty years later for the crimes.

55. A sentinel, one who has made the rounds.

56. The biblical Job was a good man subjected to disasters that decimated his family, health, and riches. Seeking to understand his situation, Job serves as an example of patience in suffering.

57. In 1857, Indian soldiers revolted against their British rulers and surrounded the town of Lucknow. Relief troops were long in coming. When one woman fell ill with a fever, she raved, "The Campbells are coming" upon hearing bagpipes. Sir Colin Campbell's command had arrived, ending the mutiny.

58. Family; Martha returned home after discovering her husband John Craine was a bigamist.

59. In his autobiography, Cody misidentifies Camp Walbach as Fort Wallach.

60. Historians alternately name Valentin Devinny or Francis Bivinny as Cody's teacher.

61. The Pike's Peak, Colorado, gold rush lasted July 1858–February 1861.

62. Russell, Majors and Waddell established the Pony Express to deliver mail via

a horseback relay system from St. Joseph, Missouri, to Sacramento, California. The enterprise lasted April 1860–October 1861.

63. The military road most likely ran from Fort Leavenworth south to Fort Scott and was used to move supplies, equipment, and troops from one fort to another.

64. Rain-in-the-Face (1835–1905), a Sioux warrior who would fight at the Battle of Little Bighorn in 1876.

65. The inadvertent use of "I" demonstrates Ingraham's reliance on Cody's autobiography. The original reads "Rain-in-the-Face turned to me and gave me to understand that as I was yet a 'papoose,' or a very young man, they would not take my life."

66. Nearly $1,400 in current value.

67. Joseph A. Slade (c. 1831–1864), a division chief on the Overland Stage Line, was infamous for his terrible temper, nevertheless both Cody and Mark Twain befriended him.

68. Some historians believe Cody participated in the Pony Express; doubters are convinced he was elsewhere on the plains, possibly Pike's Peak, or in school, citing conflicting dates or stories credited to other plainsmen.

69. In his autobiography, Cody remembered Plant's (or Plante's) Station as Ploutz's.

70. James Butler "Wild Bill" Hickok (1837–1876) was a frontiersman, Union scout, Abilene marshal, and actor in Cody's troupe.

71. An extra or spare.

72. Cody served as scout for Charles S. Clark (1837–1903) and the Ninth Kansas Cavalry; the Kiowa and Comanche, nomadic Indians of the southern plains, allied against white invasion of their lands.

73. The "Red Legs," so called for the red sheepskin leggings they wore, were Union-sanctioned volunteer guerrillas whose activities terrorized settlers on the Kansas-Missouri border. William S. Tough (or Tuff) was a horse thief and murderer.

74. Tuberculosis.

75. James "Al" Goodman (1834–1901); Julia M. Cody (1843–1928).

76. Union soldiers were so-called because they wore blue uniforms; Confederates wore gray.

PART II: "LED BY DESTINY"

1. "The evil that men do lives after them; the good is oft interred with their bones." William Shakespeare, *Julius Caesar*, act 3 scene 2.

2. "These are the times that try men's souls." Thomas Paine, *The American Crisis*.

3. Cody's account differs from Ingraham's romantic version: "A number of my old comrades and neighbors, who tried to induce me to enlist . . . I had no idea of doing anything of the kind; but one day, after having been under the influence of bad whisky, I awoke to find myself a soldier in the Seventh Kansas."

4. The Santa Fe Trail, a main transportation route from Boonville, Missouri, to

Santa Fe, New Mexico, ran through Indian Territory. Resisting constant invasion by travelers, Indians attacked wagon trains until the army forced them onto reservations.

5. The Younger family of Missouri bushwhackers (Civil War guerrillas), including Bob, Cole, Jim, and John, were later joined by Frank and Jesse James.

6. During the Civil War, Col. Charles R. Jennison led the Seventh Kansas Volunteer Cavalry into Missouri to rob and plunder.

7. Confederate Gen. Nathan Bedford Forrest's (1821–1877) troops defeated those of Union Gen. Samuel D. Sturgis (1822–1889) at the Battle of Brices Crossroads in northern Mississippi in June 1864. The Seventh Cavalry, including Cody, was engaged in the July 14–15, 1864, Battle of Tupelo. Forrest's aim to drive Unionists out of Mississippi was foiled by Union Gen. Andrew J. Smith's command. Cody had not yet enlisted at the time of the Battle of Corinth, Mississippi, in October 1862.

8. Possibly a reference to William W. Loring (1818–1886) who, like Ingraham, served the Confederacy, fought in the Mexican-American war, and joined the Egyptian Khedive's army.

9. The Nat Golden story does not appear in Cody's autobiography, but was first told by Helen Cody Wetmore. In Frank Cooper's *Thrilling Lives of Buffalo Bill and Pawnee Bill*, Cody takes Golden's papers to Gen. Braxton Bragg.

10. The unofficial flag of the Confederacy.

11. In Ingraham's novel *Buffalo Bill in Disguise* (May 1903), the character William Fredericks is discovered to be Bill Cody.

12. November 1878–February 1880.

13. This extended piece on Hickok was originally Ingraham's footnote but is here included in the text for clarity.

14. Union Gen. George A. Custer (1839–1876) served in the Civil War, then fought in the Indian wars, dying at Little Bighorn with his Seventh Cavalry.

15. *Harper's New Monthly Magazine*, February 1867.

16. In July 1870, Hickok killed Pvt. John Kile of the Seventh Cavalry in Hays City, Kansas.

17. As marshal of Abilene, Kansas, Hickok shot troublemaker Phil Coe. Hearing the ruckus, policeman Mike Williams ran up and Hickok inadvertently shot him too, then paid his funeral expenses.

18. Sterling Price (1809–1867) commanded twelve thousand Confederates aiming to regain control of Missouri.

19. Union generals William T. Sherman (1820–1891), Philip H. Sheridan (1831–1888), and Nelson A. Miles (1839–1925) served in the Civil War, then in the western Indian wars. Wounded Knee, December 1891, was commanded by Miles of the Military Division of the Missouri during which the US Army killed three hundred Sioux Indians. Cody was not present at the time. In January 1891, he was commissioned to help safeguard the Nebraska border. When the Indian wars were over, he requested demotion to Colonel; thereafter using that title.

20. In September 1864, Confederates under Price attacked Fort Davidson, Mis-

souri, in hopes of gaining weapons for three thousand unarmed soldiers. The fort soldiers counter-attacked but ran low on ammunition. Union general Thomas Ewing ordered the fort evacuated and all supplies exploded, foiling the Confederates.

21. Alert.

22. Hickok biographer Joseph Rosa insisted that while Hickok was possibly spying against Price, Cody spent most of his military career copying orders at St. Louis headquarters. Cody's claim that he was a spy "is nonsense" (Rosa, email to editor, February 16, 2014).

23. According to Cody, this happened when he and Hickok were with Lew Simpson's ill-fated wagon train.

24. Hickok was a stock-tender at one of the relay stations, not an express rider.

25. Hillbilly.

26. Confederate general John S. Marmaduke (1833–1887) commanded a division in Price's raid in September 1864.

27. Ingraham repeats Cody's misspelling of Union general John McNeil's name (1813–1891), who was known as "The Butcher of Palmyra" for executing ten Confederate prisoners of war in retribution for the capture of a Union civilian.

28. Spanish for "who knows."

29. In October 1864, the Seventh Kansas became part of the cavalry division under Union general Alfred Pleasanton (1824–1897) who, by defeating Confederate general Price's forces at Westport, Byram's Ford, and Marais des Cygnes, ended the war in Missouri.

30. In her *Memories of Buffalo Bill*, Louisa Cody claims she met him on a blind date set up by her cousin William McDonald.

31. Cody had enlisted at Fort Leavenworth, Kansas, as a private in Company H, Seventh Regiment Kansas Cavalry Volunteers and was honorably discharged as a private.

32. A demon's characteristic.

33. A benedict is a newly married man, previously a longtime bachelor. The term probably came from Shakespeare's *Much Ado about Nothing*, in which the character Benedick married late in life.

34. A pub landlord.

35. Ingraham may be referring to Henry David Thoreau's essay, "The Landlord," published October 1843 in the *United States Democratic Review*: "Likewise we look in vain east or west over the earth to find the perfect man; but each represents only some particular excellence. The Landlord is a man of more open and general sympathies, who possesses a spirit of hospitality which is its own reward, and feeds and shelters men from pure love of the creatures."

36. The Kansas Pacific Railway, started in 1855, was to run from Kansas City to Denver, Colorado, then northward. Service began fifteen years later.

37. Fort Ellsworth, established in 1864, was a supply station for the Butterfield Overland Despatch freight and stage line. By 1867, the Kansas Pacific railroad was completed to that point. Fort soldiers escorted wagon trains and guarded construction workers from Indians.

38. Winfield S. Hancock (1824–1886) was recognized as one of the Union's most brilliant commanders.

39. Sitting Bull, a Hunkpapa Sioux chief (c.1831–1890), inspired his warriors to defeat Custer and his Seventh Cavalry. In 1885 he joined Cody's Wild West for four months, eventually tiring of the crowds and white civilization.

40. Ingraham repeatedly misspells Fort Hays.

41. Whip.

42. In Cody's autobiography, the next line is "'General, how about this mule, anyhow?' I asked, at last."

43. According to biblical tradition (Jeremiah 47:4), Philistines were a warlike people and the Israelites' enemies. In a modern sense, it refers to someone lacking in culture.

44. In Numbers 22:22–28, Balaam's donkey, seeing an angel, will not move. When Balaam whips the donkey, it miraculously speaks, complaining about the punishment.

45. Traditionally, Archangel Gabriel blows a horn announcing Judgment Day. One wonders if non-Christian Indians knew who Gabriel was.

46. George A. Armes (1844–1919) led the Tenth Cavalry of colored volunteers against Indians; he once described Cody as "one of the best shots on the plains." Ingraham consistently misspells his name.

47. African-American soldiers comprised six regiments commanded by white officers, an arrangement typical of the era. Black "buffalo soldiers" were so named for their hair which resembled that of a buffalo.

48. Forces of French emperor Napoleon Bonaparte were defeated at Waterloo, Belgium, in June 1815. While decimating the British, his eastern flank was attacked by Prussians. By the time he reorganized his defenses, the panicked French had begun a chaotic retreat.

49. An intestinal disease characterized by extensive diarrhea leading to dehydration.

50. In Cody's autobiography, he intimates the opposite: that the soldiers preferred Indian fighting to battling cholera in camp.

51. Ingraham references W. S. Gilbert's opera *H.M.S. Pinafore:* "Things are seldom what they seem; Skim milk masquerades as cream."

52. Arta Lucille Cody (1866–1904). In her memories of Cody, Mrs. Cody writes that she thought of the name Arta.

53. In his autobiography, Cody writes that Webb did give Rose and himself two lots.

54. Frontiersmen referred to the .50 caliber Springfield rifle as a needle gun for its needle-like firing pin. Cody may have attended a performance of Victor Hugo's *Lucretia Borgia, or the Prisoner*, a contemporary opera.

55. A blind bridle focuses the horse's attention, preventing it from being frightened or distracted by objects to its side or rear.

56. In Cody's autobiography, the officers refer to Brigham as a Gothic steed.

57. Capt. George W. Graham, Tenth Cavalry; Second Lt. John M. Thompson, Thirty-Eighth Infantry.

58. Cody refers to a Lt. Emmick. Don Russell believes it is First Lt. Myron J. Amick.

59. According to Jeremiah 23:2–3, the Jewish people were scattered throughout the world when invaders conquered Israel.

60. 1866's $500 equals about $6,800 today.

61. Cody only worked for the Goddard Brothers for eight months, so his buffalo tally was probably closer to three thousand.

62. Dime novelist Ned Buntline cajoled Cody into performing frontier melodramas on stage. The Buffalo Bill Combination performed for fourteen seasons, 1872–1886.

63. Cody's first story was "The Haunted Valley" in *Vickery's Fireside Visitor*, April 1875. Another story, *The Pearl of the Prairies; or The Scout and the Renegade*, was published in *New York Weekly*, August 1875.

64. Nicholas M. Nolan (1835–1883) commanded buffalo soldiers over ten years.

65. A depression in the ground formed by buffalo rolling around in the dirt seeking relief from insects; wallows can range in depth from a few inches to several feet with diameters of over one hundred feet.

66. Generals William T. Sherman and Philip H. Sheridan share the notoriety for allegedly declaring that "the only good Indian was a dead Indian."

67. In Shakespeare's play, Othello (act 3, scene 3) believes that, because he no longer takes joy in soldiering, he has lost his identity. Ingraham compares Cody losing his identity as a buffalo hunter if he is no longer needed in that occupation.

68. Daingerfield Parker (1832–1925) served the Union in the Civil War and was honored for his gallantry at Gettysburg.

69. William B. Hazen (1830–1887), a Union general, later handled negotiations with American Indians.

70. Satanta (c. ?–1878); Lone Wolf (c.?–1879); Kicking Bird (1835–1875); Satauk (1810–1871).

71. In his autobiography, Cody identified it as Fort Zarah.

72. A wagon used on the plains.

73. Confidence derived from drinking alcohol.

74. William B. Royall (1825–1895) served in the military in the war with Mexico and as a Union major during the Civil War.

75. George A. Forsyth (1837–1915) is best known for soliciting fifty frontiersmen to scout Indian territory, then leading them to victory against Cheyenne Roman Nose.

76. In his autobiography, Cody refers to Major William H. Brown.

77. Place to eat or a wagon that carried food and cooking provisions.

78. Eugene A. Carr (1830–1910), an experienced Indian fighter, was also wounded several times as commander in the Union army. He was awarded the Congressional Medal of Honor.

79. According to Cody, Brown remarked on the shot breaking Lt. Alfred Bache's plate.

80. William H. Penrose (1832–1903), a Union officer, was trained as a civil-

mechanical engineer. He commanded at Gettysburg, Second Bull Run, and Fredericksburg, among other battles.

81. The animals harnessed closest to the wheels.

82. Ad libitum—"at one's pleasure."

83. A hard, dry bread easily carried as a staple in frontier diets.

84. In November 1864 Kit Carson (1809–1868) led troops in an attack on Kiowa and Comanche villages in the Texas Panhandle. Indian warriors retaliated, and fighting continued down the Canadian River to adjacent camps.

85. In his autobiography, Cody called him Little Geary.

86. W. C. Forbush.

87. William Bevins was a criminal of some repute throughout the West who, at various times, stood accused of horse theft, prison escape, and stagecoach robbery.

88. The Black Hills, considered sacred by American Indians, is a small mountain chain extending from western South Dakota to Wyoming.

89. Edward W. Ward (1843–1897) served as adjutant of a Fifth Cavalry battalion in the campaign against the Sioux and Cheyenne in western Kansas.

90. A bugle call notifying troops to mount up.

91. Belgian Jules C. A. Schenofsky offered his services for the Union during the Civil War.

92. A quote from Henry Wadsworth Longfellow's poem "Day Is Done."

93. When Congress authorized the enlistment of Indian scouts, Frank North (1840–1885), who spoke fluent Pawnee, and others were hired as officers of the Indian companies. He joined Cody's Wild West show in 1883.

94. Christopher C. Augur (1821–1898), severely wounded in the Civil War, sat on the military court investigating the surrender at Harper's Ferry. He commanded the Department of the Platte at the time of the story's Indian battle.

95. Describing the apparel of Hawaiian islanders in *Roughing It*, Twain wrote, "[A] stately 'buck' Kanaka would stalk [into church] with a woman's bonnet on, wrong side before—only this, and nothing more; after him would stride his fellow, with the legs of a pair of pantaloons tied around his neck, the rest of his person untrammeled; in his rear would come another gentleman simply gotten up in a fiery neck-tie and a striped vest."

96. In May 1869, Tall Bull's Cheyenne carried off Susanna Alderdice and Maria Weichel in an attack on settlers.

97. Edward "Fighting Jack" M. Hayes (1842–1912) served in Georgia and the Carolinas during the Civil War, in Indian campaigns, in Cuba, and the Philippines.

98. Cody claims he shot Tall Bull (1830–1869), chief of the Dog Soldiers, at Summit Springs, Colorado, in July 1869. Several others, including Frank and Luther North, refute the assertion.

99. The quote is attributed to Abraham Lincoln.

100. Ned Buntline, the pseudonym of Edward Z. C. Judson (1813–1886), was a prolific author who introduced Cody in a serial titled "Buffalo Bill: The King of the Border

Men" published in 1869 in the *New York Weekly*. Fred Maeder dramatized it for the New York stage in February 1872. Buntline also wrote the drama *Scouts of the Prairie* featuring Cody in the starring role.

101. William H. Emory (1811–1887), a civil engineer, mapped the Texas-Mexico border, served in the Civil War, and commanded the Department of the Gulf.

102. Thomas Duncan (1819–1887) commanded the Fifth Cavalry at this time and, afterward, the Department of the Platte.

103. The phrase comes from a nineteenth-century naval proverb. When one ship pursued another, both could only fire guns that pointed forward or backward.

104. Pocahontas, the daughter of Indian chief Powhatan, is credited with saving the life of Englishman John Smith in 1607.

105. Pawnee Killer, a Sioux, had allied with Tall Bull, a Cheyenne, at Summit Springs. Nelson Buck (1808–1869) and his party of eleven were surveying a line between Kansas and Nebraska and killed some Indian scouts they had come across, thus instigating Sioux retaliation. Indians massacred Buck's entire party in three separate attacks.

106. In his autobiography, Cody wrote, "I don't know any more about law than a government mule does about book-keeping."

107. A person may recover goods unlawfully withheld from him by a legal process in which the court requires the defendant to return the goods to the plaintiff until rightful ownership is determined.

108. John 5:39.

109. In his early melodramatic performances, Cody suffered severely from stage fright.

110. Paleontologist Othniel C. Marsh (1831–1899) led four expeditions to the West seeking dinosaur fossils.

111. Lawrence R. Jerome (?–1888), with his brother Leonard founded the Rochester *American*; Leonard W. Jerome (1818–1891), a New York financier; Carroll Livingston (?–1904), member of the Stock Exchange; John G. Heckscher (1837–1908), Wall Street banker; Charles L. Fitzhugh (1838–1923), Union officer, steel manufacturer; Henry E. Davies (1836–1894), author of *Ten Days on the Plains* detailing the 1870 hunting trip; M. Edward Rogers (1839–1884) of Philadelphia; J. Schuyler Crosby (1839–1914), Union officer; Chicagoan Samuel Johnson; Anson Stager (1825–1885), Union officer, superintendent at Western Union Company; Charles L. Wilson (1818–1878), owner of *Chicago Evening Herald*; Daniel Henry Rucker (1812–1910), Major General quartermaster; Morris J. Asch (1833–1902), Union surgeon.

112. Grand Duke Alexei Alexandrovich (1850–1908), son of Russian Czar Alexander II.

113. Spotted Tail (1823–1881), Brulé Sioux Chief during the Plains Wars.

114. Todd Randall was an old frontiersman with an Indian wife, considered "disreputable" by some.

115. James Egan (1837–1883), an Irish native, served in the Union's First Cavalry; entourage, servants.

116. Cody lent the Duke his rifle "Lucretia Borgia" and horse Buckskin Joe after the Duke had little success with his own weapon and horse.

117. Edward O. C. Ord (1818–1883), a Union major general, served in the Civil War and in various Indian wars.

118. John B. Studley (1831–1910), famous American actor, played the lead in *Buffalo Bill, King of the Border Men*.

119. About $1,800 in today's value.

120. John B. "Texas Jack" Omohundro (1846–1880) became a Texas cowboy after the Civil War. On a cattle-drive to Nebraska, he met Cody and the two became friends.

121. Windham Thomas Wyndham-Quin, Fourth Earl of Dunraven (1841–1926).

122. Cody's opponent, D. P. Ashburn, contested the win. It was found that the county clerk was in error, the votes improperly returned, so Ashburn rightfully claimed the seat.

123. *Scouts of the Prairie* was Cody's first melodrama.

124. Super, short for supernumerary, was a person who appeared onstage in a non-speaking role.

PART III: "HONORS EASY"

1. A phrase denoting violent action, often for the sake of sensationalism.

2. Buntline wrote *Scouts of the Prairie* for Cody's dramatic debut. Ingraham confuses it with Hiram Robbins's *Scouts of the Plains*, Cody's second drama.

3. Hickok did not join Cody's theatrical troupe until 1873 and was not present for the meeting with Buntline.

4. With only four days from renting the theater to opening night, Buntline, the press reported, wrote the play in four hours.

5. According to Cody's autobiography, Buntline urged them to "stick to it"; then Cody himself uttered the "luck" wish.

6. In Cody's first season onstage, the only professional was Giuseppina Morlacchi.

7. Over $340,000 in today's value.

8. The first season ended June 28, 1873, at Port Jervis, New York.

9. Cody's second theatrical season closed in New York City, June 30, 1874.

10. Anson Mills (1834–1924) laid out the city of El Paso, Texas, served the Union army, and commanded during the Indian wars.

11. Dunraven's yacht, *Valkyrie III*, lost in the first race of the 1895 America's Cup.

12. John M. Burke (1842–1917), Cody's press agent for the theatrical troupe and Wild West show, in 1893 wrote a biography titled *Buffalo Bill from Prairie to Palace*.

13. George Crook (1828–1890), a Union general, also led Indian campaigns in the southwest and Dakotas, particularly the 1876–1877 Great Sioux War. Powder River is in northern Wyoming.

14. Wesley Merritt (1834–1910) served in the Civil War, Spanish-American War, and as first American military governor in the Philippines.

15. In Cody's autobiography, another scout announces news of Custer's defeat.

16. Nimrod was a skillful hunter, Genesis 10:8–9.

17. In Joel 3:2, 12, the Valley of Jehoshaphat was God's seat of judgment.

18. Built in 1872, Fort Abraham Lincoln was home to the Seventh Cavalry, who were sent to North Dakota to protect Northern Pacific railroad workers. The Badlands of South Dakota consist of over 240,000 desolate acres of buttes, ravines, and prairie.

19. Charles "Buffalo Chips" White (?–1876), one of Crook's scouts, was killed at the Battle of Slim Buttes in South Dakota.

20. A compound used to ignite the charge in a cartridge.

21. Possibly Pierre-Jean DeSmet (1801–1873).

22. Alfred H. Terry (1827–1890) was to move his forces west. John Gibbon (1827–1896) was to march east, and George Crook's soldiers were to march north.

23. Because he divided his troops, Custer's command at Little Big Horn consisted of little more than 200 men.

24. General Charles King gave this order.

25. Son of a chief, his name—Yellow Hair—was mistranslated.

26. In his autobiography, Cody identifies the scout as Frank Grouard (1850–1905).

27. Cody, and Ingraham in turn, confuses Gen. Nelson Miles with Col. Anson Mills. Miles served as a Union general and was prominent in the Indian wars, commanding the Department of the Missouri.

28. Grant Marsh (1834–1916), the Missouri river steamboat captain who, it was said, "could navigate a sternwheeler through a sea of dew."

29. Edmund Rice (1841–1906), mentioned by Cody as having built a fort with trowel-bayonets which were also useful as shovels in throwing up entrenchments.

30. An extremely large and heavy 15-inch smooth-bore cannon.

31. In December 1876, Cody debuted *Red Right Hand; or Buffalo Bill's First Scalp for Custer*, written by Ingraham.

32. Joseph N. G. Whistler (1822–1899) served in the Civil War, Mexican-American war, and in skirmishes against the Apache and Navajo.

33. Edward W. Smith (d. 1883).

34. Cody closed his 1877 season at Carson City, Nevada.

35. Cody lived until January 10, 1917.

BIBLIOGRAPHY

American Heritage New History of the Civil War, ed. James M. McPherson. New York: American Heritage, 1996.

Appletons' Annual Cyclopaedia and Register of Important Events. New York: Appleton, 1862–1903, vol. 16.

Armes, George A. *Ups and Downs of an Army Officer*, Washington, DC, 1900, n.p. https://archive.org/stream/upsanddownsofana00armerich/upsanddownsofana00armerich_djvu.txt, accessed January 5, 2017.

"Author and Soldier: Prentiss Ingraham, Who Wrote One Thousand Novels and Fought in Many Wars." *Los Angeles Times*, August 28, 1904, A6.

Barry, Louise. "The Fort Leavenworth-Fort Gibson Military Road and the Founding of Fort Scott." *Kansas State Historical Society Quarterly* 11, no. 2 (May 1942): 115–129.

Burke, John. *Buffalo Bill, the Noblest Whiteskin*. New York: G. P. Putnam's Sons, 1973.

Burke, John M. *Buffalo Bill from Prairie to Palace*, Chicago: Rand McNally, 1893; rept. ed. Chris Dixon. Lincoln: University of Nebraska Press, 2012.

Burlingame, Michael. *Abraham Lincoln: A Life*, vol. 5. Baltimore, MD: Johns Hopkins University Press, 2008.

Catton, Bruce. *The Civil War*. Boston: Houghton Mifflin, 1987.

Chaky, Doreen. *Terrible Justice: Sioux Chiefs and U.S. Soldiers on the Upper Missouri, 1854–1868*. Norman: University of Oklahoma Press, 2012.

Chase, A. C. "Colonel Prentiss Ingraham: His Life and Work." *Bob Taylor's Magazine* 2, no. 6 (March 1906): 694–699.

Cody, Louisa, with Courtney Ryley Cooper. *Memories of Buffalo Bill*. New York: Appleton, 1919.

Cody, William F. *The Life of Hon. William F. Cody Known as Buffalo Bill*. Hartford: Frank E. Bliss, 1879; rept. ed. Frank Christianson. Lincoln: University of Nebraska Press, 2011.

Connelley, William E. *A Standard History of Kansas and Kansans*. Chicago: Lewis, 1918.

Cook, James W. *The Arts of Deception: Playing with Fraud in the Age of Barnum*. Cambridge, MA: Harvard University Press, 2001.

Cooper, Frank C. *Stirring Lives of Buffalo Bill Colonel Wm. F. Cody Last of the Great Scouts and Pawnee Bill Major Gordon W. Lillie White Chief of the Pawnees*. New York: S. L. Parsons, 1912.

Cutler, William G. *History of the State of Kansas*. Chicago: A. T. Andreas, 1883. http://www.kancoll.org/books/cutler/leavenworth/leavenworth-co-p1.html#TOC, accessed November 18, 2016.

Duby, George, ed. *A History of a Private Life: Passions of the Renaissance.* New York: Belknap Press, 1989.

Encyclopedia of Mormonism. New York: Macmillan, 1992; digital copyright Brigham Young University, 2001.

Etcheson, Nicole. *Bleeding Kansas: Contested Liberty in the Civil War Era.* Lawrence: University Press of Kansas, 2004.

Eyster, Wm. R., "A Rolling Stone: Incidents in the Career on Sea and Land, as Boy and Man of Col. Prentiss Ingraham, Soldier, Sailor and Wanderer." *Beadle's Boy's Library of Sport, Story and Adventure* 2, no. 25 (1884): 1–31.

Foote, Stella Adelyne. *Letters from Buffalo Bill.* Billings: Foote Publishing, 1954.

Goodman, Julia Cody. "Julia Cody Goodman's Memoirs of Buffalo Bill," ed. Don Russell. *Kansas Historical Quarterly* 28, no. 4 (Winter 1962): 442–496.

Gray, John. "Fact versus Fiction in the Kansas Boyhood of Buffalo Bill." *Kansas History* 8, no. 1 (Spring 1985): 2–20.

Grossman, James R., ed. *The Frontier in American Culture: An Exhibit at the Newberry Library, Aug. 26, 1994–Jan. 7, 1995.* Essays by Richard White and Patricia Nelson Limerick. Chicago: Newberry Library, 1994; Berkeley: University of California Press, 1994.

Hall, Jesse A., and LeRoy T. Hand. *History of Leavenworth County, Kansas.* Topeka: Historical Publishing, 1921. https://archive.org/details/historyofleavenwoohall, accessed October 24, 2016.

Harvey, Charles M. "The Dime Novel in American Life." *Atlantic Monthly* 100, 1907, 37–45.

Hedren, Paul L., ed. *The Great Sioux War 1876–77.* Helena: Montana Historical Society Press, 1991.

———, comp. *Where Are They Now? Burial Places of Officers, Physicians, and Other Military Notables of the Great Sioux War.* Norman, OK: Arthur H. Clark, 2011.

Hyde, George E. *Spotted Tail's Folk: A History of the Brule Sioux.* Norman: University of Oklahoma Press, 1961.

Ingraham, Prentiss. *Adventures of Buffalo Bill from Boyhood to Manhood.* New York: Beadle and Adams, 1881.

———. "The Classic Dime Novel and Its Gradual Disappearance," *New York Herald*, February 3, 1901.

———. *Buffalo Bill's Conquest.* New York: Street & Smith, 1908.

———. *Buffalo Bill's Iron Grip.* New York: Street & Smith, 1908.

———. *Buffalo Bill's Outlaw Hunt.* New York: Street & Smith, 1909.

———. *Buffalo Bill's Clean Sweep.* New York: Street & Smith, 1911.

———. *Buffalo Bill and the Lone Camper.* New York: Street & Smith, 1915.

———. *Buffalo Bill in Harness.* New York: Street & Smith, 1915.

Jenks, George. "Dime Novel Makers." *Bookman* 20 (October 1904): 108–114.

Johannsen, Albert. *The House of Beadle and Adams and Its Dime and Nickel Novels.* Norman: University of Oklahoma Press, 1949.

Johnson, Michael L. *Hunger for the Wild: America's Obsession with the Untamed West.* Lawrence: University Press of Kansas, 2007.

Jones, Daryl. *The Dime Novel Western.* Bowling Green, OH: Popular Press, Bowling Green State University, 1978.

Kelly, C. Brian. "Prentiss Ingraham, the Confederacy's Most Prolific Author, Found a Postwar Audience for His Hundreds of Novels." *Military History* 22, no. 4 (July 2005): 74.

Leithead, J. Edward. "Colonel Prentiss Ingraham." *Roundup* 32, no. 1 (January 1964): 10–14.

Lloyd, James B., ed. *Lives of Mississippi Authors, 1817–1967.* Jackson: University Press of Mississippi, 2009.

Lundgren, Paul. *Area Women in History: Helen Cody Wetmore, More Than Just Buffalo Bill's Little Sister.* http://www.paullundgren.com/journalism-area-woman-helen-cody-wetmore.cfm, accessed September 24, 2014.

———. "Buffalo Bill Cody, His Little Sister Helen, and Their Connection to Duluth." http://www.perfectduluthday.com/2012/03/31/buffalo-bill-cody-his-little-sister-helen-and-their-connection-to-duluth/, accessed February 15, 2017.

Majors, Alexander. *Seventy Years on the Frontier: Alexander Majors' Memoirs of a Lifetime on the Border*, ed. Prentiss Ingraham. Chicago: Rand, McNally, 1893.

Manning, Chandra. *Civil War History* 52, no. 2 (June 2006): 174–175.

McCullough, David. *The American Spirit: Who We Are and What We Stand For.* New York: Simon & Schuster, 2017.

The New American Bible. Nashville: Thomas Nelson Publishers, 1983.

Nye, Wilbur S. *Carbine and Lance: The Story of Old Fort Sill.* Norman: University of Oklahoma Press, 1983.

Parrish, Randall. *The Great Plains: The Romance of Western American Exploration, Warfare, and Settlement, 1527–1870.* Chicago: A. C. McClurg, 1907.

"Partisans, Guerillas, Irregulars and Bushwhackers: The Truth behind the Names." http://www.rulen.com/partisan/partisan.htm, accessed October 19, 2016.

Patten, Gilbert. "Dime-Novel Days." *Saturday Evening Post*, March 7, 1931: 33, 36, 52, 54, 57, 60.

———. "My Friend, Col. Prentiss Ingraham." *Reckless Ralph's Dime Novel Round-Up* 2, no. 140 (May 1944): 1–2.

Price, George F. *Across the Continent with the Fifth Cavalry.* New York: D. Van Nostrand, 1883. https://archive.org/details/acrosscontintwoopricrich, accessed September 29, 2015.

Ramos, Donna. "Utah War: U.S. Government Versus Mormon Settlers." *Wild West Magazine*, http://www.historynet.com/utah-war-us-government-versus-mormon-settlers.htm, accessed June 12, 2006.

Reader, Samuel James. "From the Diary and Reminiscences of Samuel James Reader," ed. George A. Root. *Kansas Historical Quarterly* 1, no. 1 (November 1931): 28–49.

Reddin, Paul. *Wild West Shows.* Urbana: University of Illinois Press, 1999.

Reynolds, Quentin James. *The Fiction Factory; or, From Pulp Row to Quality Street: The Story of 100 Years of Publishing at Street & Smith*. New York: Random House, 1955.

Rich, Effie Dean. *Buckskin History, Kaibab Plateau and Grand Canyon*. Unpublished manuscript, Utah State Historical Society, Salt Lake City, 1941.

Robbins, Eloise Frisbie. "The Original Military Post Road between Fort Leavenworth and Fort Scott." *Kansas State Historical Society Quarterly* 1, no. 2 (Summer 1978): 90–100.

Rosa, Joseph G. *They Called Him Wild Bill*. Norman: University of Oklahoma Press, 1974.

Russell, Don. *The Lives and Legends of Buffalo Bill*. Norman: University of Oklahoma Press, 1979.

Sagala, Sandra K. *Buffalo Bill on Stage*. Albuquerque: University of New Mexico Press, 2008.

———. "Nate Salsbury's *Black America:* Its Origin and Programs." *Points West* (Fall/Winter 2018; Spring 2019).

Sargent, George H. "The Dime Novel Finds a Niche in Americana." *Watertown (NY) Daily Times*, May 31, 1920.

Schindler, Hal. "'Buffalo Bill' Cody: Ever the Showman Tells Secret during Hunting Trip." *Salt Lake Tribune*, September 26, 1993, D1.

Sills, Joe, Jr. "Battle of the Little Bighorn." http://www.custerbattlefield.org/battle.shtml, accessed April 9, 2016.

Slagle, Jefferson D. "The Heirs of Buffalo Bill: Performing Authenticity in the Dime Western." *Canadian Review of American Studies* 39, no. 2 (2009): 119–138.

Slotkin, Richard. *Regeneration through Violence: The Mythology of the American Frontier, 1600–1860*. Middleton, CT: Wesleyan University Press, 1973.

———. *Gunfighter Nation: The Myth of the Frontier in Twentieth-Century America*. New York: HarperCollins, 1992.

Smith, Henry Nash. *Virgin Land: The American West as Symbol and Myth*. Cambridge, MA: Harvard University Press, 1978.

Spangler, Jerry. *Vermilion Dreamers, Sagebrush Schemers: An Overview of Human Occupation in House Rock Valley and the Eastern Arizona Strip*. Ogden, UT: Archaeological Alliance, 2007.

Springhall, John. *The Genesis of Mass Culture: Show Business Live in America 1840–1940*. New York: Palgrave MacMillan, 2008.

Steckmesser, Kent L. "The Frontier Hero in History and Legend." *Wisconsin Magazine of History* 46, no. 3 (Spring 1963): 168–179.

Thoreau, Henry David. "The Landlord." *United States Democratic Review* 13, no. 64 (October 1843): 427–430.

Twain, Mark. *Roughing It*. Hartford, CT: American Publishing, 1872.

Utley, Robert M., and Wilcomb E. Washburn. *Indian Wars*. Boston: Houghton Mifflin, 1977.

Walsh, Richard. *The Making of Buffalo Bill*. Indianapolis: Bobbs-Merrill, 1928, rept. Cody Family Association, 1978.

Ward, Geoffrey C. *The West: An Illustrated History.* New York: Little, Brown, 1996.
Warren, Louis S. *Buffalo Bill's America: William Cody and the Wild West Show.* New York: Vintage Books, 2005.
Wetmore, Helen Cody. *Buffalo Bill: Last of the Great Scouts.* Duluth: Duluth Press, 1899, rept. Stamford, CT: Longmeadow Press, 1994.
Whittaker, Frederick. *A Complete Life of Gen. George A. Custer.* New York: Sheldon, 1876. https://archive.org/details/completelifeofgeoowhit, accessed November 25, 2016.
Yost, Nellie Snyder. *Buffalo Bill: His Family, Friends, Fame, Failures, and Fortunes.* Chicago: Swallow Press, 1979.

Buffalo Bill Center of the West, Cody, Wyoming, MS6 William F. Cody

Websites:
http://www.arlingtoncemetery.net/gforsyth.htm
http://www.mswritersandmusicians.com/writers/prentiss-ingraham.html
http://www.nps.gov
http://www.nrcprograms.org/site/PageServer?pagename=airc_bio_main
http://www.rootsweb.ancestry.com/~neharlan/buck.html
http://www.thecivilwarmuse.com
http://www.vlib.us/old_west/forts.html
http://www.wyomingtalesandtrails.com/custer2.html

INDEX

Adventures of Buffalo Bill: From Boyhood to Manhood, 8, 311
Alderdice, Susanna, 333n96
Alexis, Grand Duke, 253, 267–270, 334n112, 335n116
American Indians. *See names of individual tribes*
Ames, Major. *See* Armes, Major George A.
Amick, First Lieutenant Myron J., 219, 220, 332n58
Arapaho, 288
Armes, Major George A., 209–211, 219, 331n46
Arms, Major. *See* Armes, Major George A.
Asch, Dr. Morris J., 266, 334n111
Ashburn, D. P., 335n122
Ash Hollow, Battle of, 84, 327n52
Augur, General Christopher, 252, 333n94
Austin, John, 235

Bache, Lieutenant Alfred, 240, 332n79
Barnhart, Mr., 327n44
Beadle and Adams, 3, 312, 326n40
Beecher, Lieutenant, 252
Bennett, James Gordon, 266, 271
Benteen, Colonel Frederick, 296
Bevins, Bill, 248, 333n87
Bivinny, Francis, 327n60
Black America, 6
Bomer, Buck, 107
Bonham, Ike, 229
Bragg, General Braxton, 329n9
Brinkline, Ned. *See* Buntline, Ned
Brouse, Major. *See* Brown, Major William H.

Brown, Major William H., 239–241, 245–246, 256–258, 261, 266, 332n76
Buck, Captain Nelson, 262, 334n105
Buck, Royal, 262‡
Buffalo Bill, King of the Border Men, 4, 333–334n100, 335n118
Buffalo Bill at Bay, 5
Buffalo Bill from Prairie to Palace, 335n12
Buffalo Bill in Disguise, 329n11
"Buffalo Chips." *See* White, Charles "Buffalo Chips"
buffalo soldiers, 331n47, 332n64
Buntline, Ned, 257, 261, 271, 272–273, 332n62
  actor, 280–286, 289
  author, 4, 8, 257, 276–277, 333–334n100
  meets Cody, 257–258
  playwright, 257, 279–280, 282, 335nn2–5
Burke, John M., 289, 335n12
Burr, Dangerfield, 4
Burrell, Mr. *See* Waddell, William
Burt, A. S., 308

Carr, General Eugene A., 9, 249, 252, 259, 332n78
  commands Fifth Cavalry, 240–244, 266, 290–291
  orders Cody after thieves, 247–248
  seeks General Penrose, 245–246
  wars with Indians, 239, 250–251, 254–256, 267
Carson, Kit, 140, 246, 333n84

Cheyenne, 84, 237–238, 238*, 295, 297, 299–300, 333n89, 333n96, 333n98
cholera, 211–222, 331nn49–50
Chrisman, George, 116–120, 129
Civil War, 2, 3, 134, 135, 202, 206, 243
   colored troops in, 221
Clark, Colonel Charles S., 134, 148, 328n72
Clifford brothers, 267
Cody, Arta, 214–215, 223, 225, 290, 331n52
Cody, Charles "Charlie" Whitney, 68, 83, 94, 103, 120, 327n43
Cody, Elijah, 19, 24, 26, 27, 37, 46, 325n6, 326n23
Cody, Eliza "Liza" (Mrs. George Myers), 68, 103, 199
Cody, Helen "Nellie" (Mrs. Hugh Wetmore)
   as Cody's sister, 52, 57, 68, 103, 112, 188, 325n7, 326n33, 327n44
   as Mrs. Hugh Wetmore, 6, 7, 10, 18*, 252†, 329n9
Cody, Isaac, 16–17, 18*, 19, 22–26, 28, 31, 325n3
   abolitionist, 35–38
   Alexander Majors's opinion of, 66
   in danger, 45–47, 49–50
   death, 64–65, 105
   elected to Kansas legislature, 44, 64, 326n29
   joins Free State Party, 40
   owns trading post, 34, 39
   settles in Salt Creek, 29–30
   wounded, 52–54
Cody, Julia
   as Cody's sister, 18*, 68, 103, 106, 120, 136–137, 325n7
   as Mrs. A. J. Goodman, 18*, 188, 328n75
Cody, Kit Carson, 261, 289–290
Cody, Louisa Frederici (Mrs. William F. Cody), 183–188
   as mother, 214–215, 223, 225, 252, 261, 289–290
   as wife, 196–200, 202, 212, 309, 330n30
Cody, Martha, 18*, 19, 51–52, 57, 68, 103–104
   death, 105–107, 327n58
Cody, May (Mrs. E. C. Bradford), 18*, 68, 103, 188, 308–309
Cody, Mrs. Isaac, 18, 22, 36, 120, 135, 169
   as mother, 34, 45–46, 65, 94, 106
   death, 137, 141, 289
   defends home, 39, 47, 49–51, 53–54
   permits Will to work, 48, 61, 67–68, 82, 327n50
Cody, Ora. See Cody, Orra
Cody, Orra, 290
Cody, Sam, 17, 19, 325n5
Cody, William Frederick "Buffalo Bill"
   actor, 271*, 273, 279–289, 290, 305, 308–309
   army courier, 134, 143–144, 149, 187, 233–236, 246–247, 304–308
   author, 225, 277–279, 332n63
   buffalo hunter, 62–63, 85, 103, 215, 217–218, 221–224, 242
   cattle herder, 48, 51, 54, 144
   death, 336n35
   dime novels featuring, 3–5, 8, 11, 277
   elected to legislature, 272
   enlists in army, 137, 142–143, 328n3, 330n31
   Frederick Williams, 159–161, 164, 329n11
   freight train messenger, 67, 71
   friend of Wild Bill Hickok, 8–9, 130*, 134, 168–169, 201, 246, 271*, 277, 287
   gold prospector, 113–115, 117
   honorable discharge, 187
   hunting guide, 266–267, 269–270, 272, 284, 287–288
   investments, 7, 309
   Jayhawker, 149, 197, 198
   joins Red Legs, 135

justice of the peace, 9, 261, 263–265
kills Yellow Hair, 8, 297–299, 300
landlord, 1, 200, 330n35
marriage, 196
meets Buntline, 257–258
meets Ingraham, 5
in Nebraska National Guard, 167*, 272
nickname, origin of, 222–224
Pony Express rider, 117–120, 128–131, 141, 276, 328n68
real estate developer, 212–214
schooling, 52, 54, 57–58, 64, 107, 112–113, 125, 278, 337n51, 338n68
stagecoach driver, 189–194, 270
trapper, 108–109, 121–122
Union spy, 150, 152, 154–163, 168–172, 181–182
Wild West show, 1, 4, 6, 7, 10, 262, 279, 309, 331n39, 333n93, 335n12
Cody, William Frederick "Buffalo Bill," as army scout, 167, 219, 271–272
for Captain Parker and General Hazen, 229–231
Chief Scout Department of the Platte, 286
Chief Scout Fifth Cavalry, 237–238, 251, 290–291, 297
for Colonel Clark, 148
for Colonel Mills, 288, 290
for General Carr, 243
for General Custer, 203
for Major Armes, 207–211
for Seventh Kansas, 166
Coe, Phil, 329n17
Comanche, 47, 134, 148, 230, 234, 326n30, 328n72, 333n84
Comstock, Billy, 222–224, 224†, 225
Cox, Major, 235
Craine, John, 327n58
Crimson Trail; or, On Custer's Last Warpath, The, 5
Crook, Doctor J. J., 200
Crook, General George, 290–291, 295, 297, 300–303, 306, 335n13, 336n19, 336n22
Crosby, Colonel J. Schuyler, 266, 334n111
Curtis, Dick, 229, 232
Cushing, Captain, 252
Custer, General George Armstrong, 2, 329n14
headed for Indian expedition, 202–205, 208
hunting with Grand Duke Alexis, 269
at Little Bighorn, 290–291, 293–297, 331n39, 335n15, 336n23
revenge for death of, 299–300, 302, 336n31
tribute to Hickok, 164–166
Cut Nose, 300

Danites, 90–93, 327nn53–55
Davies, General Henry E., 266, 267, 334n111
Denimy, Mr., 112
Denver Jim, 231, 232
DeSmet, Pierre-Jean, 336n21
Devinny, Valentin, 327n60
dime novels, 2, 3, 5, 9, 11
Douglass, John C., 68, 68*
Duluth Press, 1, 2, 7, 18, 252
Dunbar, Noel, 4
Duncan, General Thomas, 260–261, 334n102
Dunn, Charles, 326n23
Dunraven, Earl of, 272, 288, 335n11

Egan, Captain James, 269, 334n115
Emmick, Lieutenant. *See* Amick, First Lieutenant Myron J.
Emory, General William H., 259, 263, 266, 334n101
Emrich, Lieutenant. *See* Amick, First Lieutenant Myron J.
Enabling Act of Kansas, 34, 35, 325n17
Ernest, Bony, 288
Ewing, Thomas, 329–330n20

Index : 345

Fall Bull. *See* Tall Bull
Field, Luke, 51
Fifth Cavalry, 5, 263, 333n89, 334n102
    Carr commander of, 239, 266
    as Indian fighters, 299, 300, 302
    re-enforced by North, 252
Fitzhugh, General Charles L., 266, 334n111
Forbish, Lieutenant. *See* Forbush, Lieutenant W. C.
Forbush, Lieutenant W. C., 247, 333n86
Forrest, General Nathan Bedford, 150, 150*, 157–161, 163–164, 329n7
Forsyth, General George A., 238, 332n75
Free State Party, 40, 43, 65, 143
freighting company, 48, 60, 65, 81, 83–84, 102, 128, 169, 326n31

Gibbon, General John, 295, 336n26
Girard, Frank. *See* Grouard, Frank
Gobel, Steve, 56–62, 64
Goddard Brothers, 221, 332n61
Golden, Nat, 151–154, 158–164, 329n9
Goodman, James "Al," 18, 136, 328n75
Graham, Captain George W., 218–220, 331n57
Grattan, Lieutenant John, 327n52
"Great Plainsman, The," 276
Green, John, 50, 51
Grouard, Frank, 301, 336n26
Guss, General Henry R., 271

Hancock, General Winfield S., 202, 331n38
Harney, General William S., 84, 326–327n42, 327n52
Harrington, Dave, 121–128, 261
Hayes, Captain Edward "Fighting Jack" M., 254, 333n97
Hays, Captain. *See* Hayes, Captain Edward "Fighting Jack" M.
Hazen, General William B., 230–234, 236–237, 332n69
Heckscher, Major John G., 266, 334n111
Hecksher, Major J. G. *See* Heckscher, Major John G.
Hickok, James Butler "Wild Bill," 8, 130*, 185–186, 257, 328n70, 329nn16–17, 330nn23–24
    actor, 277, 279–283, 286–287, 335n3
    biography and description, 164–166
    government scout, 201, 243, 246, 247
    spy, 168–172, 182–183, 330n22
    wagon master, 130–131, 134
Hickory Point, battle of, 40, 326n27
Hutchinson, John, 80*
Hyatt, Mary or Mollie, 326n37

Indian Removal Act, 325n10
Ingraham, Joseph Holt, 2
Ingraham, Prentiss
    author of Cody biography, 2–3, 6–9, 277
    Confederate, 2–3, 150
    death, 10
    defends Indian wars, 10, 256–257
    grammar, 9, 10
    income, 4
    meets and works for Cody, 5–6
    prolific output, 4–5
    pseudonyms, 4
    reviews, 5

James, Frank and Jesse, 3, 329n5
Jennison, Charles R., 329n6
    Jay-Hawkers, 149, 197
Jerome, Lawrence R., 266, 334n111
Jerome, Leonard W., 266, 271, 334n111
Johnson, Samuel, 266, 334n111
Johnston, General Albert Sidney, 67, 81, 91, 327n42
Judson, Colonel E. Z. C. *See* Buntline, Ned

Kane, Jessie, 58–60
Kansas Pacific Railroad, 201, 209, 212–214, 222, 224*, 228, 330nn36–37
Kansas-Nebraska Act, 325n17
Kansas war, 2, 36, 38, 197, 326n20, 326n25

Kickapoo, 26, 30, 34, 325n10
Kicking Bird, 230, 332n70
Kile, Private John, 329n16
King, General Charles, 336n24
King, T. W., 4
Kiowa, 134, 148, 230, 234, 328n72, 333n84
Kislandberry, Lieutenant, 252
Knight of the Plains, 5, 164

Lane, Colonel James H., 40, 44, 326n26
Lane, Colonel Jim. *See* Lane, Colonel James H.
Langley, Rosa, 10
Last of the Great Scouts, 10
Lecompton legislature, 44
Lee, John D., 327n54
"Life in Our Childhood Home," 7
Little Geary, 247, 333n85
Little Glory. *See* Little Geary
Little Wolf, 288
Livingston, Carroll, 266, 334n111
Lone Wolf, 230, 332n70
Loring, General William W., 153, 329n8
Lorning, General. *See* Loring, General William W.
"Lucretia Borgia," 216, 218, 223, 263, 331n54, 335n116

Maeder, Fred, 333–334n100
Majors, Alexander, 48*, 67*, 82, 86, 103–104, 326n4
   author of *Seventy Years on the Frontier*, 48*, 66*, 326n31
   hires Cody, 65–69
   See also Russell, Majors & Waddell freighting company
Marmaduke, General John S., 170, 172, 330n26
Marsh, Captain Grant, 304, 336n28
Marsh, Professor Othniel C., 265–266, 334n110
Matthews, Lieutenant, 252
May Cody or Lost and Won, 308

McCall, Jack, 130*, 166
McCarthy, Bill, 71, 74–81, 85
McCarthy, Frank, 71, 74–75
McDonald, William, 330n30
McNeil, General John, 170, 172, 175, 183, 330n27
McNiel, General. *See* General John McNeil
Medley, Mr. Thomas, 287–288
Merritt, General Wesley, 291, 297–300, 335n14
Miles, General N. A. *See* Miles, General Nelson A.
Miles, General Nelson A., 2, 167, 329n19, 336n27
Milligan, Mr., 284
Mills, Colonel Anson, 288, 290, 302–304, 335n10, 336n27
Mississippi yager, 74–75, 79, 96–97, 101, 122, 327n45
Moore, Colonel, 233
Morlacchi, Giuseppina, 335n6
Mormons, 26, 67, 81, 90, 92–93, 95, 309, 326n42, 327n53
Morse, Captain, 252
Mountain Meadow Massacre, 93
Myers, George, 199

Nelson, John Y., 262, 262*, 267
Nigger Jim, 25–26
Ninth Kansas regiment, 134, 148, 328n72
Nolan, Captain Nicholas M., 227, 332n64
Norcross, Ed, 147–148
North, Captain Lute. *See* North, Captain Luther
North, Captain Luther, 252, 333n98
North, Major Frank, 252–254, 260, 266, 308, 333n93, 333n98

Old Jules, 116, 116*
Omohundro, John B. "Texas Jack," 3, 257, 271–273, 271*, 288, 305, 335n120
   as actor, 277, 279–280, 282–283, 286–287

Index : 347

Ord, General Edward O. C., 270, 335n117
Overland Trail, 26, 33, 67, 141, 326n39

Paiute, 327n54
Parker, Captain Daingerfield, 229, 232, 236, 332n68
Pawnee, 252–255, 259–260, 308, 333n93. *See also* North, Major Frank
Pawnee Killer, 262, 334n105
Penrose, General William H., 243–246, 332–333n80
Perry, Dave, 253
Pleasanton, General Alfred, 183, 330n29
Pony Express, 116–118, 120, 128–129, 131, 151, 169, 327–328n62, 328n68. *See also* Cody, William Frederick "Buffalo Bill": Pony Express rider
Pope, Alexander, 325n9
Price, General Sterling, 166–167, 170, 182–183, 329n18, 329–330n20, 330n22, 330n26, 330n29

Rain-in-the-Face, 2, 125, 328nn64–65
Randall, Todd, 268, 334n114
Red Right Hand; or Buffalo Bill's First Scalp for Custer, 5, 336n31
"Red Legged Scouts," 135, 328n73
Reeder, Governor Andrew H., 44, 326n29
Reilly, Lieutenant Burr, 263–264
Reno, Major, 296
Rice, Colonel Edmund, 304, 307–308, 336n29
Richard, Louis, 303
Rively, M. Pierce, 37–39, 326n21
Robbins, Hiram, 335n2
Rogers, Captain M. Edward, 266, 334n111
Roman Nose, 332n75
Rose, William, 212–216, 222, 331n53
rounder, 94, 327n55
Royal, Colonel William B., 238–239, 254, 258, 332n74
Rucker, General Daniel Henry, 266, 334n111

Ruff, Arthur, 267
Russell, Majors & Waddell freighting company, 48, 55, 60, 65, 80, 82*, 84, 94–95, 107, 116, 151, 169, 326n31, 327n62
Russell, William, 128, 326n31, 327n50. *See also* Russell, Majors & Waddell freighting company

Salsbury, Nate, 6
Santa Fe Trail, 148, 233, 325n11, 328–329n4
Satanta, 230–232, 237, 332n70
Satauk, 230, 332n70
Schenofsky, Jules C. A., 250, 333n91
Schinosky. *See* Schenofsky, Jules C. A.
Scotty, 227–228
Scouts of the Plains, 273, 279, 282, 283–284, 285, 335n2
Scouts of the Prairie, 333–334n100, 335n2, 335n123
Scout's Rest Ranch, 251
serialization of stories, 1, 4, 6, 7, 333–334n100
Seventh Kansas regiment, 149, 166–167, 328n3, 328nn72–73, 329nn6–7, 330n29, 330n31, 336n18
Seymour, Dick, 267
Sheridan, General Philip H., 8, 232, 233–234, 236, 243, 305, 329n19, 332n66
  Cody served under, 2, 167, 229, 237–238, 291
  with Duke Alexis, 268–270
  hunting expedition, 266, 272
Sherman, General William T., 140, 167, 228, 329n19, 332n66
"Silver Star, The," 6
Simpson, Lew, 82, 83, 92*, 117, 330n23
  captured by Danites, 89–93
  staves off Indians, 95–103
  wagon master, 81, 107, 128–129, 132
Sitamore, 230
Sitting Bull, 2, 202, 295–297, 301, 331n39

348 : *Index*

Slade, Alf. *See* Slade, Joseph A.
Slade, Joseph A., 116*, 128–129, 131, 134, 135, 328n67
slavery, 2, 9, 36, 37, 40, 61, 144, 325n17, 326n20, 326n25, 326n27
Slim Buttes, Battle of, 336n19
Smith, Captain Edward W., 305–306, 336n33
Smith, Joe. *See* Smith, Joseph
Smith, Joseph, 90–92, 92*, 327n53
Smith, General A. G. *See* Smith, General Andrew J.
Smith, General Andrew J., 150, 154–155, 160, 163, 329n7
Smith, Major Lot, 327n53
Spaulding, Captain, 260
Spotted Tail, 268–269, 334n113
Stager, General Anson, 266, 334n111
Street & Smith, 3, 277, 314
Studley, Jack. *See* Studley, John B.
Studley, John B., 271, 335n118
Sturgis, General Samuel D., 150, 329n7
subscription school, 54, 326n34
Sun, Tom, 288
Surr, Tom. *See* Sun, Tom
Sweetman, Captain, 238, 240

Tall Bull, 255, 333n96, 333n98, 334n105
Taylor, Alfred B., 4
Tenth Colored Cavalry, 209–212, 218, 227, 245, 331n46, 331n57
Terry, General Alfred H., 295, 301–302, 304–308, 336n22
Texas Jack. *See* Omohundro, John B. "Texas Jack"
Thomas, Lieutenant, 260
Thompson, Lieutenant John M., 218, 331n57
Tough, William S. *See also* Tuff, Captain William S.

Trotter, Bill, 129, 189, 191, 195
Tuff, Captain William S., 135, 328n73
Tupelo, Battle of, 150, 150*, 329n7
Twain, Mark, 84, 116*, 252, 273, 328n67, 333n95
Two Lance, 270

Union Pacific Railroad, 241, 256, 257
"Utah War," 67, 326–327n42

Valley Grove House, 120*

Waddell, William B., 48, 55. *See also* Russell, Majors & Waddell freighting company
Wallace, Lew. *See* Simpson, Lew
Ward, Lieutenant Edward W., 249–250, 333n89
Webb, W. E., 213, 215–216, 331n53
Weichel, Maria, 333n96
Weir, Colonel, 302
Wetmore, Hugh, 6, 7
Whistler, General Joseph N. G., 8, 305–306, 336n32
White, Charles "Buffalo Chips," 293, 336n19
Wild West show, 1, 4, 6, 7, 10, 262, 279, 309, 331n39, 333n93, 335n12
Williams, Mike, 329n17
Willis, John, 60–64, 326n38
Wilson, Charles, 266, 334n111
Woods, George, 89, 95, 97, 98–102
Wounded Knee, 10, 167, 329n19
Wyndham-Quin, Windham Thomas. *See* Dunraven, Earl of

Yellow Hair, 2, 8, 299–301, 336n25
Yellow Hand. *See* Yellow Hair
Young, Brigham, 326–327n42
Younger brothers, 149, 329n5